Same-Sex Marriage in the United States

Same-Sex Marriage in the United States

The Road to the Supreme Court

Jason Pierceson

ROWMAN & LITTLEFIELD PUBLISHERS, INC.
Lanham • Boulder • New York • Toronto • Plymouth, UK

Published by Rowman & Littlefield Publishers, Inc.
A wholly owned subsidary of The Rowman & Littlefield Publishing Group, Inc.
4501 Forbes Boulevard, Suite 200, Lanham, Maryland 20706
www.rowman.com

10 Thornbury Road, Plymouth PL6 7PP, United Kingdom

13-148T49.05

British Library Cataloguing in Publication Information Available

Library of Congress Cataloging-in-Publication Data

Pierceson, Jason, 1972–
Same-sex marriage in the United States : the road to the Supreme Court / Jason Pierceson.
pages cm
Includes index.
ISBN 978-1-4422-1204-6 (hbk. : alk. paper) — ISBN 978-1-4422-1206-0 (electronic)
1. Same-sex marriage—United States. 2. Same-sex marriage—Law and legislation—United States. I.
Title.
HQ1034.U5P54 2013
306.84'80973—dc23
2012049870

13-14

The paper used in this publication meets the minimum requirements of American
National Standard for Information Sciences Permanence of Paper for Printed Library
Materials, ANSI/NISO Z39.48-1992.

Printed in the United States of America

To Dylan White

Contents

Preface   ix

1 Introduction   1
2 Gay Rights and Same-Sex Marriage, 1950–1990   23
3 Same-Sex Marriage, Politics, and Law around the World   51
4 The First Modern Phase of Litigation, Backlash, and Litigation's
       Legacy: Hawaii, Washington, D.C., Alaska, Vermont, and
       Massachusetts   87
5 Same-Sex Marriage in the Midwest   119
6 Continued Progress and Backlash, 2004–2012: The East and South   151
7 Continued Progress and Backlash, 2004–2012: The West   179
8 Same-Sex Marriage and the Supreme Court   205
9 Conclusion   235

Index   243
About the Author   255

Preface

This book explores legal, political, and cultural factors behind the movement for marriage equality in the United States and the opposition to that movement with the goal of placing eventual action by the U.S. Supreme Court in context. It also examines the history of the movement for marriage equality, explores the ideas behind the movement and its opposition, and places developments in the United States in a comparative context. It is intended to be accessible and useful for scholars of law and politics, and students and citizens interested in the topic.

The book is the product of significant support and assistance. The Center for State Policy and Leadership at the University of Illinois, Springfield, provided financial support for the research and writing of the book, and I thank David Racine and others in the Center for seeing promise in this project. I thank Fulbright Canada and the Alberta Institute for American Studies and the Faculty of Law at the University of Alberta for providing support. Thanks also to Jonathan Sisk and the great staff at Rowman & Littlefield, as well as the reviewers of the manuscript, for working with me in seeing the project through to completion. Finally, thank you to Dylan White for supporting me in innumerable ways, and especially for his patience. It is not easy completing large scholarly projects while at a teaching institution, and this book would not have been possible without his support and encouragement.

Chapter One

Introduction

The issue of same-sex marriage has become one of the defining social issues in contemporary U.S. politics. State court decisions finding in favor of same-sex relationship equality claims have been central to the issue's ascent from nowhere to near the top of the national political agenda, starting with Hawaii in 1993 and continuing through the fight over Proposition 8 in California and the legalization of same-sex marriage in New York. Indeed, the fact that the California court found same-sex marriage to be a fundamental right and applied the highest level of equal protection review, strict scrutiny, in ordering same-sex marriage in the state illustrates how far the jurisprudence has evolved on this question in the last fifteen years.

There is a clear story of jurisprudential evolution from Hawaii, through Vermont, Massachusetts, New Jersey, California, Connecticut, and, remarkably, Iowa. This is also illustrated by the fact that trial court judges are increasingly willing to find in favor of same-sex marriage claims—a policy innovation role that this type of judge seldom plays. However, the same federalism that has allowed this policy innovation from courts has led to a pronounced backlash in states not wishing to be a part of this change, including Proposition 8, which banned same-sex marriage in California, the challenge to which has created a new phase in the legal and political context of same-sex marriage. Federal courts have invalidated Prop. 8, setting the stage, along with the striking down of the federal Defense of Marriage Act by federal courts, for ultimate review by the U.S. Supreme Court.

This book will tell the story of this legal and cultural shift and its backlash in order to set the stage for Supreme Court action. Rather than simply focus on jurisprudence, the book will pay special attention to the complex and interactive relationship between law and politics. Indeed, it is a fundamental assumption of this book that politics both shapes and is shaped by law. In

1

other words, in order to understand how the Supreme Court will deal with the issue of same-sex marriage, it is necessary to fully explore the legal, political, and cultural evolution of the issue and the interaction between law and politics.

An example from the heart of the country illustrates the complex dynamics involved. In 2009, the Iowa Supreme Court unanimously ruled that the state's statute prohibiting same-sex marriage was unconstitutional. As a consequence, same-sex marriage became legal in Iowa later that year. Polls taken before and after the decision, however, indicated less-than-majority support for same-sex marriage in the state. In other words, the court's constitutional interpretation did not match the policy preferences of the citizens, as reflected in opinion polls. Democrats in the state, who held majorities in the legislature and the office of governor, were able to rebuff attempts by conservative Republicans to reverse the decision through a constitutional amendment. However, the 2010 election became a referendum on the Supreme Court decision, with the significant presence of same-sex marriage in the race for governor (the Democratic incumbent, Chet Culver, was challenged by former Republican governor, Terry Branstad) and in retention elections of three of the seven justices who ruled in favor of same-sex marriage.

In a gubernatorial debate, the candidates articulated the two sides of the debate over same-sex marriage and the role of the courts. Responding to a question, from a legally married lesbian couple with children, about why their marriage should not be legal, Terry Branstad stated,

> I believe that the law, passed by the legislature and signed by me [when he was formerly governor], was appropriate, and that is to limit marriage between one man and one woman. The [Iowa] Supreme Court has struck that down, and I think the people of Iowa deserve the same opportunity as they have in thirty-one other states: vote on this critical issue. In all thirty-one states, from Maine to California, where it's come up for a vote people have restored one-man-one-woman-marriage in the [state] constitution. I'm a Catholic, and I believe in traditional marriage. I believe that we, the people of Iowa, should have the opportunity to vote on that issue.[1]

Politicians as experienced as Branstad, the former governor, are good at sending signals to multiple constituencies or emphasizing themes that will be attractive to a range of voters. Indeed, in a few brief sentences, Branstad hit upon several of the arguments against same-sex marriage, arguments more fully explored in the following chapters. First, he makes an argument against judicial activism and argues that issues of civil rights and equality should be open to popular vote, not the courts. This is a particularly strong political tactic to get votes, especially when the civil rights are those of a relatively small minority. Second, he notes the significant backlash that same-sex marriage legalization has engendered, putting him and his voters on the side of majority rule. Third, by twice referencing "one man, one woman" marriage, he references the argument that same-sex marriage will open the door to plural marriage. Finally, he invokes his religion, knowing that opposition to same-sex marriage is an issue that unites Catholics and Protestants, showing his Catholicism to be an asset in this mostly Protestant state and signaling to religious conservatives that he is one of them. Indeed, religion looms large over this issue and is the most significant source of political opposition to same-sex marriage. Of course, religious voices and perspectives supporting same-sex marriage exist, but the bulk of religious rhetoric and mobilization has been opposed to it.

Governor Chet Culver stated the following in response to a question by a woman asking why he did not stand by a campaign promise in 2006 to defend traditional marriage:

> I support, as governor, upholding the constitution of Iowa and the Constitution of the United States of America. The supreme court, in a unanimous decision, voted seven to zero to overturn the law that Terry Branstad referenced. Terry Branstad cannot have it both ways. You cannot sign a law and then have the courts overturn it and then ask the people to vote. Your [Branstad's] justice, the person you appointed to the court, made and signed the decision. Look, it's not as easy as just saying, let the people vote. If that were the case, every time the supreme court made a decision, under your theory, we should let people vote. I support three co-equal branches of government. The law changed when I was governor, and I support the supreme court decision. Iowa has always been an inclusive, welcoming place. That's why companies like Wells Fargo, Viva, IBM, Google, and Microsoft are coming here to create more jobs. We don't want to discriminate against individuals in our state.[2]

Culver made the more politically difficult argument that the United States is a constitutional democracy with limits on majority rule. He also emphasizes the theme of tolerance and inclusion, both grounded in political culture and in constitutional principles. He also defends his changed position with "the court made me do it argument," which reflects two important points about the role between law and politics: first, elected officials are often glad when courts make decisions that the official may want to make but are politically costly, and, second, judicial pronouncements are often accepted by elected officials as legitimate because they are grounded in constitutional principles. Finally, Culver invokes the wisdom of the free market in noting the pro-gay policies of leading corporations.

While Branstad won the election and three justices lost their retention election, it would be a mistake to link this solely to the issue of same-sex marriage. Certainly, economic issues were prevalent in the 2010 election cycle, and voters in Iowa, like most states, voted many incumbents out of office. But this election in this state demonstrates the continuing volatility of the issue of same-sex marriage, legally and politically, and provides a preview of the contentious politics that this issue has created in the United States, and the environment into which the Supreme Court may enter. Will the court take Culver's side in the debate and emphasize judicially mandated constitutional principles of equality and inclusion, or will the court view this issue as one best resolved by the political process in the states? While U.S. Supreme Court justices are appointed for life, will they nonetheless view what happened to the judges in Iowa as a sign that ruling in favor of same-sex marriage makes a court vulnerable to political attack and a lack of confidence in its rulings?

COURTS AND SOCIAL CHANGE

The exchange between Branstad and Culver also reflects different perspectives of scholars on the role of courts in a democracy. One version of this debate is normative, while the other is more empirical. The normative debate, or the discussion of what role judges *should* play in a democracy, pits those who advocate for judicial deference to political and legislative majorities against those who argue that these majorities require limitation out of concern for majority abuse of minority rights.

One side of this debate is represented by Alexander Bickel, who argues that judicial review is a potentially dangerous and "countermajoritarian" element in the American political system. When unelected judges trump the judgment of elected officials too often, the practice of democracy is undermined, as citizens increasingly defer to the judges and stop engaging in democratic self-governance. Bickel's solution is to urge judges, particularly those on the Supreme Court, to avoid inserting themselves into controversial politics, unless the Constitution clearly mandated intervention.[3]

Ronald Dworkin takes the opposite view, arguing that the Supreme Court should almost always protect the rights of individuals against the majority, even when the Constitution is not explicit about a right. He is not as concerned about the tension between judicial review and democracy, because this is an essential part of contemporary practice in liberal democracies, or political systems where majority rule is tempered with individual-rights protections and equality guarantees. Indeed, the view that courts should limit political majorities in the name of individual rights and equality is gaining prominence not just in the United States, but in political systems around the world, most notably in systems without a strong history of judicial review.[4]

Other scholars try to understand when, and under what conditions, courts challenge majorities and to what extent courts create change in society through the process of litigation. One perspective holds that the Supreme Court seldom challenges either strong political majorities or the strongly held views of elected officials. In other words, the court considers the possible reactions to its decisions and only rules aggressively if public or elite opinion is on its side. Consequently, the court is not a vehicle for social change outside of the political process of grassroots mobilization, elections, and lobbying.

The leading proponent of this perspective is Gerald Rosenberg in his book, *The Hollow Hope.* Rosenberg fervently argues that advocates looking for change in the courts are seriously misguided as a result of the lack of independent power that courts possess. Either the rights the advocates desire are not explicitly in the Constitution, or, more importantly, the courts are in no position politically to grant the rights requested. Furthermore, according to Rosenberg, politically premature litigation will only embolden the opponents of the rights advocates and help to create legal interpretations and policies harmful to the cause of rights expansion.

In the case of same-sex marriage, Rosenberg asserts that litigation for same-sex marriage has been disastrous, because it has not created social change but has created significant opposition, reflected by state and federal bans on same-sex marriage. And he is not alone. A leading historian of sexuality, John D'Emilio, asserts that same-sex marriage litigation "has provoked a series of defeats that constitute the greatest calamity in the history of the gay and lesbian movement in the United States."[5]

While there is some validity in these assertions, this book represents an alternative look at same-sex marriage litigation and its effects. At the very least, through a detailed examination of same-sex marriage litigation and its causes and effects, a much more complicated picture will emerge. While litigation has created a backlash, it has also created tangible social and political change, in the form of policy change and shifts in public opinion in the direction of support for the legal recognition of same-sex couples. And because the issue likely will be addressed by the U.S. Supreme Court, this examination will allow for a fuller understanding of the issues and options facing the court and avenues for potential rulings and their possible effects.

THE ROLE OF FEDERALISM

Arguably, the discussion about courts and social change is beside the point. The decentralized structure of the United States' political system creates enormous incentives for activists to turn to litigation to achieve policy objectives. In particular, federalism creates a policy vacuum, given that many policies are primarily the responsibility of states or are shared by the state and the federal government. Thus, in many policy areas, no uniform approach exists. This, of course, can be a blessing and a curse. Policy innovation can result from this decentralization, but so too can policy stagnation and a frustrating, and sometimes an unjust, lack of uniformity. This is true of same-sex relationship policies, as states historically have defined marriage as the gateway to a multitude of rights and privileges at the state (hundreds) and federal (over one thousand) levels.

The political scientist Thomas Burke argues that this decentralization creates a powerful incentive for activists to turn to litigation, especially litigation in federal court, to trump the decentralization of federalism.[6] Thus, beyond the question of the wisdom and efficacy of litigation in the long run, activists often turn to litigation because litigation is a part of the American "DNA." In addition to the structural issue of federalism, many scholars note the propensity to view questions of politics and policy in legal terms, often framed by claims of rights. Individuals who feel that their rights have been violated are often not content to defer to the view of majoritarian institutions, such as legislatures. In other words, in the U.S. context, litigation happens. It may be hopeless to urge advocates for policy change to avoid the courts completely. While same-sex marriage advocates have consciously turned to the federal courts only recently (their reluctance due to the perceived conservatism of the federal judiciary), activists and advocates for relationship equality have for some time turned to the courts for assistance, or have been dragged into the legal arena by the rights claims of couples seeking equal treatment.

Federalism, then, has played a central role in the movement for same-sex marriage. It has created opportunities both for advocates and for opponents of same-sex marriage, and it explains much of the difference between the policy stagnation in the United States compared to other nations. Many nations with more political centralization have reacted more quickly and more coherently to calls for relationship equality. As of 2012, nineteen states possess policies recognizing same-sex relationships while thirty states constitutionally ban same-sex marriage, with some banning all legal recognition. Barring significant federal intervention from Congress or the courts, this state of affairs will continue for some time. Thus, this book will primarily examine same-sex marriage litigation and advocacy, and its backlash, in the states. However, the incentive that Burke describes has been powerful for advocates of same-sex marriage, and a later chapter will examine the turn toward federal litigation and its implications. The institution most likely to break this deadlock is the U.S. Supreme Court. To understand the role that the court will play, we must explore the path of the issue to the court.

The dynamic created by federalism invokes the movie *Groundhog Day*. In that film, the character played by Bill Murray finds himself waking up every morning to the same day, Groundhog Day, in rural Pennsylvania, where he has traveled to cover the emergence of Punxsutawney Phil as a local news weatherman. He experiences the same events, over and over again, despite his best attempts to break the cycle of repetition. The fight over same-sex marriage in the states has a similar feel: as legal or political events bring the discussion to each state, the same arguments and tactics are played out, over and over. While the results sometimes differ, the sheer repetitive nature of the debate contrasts sharply with events in most other countries where legalization of same-sex marriage is a conversation at the national level, often with one big conversation and one big change that ends the debate definitively. For the foreseeable future, events in the United States will most likely reflect Murray's predicament in the film.

A PHILOSOPHICAL CONFLICT

Ultimately, the debate over same-sex marriage is between fundamentally different philosophical foundations that lead to quite different perspectives on politics and law. Three broad philosophical camps are reflected in the debate. The first is the natural law perspective. It holds that same-sex marriage is unnatural, because marriage is for human procreation, deriving from the "complementarity" of male and female reproductive systems. Indeed, any sex outside of the framework is "unnatural," and this position results in opposition to any support or sanction for sexual minorities. As we shall see, this has a strongly Christian theological component, and has its ultimate roots in the classical political thought of Aristotle. The second position, supportive of same-sex marriage, is liberal constitutionalism. This perspective holds that equality and individual rights for all citizens are protected by the Constitution or by fundamental principles of liberal democratic government. The final perspective is critical of same-sex marriage, but from the perspective of more radical social critiques, primarily through the insights of feminist and queer theory. Theorists in this category argue that marriage is an oppressive institution, especially for women, and individuals seeking liberation and equal treatment should not pursue it through this conservative institution.

Natural Law

Natural law–based objections to same-sex marriage are grounded in the classical political thought of Aristotle, continued by Catholic theologians and philosophers like Thomas Aquinas, and given new prominence by the emergence of the issue of same-sex marriage with a school of thought often referred to as the "new natural law" thinkers. Aristotle maintained that to understand the natural and political worlds, and the place of a particular thing or institution in them, one needed to look at its purpose, or *telos*. Of course, this observational approach to political theory stands in stark contrast to the scientific method that would be developed much later. In the scientific method, the scientist should be a neutral observer, and any bias will be weeded out by the process of repeated experimentation and replication by other scientists. However, the teleological approach inevitably brings in the cultural biases of the observer, as it did for Aristotle. For example, Aristotle defended slavery as natural, because it existed in his society and appeared to serve a useful purpose: allowing the elite to govern through free time created by the labor of their slaves. Indeed, for Aristotle, social and political inequality was natural in human society.

This approach is applied to the issue of same-sex marriage by new natural law thinkers and many religious activists who adopt the approach in an attempt to ground opposition to same-sex marriage in something other than purely theological terms through religious texts. The argument goes something like this: given the "complementarity" of male and female sexual organs, it is obvious that sex is naturally intended for procreation, and this can only result from the joining of the male and female. The institution of marriage, in which sex is implicit, is thus naturally connected to heterosexual procreation, and, by its nature, cannot include same-sex couples. Natural law thinkers are unfazed by the argument of same-sex marriage advocates that some heterosexual marriages do not produce children by choice or infertility. Natural law thinkers respond that the lack of functioning sex organs or individual choice does not undermine the essential nature of the marital relationship. The exceptions do not disprove the natural law rule.

This approach is exemplified by the 2009 Manhattan Declaration authored by prominent natural law philosopher Robert George, discussed below. As with Aristotle, the approach is susceptible to tremendous bias because of the tendency for preconceived notions to affect one's "natural" observations. An incident from 2010 is illustrative. Kenneth Howell, an adjunct lecturer of religion at the University of Illinois, Urbana-Champaign, and director of the Institute for Catholic Thought in Peoria, became a cause célèbre for conservatives and advocates of academic freedom when he was dismissed, but eventually reinstated, from the university over an e-mail sent to students explaining natural law approaches to sexuality, about which a student complained in regard to its homophobic content.[7] Much of the coverage and discussion of the incident focused on Howell's description of the natural law approach: "NML [natural moral law] says that Morality must be a response to REALITY. In other words, sexual acts are only appropriate for people who are complementary, not the same. How do we know this? By looking at REALITY. Men and women are complementary in their anatomy, physiology, and psychology. Men and women are not interchangeable. So, a moral sexual act has to be between persons that are fitted for that act."[8] Of course, this accurately reflects the natural law perspective.

However, a revealing portion of the e-mail largely was ignored in the discussion of the incident. Howell continued: "To the best of my knowledge, in a sexual relationship between two men, one of them tends to act as the 'woman' while the other acts as the 'man.' In this scenario, homosexual men have been known to engage in certain types of actions for which their bodies are not fitted. I don't want to be too graphic so I won't go into details but a physician has told me that these acts are deleterious to the health of one or possibly both of the men."[9] Professor Howell's description of gay men reflects what the philosopher Martha Nussbaum calls the "politics of disgust," and this often goes hand-in-hand with natural law approaches to the politics of sexual minorities, particularly when individuals and their relationships are defined as unnatural. According to Nussbaum, this politics is usually grounded in some repulsion to some aspect of the (ironically natural) human body and has been directed at women, Jews, and racial minorities, but is now primarily directed at sexual minorities. It is problematic for politics in a liberal democracy, because it represents "a fundamental refusal of another person's humanity."[10]

The natural law perspective is also deeply sexist and heterosexist by demanding fixed gender roles and excluding persons with same-sex attraction from what is good in society and making them justified outsiders to legal protection while privileging heterosexuality in all aspects of law and policy. Professor Howell clearly reflected this in his e-mail when he told his students: "Human sexuality is inherently unitive [sic] and procreative. If we encourage sexual relations that violate this basic meaning, we will end up denying something essential about our humanity, about our feminine and masculine nature."[11] This is not merely an abstract debate. Heterosexism has costs to individuals and couples, because government has connected a wide variety of rights and benefits to hetersexual marriage in order to streamline certain policy areas (welfare benefits, immigration law, parenting rights, and so on) or to create incentives for heterosexuals to marry. These are government-sponsored expressions of heterosexism.

Liberal Constitutionalism

As the litigation examined in this book will indicate, advocates for same-sex marriage in the United States ground their arguments in liberal constitutionalism. This approach views the political and legal status of sexual minorities as appropriately informed by the twin constitutional principles of individual freedom and equal treatment. Sexuality is viewed as an integral part of human identity, and nonheterosexual forms of sexuality must be recognized and protected by the state in its policies. In addition, the state should not punish or regulate those individuals falling outside the parameters of traditional heterosexuality, unless some tangible harm can be demonstrated through some form of sexual expression. Justice Anthony Kennedy expressed this perspective for a majority of the U.S. Supreme Court in the case of *Lawrence v. Texas* (2003). As he stated, "When sexuality finds overt expression in intimate conduct with another person, the conduct can be but one element in a personal bond that is more enduring. . . . These matters, involving the most intimate and personal choices a person may make in a lifetime, choices central to personal dignity and autonomy, are central to the liberty protected by the Fourteenth Amendment."[12]

Liberal constitutionalist approaches are generally accommodationist and try to work within the system, viewing the struggles of sexual minorities as similar to the struggles of other marginalized groups (racial minorities, women, etc.) and able to be rectified by applying fundamental constitutional principles to gain access to important societal and legally supported institutions, such as marriage.[13] Advocates of this approach favor secular arguments, and they strongly reject explicitly theological arguments for law and policy. This does not mean, however, that moral arguments are disfavored. Rather, moral arguments grounded in liberal constitutional principles are favored over scriptural morality, or even morality derived from natural law approaches. As Claire Snyder-Hall notes, liberalism possesses great moral content. "In its essence, liberalism constitutes a political tradition that allows moral pluralism to flourish; it emphasizes important values, like liberty, equality, human dignity, and the rule of law; it has greatly contributed to the fundamentally moral discourse of human rights; and it stands opposed to and lessens the possibility of immoral acts such as suppression of dissent, tyranny, cruelty, and hate."[14]

Liberal constitutionalists have seen promise in two prominent elements of constitutional jurisprudence for the judicial sanction of same-sex marriage: fundamental rights and equal protection jurisprudence. Despite the lack of explicit text in the Constitution, the court has defined certain rights to be fundamental, including the right to (heterosexual) marriage. The court has even extended this right to prisoners, illustrating its importance in the minds of the justices who created and support the constitutionalization of this right.[15] When a right is deemed fundamental, a high level of judicial scrutiny is triggered, referred to as strict scrutiny. Under this level of review, the government must present a "compelling interest" to justify the deprivation of the right, but this seldom works. In other words, fundamental rights can seldom be violated. This, of course, struck many liberal constitutionalists as fertile ground for the judicial enactment of same-sex marriage, and some courts have used this line of argument in doing so. However, fundamental rights analysis is inherently backward-looking, searching for rights deeply embedded in tradition. Given that same-sex marriage is a newer idea, most judges have been reluctant to use this approach.[16]

Equal protection jurisprudence has proven to be more fruitful for equal protection claims. This body of jurisprudence developed as the Supreme Court began to grapple with the meaning of the following words in the Fourteenth Amendment and their application to a wide range of discrimination (race, class, gender, sexuality, disability, etc.) in the mid-to-late twentieth century: "No state shall . . . deny to any person within its jurisdiction the equal protection of the laws." The court eventually developed a three-tiered framework, with classifications based upon race on the top tier, called a suspect classification, sex and gender in the middle tier, a semi- or quasi-suspect classification, and most other identity categories on the bottom tier. Like fundamental rights, suspect classifications trigger strict scrutiny review, quasi-suspect classifications trigger intermediate scrutiny, and the rest trigger rational basis review. In reality, these levels of review are levels of deference to discriminatory governmental policy goals, meaning that under strict scrutiny, courts will generally not defer to a government's reason for discrimination, while the rational basis test is highly deferential. This framework is the result of the fact that there may be good policy reasons for some forms of discrimination, and the Supreme Court has been unwilling to place the judiciary in the position of arbiter of all discriminatory social policies. In other words, aggressive invocation of the full power of the Equal Protection Clause exacerbates the countermajoritarian tension between judicial review and majority rule. Thus, the Supreme Court, and courts that follow its lead, has tried to balance its way through the equal protection political thicket.

Sexual orientation has traditionally fallen under the deferential rational basis test, but lesbian and gay rights–concerned liberal constitutionalists have argued that it should at least be in the same category as gender. The test used to identify suspect or quasi-suspect classifications involves three elements. Is the trait involved immutable, or unchangeable? Has the group experienced a history of discrimination? Is the group politically powerless? Many liberal constitutionalists thought that the answer to all questions was yes, thus opening the door to an equal protection–based litigation strategy for same-sex marriage. As we will see, judges have been reluctant to view sexual orientation in this manner, but many have still found bans on same-sex marriage to violate even the rational basis test, in that there is no good reason for the discrimination beyond a moral preference, which is not sufficient under rational basis review.

RADICAL CRITIQUES OF (SAME-SEX) MARRIAGE

This accommodationist approach poses a problem for more radical approaches to the legal and political status of sexual minorities, generally represented by radical feminism and queer theory. Requests for inclusion to long-standing social institutions are flawed, because membership in these institutions brings with it traditional, and oppressive, ideas about gender and sexuality. Feminists have long objected to the oppressive elements of the institution of marriage, and many have called for an abandonment of traditional marriage. Historically speaking, of course, there is much truth to this critique. For much of Anglo-American history, men held the legal, economic, and cultural keys to the institution. Even after laws were changed to correct this, traditional societal norms about gender roles continued to be reinforced by marriage and its social trappings. This led leading lesbian-feminist voices to strongly resist political and legal efforts for same-sex marriage in the 1970s and 1980s, as we will see in chapter 2.

Law professor Nancy Polikoff is a leading contemporary theorist who discusses marriage and family policy from this perspective. She is particularly concerned with not just the historical oppression represented by traditional marriage, but she argues persuasively that marriage, whether same- or opposite-sex, fails to legally and economically protect all families, especially those families not in the mainstream definition of family. Polikoff correctly notes that social welfare policy in the United States is strongly tied to marital status. Thus, many benefits and preferred status in law and policy are linked to marital status, both as a way to encourage traditional marriage and to limit welfare benefits. For instance, the most significant social welfare policy in the United States, Social Security, offers an array of benefits for spouses and former spouses. These are currently not available to same-sex couples, even if they are legally married in a state, because of the federal Defense of Marriage Act. Additionally, they are not available to other family forms, for instance, elderly sisters who live together and share their finances. Polikoff objects to this merging of the welfare state to a narrow definition of family, and she is critical of calls for same-sex marriage, which still only provides protections for some, not all, families. The movement for same-sex marriage, according to Polikoff, "positions the gay rights movement on the wrong side of the culture war over acceptable family structures. More alarming, the logic of the arguments made to win converts to marriage equality risks reversing, rather than advancing, progress for diverse family forms, including those in which many LGBT (lesbian/gay/bisexual/transgender) people live. The civil rights victory of marriage for those gay and lesbian couples who seek it may come at the expense of law reforms benefiting a wider range of families."[17] Instead of this approach, Polikoff argues for legal reform that decouples the welfare state from traditional marriage, and its same-sex equivalent, and establishes a framework for a wide variety of families and individuals. For instance, if the United States enacted a universal health-care system that covered everyone directly with government insurance, there would be no need to worry about spouses and dependents, as does the current system, even under the 2009 reforms. The question for Polikoff is how feasible is such an approach, across the spectrum of the U.S. welfare state? Her approach would require substantial legal reform and cultural transformation.[18]

Queer theorist Michael Warner argues that the liberal, litigation-based approach to same-sex marriage is irredeemably flawed. Like Polikoff, he argues that it is a largely conservative movement that ignores the need for true liberation for sexual minorities, abandoning the approach of queer theory begun in the aftermath of the 1969 Stonewall Riots. Queer theory's central approach is the elimination of shame related to sexual activity, a shame that burdens sexual minorities and that limits heterosexuality as well. Marriage, according to Warner, is the institution that enforces these limits. Instead of sexual minorities asking to be like straight people through marriage, true liberation and freedom would be served better by straights learning from sexual minorities. Indeed, Warner directs his greatest ire toward advocates of same-sex marriage, such as Andrew Sullivan and Jonathan Rauch, who argue that marriage will "civilize" lesbians and gays (mostly promiscuous gay men) and make them respectable. This approach, according to Warner, "brings the machinery of administration to bear on the realm of pleasure and intimate relations, aiming to stifle variety among living things. It authorizes the state to make one form of life—*already normative*—even more privileged."[19]

RELIGIOUS AND MORAL ROOTS OF ANTI-GAY POLITICS AND LITIGATION

While many religions are supportive of same-sex marriage and the freedom of religion supports marriage equality, given that many same-sex couples desire marriages in their faiths as a result of their religious beliefs, religion has mostly proven to be a barrier to marriage equality to date.[20] Most directly, religious leaders and organizations speak out and mobilize against rights for sexual minorities. They argue that law and policy should not support sin (of course, they assert that homosexuality is a sin—a contested proposition by theologians and nonbelievers alike) and that the "gay agenda" is asking not for equality but "special rights." As will be shown in later chapters, these arguments have been aggressively and consistently deployed in opposition to the movement for marriage equality. This approach has been particularly potent when combined with popular initiatives and referenda. As Jonathan Goldberg-Hiller has noted, "When these [same-sex] 'perversions' are said to be protected by 'special rights' . . . a fusion of voters into an outraged majority has been driven to the polls in the quest for political purification and the restoration of [heterosexual] political sovereignty."[21] This impulse transcends traditional theological divisions between Protestants, Catholics, Mormons, and so on.

Of course, this is nothing new. As James Morone argues, this dynamic has existed throughout American political history. Lacking a distinct, ethnically based identity and with a relatively open and mobile society, "Americans measure one another by a vaguely delineated, highly moralistic code of conduct." As a result, he argues, "there's always a group who seems a dubious us, who endanger our special status as a city on a hill."[22] The politics of sexuality reflects this dynamic, as sexual minorities historically have been deemed threats to society, as will be explored in chapter 2. Morone's description is also seen in more recent debates over same-sex marriage. In 1996, congressional supporters of the Defense of Marriage Act described the threat posed by sexual minorities. Republican Tom Coburn of Oklahoma agreed with his constituents that "homosexuality is immoral, that it is based on perversion." Republican David Funderburk of North Carolina feared social decline stemming from equality for sexual minorities: "As the Family Research Council points out: Homosexuality has been discouraged in all cultures because it is inherently wrong and harmful to individuals, families and societies." Republican Robert Barr of Georgia (who, now out of Congress, supports marriage equality) extended this line of reasoning further: "[Same-sex marriage] is an issue that is being used to divide America. It is part of a deliberate, coldly calculated power move to confront the basic social institutions on which our country not only was founded but has prospered and will continue to prosper."[23]

Barr's statement reflects a perspective against same-sex marriage that is not explicitly theological but is derived from neoconservative approaches to social policy. Neoconservatism arose in the 1970s as a reaction to the liberal social policies of the Great Society of the 1960s. Neoconservatives critique these policies for an excessive reliance on governmental solutions to social problems, such as poverty. For neoconservatives, a healthy society was created not by government policy, but by nongovernmental social norms and structures that maintain a healthy society. The rise of out-of-wedlock births was one of their central concerns, and they argued that many social pathologies stemmed from this social phenomenon. To counter this, they argued for a strengthening of social norms privileging heterosexual, monogamous marriage as the only appropriate institution for procreation. In their view, government policy should reinforce this perspective, and policies that undermined this approach ought to be changed or prevented. In addition, they valued religious norms and practices that upheld important social institutions, such as marriage. These were the glue that held society together, not the policies of government, but government could undermine or destroy them.[24] This explains why many nonreligious individuals oppose same-sex marriage. However, the secular and religious arguments are usually combined in the public arena, and both continue to paint those who demand same-sex marriage as threats to society. It is clear that the issue of same-sex marriage is not your everyday area of public policy. While proponents view it as necessary to live up to fundamental American values of individual rights and equal treatment, opponents view it as a threat to civilization itself, tapping into the long-standing narrative of sexual minorities as devious and a threat to the nation, and this is often supported by theological arguments.

However, as other citizens and policy makers have increasingly questioned this approach as too theocratic, another religion-based argument has emerged. Increasingly, opponents of marriage equality and LGBT rights in general argue that state recognition of these rights violates religious freedom. It is an attempt to neutralize the rights claims of sexual minorities with rights claims by opponents of sexual equality. For instance, in 2007 President George W. Bush threatened to veto the Employment Non-Discrimination Act (ENDA), and its protection for sexual minorities, by citing the fear that the statute would interfere with the free exercise of religion by making religiously based anti-gay perspectives illegal.[25]

"The Manhattan Declaration: A Call of Christian Conscience," a document released in 2009, represents contemporary opposition to same-sex marriage that draws from both theological and neoconservative perspectives. The document reflects an attempt by its authors to bring together "Orthodox, Catholic, and Evangelical Christians" in a statement of opposition to same-sex marriage. The document begins with a preamble seemingly intended to counter the argument that opponents of equality for sexual minorities are on the side of oppression by noting that "Christians are heirs of a 2,000-year tradition of proclaiming God's word, seeking justice in our societies, resisting tyranny, and reaching out with compassion to the poor, oppressed and suffering." Notably, the document downplays the traditional theological arguments about the sinfulness of homosexuality, opting instead to emphasize and intertwine the theological and neoconservative arguments about monogamous, heterosexual marriage. Indeed, the neoconservative arguments play a central role in the authors' opposition to same-sex marriage:

> Marriage then, is the first institution of human society—indeed it is the institution on which all other human institutions have their foundation. In the Christian tradition we refer to marriage as "holy matrimony" to signal the fact that it is an institution ordained by God, and blessed by Christ in his participation at a wedding in Cana of Galilee. In the Bible, God Himself blesses and holds marriage in the highest esteem.
> Vast human experience confirms that marriage is the original and most important institution for sustaining the health, education, and welfare of all persons in a society. Where marriage is honored, and where there is a flourishing marriage culture, everyone benefits—the spouses themselves, their children, the communities and societies in which they live. Where the marriage culture begins to erode, social pathologies of every sort quickly manifest themselves.

However, despite this approach that seemingly takes a softer tone toward sexual minorities, the document clearly does not envision LGBT individuals as legitimate rights bearers and equal citizens; rather, the authors refer to "immoral sexual practices" not to be protected by the state in the name of individual freedom and self-fulfillment, but to be condemned as sinful with those who commit the sin worthy of pity and compassion, but not equality ("No one has a civil right to have a non-marital relationship treated as marriage."). Additionally, the document cleverly, and repeatedly, joins calls for same-sex marriage with calls for multiple partner marriage as equivalent threats to marriage and society, even equating same-sex marriage with incest, though it stops short of a common comparison to bestiality.[26] The document also calls same-sex marriage a direct and real threat to religious liberty, thus fighting libertarian calls for sexual freedom with libertarian calls for religious freedom.

The declaration achieved cultural significance in 2010, though not for the reason its authors intended. Apple removed the Manhattan Declaration application from its menu of iPhone applications, stating that it violated company policy, as it was "objectionable and potentially harmful to others."[27] Apple thus sided with liberal constitutionalists and against the natural law perspective, indicating that in certain elements of American culture, these arguments struggle for respectability.

However, the religious perspective on same-sex marriage is amplified by the disproportionate influence of religious conservatives in the Republican Party. For instance, while public opinion was fairly evenly divided on support for a federal constitutional amendment to ban same-sex marriage (constitutional amendments normally require super-majority support to sustain the amendment process), this policy position was placed in the Republican Party platform in 2004 and 2008, largely through the advocacy of, and desire for the support of, religious conservatives. In 2010, despite overwhelming public support (generally 70 percent or higher in opinion polls) for the repeal of "Don't Ask, Don't Tell," the Republican members of Congress were mostly opposed to the repeal, including vehement opposition from the 2008 party nominee for the presidency, John McCain. This phenomenon is not isolated to lesbian and gay rights. In 2005, the Republican-controlled Congress enacted special, and highly unusual, legislation related to the Terri Schiavo controversy in Florida, largely from pressure from religious conservatives and in opposition to overwhelming public opinion.

This dynamic is also evident in the rise of the Tea Party movement and its influence on the Republican Party. While some leaders of the movement described it as a nonpartisan movement whose adherents are primarily concerned with fiscal conservatism, the reality is quite different. The movement is composed of traditional conservatives who emphasize social conservatism as much as economic conservatism. During the 2010 election, the Tea Party movement drove Republican Party politics, and the results of this were seen in the attack on Planned Parenthood by the Republican House majority in 2011, and the plethora of socially conservative policies enacted by state legislatures with new Republican control in the wake of the election. In particular, Republican-controlled legislatures enacted extensive restrictions on abortion rights, with some states essentially outlawing abortion, and continued attempts to ban same-sex marriage or similar arrangements. Thus, in the political arena, through one of the two major political parties, the arguments of religious conservatives hold tremendous sway, to the detriment of equality for sexual minorities and often in opposition to public opinion.

This has resulted in the Republican Party's, with a few high-profile exceptions, strong opposition to a variety of lesbian and gay rights initiatives. Such strong opposition from a party in a multiparty political system could be diffused by support in other parties; however, in the U.S. two-party system, this is a significant barrier for change, both nationally and in the states. The role of political independents further complicates the situation. While polls indicate that independents have views on lesbian and gay rights closer to those of Democrats, their support for Republican candidates, as demonstrated in the 2010 election, can shift the political ground toward opposition to lesbian and gay rights, despite their supportive policy preferences. This explains why, despite public support for gay rights initiatives such as federal protection from employment discrimination and some form of relationship recognition, no pro-gay legislation will be enacted in Congress, given the Republican-controlled House of Representatives starting in 2011, until the entire Congress reverts to the Democrats or substantial change occurs in the Republican Party.[28] In other words, the U.S. party system distorts the relationship between citizen preferences and policy positions of parties and elected officials on policies and laws concerning sexual minorities.

Consequently, advocates of same-sex marriage have found courts to be a more hospitable environment for their arguments, resulting in another incentive to use litigation to achieve their goals. In the political realm, a wide range of arguments, including explicitly theological arguments, are present, especially if they serve an electoral purpose, such as appealing to a powerful constituency. In other words, political expediency is the rule. However, courts are increasingly seen as the realm of the rational argument.[29] Indeed, the Supreme Court has consistently ruled that any law violating a fundamental right (including marriage) or denying equal treatment to a class of persons must have a rationale beyond majoritarian morality. Thus, litigation shields advocates of same-sex marriage from arguments present in the political arena and potentially detrimental to their cause. This further explains the attempt by religious opponents of same-sex marriage to invoke the secular, neoconservative arguments, as did the authors of the Manhattan Declaration, a spillover effect from the legal to political realms.

The explicitly religiously based opposition to same-sex marriage has led the political theorist Gordon Babst to label the ban on same-sex marriage a "shadow establishment" of religion. As he notes, "The morals regime that gives sense to the new national ban on same-sex marriage is a religiously inspired heteronormative order that has subjected its non-heterosexual of citizens to administration by the civil authority, where other citizens are not burdened."[30] He also notes that bans on same-sex marriage violate the religious freedom and rights of conscious individuals wishing to form relationships with persons of the same gender. Indeed, this is more of a real violation of religious freedom than is the harm claimed by opponents of same-sex marriage. Being required to acknowledge relationships or identities that one finds offensive is milder than is being prevented from pursuing one's life as one sees fit. It is the difference between mere offense and state-enforced stifling of an individual's conception of the good and the means to carry it out.

POLITICAL AND LEGAL CULTURE

The movement for marriage equality has faced another barrier stemming from the political culture of the United States. In the United States, freedom tends to be viewed primarily in negative terms, or freedom from government interference. Arguments for positive freedom, or the affirmative obligation of the government to assist individuals to achieve their full potential, tend to gain less traction. This differs from other nations where arguments about positive freedom are more uniformly accepted. Take health care, for instance. Proponents of government-sponsored universal coverage often frame their demands by referencing a positive right to health care. After all, they argue, it is difficult to be truly free if you are inhibited by illness and cannot afford to get cured. Opponents assert that the Constitution only protects the negative rights of the Bill of Rights and that aggressive rights claims beyond this violate the understood parameters of American political custom and practice.

Applied to the debate over the rights of sexual minorities, this element of U.S. political culture has made some LGBT rights claims more politically and legally palatable than others. For instance, calls to eliminate sodomy laws, while still meeting moralistic resistance, were met with significant success in state courts in the 1990s and 2000s with little political backlash, while attempts to legalize were met with far greater resistance and a significant backlash. Sodomy laws invoke notions of negative freedom (government should stay out of your bedroom), while marriage equality requires the state to recognize and give status and rights to same-sex couples, clearly positive freedom.[31] During the debate over the Defense of Marriage Act in Congress in 2006, progressive Democrat Ron Wyden framed opposition to the act banning same-sex marriage in federal law in terms of negative freedom, despite the fact that marriage equality requires more than this. Quite simply, Wyden knew that a negative freedom argument would be the only hope at derailing the legislation. As he stated, "Not once has a gay or lesbian

Oregonian come to me and asked that the Federal Government endorse their lifestyle. They simply ask to be left alone. In this regard, they are very similar to what I hear from ranchers and small business owners and fishermen and scores of other citizens."[32] Interestingly, as we will see in a later chapter, marriage equality advocates adopted a similar strategy in Western states where libertarian, negative freedom serves as a particularly prominent hook on which to hang calls for relationship equality, especially when calls for the state affirmation of same-sex relationships was not a winning political strategy.

Significant differences in state legal culture will also be evident in the following pages. Differences in state constitutional provisions, methods of judicial appointment, case law and precedents, and judicial norms, especially concerning judicial policy-making aggressiveness, will shape the varied responses to marriage equality litigation. Marriage equality activists will use these differences to select the states where the legal culture is most favorable to their arguments, a process known as forum shopping.

CONCLUSION AND ORGANIZATION OF THE BOOK

Same-sex marriage is one of the most vexing contemporary issues that evoke fundamental debates in U.S. politics over the role of courts, states versus the federal government, and the proper role of religion in politics and law. It is also a case that can teach students of U.S. politics and law a great deal about those questions. These debates and empirical insights will be explored in the pages that follow.

Chapter 2 explores the history of relationship equality, or lack thereof, from the early lesbian and gay rights movement in the United States to the late 1980s. During this period, much more activism and activity occurred than is generally known. The struggle for same-sex marriage did not begin in 1993 in Hawaii. As long as there has been a stable, though marginalized, lesbian and gay community, many of its members have viewed the right to marriage as central to their citizenship. Chapter 3 chronicles same-sex marriage developments around the world. Increasingly, the United States is lagging behind countries in Europe and South America, with the lack of cohabitation frameworks in law and policy, the disproportionate influence of religious conservatism, and federalism to blame for this relative policy stagnation. Chapter 4 tells the story of the first modern same-sex marriage litigation in Washington, D.C., Hawaii, Alaska, Vermont, and Massachusetts. Chapter 5 explores the unique political and legal context of relationship equality in the Midwest, particularly in light of the important Iowa Supreme Court decision in 2009. Chapters 6 and 7 focus on the progress and backlash since 2004 outside of the Midwest. Chapter 8 explores the increased intervention of federal courts in the same-sex marriage debate, largely through challenges to the Defense of Marriage Act and Proposition 8. The final chapter makes the case for the importance of litigation in the success of the movement, as well as summarizing the role of religion and federalism in the U.S. movement for marriage equality.

NOTES

1. Des Moines Register Governor's Debate 2010, October 21, 2010. Transcribed from the debate video, archived at http://www.iptv.org/iowapress/story.cfm/1596/video/drg_20101021_2010_debates.
2. Des Moines Register Governor's Debate 2010.
3. Alexander M. Bickel, *The Least Dangerous Branch: The Supreme Court at the Bar of Politics* (New Haven: Yale University Press, 1986).
4. Ronald Dworkin, *Freedom's Law: The Moral Reading of the Constitution* (Cambridge: Harvard University Press, 1996).
5. John D'Emilio, "Will the Courts Set Us Free: Reflections on the Campaign for Same-Sex Marriage," in Craig Rimmerman and Clyde Wylcox, eds., *The Politics of Same-Sex Marriage* (Chicago: University of Chicago Press, 2007), 45; Gerald Rosenberg, *The Hollow Hope: Can Courts Bring About Social Change*, 2nd ed. (Chicago: University of Chicago Press, 2008).
6. Thomas F. Burke, *Lawyers, Lawsuits, and Legal Rights: The Battle over Litigation in American Society* (Berkeley: University of California Press, 2004).
7. Jodi Heckel, "Instructor of Catholicism at UI claims loss of job violates academic freedom," *News-Gazette*, July 9, 2010, http://www.news-gazette.com/news/university-illinois/2010-07-09/instructor-catholicism-ui-claims-loss-job-violates-academic-free.
8. Jodi Heckel, "E-mail that prompted complaint over UI religion class instructor," *News-Gazette*, July 9, 2010, http://www.news-gazette.com/news/religion/2010-07-09/e-mail-prompted-complaint-over-ui-religion-class-instructor.html.
9. Heckel, "E-mail."
10. Martha Nussbaum, *From Disgust to Humanity: Sexual Orientation & Constitutional Law* (New York: Oxford University Press, 2010), xiii.
11. Heckel, "E-mail."
12. 123 S.Ct. 2472 (2003), 2478, 2481.
13. I have argued elsewhere that calls for equality and inclusion for sexual minorities are supported by American constitutionalism and the American political tradition. See Jason Pierceson, "Same-Sex Marriage and the American Political Tradition," in *Moral Argument, Religion, and Same-Sex Marriage: Advancing the Public Good* (Lanham, MD: Lexington Books, 2009), 119–34.
14. R. Clare Snyder-Hall, "Marriage Equality and the Morality of Liberalism: The California Decision," in *Moral Argument, Religion, and Same-Sex Marriage: Advancing the Public Good* (Lanham, MD: Lexington Books, 2009), 101–18.
15. *Turner v. Safley*, 482 U.S. 78 (1987).
16. For an argument in favor of applying a fundamental rights approach to same-sex marriage, see Evan Gerstmann, *Same-Sex Marriage and the Constitution*, 2nd ed. (New York: Cambridge University Press, 2008).
17. Nancy D. Polikoff, *Beyond (Straight and Gay) Marriage: Valuing All Families under the Law* (Boston: Beacon Press, 2008), 98.
18. While I agree with the problem that Polikoff identifies, I am more critical of her criticisms of the tactics of the same-sex marriage movement and her path to reform. See Jason Pierceson, "Same-Sex Marriage and the American Political Tradition," in *Moral Argument, Religion, and Same-Sex Marriage: Advancing the Public Good* (Lanham, MD: Lexington Books, 2009), 119–34.

19. Michael Warner, *The Trouble with Normal: Sex, Politics, and the Ethics of Queer Life* (New York: The Free Press, 1999), 112.

20. See, for instance, Emily R. Gill, *An Argument for Same-Sex Marriage: Religious Freedom, Sexual Freedom, and Public Expressions of Inequality* (Washington, DC: Georgetown University Press, 2012).

21. Jonathan Goldberg-Hiller, *The Limits to Union: Same-Sex Marriage and the Politics of Civil Rights* (Ann Arbor: University of Michigan Press, 2002), 45–46.

22. James Morone, *Hellfire Nation: The Politics of Sin in American History* (New Haven: Yale University Press, 2003), 12.

23. *Journal of the House of Representatives of the United States*, July 11, 1996, H7444, H7487.

24. See Mark Gerson, ed., *The Essential Neoconservative Reader* (Boston Addison-Wesley, 2006).

25. George W. Bush, "Statement of Administration Policy: H.R. 3685—The Employment Non-Discrimination Act," October 23, 2007. Online by Gerhard Peters and John T. Woolley, The American Presidency Project, http://www.presidency.ucsb.edu/ws/?pid=75944.

26. Former senator and 2012 presidential candidate Rick Santorum made such a comparison while in office in 2003 in an interview with the Associated Press. Santorum's actual words are illustrative, as they fit with the overall thrust of the Manhattan Declaration: "We have laws in states, like the one at the Supreme Court right now, that has sodomy laws and they were there for a purpose. Because, again, I would argue, they undermine the basic tenets of our society and the family. And if the Supreme Court says that you have the right to consensual sex within your home, then you have the right to bigamy, you have the right to polygamy, you have the right to incest, you have the right to adultery. You have the right to anything. Does that undermine the fabric of our society? I would argue yes, it does. It all comes from, I would argue, this right to privacy that doesn't exist in my opinion in the United States Constitution, this right that was created, it was created in Griswold—Griswold was the contraceptive case—and abortion. And now we're just extending it out. And the further you extend it out, the more you—this freedom actually intervenes and affects the family. You say, well, it's my individual freedom. Yes, but it destroys the basic unit of our society because it condones behavior that's antithetical to strong healthy families. Whether it's polygamy, whether it's adultery, whether it's sodomy, all of those things, are antithetical to a healthy, stable, traditional family.

Every society in the history of man has upheld the institution of marriage as a bond between a man and a woman. Why? Because society is based on one thing: that society is based on the future of the society. And that's what? Children. Monogamous relationships. In every society, the definition of marriage has not ever to my knowledge included homosexuality. That's not to pick on homosexuality. It's not, you know, man on child, man on dog, or whatever the case may be. It is one thing. And when you destroy that you have a dramatic impact on the quality." "Excerpt from Santorum interview," *Associated Press*, February 23, 2003, http://www.usatoday.com/news/washington/2003-04-23-santorum-excerpt_x.htm.

27. Rebecca D'Souza, "Apple rejects Manhattan Declaration app," *Manufacturing Digital*, January 2, 2011, http://www.manufacturingdigital.com/sectors/electronics/apple-rejects-manhattan-declaration-app.

28. Donovan Slack, "Hopes for Gay-Rights Gains Shift to Courts," *Boston Globe*, January 2, 2011, http://www.boston.com/news/nation/articles/2011/01/02/hopes_for_gay_rights_gains_shift_to_courts/?page=full.

29. Evan Gerstmann, "Litigating Same-Sex Marriage: Might the Courts Actually Be Bastions of Rationality?" *Political Science and Politics* 38:2 (2005), 217–20.

30. Gordon A. Babst, *Liberal Constitutionalism, Marriage, and Sexual Orientation: A Contemporary Case for Dis-Establishment* (New York: Peter Lang, 2002), 38.

31. See Jason Pierceson, *Courts, Liberalism, and Rights: Gay Law and Politics in the United States and Canada* (Philadelphia: Temple University Press, 2005).

32. *Journal of the Senate of the United States*, September 10, 1996, S10124.

Chapter Two

Gay Rights and Same-Sex Marriage, 1950–1990

While the push for same-sex marriage has moved to the forefront of the lesbian and gay rights movement, sustained political and legal mobilization for marriage equality is a development of the past twenty years. In fact, many in the LGBT rights movement argue that activism for same-sex marriage has eclipsed equally important, or more important, issues such as anti-gay violence, employment and public accommodation discrimination, LGBT youth rights, and a more general project of liberation from traditional societal norms about gender roles and practices. On this front, many feminist and queer theorists argue that the movement for marriage equality reinforces traditional gender roles and inhibits sexual liberation, a topic explored later in this chapter. Despite these objections, developments by the 1980s pushed the issue of same-sex relationships and their recognition and support by the state to the forefront of the movement. Before these more contemporary events are examined, it is necessary to explore the early LGBT rights movement and its relationship to same-sex marriage.

THE EARLY LESBIAN AND GAY RIGHTS MOVEMENT IN THE UNITED STATES

With the significant amount of social progress that has occurred on behalf of sexual minorities in the past decade, it is difficult to imagine that just a few short decades ago, almost all leading societal institutions condemned or were hostile toward sexual minorities, including organized religion, the medical profession, and the government. In other words, there was not just prejudice against sexual minorities; they were under attack from almost all quarters in society and there was little social, political, or legal space in which to allow openness about sexuality.

Before there was a movement, an identity around which to mobilize was required. The term "homosexual" did not exist until the late nineteenth century. Before this, same-sex acts were noted, but these were condemned along with other nonprocreative sex acts, all often lumped into the category of "sodomy." In the United States, these acts were forbidden by the law, largely as the result of prohibitions stemming from English common law. However, by the late 1800s, communities of persons with same-sex attractions began to form in urban areas. While same-sex relationships existed prior to this, they were not generally visible, given social stigma and legal sanctions. As these communities became more visible, they threatened deeply embedded gender roles. This triggered a desire to use the law to not just prohibit sex acts but to prohibit, and even eliminate, persons with same-sex attraction, especially by the 1930s and the decades immediately following. This led to the Lavender Scare, the gay counterpart to the Red Scare of the 1950s.[1]

Several mid-twentieth-century developments aided the development of the early lesbian and gay rights movement while also contributing to the legal and political movement to regulate sexual minorities. World War II accelerated the pace of lesbian and gay community formation through massive mobilization and demobilization of men and women. For many of these individuals with same-sex attraction, the war was the first time they came into contact with other gays and lesbians. When the war ended, many of these individuals chose to organize their lives around their sexuality, some choosing to stay in port cities such as San Francisco, Los Angeles, and New York, while others went back home with their new identities. In addition, many lesbians and gay men moved to Washington, D.C., to find jobs in the expanding federal government that started during the New Deal and continued through and after World War II. Given the continuing social stigma, however, new political activism was not the result. Rather, social communities formed, but they were generally not open. Instead, much of the social activity was confined to private residences and other relatively protected social settings, such as bars. In other words, the growth of urban lesbian and gay communities continued, but this did not automatically result in political power and mobilization. If anything, this social organization triggered increased backlash against this developing community. And the necessarily secretive nature of the community, imposed by social stigma, furthered the public perception of deviance and threat.[2]

The publication of *Sexual Behavior in the Human Male* by Alfred Kinsey (The Kinsey Report) in 1948 both reflected the increased social mobilization and awareness of sexual minorities and further accelerated their formation, even catalyzing limited political theorizing and mobilization. Kinsey's findings of a range and fluidity of sexualities, with a significant percentage of exclusively homosexual individuals, shocked and frightened the heterosexual majority, but it also gave expert legitimacy to the early lesbian gay rights movement, as well as providing hope for lesbian, gay, and bisexual individuals. A statement from a U.S. Senate report from 1950 disturbingly reflects the backlash: "Sex perverts, like all other persons who by their overt acts violate moral codes and laws and the accepted standards of conduct, must be treated as transgressors and dealt with accordingly."[3] Lesbians and gay men were routinely called sex perverts and sexual deviants by those in and out of government. As a result of this and other actions, the government of the United States was at war with sexual minorities, as it was at war with communists during the Cold War. Both were seen as threats to the nation's morality and security. According to the historian David K. Johnson, this "Lavender scare . . . permeated 1950s political culture [and] . . . it sparked a moral panic within mainstream American culture and became the basis for a federal government policy that lasted nearly twenty-five years and affected innumerable people's lives."[4]

Despite this hostile environment, a lesbian and gay rights movement began to take shape during this period, but same-sex marriage generally was the last thing on the mind of these advocates. Their concern was to reduce the social stigma, and they mostly argued for a libertarian "live and let live" approach to the legal status of sexual minorities. However, even this level of organization and advocacy was difficult and dangerous. The organizations formed in this decade, the Mattachine Society (1950) and the Daughters of Bilitis (1953), did not function like open, direct-action groups such as the NAACP. Indeed, the Mattachine Society was founded by a former communist, Harry Hay, and operated in a fairly clandestine manner to avoid public scrutiny and potential governmental regulation and punishment, as it essentially was illegal to be gay or lesbian during this period of time. These activists focused on community building and limited political discussion.

SAME-SEX MARRIAGE IS CONTEMPLATED

The Homosexual in America by Donald Webster Cory,[5] published in 1951, was one of the first extended discussions of the social, political, and legal status of sexual minorities in the United States. The very presence of the book, as well as its ideas, motivated many activists in the early lesbian and gay rights movement. However, same-sex marriage, as currently conceived, was not a significant part of Cory's analysis; in fact, his conception of marriage was mostly heteronormative. An argument for a libertarian approach to the legal status of sexual minorities was the primary political legal thrust of the book. Cory also repeatedly analogized the experiences and problems of sexual minorities to the situation of other minorities, such as African Americans and Jewish Americans, demonstrating the influence of emerging civil rights concerns and rhetoric. As he stated: "It is my contention that the lifting of social and economic discrimination is the only practical and justifiable program that has been suggested for dealing with the homosexual. That such a program implies a broadening of the democratic structure of America by expanding liberties to a new group and in a new direction should make it more attractive to all Americans."[6]

While one could read this call as also including a demand for something like contemporary calls for same-sex marriage, as William Eskridge and Darren Spedale argue,[7] Cory's analysis suffered from such a thorough sexism and heteronormative bias that calling him an advocate for same-sex marriage is problematic. For Cory, marriage was deeply linked to gender roles, and heterosexual marriage was the ideal, even for many gay men. While he recognized that men could establish relationships with each other (indeed, he mostly discusses gay men and ignores or marginalizes lesbians), he saw marriage as something quite distinct from these relationships. The key to marriage was the influence of women on men, even gay men. Marriage constrained the male sexual impulse, and the presence of a woman in the relationship brought stability, especially when children are involved. According to Cory, marriage created "a self-imposed discipline with iron rigidity."[8]

Cory's views on marriage, then, demonstrate how far notions of same-sex marriage were from contemporary notions. Calls for equality in access to the institution of marriage were undermined by strong heteronormative notions about marriage and more immediate needs, such as the need to be free from the intrusion, regulation, and discrimination by the state and society manifested by the Lavender Scare. Cory's political agenda was clearly libertarian: "The homosexual, first and foremost, wants recognition of the fact that he is doing no one any harm. He wants to live and let live, to punish and to be punished when there are transgressions, and to go about the ordinary and everyday pursuits of life, unhindered either by law or by an unwritten hostility which is even more effectual than the written law."[9]

Same-sex couples lived together and shared their lives and finances without religious or state sanction. For example, Boston marriages, a term dating from the 1800s, referred to the relationship between two cohabiting women in New England, with some relationships sexual in nature, some not.[10] Cory noted this phenomenon, but he could not conceive of it as a marital relationship; however, many same-sex couples considered themselves married without the public sanction. These relationships would combine with more political awareness by the 1960s and 1970s and create the movement for same-sex marriage.

Indeed, lesbian and gay rights advocates did not begin to engage in sustained public activism until the mid-1960s. Among many others, Franklin Kameny was a leader in the effort to model the lesbian and gay rights movement along the lines of the civil rights movement for African Americans. This movement is generally referred to as the homophile movement (after what the activists chose to call it in order to deemphasize sex and emphasize civil rights elements), in contrast to the more radical gay liberation movement triggered by the Stonewall Riots in 1969. For liberation activists and thinkers, same-sex marriage would not be a central concern, while for activists such as Kameny, marriage equality was a logical extension of their calls for equality within the American political and legal tradition. While not directly advocating same-sex marriage at the start of his activist career, Kameny's analysis of the barriers facing sexual minorities and his proposed solutions would soon lead him and others to envision and work for the legalization of same-sex marriage. In particular, by the 1970s, Kameny expected that same-sex marriage would become a reality, and he began to work to legalize it in Washington, D.C. Marriage was also discussed in the pages of the *Ladder*, the magazine of the Daughters of Bilitis, in the 1960s, reflecting the fact that many lesbian couples were considering themselves married, though without state sanction or benefits. [11]

This was part of a larger attempt, after the Stonewall Riots in 1969, by activists and everyday citizens to legalize same-sex marriage, particularly those whose thinking about lesbian and gay rights stayed within a liberal, reformist framework. Notably, however, some radical activists challenged heteronormative approaches to marriage in the immediate wake of the Stonewall Riots, and viewed activism on marriage as central to the movement for gay liberation. In 1971, activists from the Gay Activists Alliance in New York City took over the Marriage License Bureau and threw an engagement party for two same-sex couples. This protest responded to a threat from the city clerk to sue religious officials performing same-sex union ceremonies. [12] Soon, however, pursuing the right to equal marriage would be seen as a conservative approach in the movement.

THE EARLY SAME-SEX MARRIAGE CASES

The more reformist approach resulted in three unsuccessful legal challenges stemming from same-sex couples filing for marriage licenses in Minnesota, Kentucky, and Washington State. Activists were encouraged that many marriage statutes did not specify the gender of the parties to a marriage, nor did the statutes specifically prohibit same-sex marriage. They viewed this state of affairs as a backdoor way to legalize same-sex marriage, but they ran up against a culture and legal system imbued with a thoroughly heteronormative view of marriage. They were eventually laughed out of court by judges highly dismissive of their claims.

The Supreme Court case of *Loving v. Virginia* (1967) also catalyzed action on same-sex marriage. While this case did not deal with same-sex marriage, the decision invalidated state bans on interracial marriage (sixteen states still had such bans), and, in doing so, brought attention to the constitutional protections for marriage. While controversial, advocates for same-sex marriage would continue to use *Loving* as a political and legal precedent to the present day, largely because of the decision's attack on the white supremacy's undergirding of bans on interracial marriage. These bans were in place primarily to maintain the "purity" of the white race. Advocates for same-sex marriage saw inspiration for ridding marriage of heterosexist supremacy and in the decision's language, which discussed marriage as a fundamental right. As Chief Justice Earl Warren declared, "The freedom to marry has long been recognized as one of the vital personal rights essential to the orderly pursuit of happiness by free men. Marriage is one of the 'basic civil rights of man,' fundamental to our very existence and survival."[13] The latter sentence would become the source of significant contestation, with same-sex marriage advocates viewing it as applying to same-sex couples, while conservative opponents would frame this institution central to our survival as heterosexual-only, as we saw in chapter 1. The court's elevation of marriage to the status of a fundamental right in this and other cases invited the debate, though it took several decades to be fully engaged.

Jack Baker and Michael McConnell applied for a marriage license in Minnesota in 1970. Their case, *Baker v. Nelson*, reverberates in contemporary federal litigation, because it eventually reached the U.S. Supreme Court. They were activists hoping to give national media attention to the issue of same-sex marriage. In this strategy, they were successful, profiled in *Look* magazine in 1971. Their legal strategy was not as successful.[14] Their request for a state court to mandate the granting of a marriage license to them was declined.[15] On appeal before the Minnesota Supreme Court, they made several arguments, but three were most relevant for the litigation. First, lacking an explicit ban on same-sex marriage, Minnesota law required it. Second, they invoked emerging right-to-privacy jurisprudence as represented by cases such as *Griswold v. Connecticut* (1965). Finally, they made an equal protection argument inspired by *Loving*.[16]

The Minnesota high court judges refused to challenge the state's marriage framework on either statutory or constitutional grounds. They assumed that marriage was, by definition, heterosexual. As they stated, "It is unrealistic to think that the original draftsmen of our marriage statutes . . . would have used the term in any different sense."[17] The privacy and equal protection arguments were dismissed as well. For instance, the court held that *Loving* did not establish a broad right to marry but only represented opposition to "patent racial discrimination," adding "in commonsense and in a constitutional sense, there is a clear distinction between a marital restriction based merely upon race and one based upon the fundamental difference in sex."[18] Fundamentally, the court viewed marriage as an institution designed for the social goods of procreation and child rearing, not an individual right.

The decision to appeal to the U.S. Supreme Court would create a powerful negative precedent for the movement in the contemporary phase of the litigation strategy. The court rejected the appeal in a one-sentence ruling: "Appeal from Sup. Ct. Minn. dismissed for want of substantial federal question."[19] In other words, there were no federal constitutional provisions or areas of jurisprudence to support the claims of same-sex couples who wish to be married. This put the Supreme Court's stamp of disapproval on the emerging movement for marriage equality. The full effects of this decision will be explored in chapter 8.

Baker and McConnell were not the only couples who went to court in the early 1970s. A lesbian couple's application for a marriage license was denied, and the Kentucky Court of Appeals dismissed their constitutional arguments after they chose to litigate the denial of the license. Like the Minnesota court, these judges, in the case of *Jones v. Hallahan*,[20] demonstrated no need to go beyond the assertion that marriage was heterosexual-only: "In substance, the relationship proposed by the appellants does not authorize the issuance of a marriage license because what they propose is not marriage," the court declared.[21]

Litigation in Washington State included gender discrimination arguments, because this litigation relied significantly on the state's recently enacted equal rights amendment.[22] Indeed, the same-sex couple who sued after the denial of a marriage license, Paul Barwick and John Singer, were inspired to bring litigation after a meeting with a state senator in 1971 who "told them about efforts to update state laws and with a wink and nod explained that marriage was now defined in laws as a contract between two people—not specifying a man and a woman." Both were activists who lived in a commune of gay activists in Seattle, and Singer was especially focused on challenging gender norms. He wore a dress and other gender norm–challenging clothing to work at the Equal Employment Opportunity Commission and was fired for doing so.[23] As with the Gay Activists Alliance in New York, the radical Seattle Gay Liberation Front supported the lawsuit, viewing its potential to change the institution of marriage rather than a conservative attempt at acceptance. According to a spokesperson, "The state has no right to specify the structure of our emotional and sexual life, any more than it may specify our religion."[24] Reflecting on their efforts decades later, Barwick made explicit their motivation: "[We] really believed we'd never be equal until we had the right to get married. Choosing your partner is the most personal basic right you have through life. You'll never be equal until you have that."[25]

In addition to the legal arguments, lawyers for the couple submitted a forty-page Brandeis brief filled with sociological, scientific/medical, and theological arguments for the legitimacy of homosexuality and same-sex marriage.[26] Also, given the lack of supportive precedents, the couple cited a recent law review article that addressed the issue of same-sex marriage.[27] That article noted the similarities between sexual and racial minorities, highlighted how emerging privacy jurisprudence privileged marriage (thus arguably opening the door to same-sex marriage), and noted that if the federal Equal Rights Amendment were added to the Constitution, it would strengthen constitutional claims for same-sex marriage.

Despite praising the couple for submitting such material, the judges on the Washington Supreme Court found it to be irrelevant. They, too, provided a formalistic and deferential interpretation of the law concerning marriage. No constitutional arguments could undo the heterosexual definition of marriage, in their view. Despite seeing problems with the procreation argument, the court ultimately upheld its centrality in the status quo definition of marriage. As they declared:

> In the instant case, it is apparent that the state's refusal to grant a license allowing the appellants to marry one another is not based upon appellants' status as males, but rather it is based upon the state's recognition that our society as a whole views marriage as the appropriate and desirable forum for procreation and the rearing of children. This is true even though married couples are not required to become parents. . . . The fact remains that marriage exists as a protected legal institution primarily because of societal values associated with the propagation of the human race.[28]

The more sophisticated litigation strategy in this case caused the Washington court to more seriously contemplate same-sex marriage as a legal requirement, but the judges were unwilling to innovate at this point—a third strike for early same-sex marriage litigation that put an end to any thought of a coordinated litigation strategy for nearly two decades. According to Arthur Leonard, "These simultaneous losses convinced public-interest lawyers working on lesbian and gay issues (who had not represented the petitioners in these cases) that further attempts to seek same-sex marriage were futile."[29]

SAME-SEX MARRIAGE ACTIVISM IN THE 1970s AFTER THE LITIGATION FAILURES

Despite these legal setbacks, throughout the 1970s and 1980s, activists in large cities advocated for recognition of same-sex relationships through marriage or domestic partnership frameworks. Kameny, along with others, saw great opportunity for the legalization of same-sex marriage in his home city of Washington, D.C., which functions more like a state than a city for marriage policy. By the early 1970s, Kameny clearly viewed marriage equality as demanded by constitutional principles and as a last legal and social step toward respectability for sexual minorities. He also recognized the tangible benefits in law and social policy stemming from marriage, and he understood how changes in societal norms about reproduction were beginning to unmoor marriage from procreation. As he noted in a 1975 survey of the legal landscape for sexual minorities, "With the growing use of contraception and sterilization, with an absence of a ban on marriages between those psychologically or chronologically incapable of reproduction, and with the rapid relaxation of restrictions on adoption, denial of marriage to homosexuals on frequently adduced grounds which define marriage and its purposes in terms related solely to procreation and related considerations, is clearly untenable."[30]

Kameny's first impulse to achieve same-sex marriage was to follow the model of others at the time—a same-sex couple applying for a marriage license—according to a press release drafted by Kameny in 1972. As he wrote, "This is another of the efforts by homosexuals to place their relationships and entire life style on par with those of heterosexuals, and to achieve full equality in society. All rights and benefits of government and law available to heterosexual citizens are, by right, available to homosexual citizens."[31] By this time, however, the Mattachine Society of D.C. was losing clout, eclipsed by more radical groups whose interests did not include fights for marriage equality. And this effort by Kameny was sandwiched in between a run for Congress (to be the nonvoting delegate from D.C.) and a successful effort to lobby the American Psychological Association to stop considering homosexuality as an illness. In other words—after the initial activism for same-sex marriage—the negative court response, the need for the movement to address other issues, an emboldened Religious Right, and the critique of marriage and other forms of traditionalism in the gay liberation and lesbian-feminist movements combined to marginalize these efforts.

However, in some urban areas, including Washington, D.C., efforts to recognize and protect same-sex couples continued, eventually resulting in municipal domestic partnership laws by the 1980s. Legislation, not litigation, was the goal of this round of activism. Of any urban area, Washington, D.C., held the most promise, because, as previously noted, it functioned as a state for marriage law. In addition, lesbian and gay activists in D.C. were more politically inclined and astute than activists in other cities, given their location, and they possessed connections to other legal and political activist groups. The events in D.C. represent the most significant legislative attempt to enact same-sex marriage, or its rough equivalent, until the 1990s, and the eventual failure of this attempt led to one of the early lawsuits of the second phase of same-sex marriage litigation.

The application for a marriage license planned in Kameny's press release was eventually replaced by a religious marriage of two men, Jack Allen Spainhour and Michael Floyd Burns, in July of 1972 in the Metropolitan Community Church (MCC) in D.C. The story in the *Washington Post* about the event was titled, "Homosexuals 'Wed' in 'Holy Union,'" and it interestingly focused on the domestic duties of the couple, indicating the extent to which marriage was still an institution with rigid gender roles at the time, with "women's work" in the home. The paper noted that the two men "envisage a life together in which Spainhour will do much of the cooking, Burns will wash dishes and both will pitch in on house cleaning." The story also noted that one of the religious officiants at the ceremony had performed twenty-five such ceremonies.[32]

Indeed, much of the story of same-sex marriage in the 1970s involves same-sex couples looking for, and sometimes finding, religious sanction for their relationships, even if the law did not recognize their relationships. By 1975, Rev. Troy Perry, founder of the Metropolitan Community Church, had performed three hundred religious marriages of same-sex couples, having performed the first ceremony in 1969.[33] In 1976, a D.C. Episcopal priest got into trouble with the bishop for planning a union of two men, largely based on his interpretation that the national Episcopal convention's statement that called homosexuals "children of God" and deserving of the "love, acceptance, and pastoral care of the church" supported same-sex marriage.[34] The convention also adopted a resolution stating "that this General Convention expresses its conviction that homosexual persons are entitled to equal protection of the laws with all other citizens, and calls upon our society to see that such protection is provided in actuality."[35] Thus, religious progressives were affected by the gay liberation movement, and this created, admittedly very limited, space for religiously sanctioned same-sex marriages.

The 1972 presidential race, particularly the campaign of George McGovern and his successful attempt to win the Democratic nomination, represents the first time that lesbian and gay rights were addressed in a national election. This was the first presidential election after the Stonewall Riots, and lesbian and gay rights activists saw opportunity in the Democratic Party, as did the women's movement, and Democrats saw lesbians and gay men as a new constituency, especially in urban areas. This new dynamic, however, caused problems for the party, given the continued strong stigma against sexual minorities. For instance, Jack Baker of *Baker v. Nelson* (one of the early same-sex marriage cases) successfully lobbied for a statement in the Minnesota Democratic-Farmer-Labor (the name of the Democratic Party in Minnesota) Party platform endorsing same-sex marriage. *Washington Post* columnist David Broder noted the problem this created for McGovern when the "McGovern-dominated liberal coalition overrode warnings from the Democratic governor that they were playing into the Republicans' hands and pushed through a resolution sanctioning homosexual 'marriage.'"[36] While not going as far as the Minnesota party, the McGovern campaign actively courted lesbian and gay voters by releasing a statement criticizing the legal treatments of gays and calling for an end to employment discrimination.[37]

This backlash culminated in the rejection of a strong lesbian and gay rights platform (with no mention of marriage equality, however) at the 1972 national convention by the Democrats. Two openly gay delegates were allowed to speak in support of the platform (the first ever at a convention), and relationship equality was mentioned by one of the speakers, Jim Foster: "We come to you affirming our pride in our lifestyles, *affirming the validity of our right to see and maintain meaningful emotional relationships* [italics added], and affirming our right to participate in the life of the country on an equal basis with every other citizen."[38]

Foster's approach reflects that of Kameny and other liberal, reformist approaches, but it was drowned out by the homophobia in the Democratic Party and, more broadly, by the radical voices in the gay liberation and feminist movements. To counter Foster and Madeline Davis, an openly lesbian delegate who also spoke at the convention, party leaders sent delegate Kathleen Wilch, who declared that the pro-gay platform provision would "commit the Democratic Party to seek repeal of all laws involving the protection of children from sexual approaches by adults."[39] While driven by homophobia and crass political considerations, this statement contained a kernel of truth, as the gay liberation movement often advocated the repeal of age of consent laws in the interest of sexual freedom.

Activism on behalf of same-sex marriage waned in the wake of the court defeats, but the movement appeared to gain new energy in 1975 with an attempt to legalize same-sex marriage in Washington, D.C., and with more relatively high-profile applications for marriage licenses by same-sex couples in Arizona, Colorado, Illinois, and Maryland. Same-sex couples throughout the decade envisioned religious and legal support for same-sex marriage, despite the larger movement's trend away from marriage advocacy.

SAME-SEX COUPLES PERSIST IN GETTING LICENSES (AND GOING TO COURT)

In a wave similar to the years immediately after the Stonewall Riots, same-sex couples applied for marriage licenses in large cities and college towns in 1975. The first application was denied in Phoenix in January, followed by license denials in Maryland and Illinois. However, a county clerk in Boulder, Colorado, Clela Rorex, began granting licenses to same-sex couples in March 1975 and eventually granted six licenses. These developments received national attention, and one of the couples involved eventually filed a federal lawsuit to have their marriage recognized for immigration purposes. *Time* magazine took note of the desire for some same-sex couples to be married in a September 1975 story entitled, "Homosexuality: Gays on the March," and the Boulder marriages were the subject of a prominent story in the *New York Times*, with the article's author referring to Colorado as a "mini-Nevada" for gay and lesbian couples.[40] These actions were not coordinated by any national or regional advocacy organizations but were the result of the continued view of same-sex couples that their relationships were as valuable as straight relationships. For example, a lesbian couple who applied for a marriage license in Chicago were criticized by activists in that city as naïve and their actions harmful to the cause.[41]

In Boulder, Rorex began granting marriage licenses to same-sex couples after she received a legal opinion from the assistant district attorney in Boulder stating that same-sex marriages were not prohibited. William Wise, the author of the opinion, reflected a libertarian approach for his rationale when he noted, "Who's it [same-sex marriage] going to hurt?"[42] The opinion was triggered by an inquiry from a lesbian couple about the legality of same-sex marriage in the state.[43] The first license was granted to a male couple who applied for a license in Boulder after being turned down in El Paso County. In fact, that county's clerk advised them to try in, presumably more liberal, Boulder. The couple was married previously in a religious ceremony in an MCC church in 1973 but decided to legalize their union.[44] After an intense backlash, mostly from churches in the Boulder area, and after the state attorney general produced an opinion arguing against the legality of same-sex marriage, Rorex stopped granting licenses to same-sex couples.[45]

Reaction to the events in Boulder, as reflected in the pages of the local newspaper, foreshadowed more contemporary debates, with opponents of Rorex's actions citing the Bible and her defenders citing political and legal principles. While viewing the union of two men "personally repugnant," one local resident nonetheless noted that "The Constitution . . . goes to great lengths to protect the rights of the individual, no matter how he may deviate from society's accepted norms."[46] This was a letter written in reaction to a scathing critique of Rorex by the paper's editors, who noted that merely being required to cover the story was "sad and repugnant." As they further stated, "We support the principle that consenting adults have the right of relationship privacy. But special and public recognition in law of patently deviant and reprehensible conduct is unacceptable to the general citizenry."[47]

For at least one couple (and likely most couples), applying for a marriage license was more than a symbolic gesture. Richard Adams and Anthony Sullivan applied for a marriage license with the specific goal of allowing Sullivan, an Australian whose visa was expiring, to remain in the United States.[48] They first tried to keep Sullivan in the country by having him marry a woman, but the Immigration and Naturalization Service revoked his status to stay after the agency determined that the marriage was not a genuine marriage.[49] Upon receiving the license in Boulder, the couple went to federal court to secure the recognition of the marriage under federal immigration law, allowing Sullivan to stay in the country. The case, *Adams v. Howerton* (1982), made it all the way to the Supreme Court, but courts at all levels ruled against the couple, with all judges unwilling to view their marriage as valid.[50] The federal judges sided with the state judges from the early 1970s (and the U.S. Supreme Court justices who refused to hear a challenge to the same-sex marriage ban) in asserting that marriage was inherently heterosexual. However, the district court judge, Irving Hill, foresaw some form of legal protections for same-sex couples, though not marriage: "The time may come, far in the future, when contracts and arrangements between persons of the same sex who abide together will be recognized and enforced under state law. When that time comes, property rights and perhaps even mutual obligations of support may well be held to flow from such relationships. . . . At most, they would become personal relationships having some, but not all, of the legal attributes of marriage."[51] Judge Hill, a Lyndon Johnson appointee and chief judge of the Central District, thus had one foot planted in heteronormative decisions of the early 1970s but also had another foot planted in an evolving legal and political egalitarianism for sexual minorities. Indeed, Hill's decision references a 1979 *University of Pennsylvania Law Review* article calling for "quasi-marriage," or civil unions in today's parlance.

THE DIXON BILL IN WASHINGTON, D.C.

Same-sex marriage became legal in the District of Columbia in 2010, the culmination of a process started in 1975 when a member of the city council, Arrington Dixon, proposed a bill that would have effectively legalized same-sex marriage. Reflecting the larger societal changes in marriage and divorce (discussed more fully later), Dixon's bill was a general reform of the District's laws relating to marriage and divorce, but the language he proposed for spouses was gender-neutral, thus potentially opening the door for same-sex marriage. While the bill was primarily focused on reforming traditional marriage by allowing for no-fault divorce, Dixon knew that the neutral language he proposed (the bill referred to a marriage between two "persons") would lead to a debate on same-sex marriage. As he stated, "We wanted to start a dialogue [on same-sex marriage], to raise the issue to the consciousness of the community."[52]

This proposal followed the high-profile discussion of the marriages in Colorado by only a few weeks, and it came on the heels of the granting of a marriage license to a lesbian couple in neighboring Maryland. This license was granted because of a confused county clerk who thought that one of the women was a man (one of the women applied for the license with a male friend, not the other woman, but gave her partner's name), or simply assumed that it was a male-female couple. Same-sex couples also applied for licenses in 1972 in Baltimore, prompting the enactment of a law to specifically prohibit same-sex marriage. Frank Kameny knew the couple from Maryland. Indeed, he commented on the situation in the *Baltimore Sun* while noting the developments in D.C. with the Dixon bill, reflecting a focused attempt to create political awareness of the issue in the region.[53] Indeed, coverage of the Maryland marriage coincided with the hearings on the Dixon bill in July of 1975, at which Kameny testified.

The effort in D.C. was initiated by Dixon without the coordination or support of the lesbian and gay community in the city. Indeed, a 1974 document outlining the priorities of the Gay Activists Alliance (GAA), the most prominent gay advocacy group in the city at the time, said nothing about marriage, instead focusing on challenging police entrapment, creating a gay and lesbian community center, and ensuring enforcement of a newly enacted antidiscrimination ordinance.[54] However, once the language of the bill was shared with activists, an intense lobbying effort commenced. While the bill would have faced a potential veto from Congress, activists in D.C. took the proposed bill seriously. By the fall of 1975, especially after it became clear that opposition to the same-sex marriage provision was forming, a loose coalition of organizations spearheaded by the GAA began to strategize and lobby for Dixon's bill.

Interestingly, at first, opposition to the bill was muted, and many in D.C., including Councilman Dixon, thought that the bill would be enacted without substantial change. The muted reaction likely was aided by the fact that the bill dealt with many marriage and family law issues, most of them popular. Dixon noted in July, a few months after the bill was introduced, that feedback on the bill "weighted 3 to 1 in favor" and that other members of the council voiced their support.[55] Hearings were held in July, and advocates, including Frank Kameny, testified in favor of legalizing same-sex marriage with little immediate backlash. This testimony also included a recommendation that the bill include a ban on lesbian and gay parents in child custody cases. Dixon added this amendment.[56]

By the fall, however, religious opposition arose, but not only concerning possible same-sex marriage legalization. A coalition of city ministers were seemingly more concerned about the council's attempt to legalize gambling and small amounts of marijuana possession.[57] In other words, same-sex marriage, while controversial, was not the primary concern of some religious leaders, as it would become in later years. In an attempt to shield the issue from politics and the emerging opposition, the GAA's first action was writing to the city council requesting the creation of a commission to study the issue of same-sex marriage and report back a year later.[58] When this approach failed, a more intense, behind-the-scenes lobbying effort commenced. Advocates discussed reaching out to groups such as the League of Women Voters, the National Organization for Women, the American Civil Liberties Union, and Americans for Democratic Action to form a coalition beyond the lesbian and gay community. Outreach to supportive religious leaders was also planned.[59] However, before much of this plan was fully realized, Alderman Dixon pulled the same-sex marriage provision of the bill in December of 1975 as a way to salvage the divorce-related aspects of the bill.[60]

EXPLAINING THE PERSISTENCE OF SAME-SEX MARRIAGE IN THE 1970s: LEGAL CONSCIOUSNESS, CHANGING GENDER JURISPRUDENCE AND THE ERA, AND THE TOTAL TRANSFORMATION OF MARRIAGE THROUGH DIVORCE

Clearly, 1975 was an active year for same-sex marriage, even after the litigation earlier in the decade had subsided. The concept of same-sex marriage was still in the mind of individuals, and some thought that political change was possible. Same-sex marriage continued to be contemplated, despite deep cultural resistance and dismissiveness, for three reasons. First, the ideas of same-sex marriage continued in the consciousness of lesbian and gay individuals and couples, despite the legal failures and seemingly intractable barriers to its enactment. Second, politics surrounding the ratification of the Equal Rights Amendment (ERA), passed by Congress in 1970, as well as general legal and political developments surrounding gender discrimination, kept the idea of same-sex marriage in the public arena, with both positive and (mostly) negative consequences for the politics of same-sex marriage in the 1970s.[61] In other words, the struggle for same-sex marriage has strong legal and political connections to the politics of gender, in addition to sexual orientation politics. Finally, the trend toward no-fault divorce, completed by the 1970s, provided a signal to same-sex couples that marriage ceased to be an institution for the raising of children, instead becoming a vehicle to pursue happiness through finding one's "soul mate."

Legal Consciousness and Same-Sex Marriage

Socio-legal scholars define legal consciousness as a form of legal awareness and activity by average citizens, as opposed to traditional legal actors. This awareness and interaction with the law by citizens can both restrict and encourage their legal ideas and actions, either by fear of the law or by a sense of justice motivating challenges to the law. Resistance to the law is an element of legal consciousness that is present in the early struggle for same-sex marriage. According to leading scholars of legal consciousness Patricia Ewick and Susan Silbey, "Foot-dragging, omissions, ploys, small deceits, humor, and making scenes are typical forms of resistance for those up against the law." These tactics are usually used "with a strong sense of justice and right."[62] Certainly, activists like Kameny, Jack Baker, and Clela Rorex were up against the law, and they resisted in the best way that they could.

Rorex claimed that she was acting within her administrative discretion, given what she and the assistant district attorney saw to be vagueness in the law about the legality of same-sex marriage, but she used her discretion in the direction of equality. Clearly, she knew that her position was a strong challenge to the existing legal order, but her ploy was clearly designed to create awareness and shake things up a bit. Legal consciousness was thus central to the persistence of same-sex marriage advocacy throughout the decade of the 1970s. In the shadow of the homophile movement and gay liberation, many progressive individuals and same-sex couples thought that the law was on their side, but they recognized the overwhelming consensus against them. This only fueled their resistance to the legal status quo. This approach would be central to the movement for same-sex marriage decades later, most notably in 2004 when the mayors of San Francisco (Gavin Newsom) and New Paltz, New York (Jason West) began marrying same-sex couples in defiance of state law. As Nancy Nicol and Miriam Smith describe the role of legal consciousness:

> By asserting that their relationships were equal to those of opposite sex couples, same-sex couples and their allies drew on the power of the law as a cultural sanction, as a sign of social worth and approval while, at the same time, they subverted the law. . . . By issuing marriage licenses, Newsom, West, and other leaders asserted their right to directly participate in the creation of law, asserting that law rests on the community's consent to it (or rejection of it) and shifting the question of legal legitimacy away from the courts and toward the grass roots of the community.[63]

While the actions of Newsom and West were more noticed, given the maturation of the movement from 1975 to 2004, their tactics were the same as the early activists, all driven by legal consciousness and justice-driven resistance.

The Revolution in Gender Law and Politics: The Supreme Court and the ERA

In the late 1960s and early 1970s, the women's rights movement engaged in a litigation strategy to secure legal equality on the basis of gender. The ultimate goal was to convince the Supreme Court to view gender discrimination as it viewed race, as a suspect classification triggering strict scrutiny. The results of this effort were mixed. On the one hand the court came close to taking this approach, and it began to take claims of gender-based discrimination seriously. On the other, the court ultimately balked at viewing race and gender in the same light, instead opting to view gender as a "semi-suspect" classification triggering "intermediate" or "heightened" scrutiny. This failure reenergized the movement to enact the Equal Rights Amendment (ERA), but the legal strategy, along with the women's movement in general, significantly increased the awareness of the issue of gender discrimination. This generated advocacy for LGBT rights and same-sex marriage, as the link between gender and sexuality became clear, both for progressive activists and for conservative opponents. The new thinking about gender led to activism on same-sex marriage. As Peggy Pascoe describes the dynamic:

> A small but determined group of lesbian and gay couples saw in these developments reason to hope that they might win the right to same-sex marriage. They made connections everywhere. They used feminist insistence on the use of nonsexist language to support their claim that laws that defined marriage as a contract between "parties" could be interpreted to include same-sex couples. They thought it logical that a Supreme Court that found "race" an "unsupportable" basis on which to deny entrance to the civil right of marriage could be persuaded to say the same about "sex." And they believed that, as they put it, allowing George to marry Sally, but forbidding Linda to do the same thing, was sex discrimination, and so a violation of both the constitutional guarantee of equal protection and the proposed Equal Rights Amendment. [64]

Recall that this approach was evident in the case of *Singer v. Hara* from Washington State. In addition, at the time of the Colorado controversy, Clela Rorex was the president of the local chapter of the National Organization for Women (NOW). Her sense of justice on issues of gender equality clearly spilled over into her approach to the issue of same-sex marriage. In addition,

an assistant clerk in her office was gay and received one of the marriage
licenses she granted, reflecting yet another feminist-gay alliance and shared
legal consciousness among some activists.[65]

This alliance was clear in the movement for marriage in D.C. as well,
mostly in the activism of Eva Freund, a lesbian with strong connections to
the D.C. chapter of NOW. In the fall of 1975, she successfully lobbied D.C.-
area NOW chapters to support the Dixon bill. Kameny was also influenced
by the connection between gender and same-sex marriage. In 1991 he wrote
to Craig Dean, a plaintiff in a same-sex marriage case in the District, object-
ing to the fact that Dean, his partner, and his lawyers were making an equal
protection argument based on sexual orientation. "As a matter of fact and
logic," Kameny wrote, "it is not that at all. Neither of you is being discriminated against because you are Gay. You are being discriminated against
because of your sex, and this is a case of *gender* discrimination." Kameny
(correctly) thought that a gender claim was supported by stronger equal
protection doctrine and fewer "cultural prejudices," and that failure would
result if they "continue[d] to grind the sexual-orientation-discrimination
axe."[66] Kameny's position is both tactical and the inevitable result of two
decades of dealing with the link between gender and same-sex marriage.

This alliance was less solid in the fight over the ERA, as opponents used
the specter of same-sex marriage as an argument against the amendment,
along with unisex toilets and women in military combat. These arguments
began in the debates over the ERA in Congress at the start of the decade and
helped to defeat the amendment in crucial state ratification efforts by the end
of the decade. Supporters of the ERA felt that they had no choice but to
separate themselves from same-sex marriage, for the good of the movement,
but the issue had great salience for conservative opponents and supporters of
same-sex marriage. The debate over the ERA kept the issue of same-sex
marriage in the public mind, but the perception was mostly negative.[67]

Divorce

The movement for same-sex marriage must be understood against the back-
drop of substantial changes occurring in the institution of marriage throughout the twentieth century. Most notably, marriage shifted from an institution
with specific societal functions, such as property allocation and child rearing,
to an institution in which individuals found soul mates for their benefit, not
the benefit of society. This turn toward companionate marriage transformed
the relationship between individuals and marriage. Marriage was transformed into a fundamental individual right, driven by the desires and aspirations of individuals, rather than a social utility. The rise of easy divorce was a
natural outgrowth of this movement. If a marriage ceased to properly serve
the individuals in it, it should be ended, allowing the parties to find new

companions. This was especially true if the relationship became abusive, physically or mentally, as this would prevent an individual in the marriage from achieving happiness and their full potential.[68]

Indeed, one of the goals of the early women's rights movement was the liberalization of divorce laws, allowing women to escape bad marriages with some property and the ability to have custody of their children, as both were under the complete control of men. For Elizabeth Cady Stanton, a leading nineteenth-century feminist, marriage was a form of slavery for women, and the liberalization of divorce laws would emancipate women and make the institution of marriage a relationship between equals. As she described the situation for women in the 1870s,

> From a woman's stand-point I see that marriage, as an individual tie, is slavery for woman, because law, religion and public sentiment all combine, under this idea, to hold her true to this relation, whatever it may be, and there is no other human slavery that knows such depths of degradation as a wife chained to a man whom she neither loves nor respects, no other slavery so disastrous in its consequence on the race, or to individual respect, growth and development.[69]

A century later, no-fault divorce became the legal standard in the United States. Herbert Jacob called this legal transformation a "silent revolution." This fundamental policy change occurred in state legislatures without much contestation or political visibility and transformed marriage from an expected lifelong commitment, with the assumption of child rearing and male domination, to a much more egalitarian, companionate model of marriage. The new version of heterosexual marriage, no longer explicitly tied to reproduction and focusing on soul mates rather than societal functionality, encouraged gays and lesbians to view their relationships in similar terms, especially as reproductive technology changed the reproduction calculation for same-sex couples (as Kameny noted above). Whereas in the 1950s Cory could not quite fully envision the contemporary concept of same-sex marriage, this was conceivable just a few decades later. Legally, Cady Stanton's vision had been realized, and this had implications for nonheterosexual relationships. In other words, the calls for same-sex marriage by the 1970s resulted significantly from the transformation of the institution made by heterosexuals.[70]

1977: THE TEMPORARY END OF SERIOUS SAME-SEX MARRIAGE ADVOCACY AND THE TURN TO DOMESTIC PARTNERSHIPS AND OTHER STRATEGIES

The year 1977 marked a clear end of early same-sex marriage advocacy in the United States for at least a decade. In response to continued requests by same-sex couples in California, the state enacted an explicit ban on same-sex marriage. Legislators in Colorado, Florida, Utah, Illinois, Minnesota, and Wyoming also revised their marriage statutes to specifically prohibit same-sex marriage in 1977.[71] Additionally, the emerging Religious Right was successful in repealing a gay rights ordinance in Miami-Dade County, Florida—a significant setback for the cause of lesbian and gay rights—and the Florida legislature failed to pass the ERA, dealing a severe blow to its chances for ratification. Arguments that the ERA would legalize same-sex marriage were prominent in the debate.[72]

Applications by same-sex couples for marriage licenses had become fairly routine (several each week) in Los Angeles by 1977, and the county clerk in neighboring Orange County felt vulnerable to a legal challenge from same-sex couples, given that the law authorized marriages to "unmarried persons," the gender-specific language having been removed in 1971. One Los Angeles couple and their lawyer indicated that they would be bringing a class action lawsuit stemming from the denial of their marriage license. As a result, the legislature enacted a law explicitly banning same-sex marriage, signed by Governor Jerry Brown.[73] Ironically, Brown would refuse to defend California's Proposition 8 banning same-sex marriage decades later while serving as attorney general and again as governor.

While not a close vote in the legislature, the vote was far from unanimous (48 to 16 in the House and 23 to 5 in the Senate), and some members argued against the ban by emphasizing that same-sex couples needed legal rights and benefits as a result of increased cohabitation. The idea of a separate bill extending some rights to same-sex couples was discussed in a committee, but the moral argument against the sanctioning of same-sex relationships prevailed.[74]

While the backlash was strong and set back the movement for same-sex marriage, law and policy change on behalf of same-sex couples did not end. Because unmarried cohabitation was becoming more common for heterosexuals as a result of changing attitudes about marriage, reflected by no-fault divorce, contemplating the legal arrangements for cohabitating same-sex couples became more common. In 1977, the lawyer for Michelle Triola, a woman who successfully sued actor Lee Marvin for a potential share of his earning while the two cohabitated, predicted that family law allowing for more cohabitation rights would include same-sex couples.[75] In addition, the issue of cohabitation for opposite-sex couples surfaced in the 1970s and 1980s in many European countries. While the Marvin case made headlines in the United States, policies creating rights based on cohabitation were much more common in Europe or in countries such as Canada with common law marriage frameworks. Despite the optimism of Triola's lawyer, the United States continued to privilege traditional marriage as the avenue to rights and benefits for couples, even while making divorce much easier. This created a much narrower path for same-sex couples to receive rights and benefits for their relationships. Also, continuing to elevate marriage as a legal and cultural status made same-sex couples argue why they "belonged" and led opponents of same-sex marriage to fight strenuously to maintain the privileged status of heterosexual relationships. Thus, as opposed to the Canadian and European contexts, there would be no significant national path to rights for U.S. same-sex couples through cohabitation.

However, the idea of a separate legal framework for same-sex couples continued in some cities with significant populations of sexual minorities, but cities could not challenge the privileged status of marriage in state law. These laws were quite minimal in their effects—they applied initially only to city employees—but they were symbolically important for same-sex couples still desiring recognition and respect. As Harry Britt, the author of a proposed domestic partnership ordinance in San Francisco, stated: "Society may not allow me to marry a partner of my own sex. Nonetheless, I know that I can care very deeply for people and society offers me no way to recognize those feelings in a legitimate, official way."[76]

The movement for domestic partnerships began in Berkeley, California, in 1979 by a University of California, Berkeley, employee, Tom Broughman, who felt discrimination after he was not able to count his partner as a beneficiary for health insurance, but the spouses of university employees, of course, could. This was particularly galling, because Berkeley had recently enacted an antidiscrimination ordinance based on sexual orientation. Broughman's lobbying efforts in Berkeley initially failed to change policy, but his idea caught on. Britt saw a presentation by Broughman and decided to pursue the issue in San Francisco, where he was a city supervisor (or member of the city council).[77]

The San Francisco ordinance, which would have provided health insurance, bereavement leave, and hospital visitation rights for same-sex city employees, was passed by the Board of Supervisors but vetoed by then-mayor Diane Feinstein. Feinstein argued that the costs of the potential policy were unclear, and she objected to the fact that it did not cover a broader range of dependents, such as blood relatives, a clear attempt to de-gay the issue. Even this relatively minimal policy triggered a traditional moralistic backlash, exemplified by the city's Catholic archbishop's statement arguing that the policy would "further erode the moral foundation of civilized society," issued one day before Feinstein's veto.[78] Due to the persistent efforts of Broughman and his allies, including aggressive grassroots politicking to elect pro–domestic partnership candidates to the city council, Berkeley, California, was the first city to enact a domestic partnership ordinance covering municipal employees in 1984, followed by Los Angeles, Madison, Seattle, and West Hollywood in the 1980s.[79] In these cities, too, debates over a minimal set of rights for a subset of the LGBT community (municipal workers) allowed advocates in progressive jurisdictions to continue the argument about relationship equality and opponents to frame the issue as one of immorality and civilizational threat, continuing to set the stage for contemporary fights over same-sex marriage.

Indeed, after Feinstein's veto in San Francisco, the fight over same-sex relationship recognition continued in the city as a preview of future debates and tactics, with conservative activists using popular referenda to overturn a domestic partnership ordinance. The board of supervisors passed another partnership bill in 1989, but this had the support of Mayor Art Agnos. Conservatives pursued a referendum to defeat the measure later in the year and were successful. However, partnership supporters ultimately prevailed with a popular initiative enacting domestic partnerships in 1990, secured by a defeat of a repeal referendum in 1991. [80]

These policies proliferated in large cities and college towns over the next several decades. Some were simply symbolic registries, given that cities cannot generally extend many benefits beyond their employees (this falls under the jurisdiction of state and federal law). More recently some cities have enacted ordinances mandating that companies doing business with the city must offer domestic partner benefits to the company's employees, and such business and corporate coverage has become common in recent years. According to the Human Rights Campaign, 59 percent of Fortune 500 companies offered these benefits in 2011. A software company, Lotus, started this trend in 1992, as the first publicly traded company to offer such benefits. Local domestic partnership laws have also been used to mobilize opposition to state constitutional bans on same-sex relationship recognition. For instance, in the run-up to the placing of such an amendment on the ballot in Minnesota in 2012, eleven cities enacted ordinances in 2010 and 2011. [81]

Reflective of both the desire of same-sex couples to gain legal protections and benefits and the depth of societal and legal resistance, the adoption of one partner by the other in order to secure benefits stemming from a parental relationship was another legal avenue attempted by some same-sex couples. Such a case made it to the New York Court of Appeals in 1984 with the support of the leading lesbian and gay rights litigation group, Lambda Legal Defense and Education Fund, which filed an amicus curiae brief, indicating support for the strategy from the leading LGBT litigants of the period. The court rejected the attempt by one male to adopt his partner largely by focusing on the assumed sexual activity in the relationship, arguing that this was not in line with the goals and purposes of the state's adoption statute (indeed, it was "utterly repugnant to the relationship between parent and child"), even though adult adoption was allowed. [82] A dissenting judge noted that nothing in the adoption law precluded this arrangement. The dissent also noted that the court had recently ruled the state's sodomy law unconstitutional under the doctrine of the right to privacy and argued that the adoption statute did not require an inquiry into "the sexual habits of the parties," largely agreeing with the arguments of Lambda Legal.[83] That group saw this case as part of an increasing trend of courts recognizing and protecting nontraditional families, relying on precedents relating to changes in heterosexual families, yet again linking expanded rights for lesbian and gay couples to broader changes in family law and policy.[84]

The need for legal protections for same-sex couples became less symbolic and more tangible as a result of the AIDS crisis, starting in the early 1980s. As partners died and families swooped in to make funeral arrangements and take property from surviving partners, and as partners were denied hospital visitation rights, it became clear that basic legal protections were needed.[85] Indeed, a large portion of the litigation load of Lambda Legal was AIDS-related during this period.[86] A significant state court decision in New York in 1989 that defined same-sex couples as a family resulted from such a situation. The case, *Braschi v. Stahl Associates* (1989), stemmed from a dispute over the right to a rent-controlled apartment in New York City after the death of a same-sex partner from complications due to AIDS. Under the law, same-sex partners were not explicitly defined as family members entitled to continue possession of an apartment and its controlled rent. The New York Court of Appeals (the state's highest court) ruled that a same-sex partner was a family member for the purposes of the statute, arguing that "a family includes two adult lifetime partners whose relationship is long term and characterized by an emotional and financial commitment and interdependence."[87]

The decision spurred the city of New York to provide more protections and benefits for same-sex couples, but its real legacy was more symbolic and more consequential, according to Carlos Ball:

> The importance of *Braschi* lies not so much in the way in which future courts relied on its holdings and reasoning . . . but rather in the fact that the highest court of New York adopted the movement's position on what constitutes a family. In doing so, it provided considerable legitimacy to the movement's claim that LGBT people were as capable of forming loving and lasting familial ties as were straight people.[88]

By the late 1980s and early 1990s, then, the inclusion of same-sex couples and families in the laws of the country was gaining legitimacy in legal circles. Finally, one branch of the government was beginning to embrace the arguments made by LGBT activists for decades.

The tragic circumstances of a lesbian couple in Minnesota further heightened the awareness in the LGBT community about the lack of legal protections for same-sex couples. Sharon Kowalski was severely injured in an automobile accident in 1983 and was rendered unable to care for herself. At the time, she was in a four-year relationship with Karen Thompson in St. Cloud, Minnesota. A guardianship struggle ensued between Thompson and Kowalski's family. Ultimately, a state appeals court found in Thompson's favor, describing their relationship as a "family of affinity, which ought to be accorded respect," representing yet another court recognition of same-sex couples.[89] The case received a great deal of attention in the LGBT media, and caused many same-sex couples to ponder the legal status of their relationships, especially outside of urban centers, and resulted in a national protest in 1988. According to Casey Charles, "Thompson's petition for guardianship raised issues . . . that paralleled those of AIDS while displacing the settings of these questions from urban enclaves to the 'wholesome' Midwest, where two lesbians confronted homophobic forces on the Iron Range."[90]

Thus, by the late 1980s, the issue of relationship equality was reemerging through domestic partnership advocacy in urban areas and through litigation. The media began to frame the issue as being about marriage equality, and advocates for same-sex marriage began to advocate for same-sex marriage in prominent media outlets.[91] It was only natural that the legal consciousness of same-sex couples would be reenergized and they would go back to court. While the early 1970s cases constrained the movement for same-sex marriage, they did not completely eliminate activism in the short or long term. The allure of the idea, and the practical need for relationship equality, proved to be quite strong.

NOTES

1. See George Chauncey, *Gay New York: Gender, Urban Culture, and the Making of the Gay World, 1890–1940* (New York: Basic Books, 1994); and William N. Eskridge, Jr., *Gaylaw: Challenging the Apartheid of the Closet* (Cambridge, MA: Harvard University Press, 1999).
2. David K. Johnson, *The Lavender Scare: The Cold War Persecution of Gays and Lesbians in the Federal Government* (Chicago: University of Chicago Press, 2004).
3. United States Senate, Committee on Expenditures in the Executive Departments. Report from the Subcommittee on Investigations, by Mr. Hoey, 1950, in *We Are Everywhere: A Historical Sourcebook of Gay and Lesbian Politics*, Mark Blasius and Shane Phelan, eds. (New York: Routledge, 1997).
4. Johnson, *The Lavender Scare*, 9.
5. This was a pseudonym for Edward Sagarin.
6. Donald Webster Cory, *The Homosexual in America: A Subjective Approach* (New York: Greenberg, 1951), 48.
7. William N. Eskridge, Jr., and Darren Spedale, *Gay Marriage: For Better or for Worse* (New York: Oxford University Press, 2006), 14.
8. Cory, 202.
9. Cory, 227.
10. Lillian Faderman, *Surpassing the Love of Men: Romantic Friendship and Love between Women from the Renaissance to the Present* (New York: Morrow, 1981).
11. Eskridge and Spedale, 15.
12. Randolfe Wicker, "Gay Marriage Bureau Takeover, Part I," http://www.youtube.com/watch?v=Z7NU8B1EGnU.
13. *Loving v. Virginia*, 388 U.S. 1 (1967), 12.
14. David L. Chambers, "Couples: Marriage, Civil Union, and Domestic Partnership," in *Creating Change: Sexuality, Public Policy, and Civil Rights*, John D'Emilio et al., eds. (New York: St. Martin's Press, 2000), 283–84.

15. *Baker v. Nelson,* 191 N.W. 2d 185 (Minn. 1971).

16. *Baker,* 185–86.

17. *Baker,* 186.

18. *Baker,* 187.

19. *Baker v. Nelson,* 409 U.S. 810 (1972).

20. *Jones v. Hallahan,* 501 S.W. 2d 588 (Ky. 1973).

21. *Jones,* 590.

22. *Singer v. Hara,* 522 P. 2d 1187 (Wash. Ct. App. 1974), 1188.

23. Lornet Turnbull, "Gay Man Sees Big Changes Since '72 Suit," *Seattle Times*, April 4, 2006, http://seattletimes.nwsource.com/html/localnews/2002908816_pbarwick04m.html. Singer eventually was reinstated after a lengthy court battle, the reinstatement triggered by the change in federal policy overturning the ban on lesbian and gay employees in 1975. He changed his name to Faygele ben Miriam, which means, according to ben Miriam, in Yiddish, "Faggot son of Miriam." Susan Chadwick, "Gay Wins Six-Year Battle," *Seattle Post-Intelligencer*, September 17, 1970, D20.

24. "'Gay' Groups Back License Seekers," *Seattle Post-Intelligencer*, September 26, 1971, E4.

25. Monica Guzman, "Seattle Gay Rights Pioneer Reflects on Activism," *Seattle's Big Blog*, November 3, 2009, http://blog.seattlepi.com/thebigblog/2009/11/03/seattle-gay-rights-pioneer-reflects-on-activism/.

26. *Singer v. Hara,* footnote 1.

27. The article cited was "The Legality of Homosexual Marriage," *Yale Law Journal* 82 (1973), as cited in *Singer* at 1193.

28. *Singer v. Hara,* 1195.

29. Leonard, *Homosexuality and the Constitution*, ix–x.

30. Franklin E. Kameny, "Action on the Gay Legal Front," unpublished manuscript, 1975. Kameny Papers, Library of Congress. Copy on file with the author.

31. Draft news release, Franklin E. Kameny, "Two Homosexual Men to Apply for D.C. Marriage License," June 30, 1972, Papers of Franklin Kameny, Manuscript Division, Library of Congress. Copy on file with the author.

32. William R MacKaye, "Homosexuals 'Wed' in 'Holy Union,'" *Washington Post*, July 9, 1972, D3.

33. "Homosexuality: Gays on the March," *Time*, September 8, 1975, http://www.time.com/time/magazine/article/0,9171,917784,00.html.

34. Marjorie Hyer, "Homosexual Marriage Plans Cause Episcopal Problems," *Washington Post*, November 12, 1976, C2.

35. Resolution 1976-A071, http://www.episcopalarchives.org/cgi-bin/acts/acts_resolution-complete.pl?resolution=1976-A071.

36. David Broder, "McGovern's Radicals," *Washington Post*, June 20, 1972, A19.

37. Bruce Miroff, *The Liberals' Moment: The McGovern Insurgency and the Identity Crisis of the Democratic Party* (Lawrence, KS: University Press of Kansas, 2007), 216.

38. Dudley Clendinen and Adam Nagourney, *Out for Good: The Struggle to Build a Gay Rights Movement in America* (New York: Simon & Schuster, 1999), 134.

39. Clendinen and Nagourney, 135.

40. Grace Lichtenstein, "Homosexual Weddings Stir Controversy in Colorado," *New York Times*, April 27, 1975, 49.

41. Tracy Baim, *Out and Proud in Chicago: An Overview of the City's Gay Community* (Chicago: Agate Surrey, 2008), 88.

42. "Homosexuality: Gays on the March," *Time*.

43. Tony Stroh, "Legal Flak Expected in Licensing of Gays," *Boulder Daily Camera*, March 28, 1975, 2.

44. Tony Stroh, "County Clerk Issues Marriage Licenses," *Boulder Daily Camera*, March 27, 1975, 1.

45. Tony Stroh, "Rorex Won't Issue More Licenses to Gays," *Boulder Daily Camera*, April 26, 1975, 26. Also see interview with Clela Rorex, "1975: Clela Rorex Issues America's First Same-Sex Marriage License," *Huffington Post*, October 17, 2010, http://www.huffingtonpost.com/tom-gregory/1975-clela-rorex-issues-a_b_765534.html.

46. "Defense of Homosexual Marriage," *Boulder Daily Camera*, April 3, 1975, 4.

47. "Distortion of the Intent of the Law," *Boulder Daily Camera*, March 30, 1975, 10.

48. Tony Stroh, "Male Couple Married Outside Clerk's Office," *Boulder Daily Camera*, April 22, 1975, 1.

49. *Adams v. Howerton*, 486 F. Supp. 1119 (C.D.Cal.1980), 1120.

50. *Adams v. Howerton*, cert. denied, 458 U.S. 1111 (1982).

51. *Adams v. Howerton* (1980), 1125.

52. Quoted in David Aiken, "D.C. Council," January 21, 1976, draft article for *The Advocate* archived at the Rainbow History Project, http://www.rainbowhistory.org/dcouncil012176.pdf. Aiken was a member of the GAA in D.C. and was the D.C. correspondent for *The Advocate*.

53. Robert A. Erlandson, "State Rules Montgomery Clerk Can't Revoke Two-Woman Marriage," *Baltimore Sun*, July 10, 1975, C1; Bill Richards, "Maryland Legal Officials Ponder Legality of 2 Women's Marriage," *Washington Post*, July 2, 1975, C1.

54. "What We're Into: Some 1974-5GAA Projects," archived at the Rainbow History Project, http://www.rainbowhistory.org/gaareport74.pdf.

55. Patricia Camp, "Divorce Bill Chance 'Excellent,'" *Washington Post*, July 9, 1975, C2.

56. "Report of Meeting on Gay Marriage/Child Custody/No-Fault Divorce Called by Gay Activists Alliance, November 7, 1975," Franklin Kameny Papers, Library of Congress.

57. LaBarbara Bowman, "Ministers Oppose Bills," *Washington Post*, September 24, 1975, B3.

58. "Minutes of the Gay Activists Alliance of D.C.," September 23, 1975, Franklin Kameny Papers, Library of Congress.

59. "Report of Meeting on Gay Marriage/Child Custody/No-Fault Divorce."

60. LaBarbara Bowman, "Dixon Drops Bill for Homosexuals," *Washington Post*, December 24, 1975.

61. See Peggy Pascoe, "Sex, Gender, and Same-Sex Marriage," in *Is Academic Feminism Dead? Theory in Practice*, The Social Justice Group at the Center for Advanced Feminist Studies, University of Minnesota, ed. (New York: New York University Press, 2000).

62. Patricia Ewick and Susan S. Silbey, *The Common Place of Law: Stories from Everyday Life* (Chicago: University of Chicago Press, 1998), 48–49.

63. Nancy Nicol and Miriam Smith, "Legal Struggles and Political Resistance: Same-Sex Marriage in Canada and the United States," in *Same-Sex Marriage in the Americas*, Jason Pierceson, et al., eds. (Lanham, MD: Lexington Books), 191.

64. Pascoe, 91.

65. "Clela Rorex: Gay Marriage Pioneer," *Daily Kos*, http://www.dailykos.com/story/2011/06/24/988562/-Clela-Rorex:-Gay-marriage-pioneer.

66. Letter from Franklin E. Kameny to Craig R. Dean, July 23, 1991, Kameny Papers, Library of Congress, copy on file with the author. The "axe" quote is from a letter from Kameny to Dean's lawyer, William N. Eskridge, Jr., dated February 12, 1992. Kameny Papers, Library of Congress, copy on file with the author.

67. See Pascoe, 97–102, for a more detailed discussion on the connection between the ERA and the movement for same-sex marriage.

68. See Nancy F. Cott, *Public Vows: A History of Marriage and the Nation* (Cambridge: Harvard University Press, 2002).

69. Elizabeth Cady Stanton, "On Marriage and Divorce," 1871, http://gos.sbc.edu/s/stantoncady3.html.

70. Herbert Jacob, *The Silent Revolution: The Transformation of Divorce Law in the United States* (Chicago: University of Chicago Press, 1988), 1–5, 25.

71. Pascoe, 86.

72. Pascoe, 101.

73. Myrna Oliver, "Gay Couple Can't Wed," *Los Angeles Times*, March 16, 1977, D6; Bud Lembke, "County Won't Ask for Change in Law," *Los Angeles Times*, December 16, 1976, OC12.

74. Robert Fairbanks, "Assembly OKs Ban on Gay Marriages," *Los Angeles Times*, April 22, 1977, B20; "Senate Gets Bill to Ban Gay Marriages," *Los Angeles Times*, June 15, 1977, A28; "Senate Approves Measure Banning Gay Marriages," *Los Angeles Times*, August 12, 1977, B33.

75. Pat B. Anderson, "Lovers' Property Law Predicted," *Los Angeles Times*, March 20, 1977, GB7. Triola received nothing in the end, and the case did little to change the privilege status of marriage in the law. See Nancy D. Polikoff, *Beyond (Straight and Gay) Marriage: Valuing All Families under the Law* (Boston: Beacon Press, 2008), 176–77. The case is *Marvin v. Marvin*, 18 Cal. 3d 660 (1976).

76. Phillip Hager, "S.F. OKs Ordinance to Bestow Recognition on Gay Couples," *Los Angeles Times*, November 24, 1982, A3.

77. Leland Traiman, "A Brief History of Domestic Partnerships," *The Gay & Lesbian Review Worldwide*, July–August 2008, 23–24.

78. Philip Hager, "S.F. Mayor Vetoes Disputed Law on Live-In Lovers," *Los Angeles Times*, December 10, A10.

79. Carlos A. Ball, *From the Closet to the Courtroom: Five LGBT Lawsuits That Have Changed Our Nation* (Boston: Beacon Press, 2010), 57.

80. See Robert W. Bailey, *Gay Politics, Urban Politics: Identity and Economics in the Urban Setting* (New York: Columbia University Press, 1999), 310–18. Bailey attributes the defeat in 1989 to a fear of budget consequences due to the AIDS crisis and the effects of the 1989 earthquake in the city. This depressed turnout and gave disproportionate influence to absentee ballots mostly utilized by older voters.

81. Traiman, 24; Peter Nicholas and Mike Strong, *The Geography of Love: Same-Sex Marriage and Relationship Recognition in America (The Story in Maps)*, 2nd ed. (Self-published monograph, 2011), 18–21; "Human Rights Campaign Applauds Introduction of Domestic Partnership Benefits and Obligations Act," HRC Press Release, November 18, 2011, http://www.hrc.org/press-releases/entry/human-rights-campaign-applauds-introduction-of-domestic-partnership-benefit.

82. *In the Matter of the Adoption of Robert Paul P.*, 471 N.E.2d 424 (N.Y. 1984), 425.

83. *In the Matter of the Adoption of Robert Paul P.*, 427–29.

84. *In the Matter of the Adoption of Robert Paul P.*, discussion of amicus brief in headnotes.

85. See George Chauncey, *Why Marriage: The History Shaping Today's Debate (New York: Basic Books, 2004)*.

86. Ellen Ann Andersen, *Out of the Closets & Into the Courts: Legal Opportunity Structure and Gay Rights Litigation* (Ann Arbor: University of Michigan Press, 2005), 38.

87. 543 N.E.2d 49 (N.Y. 1989), 55.

88. Ball, 55.

89. *In re Guardianship of Kowalski*, 478 N.W.2d 790 (Minn. Ct. App.1991).

90. Casey Charles, *The Sharon Kowalski Case: Lesbian and Gay Rights on Trial* (Lawrence: University Press of Kansas, 2002), 6–7.

91. Walter Isaacson, "Ethics: Should Gays Have Marriage Rights," *Time*, November 20, 1989, http://www.time.com/time/magazine/article/0,9171,959077,00.html.

Chapter Three

Same-Sex Marriage, Politics, and Law around the World

Citizens of the United States like to think of themselves as leading the cause of human rights around the world, or that their country is the most advanced political and socially. Concerning same-sex marriage, however, this is far from true. While same-sex relationships are still not recognized in most states and at the national level, thirty countries recognize same-sex relationships nationally through marriage or similar status. Denmark was the first country to create such recognition in 1989. Looking globally and comparing these developments to the situation in the United States can shed light on the factors that lead to same-sex relationship recognition or the reasons for political and legal stagnation, as is the case in the United States. In addition, while foreign law is not directly applicable in U.S. courts, foreign policy developments and legal rulings and doctrines have recently made their way into Supreme Court decisions, and these developments will almost certainly play some role in litigation concerning same-sex marriage in the court.

This chapter will explore same-sex marriage developments around the world. However, it should be noted that the creation of laws and policies protecting same-sex couples is not a worldwide phenomenon. Progress has been made in Europe, Australia and New Zealand, South America, and North America, with little positive activity in Asia and Africa, with the notable exception of South Africa's legalization of same-sex marriage in 2006. Even where positive change has occurred, it has not been complete or without significant opposition, indicating that any attempt to rank the "goodness" of a country in terms of same-sex marriage is problematic. The LGBT rights movement is still relatively new in the world, and engagement with equality claims for sexual minorities is varied and contingent upon unique regional and national cultural, political, and legal differences.

In the United States, litigation is central to the movement for same-sex marriage; however, as table 3.1 indicates, this is not true for most countries. Indeed, strong judicial review is relatively rare in other liberal democracies. In those countries, it is more typical for the national legislature to have final say on law and policy. Judges narrowly interpret the law and grant significant deference to the legislature. The refusal of the Constitutional Council of France to mandate same-sex marriage in 2010, instead deferring to the legislature on the question, is a prominent example of this, as is a similar stance taken by the European Court of Human Rights. These civil law systems are the greatest in number among liberal democracies and contrast with the handful of common law systems, such as the United Kingdom, Canada, Australia, New Zealand, and the United States. In these systems, judges are traditionally given greater autonomy to shape the law through their interpretations and by virtue of the fact that judicial decisions have the full force of the law beyond the parties in a particular case, through the doctrine of *stare decisis*. Even in these systems, however, legislative supremacy is, or was, a fundamental element of the political system. For instance, as will be discussed, Canada operated under the doctrine of parliamentary supremacy until the last couple of decades, when a new bill of rights, the Charter of Rights and Freedoms, was enacted and aggressively enforced by the Supreme Court of Canada.

In other words, significant exceptions to the common law/civil law dichotomy exist, including a trend toward increased judicial policy making overall. Scholars refer to this trend as the "judicialization of politics," or when courts begin to make decisions traditionally made by legislatures or executives. Additionally, this politics involves the increased use of rights claims in court by individuals or groups who feel shut out by the majoritarian political process.[1] While not all protections for same-sex couples have involved the judicialization of politics, the issue of the legal status of same-sex couples has propelled the judicialization of politics in several national contexts.

Thus, courts have been useful, but far from the only, institutions in advancing rights and protections for same-sex couples. Much progress has been driven by traditional politics, with activists, interest groups/nongovernmental organizations, and political parties leading the way. Progress is also the result of shifts in cultural assumptions about marriage and the family, changes in public opinion relating to sexual minorities, and the relative weakness of religion as a political force, all issues explored in specific national contexts in the remainder of this chapter. Finally, unlike the United States, most countries that have legalized same-sex marriage or an equivalent framework have centralized political systems with jurisdiction over matters of family law housed in the national government, allowing for more swift and uniform policy making.

Table 3.1. National-Level Same-Sex Relationship Recognition around the World

Country	Name of Legal Status	Year Enacted	Judicial Mandate?
Sweden	Registered partnership	1995	No
Iceland	Registered partnership	1996	No
The Netherlands	Registered partnership	1997	No
France	Civil PACS	1999	No
Canada	Common law marriage	1999	Yes
Belgium	Statutory cohabitation	1998	No
The Netherlands	Marriage	2001	No
Germany	Registered partnership	2001	Mixed
Finland	Registered partnership	2002	No
Belgium	Marriage	2003	No
United Kingdom	Civil partnership	2004	No
Luxembourg	Civil partnership	2004	No
Spain	Marriage	2005	No
Canada	Marriage	2005	Yes
Andorra	Stable union	2005	No
Switzerland	Registered partnership	2005	No
New Zealand	Civil union	2005	No
South Africa	Marriage	2006	Yes
Czech Republic	Registered partnership	2006	No
Slovenia	Registered partnership	2006	Yes
Uruguay	Civil union	2008	No
Hungary	Registered partnership	2009	Yes
Norway	Marriage	2009	No
Sweden	Marriage	2009	No
Colombia	Civil union	2009	Yes
Ecuador	Civil union	2009	No
Austria	Registered partnership	2010	No
Iceland	Marriage	2010	No
Argentina	Marriage	2010	Mixed
Portugal	Marriage	2010	No
Mexico*	Marriage	2010	Yes
Ireland	Civil partnership	2010	No
Lichtenstein	Registered partnership	2011	No

| Brazil | Stable unions/Marriage | 2011 | Yes |
| *Denmark* | Marriage | 2012 | No |

*Same-sex marriage is legal only in Mexico City, but a ruling by the Supreme Court in Mexico mandates the recognition of these marriages by other states in Mexico. Italics indicate an "upgrade" in policy.

EUROPE: THE BEGINNING

A key to understanding the proliferation of legal protections for same-sex couples in Europe, especially northern Europe, is the fact that cohabitation gained more legal recognition there than in the United States. While the phenomenon of cohabitation increased in both regions, the law largely ignored the situation in the United States, while many European governments linked cohabitation with rights and social welfare benefits in a response to changing social reality. This was connected to another difference between U.S. and European politics. Europe possesses a stronger tradition of entitlement to governmental programs and benefits of the welfare state. In the United States, provisions of the welfare state are often tied to a certain status, as a way to reward those who are seen as most deserving of the benefits. Marriage continued to serve as a vehicle for the deserving status, as a way to raise the bar for those desiring benefits. (Recall the ineffectual legacy of the *Marvin* case discussed in the previous chapter.) For instance, in order to "deserve" survivor benefits after the death of a companion, one must have been married to that person under Social Security. People cannot simply take the "easy" way out and live together for a period of time. In Europe (and Canada), these more informal relationships increasingly opened the door to benefits. This linking of nonmarital status to government policies eventually opened the door more easily to benefits for same-sex couples. However, progress for same-sex couples in Europe was limited by an initial reluctance by policy makers to extend parenting rights to same-sex couples. This contrasts with the situation in the United States, where parenting rights were extended in many states well before relationship recognition. In the U.S. case, courts were central to this expansion of rights, relying on the "best interest of the child" standard in family law.[2] The notion that only heterosexual marriage is the proper avenue for child rearing was powerful in Europe as it was in the United States, but arguments for the equal treatment of same-sex couples in terms of other aspects of marriage were stronger.

Most European countries operate under parliamentary and civil law systems. This tends to limit judicial policy making, as noted above. Indeed, progress in Europe has been driven primarily by nonjudicial politics. In addition, Europe's politics have become much more secularized in the past several decades, as religiously based politics have increased in the United

States. While conservative religious voices, even official state churches, expressed opposition to relationship equality for same-sex couples, this opposition did not automatically translate into barriers in the policy arena.

Scandinavia: Denmark Makes History and the Dominoes Fall

Denmark's 1989 Registered Partnership Act was the first instance of a national jurisdiction granting relationship rights to same-sex couples. This was followed by similar policies in Norway in 1993, Sweden in 1995, Iceland in 1996, and Finland in 2002. The Danish approach created the new category of "registered partner" for same-sex couples that mirrored the country's marriage statute, with the glaring exception of adoption rights. Most of these countries eventually amended their laws to include parenting rights, and Finland's law did not include this exclusion. More recently Norway (2009), Sweden (2009), Iceland (2010), and Denmark (2012) have "upgraded" to same-sex marriage as public opinion in those countries shifted substantially in favor of marriage equality. In fact, Iceland's prime minister, Johanna Sigurdardottir, is a married lesbian, and was in office when the marriage legislation was enacted and worked toward its passage. In these parliamentary and civil law systems with weak judicial policy making, the policy debate was located exclusively in the political process, among advocacy groups, legislative commissions (used widely in the region to investigate new policy areas and make legislative recommendations), and legislators with support from parties on the left.

Before the enactment of registered partnerships in Denmark in 1989, the policy conversation had been percolating in the country since the late 1960s when the Socialist People's Party first broached the issue of relationship equality for same-sex couples. In fact, a committee to study the issue was appointed by parliament in 1969. The leading lesbian and gay rights group in the country, Society of 1948, advocated not same-sex marriage but government-recognized partnerships out of political expediency and discomfort with the institution of marriage by feminists in the movement. However, the committee consistently rejected this approach as it studied the issue for over a decade, invoking a traditional definition of marriage and a fear that approval of same-sex relationships on par with marriage would undermine Danish marriages in other countries, as these countries showed disapproval of a more radical approach. Instead, the committee eventually supported a gradual expansion of rights for same-sex couples.[3]

Dissatisfied with this approach, activists pushed for a new commission focused more narrowly on sexual minorities, rather than the broader topic of marriage in Danish society. While this commission was established in 1984, it stalled on a recommendation for relationship equality, causing activists to go directly to parliament with a registered partnership bill that was introduced in 1987 with the support of leftist parties. In the meantime, the new commission recommended against registered partnerships, calling for a more limited and piecemeal approach, citing the old idea of a backlash outside of Denmark and a belief that formal partnerships were not needed, because most same-sex couples were closeted and would stay that way. This, of course, undermined legislative efforts, especially as the government embraced the recommendation and rationales. Conservative opposition grew, especially from the Conservative People's Party. The debate was interrupted by an election, but the bill was reintroduced in the new parliament in 1988. In the new debate, the AIDS crisis drove much of the argument, with advocates arguing that partnerships would dampen promiscuity, while opponents argued that the bill would invite more same-sex sexual activity, especially from persons from other countries. The bill eventually passed after heated debate, the explicit removal of parenting rights from the new legal status, and a free vote for members of parliament. In parliamentary systems, parties generally dictate how party members will vote on important legislation, unless parties free their members to vote their conscience or follow the perceived wishes of their constituents. The final vote was 71 to 47, with five abstentions.

William Eskridge and Darren Spedale attribute the enactment of registered partnerships to the liberal nature of Christianity in Denmark. They note that natural law arguments were presented by opponents, but these did not carry the day. Instead, the values of tolerance and resistance to the imposition of one religious worldview, central to Danish Lutheranism, diminished the religious resistance to registered partnerships.[4] Martin DuPuis also notes the relative progressiveness of Denmark on questions of sexuality, having eliminating sodomy laws in 1933; supportive public opinion; and the country's egalitarian political culture. As he states, "Proponents' arguments centered around the principles of equality, freedom and justice. It was suggested that the realization of these principles had value in their own right. Legal equality implied an official, societal acknowledgement of the equal value of homosexual and heterosexual relationships."[5] The effects of this law were enormous, particularly in the rest of Scandinavia. Also recall that this spurred advocacy in the United States, as discussed in chapter 2. It was the start of several decades of relationship equality progress in Europe and throughout the world.

Following the dynamic of what political scientists call "policy diffusion," Norway adopted a nearly identical law in 1993, after a newly energized activist community inspired by Denmark created a media campaign designed to appeal to Norwegians' sense of fairness and to neutralize a more powerful conservative opposition than in Denmark. Fortunately for advocates, opponents were not as organized and savvy, and appeared intolerant. The conservative government called for the enactment of a registered partnership law in

1992, and it was enacted the following year.[6] Yuval Merin describes legislative supporters as drawing upon Norway's strong welfare state tradition. As he describes the dynamic, "The members of Parliament who supported the bill advocated justice in the distribution of rights and duties and the freedom of all citizens to choose their own lifestyle. They also emphasized the welfare of individuals and couples and the need to improve the position of lesbians and gays in a welfare society."[7]

Sweden soon followed in 1995, but it is important to note that the country had previously enacted a cohabitation law that included same-sex couples in 1987. This law was enacted on the basis of a parliamentary commission's recommendation for such a law in 1984, having rejected both marriage equality and registered partnerships as viable or necessary alternatives. As in Denmark, discussion about the status of same-sex relationships had been percolating since the late 1960s. After Denmark's law was enacted, another committee was appointed to study the possibility of a similar law. It recommended the enactment of such a policy to make same-sex couples more equivalent to opposite-sex couples. Soon after, the law was passed by parliament.[8] Iceland followed the Danish model in 1996, while things took a bit longer in more conservative Finland (2002), both after positive committee recommendations.[9]

The Rest of Europe: Varied Approaches but a Trend toward Equality

After the activity in Scandinavia, many other European countries enacted relationship equality policies. Some continued with the registered partnership approach, while others enacted full marriage equality, with the Netherlands the first country in the world to enact same-sex marriage in 2001, followed on the continent by Belgium (2003) and Spain (2005). The next countries to follow this lead were the Scandinavian "upgrades" to marriage of Sweden (2009), Norway (2009), Iceland (2010), and Denmark (2012), along with Portugal (2010). In this policy conversation, national and supranational courts were largely absent or not willing to challenge legislative approaches that included less than full marriage equality. However, the rapid proliferation of relationship equality policies throughout the continent over the course of two decades contrasts with the slow progress in the United States and clearly challenges the notion of the United States as a human rights leader.

France: PACS May Lead to Marriage If the Socialists Have Their Way

Despite its reputation for sexual libertinism, France has not treated sexual minorities well in policy and law. Bias against sexual minorities in criminal law was eliminated in the early 1980s under a Socialist government, and an antidiscrimination law was enacted in 1985. However, relationship equality policy has been late in coming and largely unequal. Reflecting the civil law tradition in the country, the courts in France have been unwilling to challenge the political and legal status quo. In 1989, the Court of Cassation (the nation's highest court, separate from the Constitutional Council) ruled that Air France was not obligated to offer domestic partner benefits to same-sex couples. Only heterosexual couples could receive these benefits. The court ruled similarly in 1997 concerning same-sex couples' right to a housing lease. [10] The court thus actively rejected the Scandinavian model of including same-sex couples in cohabitation frameworks. In 2011, the Constitutional Council ruled, by request of the Court of Cassation, that same-sex marriage was not mandated by the French constitution, ruling explicitly that the decision to create this status was the prerogative of the National Assembly, not the courts. [11]

Despite these barriers, however, France accelerated expansion of relationship equality policies outside of Scandinavia with the enactment of civil PACS in 1999. These are a separate category from marriage, open to both same-sex and opposite-sex couples. France's dislike for policy making based on differences or distinctions drove this particular solution to the problem of relationship inequality. The republican tradition in French politics, law, and culture emphasizes universality and commonality. France struggles with multiculturalism or identity outside of French culture and identity. As a result, a separate category for lesbian and gay relationships was out of the question, as was same-sex marriage on par with heterosexual marriage, due to French heterosexism. PACS were a significant policy change, however, especially from such a prominent European nation. The Socialist Party, with its legislative majority at the time, was committed to this policy change. Beyond the name difference, rights under PACS are far fewer than under marriage. Most notably, adoption rights are lacking, thus continuing the European discomfort with same-sex parenting. Interestingly, over time, PACS have become more popular with heterosexual couples not wanting to get married but desiring legal protections.

More recently, a lesbian couple commenced legal action, arguing that the denial of same-sex marriage violated their rights as French citizens. As noted above, however, this effort was not successful, but it represents a level of judicialization not seen in many other Western European contexts. After the Constitutional Council passed the buck to the legislature, the National Assembly considered a same-sex marriage bill in 2011, but it was defeated. It was supported by the Socialists but opposed by the party in power, Nicolas Sarkozy's conservative UMP party. After Sarkozy, who ran on an explicitly heterosexist definition of marriage in trying to shore up his support on the Right and with French Catholics, lost the 2012 election to Socialist Francois Hollande (who ran supporting same-sex marriage), the new government indicated that it would work to enact a same-sex marriage law with parenting rights. Recent polls show strong majority support for same-sex marriage among the public. [12]

The Marriage Countries outside of Scandinavia: The Netherlands, Belgium, Spain, and Portugal

Activism combined with favorable party politics (usually the coming to power of secular parties on the left), as well as geographic proximity, led to the enactment of same-sex marriage in some Western European nations. In the Netherlands, with the elimination of the Christian Democrats as a governing party in 1994, registered partnerships (open to all couples, like French PACS) were enacted in 1997. Following the European pattern, adoption rights were not included, however. A commission recommended that this be remedied, and activists continued to argue that registered partnerships were not enough. Ultimately, a same-sex marriage law was passed late in 2000, taking effect in 2001. Next door in Belgium, a similar dynamic fueled the creation of relationship equality policy. The Christian Democrats lost power in 1999 after nearly fifty years of party rule. A more secular coalition of parties on the left led to the enactment of same-sex marriage in 2003. A weak gender-neutral cohabitation law passed in 1998, effective in 2000, preceded the same-sex marriage law. Belgium thus initially reacted minimally to the domestic partner/cohabitation policies emerging in Europe, but the defeat of a religious party allowed policy makers and activists to turn toward the model of its more progressive neighbor, the Netherlands. [13]

Spain's legalization of same-sex marriage in 2005 came as a surprise to many, especially given the strong influence of the Catholic Church, but was the result of the election of the Socialist Party, whose leader committed the party to same-sex marriage in 2001. In addition, by 2004, limited domestic partnership registries had been enacted in twelve of seventeen regions, called autonomous communities, and public opinion strongly supported same-sex marriage. However, after the loss of the Socialists in the 2011 election to the much more conservative Popular Party, the future of same-sex marriage in Spain is in doubt. The party challenged the law before the Constitutional Court after it was enacted (the court affirmed the law), and the church has continued to mobilize against the law, organizing marches and demonstrations. However, given strong public support, repeal appears unlikely. [14]

Neighboring Portugal legalized same-sex marriage in 2010. Developments in Spain were a strong influence. According to the Socialist prime minister, Jose Socrates, who spearheaded the policy change, "Spain was very important for me and for my party." However, litigation also played a role. In the year following the enactment of Spain's law, a lesbian couple in Lisbon applied for a marriage license but were denied. Ultimately, the Constitutional

Court ruled 3 to 2 in 2009 that same-sex marriage was not mandated by the constitution, despite protections against sexual orientation discrimination in the document. This helped to spur the activity in the parliament (the Assembly of the Republic) that eventually led to the same-sex marriage law. Socrates and his party successfully ran for reelection in 2009 on a platform that included a commitment to legalize same-sex marriage. Adoption rights were rejected by the assembly, however. [15]

Less Than Marriage and Resistance in the Rest of Europe

Despite these notable same-sex marriage policies, most countries in Europe have enacted policies less than marriage, like the first round of Scandinavian policy change and France, or have resisted the enactment of relationship equality policy. Most of this has occurred without judicial intervention, with a few notable exceptions. In particular, countries with conservative governing parties have been resistant to favorable policy change, and Eastern Europe has proven to be inhospitable territory for relationship equality claims.

Because of the strong role in governing in the past several decades, the Christian Democrats in Germany have stunted the nation's progress on relationship equality, relative to other leading European nations. However, a window of opportunity opened in 1998 with the election of a coalition government of Social Democrats and Greens. The Life Partnership Act was passed in 2001 granting same-sex couples a limited menu of rights, but this was expanded in 2004. The election of the Christian Democrats as the leading coalition party in 2005 effectively ended further policy expansion. Public support for same-sex marriage in Germany is lower than in other Western European countries, but it is still a majority. The Social Democrats support same-sex marriage, and the party's fortunes (and other parties on the left) in the 2013 national elections will largely dictate the future of marriage equality policy in Germany, because the Constitutional Court has been reluctant to aggressively challenge the status quo. Legal challenges to the ban on same-sex marriage in Germany started as early as 1992 when a same-sex couple challenged their denial of a marriage license in court. The Constitutional Court ruled against the couple, holding that the right to marriage in the German constitution was heterosexual-only, but the court also indicated that the unequal treatment for same-sex couples was potentially unconstitutional. More recently, the court has ruled that same-sex couples are entitled to equal pension benefits and federal tax treatment, thus pushing the government little-by-little to fully recognize same-sex relationships, but stopping short of mandating full equality. [16]

In 2004, the center-left Labour Party in the United Kingdom created civil partnerships for same-sex couples. Given the doctrine of parliamentary supremacy, litigation for marriage equality has never been an option. More recently, the coalition government of conservative Tories and Liberal Democrats has pledged to enact same-sex marriage by 2015 for England and Wales (Tory Prime Minister David Cameron has come out strongly in support of marriage equality), but some Conservative MPs have balked at this. Religious opposition to the idea has also been strong, especially from the Church of England. The Conservatives will not enforce party discipline for the vote, but enough support likely exists among Liberal Democrats and Labour Party members to guarantee success. Following recent patterns of political devolution in the United Kingdom, the government of Scotland is separately considering legalizing same-sex marriage by the end of 2013. The governing party, the Scottish Nationalist Party, as well as all opposition parties, supports the policy, reflective of strong levels of public support in Scotland. [17]

In 2006, a high court judge in Ireland ruled that same-sex marriage was not required by the constitution, but the judge invited the government to treat same-sex couples equally. The Supreme Court is expected to rule on the case. Six years after its neighbor across the Irish Sea, the government of Ireland enacted civil partnerships, a noteworthy development in heavily Catholic Ireland. Enshrining same-sex marriage into the constitution may be an option at an upcoming constitutional convention. [18]

Same-sex relationship recognition has proliferated throughout the rest of Western and Central Europe. Representing an interesting outlier to the European approach, registered partnerships were approved by voters in Switzerland in a 2005 referendum. Same-sex partnerships have also been approved legislatively in the small European countries of Andorra (2005), Lichtenstein (2011), and Luxembourg (2004), as well as the semi-U.K.-independent Isle of Man (2011) and Jersey (2011). Voters in Lichtenstein approved of the law in a popular referendum after conservatives challenged the law. Austria enacted registered partnerships in 2010 through a coalition of parties on the left, as did the Czech Republic in 2006. However, most of these policies fall short of the rights and benefits offered with marriage, especially parenting rights, thus generally following the European model of frameworks outside of the marriage countries.

In Southern and Eastern Europe, however, the road to relationship equality has been considerably rockier. Most countries in these areas of Europe are uncovered by relationship equality policies, with Italy being the most notable exception to Europe's policy proliferation. There, the Constitutional Court ruled that same-sex marriages were not required by the constitution, and the recent politics in Italy have not been favorable for same-sex couples. However, a 2012 decision by the Court of Cassation could provide an opening for policy change. The court ruled that a same-sex couple was entitled to "family life" and certain benefits, but in this civil law system, the court does not have the power to set broad policy. In Slovenia, registered partnership laws were enacted in 2005 and 2006, but more recent efforts by the center-left government to enact same-sex marriage have met significant popular resistance, especially over the issue of same-sex adoption. The government action was triggered by a Constitutional Court decision holding that separate frameworks for relationship recognition was a form of sexual orientation discrimination prohibited by the nation's constitution. The same-sex marriage law, without adoption rights, was enacted in 2011, but this was vetoed by a popular referendum, initiated by religious conservatives, in March of 2012 with 55 percent of voters opposing the law.[19]

The movement for same-sex marriage in Hungary has been negatively affected by sweeping, and controversial, constitutional changes initiated by the center-right party, Fidesz, elected in 2011 with 53 percent of the vote but 68 percent of the seats in parliament. The party has used the constitutional changes to consolidate and expand its power. And according to the comparative constitutional scholar, Kim Lane Sheppele, "[T]he new constitution also accepts conservative Christian doctrine as state policy, in a country where only 21% of the population attends any religious services at all. The fetus is protected from the moment of conception. Marriage is legal only between a man and a woman." The previous government of center-left parties created strong same-sex registered partnerships (without adoption rights) in 2009. Interestingly, this followed the invalidation by the Constitutional Court of a previous law creating registered partnerships for all couples, on the grounds that this was too close to marriage, an institution protected by the constitution. But the court also ruled that same-sex couples should be recognized under some type of legal framework.[20]

Any discussion of politics and law in Europe must take account of the supranational institutions of the European Union, the European Parliament and the European Court of Human Rights. In addition, according to Kelly Kollman, the developments in Europe were influenced by human rights activists throughout Europe. "Today," according to Kollman, "the European LGBT advocacy network comprises transnationally linked national organizations, international human rights NGOs [nongovernmental organizations] and sympathetic policy elites." Kollman demonstrates that countries most exposed to these networks have seen the most policy change. Both the parliament and the court have supported some recognition of same-sex relationships, but their decisions are mostly advisory. However, they have a strong indirect effect by adding to the creation of norms, in this case norms of relationship recognition, used by activists in their distinct national settings. These norms have also been invoked by activists in litigation challenging the lack of marriage equality in some nations of the European Union. Contrary to the activists' wishes, the Court of Human Rights explicitly ruled in 2012, in a challenge to the inequality of French PACS, that European Union members are not required to enact same-sex marriage under the European Convention on Human Rights, yet another deferential court decision on the continent.

The court ruled similarly in a case from Austria in 2010, stating "marriage has deep-rooted social and cultural connotations which may differ largely from one society to another. The court reiterates that it must not rush to substitute its own judgment in place of that of the national authorities, who are best placed to assess and respond to the needs of society."[21]

To summarize the situation in Europe, the relationship policies begun in the North have spread throughout the continent in an uneven pattern, with center-left governments creating policy change when elections give them power and activists have mobilized, often using international and regional human rights norms. While courts have created opportunities for activists in some countries, most have followed the deferential norm common in civil law systems, to the extent litigation has been invoked at all. In addition, institutions of the European Union, while supportive of relationship equality, have been reluctant to impose a uniform legal approach. In some ways, the progress in Europe mirrors that of the state-by-state approach of the United States. (Of course, the U.S. federal government is a much stronger political and legal force than the European Union.) Until there is a uniform approach imposed on each decentralized region, this patchwork approach will likely continue for some time to come. In the United States this would be imposed by Congress or the Supreme Court; in Europe, the EU institutions. Neither set of institutions appears ready or willing to do this at the present political moment. The European Union is in financial and political turmoil, as of 2102, and it seems unlikely that Republicans in Congress and conservatives on the Supreme Court would challenge those states that have banned same-sex marriage.

CANADA AND SOUTH AFRICA: JUDICIALIZATION AND THE POWER OF NEW CONSTITUTIONS

In some countries, the enactment of same-sex marriage or similar approaches is linked to new or relatively new constitutions with robust rights protections and equality provisions that then become raw material for courts to compel the creation of LGBT-friendly policies, particularly in common law systems. This was the case in the legalization of same-sex marriage in Canada in 2005 and South Africa in 2006. Certainly, other factors were involved: changes in public opinion and grassroots mobilization and activism, for instance. This more traditional politics was greatly assisted by the constitutional revolutions in the two countries, thus differing from the European model of party politics and parliamentary-driven policy change. These two cases also illustrate the limits of U.S. constitutionalism for progressive legal and social change.

Canada

In terms of LGBT rights, Canada and the United States were similar until the late 1990s. While Canada repealed its sodomy law in 1969, the general approach on the political and legal status of sexual minorities was similar, as both countries failed to provide benefits for same-sex couples. Indeed, the response to the application of same-sex couples was similar in both countries—a general dismissiveness.[22] However, the movement for same-sex marriage met a very different set of cultural, legal, and political settings in the two countries by the late 1990s when legal and policy change accelerated in Canada while moving much more slowly in the United States. A new constitution, a newly assertive Supreme Court, more supportive public opinion, a history of cohabitation policies, and marriage policy jurisdiction at the federal, not provincial (or state in the United States, including popular referenda in states) level contributed to a more-rapid change in Canada than has occured in the United States.[23]

The Charter of Rights and Freedoms, enacted in 1982, transformed the Canadian political and legal systems. The charter included an array of individual rights and equality provisions and represented Canada's first constitutional-level definition of these rights and protections. A previous statutory bill of rights did not trump legislative enactments. Indeed, before the charter, politics in Canada looked more like the politics of the United Kingdom than of the United States, with parliamentary supremacy as the operating rule. The legislative branch generally defined the extent of individual rights and equal protection, and the courts seldom challenged this approach. The judiciary did not define the extent of individual rights; it merely was the highest court resolving legal disputes, but it did not overturn acts of the government as a standard practice.

However, soon after the enactment of the charter, the Supreme Court began to assert itself as the enforcer of the charter's provisions and, thereby, as a more powerful institution. By the 1990s, this was true of LGBT rights, and this accelerated the process of same-sex relationship recognition that began in reaction to increased cohabitation, as in Europe. Indeed, dynamics similar to those in the United States in the 1980s, particularly the AIDS crisis, led to activism in Canadian cities and provinces to recognize same-sex relationships either in new domestic partnership frameworks or by broadening the definition of spouse under various social welfare provisions. Unlike the United States, and more like Europe, Canada recognized cohabitating opposite-sex couples in many aspects of law and policy by the time that same-sex couples began to make demands for recognition. As Canadian political scientist David Rayside notes: "As much as in any country, the state regulation of marriage had been moving away from moral arbitration and treating marriage as the only legitimate conjugal relationship. The recognition of gay and lesbian partnerships was eventually seen as simply a logical extension of these earlier changes."[24] For example, significant change occurred in British Columbia in the early 1990s under the social democratic New Democratic Party with a series of laws (mostly relating to health care, a significant provincial policy area) recognizing same-sex relationships, primarily by broadening the definition of spouse to include same-sex couples.[25]

Using the charter, courts in Canada greatly accelerated the movement for relationship recognition by the late 1990s. The decision of the Supreme Court of Canada in *M. v. H.* in 1999 is a pivotal moment in the evolution of same-sex marriage policy. In that case, the high court ruled that a lesbian couple was entitled to the same benefits as heterosexual couples under Canada's common law marriage framework, including spousal support after the dissolution of a relationship. The court applied the equality provision of the charter and mandated similar treatment for same-sex couples, noting that "The exclusion of same-sex partners from the benefits of . . . [the common law statute] promotes the view that M., and individuals in same-sex relationships generally, are less worthy of recognition and protection. . . . Such exclusion perpetuates the disadvantages suffered by individuals in same-sex relationships and contributes to the erasure of their existence."[26]

This outcome was facilitated by a change in Canadian jurisprudence concerning sexual minorities that occurred in the decade of the 1990s. While the charter does not specifically identify sexual orientation as a category of equality protection, the Supreme Court ruled that sexual orientation was analogous to the categories actually listed in the charter in *Egan v. Canada* (1995), thus providing sexual orientation full protection under the charter. As the court stated in *Law v. Canada*, "The purpose of s. 15(1) is to prevent the violation of essential human dignity and freedom through the imposition of disadvantage, stereotyping, or political or social prejudice."[27] This is clear judicialization: a powerful constitutional provision was expanded without input from the legislature and after the legislative committee drafting the charter rejected the inclusion of sexual orientation in 1980.[28] Granted, it took the court over a decade to make this pronouncement, while the LGBT movement was growing and gaining influence and while public opinion was evolving in a more favorable direction, but the leadership of the judicial branch was enormously consequential for equality. David Rayside makes the important point that the courts did not act alone in the movement for marriage equality in Canada and were generally following shifts in public opinion, but that politicians were often willing to defer to their extension of policies protecting same-sex couples.[29] Absent court intervention, it is likely that change would have occurred more slowly and less broadly.

The decision in *M. v. H.* spawned two important results. First, the government amended the common law marriage statutes to include same-sex partners—a concrete, judicially driven policy change. Second, activists emboldened by the decision began to litigate for full marriage equality. Indeed, challenges to the exclusion of same-sex couples from solemnized marriage were brought in several provincial and territorial courts.[30] In the span of two years (2003–2004), these courts ruled that same-sex marriage was required by the charter. Geographically, these decisions in British Columbia, Manitoba, Nova Scotia, Ontario, Quebec, and Yukon covered nearly the entire country. As a result, the Liberal government began drafting same-sex marriage legislation in 2003, and this was enacted in 2005 after the Supreme Court gave its approval in a 2004 reference decision and after an election in which the Liberals held on to power. A vote in the parliament to repeal the law after the election of a Conservative government in 2005 failed, further enshrining this largely judicially driven policy.

Clearly, once the policy issue became constitutionalized, it was more difficult for the political process to resist the momentum for same-sex marriage stemming from the judiciary. While grassroots movements for LGBT equality contributed to a more favorable political climate, the issue was not one that the Liberal government saw as central to its electoral chances. Indeed, many Liberal MPs opposed same-sex marriage, especially those from rural ridings. Votes on same-sex marriage were "free votes," with parties refusing to enforce strict party discipline, particularly with the electoral fortunes of the Liberal Party fading. The defeat of the party in 2005, however, more directly was related to voter fatigue with the party and scandals that plagued the party. Same-sex marriage was a topic of debate during the 2005 election, but it did not play anything like the same role played by the issue in the United States in 2004, where eleven states voted on anti-same-sex marriage referenda in a strategy to assist in the reelection of Republican and same-sex marriage opponent George W. Bush. In Canada, these referenda do not exist, and the national government has jurisdiction over marriage policy. The issue likely prevented the Conservatives under Stephen Harper from winning a majority of seats in parliament until 2011, as the party's conservative position on social issues was emphasized by opponents in a nation becoming increasingly socially liberal.

Judicialization can be seen in the Canadian case also through the use of legal frames and language by political actors. In response to *M. v. H.*, the Liberal government proposed legislation to comply with the decision. Justice Minister Anne McLellan echoed the court decision by stating that the proposed law "ensures that federal laws reflected the core values of Canadians, values that are enshrined in the Canadian Charter of Rights and Freedoms. The fundamental tenets of Canadian society—fairness, tolerance, respect and equality—are touchstones of our national identity and serve to enhance our international reputation."[31] The government was not prepared to address the issue of relationship discrimination until the judicial intervention, but the government used the judicial language of constitutionalism to support and protect the proposed legislation.

In addition, despite the election of a Conservative majority government in May of 2011, it is unlikely that the same-sex marriage law will be repealed, given the constitutionalization of the issue. While many Conservative MPs would like a repeal of the same-sex marriage law, as they would also like a revising of abortion policy, the Conservatives will likely continue to avoid these issues, given more liberal public opinion and the role of the charter.[32] In the United States, however, opposition to same-sex marriage is still a significant part of Republican Party politics.

This difference is primarily the result of a much less potent Religious Right in Canada. While conservative evangelical Protestants and socially conservative Catholics (especially church leaders) in Canada share the same anti-gay views of their U.S. counterparts, they are much smaller in number and do not exert the same influence on the Conservative Party as do religious conservatives in the Republican Party.[33] Their socially conservative positions are usually downplayed by the Conservatives in national elections. In largely Catholic Quebec, the church has lost influence and political clout as the province has become more secular in its approach to politics, similar to the situation in Europe.[34]

Religious conservatives have been stymied in their efforts in Canada largely through the nature of the political party system in Canada. Party leaders exert enormous control over elected party members and candidates, as well as the positions of the party. While religious mobilization increased during the Canadian debates over same-sex marriage in the 2000s, because of non-party-enforced free votes, the overall approach of the Conservative Party was to deemphasize the issue to maintain national viability as public opinion shifted in favor of same-sex marriage and as it sought out urban and suburban votes.[35] Overall, despite the free votes, the party system in Canada facilitated the enactment of same-sex marriage, as three of the four major parties supported the policy by 2004.

South Africa

South Africa's 1996 post-apartheid constitution contains a remarkable provision: it explicitly lists sexual orientation as a category protected from discrimination, making South Africa's constitution the first in the world to do so.[36] This set the stage for the judicial creation of a range of LGBT rights, culminating in the court-mandated, and rather remarkable, enactment of marriage equality in 2006. According to South African legal commentator Pierre de Vos, "Given the fact that South Africa is not a developed country and given, moreover, that attitudes towards same-sex desire amongst ordinary

South Africans can hardly be described as enlightened, the adoption of legislation that now allows same-sex couples the choice of entering into a marriage seems little short of revolutionary."[37] Indeed, events in South Africa represent the greatest level of judicialization yet seen in the movement for relationship equality. Without judicial intervention, it is unlikely that the country would have seen the same extent of equality in its marriage policy.

Success in South Africa was the result of a gradualist litigation strategy. Activists, primarily represented by the National Coalition for Gay and Lesbian Equality, intended to create a series of precedents that would eventually lead to the legalization of same-sex marriage, and they knew that the South African judiciary would be their ally, not parliament.[38] Over the course of a few short years, the courts expanded the rights of sexual minorities by striking down the country's sodomy law and expanding rights for same-sex couples in adoption/child custody, pension rights, and immigration. By the time that challenges to the traditional definition of marriage in South African law commenced, a strong jurisprudence was firmly established, protecting sexual minorities from discrimination and affirming their dignity, creating, in retrospect, inevitability for the judicial recognition of full relationship equality.

The same-sex marriage case, *Minister of Home Affairs and Another v. Fourie and Another* (2005), was the result of uncoordinated litigation brought by a lesbian couple in 2002, later joined by the Equality Project representing the activist community. Due to strategic legal errors made by the couple and their lawyers, the case did not reach the Constitutional Court until 2005, but the couple achieved a victory in the Supreme Court of Appeal in 2004. The author of that decision, Edwin Cameron, had, a decade earlier, published a law review article that provided the jurisprudential foundation for the litigation strategy.[39] Now, as a judge, he transposed those principles from the pages of a law review to actual law. Ruling in favor of the couple, Justice Cameron held, as described by the Constitutional Court, that "the exclusionary definition of marriage injures gays and lesbians because it implies a judgment on them. It suggests not only that their relationships . . . are inferior, but that they themselves can never be fully part of the community of moral equals that the constitution promises to create for all."[40] Cameron's remedy was to change the common law definition of marriage to include same-sex couples, thereby mandating equality without legislative action. On appeal, the Constitutional Court was as robust jurisprudentially, but its remedy, in a nod to public opinion opposing same-sex marriage, was less aggressive, inviting parliament to craft a remedy within a year. However, parliament could not create a "separate but equal" arrangement. Essentially the court took political pressure off itself, while still mandating a high level of equality.[41]

Reflecting the high level of public opposition to the ruling, parliament did not begin seriously considering the issue until July of 2006 (the decision was the previous December) when the governing African National Congress Party (ANC) proposed two versions of legislation. The first was a bill creating gender-neutral language in the Marriage Act, thereby simply and directly legalizing same-sex marriage, but this was soon pulled from consideration due to opposition from within the party. Next, the ANC government proposed civil partnerships for same-sex couples under separate legislation from the Marriage Act, keeping marriage heterosexual-only. While this may have been more palatable for party members, the LGBT activist community strongly objected, arguing that this contravened the Constitutional Court's mandate. Meanwhile, hearings were held throughout the country, where blatant homophobia and heterosexism were on full display, fueled by religious perspectives and the argument that homosexuality was "un-African."[42]

Despite this, the ANC presented a revised bill to parliament that created a complicated legal framework, but one more consistent with the *Fourie* decision. It allowed both same-sex and opposite-sex couples to enter into a marriage or civil partnership, thus eliminating the separate but equal problem. It also granted to civil officials, in addition to religious officials, the right to refuse to perform a same-sex ceremony. The move from a gender-neutral marriage statute and the exemption for civil officials were attempts to placate more conservative members of the party, but LGBT activists were willing to go along, given the level of equality promoted by the bill. Ultimately, through party discipline and its significant majority, the ANC pushed the bill through parliament by a vote of 230 to 41, with three abstentions in the National Assembly and 36 to 11, with one abstention in the National Council of Provinces.[43]

As noted above, arguments from African traditionalists about the lack of same-sex relationships in African culture played prominently in the debate. They argued that homosexuality was introduced by Western colonizers. While this claim is not historically true (for example, same-sex relationships are a part of traditional African culture and the Western colonizers brought the *condemnation* of homosexuality and sodomy laws to the continent), it was politically and culturally powerful and helps to explain the strong resistance to LGBT rights on the continent of Africa. African traditionalism affects South African marriage policy further in the country's Customary Marriages Act, which recognizes polygamous marriages, as practiced by some Africans. Indeed, the current president of the country, Jacob Zuma, is a polygamist. These marriages are not gender-neutral, however. They are based on patriarchal family structure, with one male husband and several female wives. As a result, same-sex relationships were not included in this legal framework.[44]

The outcome in South Africa, in the face of tremendous cultural barriers, was strongly driven by the implications of the country's recent transition from a racist totalitarian state to a liberal democracy. As Justice Albie Sachs of the Constitutional Court put it, "Our Constitution represents a radical rupture with a past based on tolerance and exclusion, and the movement forward to the acceptance of the need to develop a society based on equality and respect by all for all."[45] This dynamic also drove change in countries like Spain, Portugal, and Argentina.[46] While it would be inaccurate to claim that this is a guarantee of success for LGBT rights claims, as not all formerly totalitarian countries have expanded rights for sexual minorities, it highlights an aspect of politics in politically "developed" nations like the United States that is potentially problematic for the expansion of rights. "Just world syndrome" describes a phenomenon in which citizens feel that their political and legal system has achieved the fullest freedom and equality reasonably possible, and they tend to discount or reject calls for further expansion of rights and equality.[47] This way of thinking is especially powerful in the United States and helps to explain the lack of progress for sexual minorities in contrast to nations long thought to be far behind the United States in political and legal development. The transition from totalitarianism also creates an opportunity to start new legal traditions and approaches. As Edwin Cameron declared in 1993, in creating a new constitution and equality jurisprudence "we operate free of the burdens of legal history: we can therefore try to do better than the majority of the United States Supreme Court in *Bowers v. Hardwick* managed to do."[48]

AUSTRALIA AND NEW ZEALAND: A EUROPEAN-STYLE APPROACH

In Australia, same-sex couples receive recognition and benefits as de facto couples, in a manner similar to opposite-sex unmarried couples. Some states grant civil unions, but marriage is prohibited by a 2004 law. Thus, like Canada, same-sex couples were allowed into a legal framework for cohabitating couples; however, unlike Canada, courts have not been involved, as Australia lacks a bill of rights and a strong tradition of judicial policy making in this Westminster parliamentary system.[49] Like activists in Europe, Australian marriage equality advocates have been forced to deal exclusively in the political area, with limited results. Prospects for the enactment of full marriage equality appear uncertain for the near future, despite the fact that public opinion is overwhelmingly in support of same-sex marriage.

Unique party politics are the main reason for the lack of success to date. Under the center-right government of Prime Minister John Howard (1996–2007), federal recognition of same-sex marriage was out of the question. His government enacted amendments to the Marriage Act in 2004 explicitly limiting marriage to one man and one woman and prohibiting the recognition of foreign same-sex marriages. The amendments were also passed with support from the center-left Labor Party, the other main national party in addition to Howard's Liberal Party. Howard even forbade his government officials to cooperate with a Human Rights and Equal Opportunity Commission study of the inequality faced by same-sex couples.[50] The commission identified extensive discrimination against same-sex couples, finding fifty-eight federal laws that discriminated against them, and recommended amending these laws. The commission also emphasized the challenges and unequal treatment faced by the children of lesbian and gay parents. Lacking a domestic bill of rights, the commission focused on how the legal status quo in Australia contravened international law, thus framing its analysis in the language of rights and equal treatment, not simply majoritarian policy. In particular, the commission cited the International Covenant on Civil and Political Rights and the Convention on the Rights of the Child.[51]

During the Howard years, Labor control of several state governments led to the subnational recognition of same-sex relationships with domestic partnership registries. The election of a Labor government in 2007 opened up the federal policy realm, but the Labor leaders were reluctant to embrace same-sex marriage, even telling the Australian Christian Lobby that the new government would not support same-sex marriage or civil unions. Labor leaders were fearful of alienating working-class Catholic voters, once the centerpiece of their party.[52] In this respect, the politics of same-sex marriage mirrors the politics in the United States with the strong political influence of religious conservatism. However, the new government followed the recommendations of the commission and amended a slew of laws to create rights and recognition for de facto same-sex couples and their children.

The policy debate advanced further in 2011. Responding to pressure from advocates, members of the Green Party (a coalition member after Labor failed to achieve a majority in the 2010 election) and more progressive Labor Party members (especially openly gay Finance Minister Penny Wong), Prime Minister Julia Gillard agreed to change the party platform to endorse same-sex marriage and call for a conscience vote on the issue in 2012, even though she personally opposed marriage equality. However, this is no guarantee of success, given that the government will not present the bill (it will be a private member's bill) and opposition within the party and from other parties will likely prevent the enactment of a same-sex marriage bill. Despite strong public support (a 2011 poll found 62 percent support), Gillard is wary of losing seats in more conservative and rural areas of the country in the next election and losing her already precarious position as prime minister.[53]

National policy change occurred early in neighboring, and politically similar, New Zealand with the enactment of a civil union law in 2004. The law, however, does not include full parenting rights. Only "spouses" can adopt jointly. The law applies to both same-sex and opposite-sex couples and was enacted through a conscience vote over the strong objections of religious conservatives and with the support of members of the Labour and Green parties.

Interestingly, however, a same-sex marriage lawsuit was commenced in New Zealand. Like Canada, New Zealand was home to a movement calling for a constitutional bill of rights in the 1980s. Initially, this movement included a call for judicial enforcement of these rights. However, public opinion did not support such a move, and parliament eventually enacted a statutory bill of rights in 1990, including a provision explicitly maintaining parliamentary supremacy and limiting judicial enforcement of the new rights. According to Paul Rishworth, "New Zealand's citizenry was comfortable with contentious policy issues being resolved by elected representatives in Parliament rather than by judges."[54] More importantly, sexual orientation was included as a category in a 1993 civil rights law, the Human Rights Act. This, combined with the emerging of the global movement for relationship equality by the 1990s, triggered a lawsuit by three lesbian couples who applied for a marriage license but were denied. They argued that the denial was a violation of the civil rights law. The Court of Appeal (the highest court in New Zealand at the time) ruled against them, arguing that the 1955 Marriage Act, though lacking a clear definition of marriage, envisioned only opposite-sex marriage. One judge would have ruled in their favor, but four other judges overruled him. Thus, the doctrine of parliamentary supremacy was maintained, but with the first formal statement of a potential legal deficiency.[55] The couples then pursued their claim with the United Nations Human Rights Committee International Covenant of Civil and Political Rights but were denied as well, with the argument that the covenant itself defines marriage heterosexually.[56] Even in a political culture that emphasizes parliamentary definition of rights, these couples made serious and persistent rights claims in judicial or quasi-judicial forums.

Nonetheless, the new civil rights framework still led to policy change, though without the courts driving the process. The Human Rights Act required a review of all existing statutes for potential inconsistencies within those statutes. Additionally, in the year 2000, the act would supersede existing laws, achieving a quasi-constitutional status. This caused the government to conclude in 2001 that the rights and benefits in the law for opposite-sex de facto couples should be applied to same-sex couples to be consistent with the act. The 2004 civil union law and a companion law were the vehicle to rectify the unequal treatment, not same-sex marriage.[57] However, given recent electoral victories of the conservative National Party, an upgrade to full marriage appears unlikely in the near future.

Thus, Australia and New Zealand have followed the European approach to relationship equality, with legislative policy making and marginal involvement from courts. To date, this has resulted in less than full marriage equality, despite public opinion favoring this. The lack of a constitutional bill of rights, as opposed to their fellow Commonwealth countries of Canada and South Africa, has limited the options for advocates and has resulted in less progress for relationship equality.

LATIN AMERICA: RAPID CHANGE IN A SEEMINGLY UNLIKELY REGION

As of 2011, same-sex relationships are recognized in several jurisdictions in Latin America through some form of civil unions or same-sex marriage: Uruguay (2008), Colombia (2009/2011), Ecuador (2009), Argentina (2010), Mexico (2010), and Brazil (2011). This represents about 75 percent of the population of South America. Serious conversations about recognizing same-sex couples have taken place in Chile, Paraguay, and Peru. This rapid change is the result of political parties on the left becoming more accepting of LGBT rights; the decline of religion as a political force; policy diffusion from Europe, especially Spain and Portugal, and within Latin America; and increased aggressiveness from courts mandating equality.[58]

This change is remarkable, given the history of sexuality in Latin America. Interestingly, the legal barriers for sexual minorities have not been as significant, as sodomy was decriminalized in most of Latin America in the nineteenth century, following decriminalization in the Spanish code in 1822, which itself followed the decriminalization of the Napoleonic code in 1804. In other words, sodomy laws are a legacy of British influence. Outside of British-influenced parts of the Caribbean and Belize in Central America, these legal barriers are not present in Latin America. However, other cultural and political barriers stifled progress for sexual minorities in Latin America. The creation of an identity based upon sexual diversity has been hampered by cultural forces. LGBT youth live at home during early adulthood, thereby constraining political activism by limiting social connections. Creating identity around sexuality is also impeded by cultural assumptions relating to sex roles, in that individuals who take an active role in sex generally are still considered heterosexual and many engage in same-sex sexual activity while in heterosexual marriages. While this is also common in other cultures, it is less stigmatized in Latin America. Like the United States, religious opposition, especially from the Catholic Church but also from evangelical Protestants, to LGBT rights is significant, but this appears to be waning. While progress in Europe has been driven by political parties on the left, leftist political parties in Latin America have been heavily influenced by the homophobia of Marxist parties, resulting from simple homophobia to a more complicated resistance to any non-class-based politics. These parties have historically seen their main focus as economic, rather than cultural. Finally, at the very time that lesbian and gay rights movements were forming in Europe, Canada, and the United States, many Latin American countries were ruled by military dictatorships, and nascent movements for sexual liberation were generally not tolerated and subjected to violence. A more recent turn to democratization in the region has created an opportunity for political organizing around issues of sexuality, and this has facilitated the recent, rapid change discussed above.[59]

Despite this progress, however, great variation exists for same-sex marriage in public opinion in Latin America and the Caribbean, according to one study, with the highest support in Argentina and Uruguay and lowest support in Guyana and Jamaica. The study found that higher levels of education and economic development explain higher levels of support for same-sex marriage. "Higher economic development and education tend to be linked with greater tolerance because they stimulate individual value priorities that are conducive to greater openness to diversity," according to the study's authors.[60]

Courts have also played a substantial role in the policy change in Latin America, often leading to policy changes seemingly not supported by public opinion. With the exception of Uruguay and Ecuador, courts were involved in all of the positive policy change for same-sex couples, to varying degrees. This is an interesting development, because strong judicial policy making generally is not a feature of politics in Latin America. Judicial innovation has historically been confined to countries with a common law tradition, mostly former colonies of England. Lawyers and judges in these systems are often socialized into favoring legal innovation. The law is to be interpreted in ways that further policy goals and is considered malleable and adaptable at the hands of judges and lawyers. Additionally, through the doctrine of *stare decisis*, judicial decisions affect not just the parties of a case, but anyone similarly situated. In other words, judicial decisions can be broadly applicable, adding to the policy-making power of judges. Most of the rest of the world, however, operates under a civil law system in which the written law, mostly law enacted by legislative bodies, is paramount. Judges do not see themselves as policy innovators; rather, according to Laura Saldivia, as "technocrats, who must solve problems in concrete and individual cases following . . . the codes of law or the constitution."[61] In addition, judicial decisions generally do not apply to parties other than those in the litigation, thereby limiting the impact of an innovative ruling.

This distinction between civil and common law systems is beginning to break down in Latin America, as judges have become more assertive policy makers on a range of issues, including same-sex relationship equality. Latin American judges are increasingly defining rights not explicitly defined in statutes or codes. As Javier Couso notes, this change is driven by lawyers and judges educated in the United States and socialized into common law, judge-empowered approaches and by an attempt by judges in Latin America to overcome the legacy of deference to other branches common during the era of military dictatorships.[62]

Uruguay and Ecuador: Change without Courts

In 2008, Uruguay was the first nation to recognize and protect same-sex couples at a national level. The enactment of civil unions (*union concubinaria*) was not driven by judicial mandates, but was the result of political party dynamics. In particular, the election of the Broad Front, a coalition of parties on the left, in 2004, and the pushing of activists within the party, led to the enactment of the new law. In particular, the impetus for the law came from a popular legislator, Margarita Percovich, who had also been active in the feminist movement in Uruguay. The law did not originally include adoption rights, but these rights were quickly created by the legislature. Since the enactment of civil unions, the government has also lifted the ban on lesbians and gays in the military. While nearly 60 percent of Uruguayans identify as Catholic, the church's opposition to LGBT rights progress has been muted by the increased secularization of the nation's politics. The Broad Front won even more political power in the 2009 election, leading to, in addition to the approval of same-sex marriage in neighboring Argentina in late 2010 discussed below, the introduction of a bill in Congress to modify the marriage code to include same-sex couples, with passage expected in 2013. Reflecting late but important judicialization, courts have begun to recognize foreign same-sex marriages, creating the potential for couples to marry in Argentina and return home to Uruguay and placing more pressure on the legislature to enact a same-sex marriage law. Uruguay has thus become one of the most progressive jurisdictions in the Americas on the question of LGBT rights. It is generally the most stable and egalitarian democracy in South America.[63]

Like Uruguay, Ecuador is a small country, but its political system is quite different. In Ecuador, politics is dominated by strong and populist presidential leadership, and this phenomenon led to the enactment of civil unions in the country in 2008 through constitutional referendum. Leftist President Rafael Correa led Ecuadoreans to approve a new constitution that expanded the president's powers and included new individual and social rights provisions, including Article 68: "The stable and monogamous union between two persons, free of matrimonial bond, who form a de facto couple, since the time and under the conditions and circumstances that the law provides, will generate the same rights and obligations that families, built through the marriage, are holding. Adoption will only correspond to couples of different sexes." Another provision, Article 67, declares, as requested by the Catholic Church, that marriage is only between a man and a woman. Thus, the new constitution contains both progressive and traditional views of sexuality and marriage, but the civil union provision was likely only because of the generally more popular constitution as a whole. Public support for same-sex marriage in Ecuador is very low.[64] While Correa made strong public statements on behalf of sexual minorities, it is unlikely that an independent referendum on relationship equality would have been approved.

Court-Facilitated Change: Colombia, Brazil, Mexico, and Argentina

The judiciary in Colombia, especially the Colombian Constitutional Court, is one of the most activist in South America, inspired by a 1991 constitution with a wide range of individual rights. In addition, barriers to bringing constitutional litigation are quite low through citizen lawsuits called *tutelas*, opening the courthouse door to a wide array of individuals desiring to change policy through constitutional litigation.[65] LGBT rights groups have used this to their advantage and have succeeded in expanding rights and protections for same-sex relationships through litigation. In a country where the Catholic Church wields enormous power, the turn to litigation has been crucial for achieving success, as the legislative arena has been more hostile to relationship equality claims. Most recently, the Constitutional Court has given the legislature two years (from 2011) to resolve the constitutional violation stemming from the denial of full equality for same-sex couples. This approach mirrors that of South Africa, with a series of court decisions expanding rights and protections for same-sex couples, followed by a finding that prohibitions on same-sex marriage are unconstitutional, but with a legislative mandate to correct the problem. Also, the jurisprudential "hook" for the Constitutional Court was the fact that nonmarital cohabitation is recognized in the 1991 constitution.

A ruling from the Constitutional Court in 2007 began the process of expanding rights for same-sex couples. In that case, the court found that couples were entitled to health and social security benefits. In 2009, the court ruled that all of the benefits open to heterosexual de facto couples (cohabitating more than two years) were required for same-sex couples, as these relationships deserved the same respect and dignity, and that failure to recognize these relationships impeded the individual development of the parties.[66] Emboldened by these victories, activists, led by Colombia Diversa, went back to court arguing that the Civil Code's definition of marriage as one man and one woman for procreative purposes was unconstitutional. They won a partial victory. For the first time, the court ruled that same-sex couples have the right to form a family. This is crucial, given that the constitution contains language about the family in Article 42: "The family is the basic nucleus of society. It is formed on the basis of natural or legal ties, by the free decision of a man and woman to contract matrimony or by their responsible resolve to comply with it." While this is clearly a heterosexual definition, the court ruled that same-sex marriage was not prohibited by this language, and the judges reaffirmed the previous line of reasoning that the exclusion of same-sex couples was discriminatory. Despite this far-reaching finding, they ordered Congress to enact legislation guaranteeing equal treatment; however, if Congress did not act within two years, the decision authorized same-sex couples to go before a judge or notary public to be married.[67]

It is unlikely that Congress will act to comply with the decision. The influence of the Catholic Church is quite strong on the institution, and public opinion does not support same-sex marriage.[68] In 2007, a bill granting rights to same-sex couples, consistent with the Constitutional Court case of that year, was scuttled at the last minute, despite previous passage by both chambers, due to pressure from the church.[69] In response to the 2011 decision, some legislators have called for a national referendum on the question. At any rate, same-sex marriage is set to become legal on June 20, 2013, or sooner if Congress complies with the decision. Clearly, the court pushed the issue of relationship equality beyond the boundaries of traditional politics.

After many years of little progress on relationship equality, courts in Brazil dramatically expanded the rights of same-sex couples nationally in 2011, creating "stable unions" with upgrades to same-sex marriage granted from several judges. Two political factors led to the turn to courts. First, the Brazilian political system is designed to resist change, given the many veto players in the system. Thus, the system is status quo–oriented. For instance, civil union legislation was first introduced in the National Congress in 1995 but repeatedly has stalled. Second, the LGBT activist community in Brazil has not been as focused as movements in other Latin American countries, instead focusing on issues such as violence against sexual minorities.[70]

Legal factors also facilitated the judicialization of the issue. The Citizen Constitution, put into effect in 1988 after the end of the military dictatorship in 1985, contains strong equality provisions that have been interpreted recently by courts to include sexuality, despite the rejection of the inclusion of sexual orientation during the constitution's drafting. Like Canada, this has been "read into" the constitution, linked to prohibitions on sex discrimination in the text. Conversely, as with many Latin American countries, heterosexually defined marriage is mentioned in the constitution, specifically Article 226, Paragraph 3: "For the purpose of protection by the state, the stable union between a man and a woman is recognized as a family entity, and the law should facilitate its conversion into marriage." This would appear to close the door on litigation for same-sex marriage, but this was not the case. Courts have used the equality provisions to expand the definition of family and grant rights to same-sex couples in stable unions. In the Civil Code, many of the rights of marriage are granted to stable unions, Brazil's version of cohabitation recognition. In addition, the Federal Supreme Court (Supreme Federal Tribunal or STF) possesses broad powers in this civil law nation. It has the sole constitutional power to make rulings binding on more than the parties in a case, including other branches of government, and it can hear abstract cases in original jurisdiction, or cases challenging the constitutionality of a law brought by a certain group of public officials, political parties, and certain civil society associations. As a result, activists have relatively easy access to the STF, and this court has sweeping authority to rule on the constitutionality of governmental policies. [71]

Several challenges to the exclusion of same-sex couples have been commenced in recent years with varying degrees of success, but the most successful was clearly the abstract cases brought by the attorney general and the governor of Rio de Janeiro on behalf of same-sex couples, thus demonstrating the support of the executive branch in Brazil. Indeed, according to Javier Corrales, "The reason state actors in Brazil reached out to the courts is that they were already issuing important rights to same-sex couples—such as pension privileges and health insurance benefits—and they wanted the court to lock in those practices." [72] These challenges were combined in a unanimous decision by the STF that stable unions included same-sex couples. According to Minister Carmen Lucia, "Those who make their choice for civil union cannot be unequal in their citizenship. No one can be considered a different and lower class of citizens, because they made their emotional and sexual choice apart from the majority." [73] In the wake of the decision, numerous judges have granted same-sex marriages to same-sex couples in stable unions, although this only affects the couples in each case, as only the STF can mandate broader changes. Some requests for conversions to marriage have been denied by judges, but the Superior Court of Justice (Superior Tribunal of Justice) overruled these denials on a vote of 4 to 1, declaring "sexual orientation should not serve as a pretext for excluding families from the legal protection that marriage represents." [74] Clearly, a great deal of legal momentum exists for the complete legalization of same-sex marriage in Brazil.

As a result of grassroots activism (especially an alliance between feminist and LGBT activists), leftist party politics, and supportive public opinion, same-sex marriage was legalized in Mexico City in 2010, after civil unions were enacted in 2006. The state of Coahuila also enacted civil unions in 2006. [75] The federal government, opposed to same-sex marriage, responded to the Mexico City law by challenging it in court, but this strategy backfired. The court approved the law and extended its reach by ruling that marriages

from Mexico City should be recognized by other states as a result of the
Mexican constitution's version of the full faith and credit clause of the U.S.
Constitution. However, outside of Mexico City, support for same-sex mar-
riage is quite low, and it is unlikely that many states will follow the lead of
Mexico City and Coahuila.

The fact that marriage is defined by states in Mexico allowed activists in
Mexico City to use the more progressive politics of that jurisdiction to
strongly advocate for relationship equality. In a sense, Mexico City was
Uruguay at the state level. Activism began early in the last decade with
public demonstrations, including a same-sex "kiss-in" in 2001 on Valentine's
Day. This activism was triggered by the historic election in 2000 in which the
one-party stranglehold on Mexican politics by the Industrial Revolutionary
Party (PRI) was broken after seventy years. In Mexico City, a leftist mayor
supportive of LGBT rights was elected, as were openly gay members of the
district's legislative assembly.[76] This trend continued with the legislative
enactment of same-sex marriage and adoption in late 2009 (effective in
2010), led by the leftist Democratic Revolution Party. While support for
same-sex marriage is low nationally, support is at or near 50 percent in
Mexico City.[77]

While the Supreme Court has been most assertive in resolving disputes
between political branches, and not on individual rights claims, the court's
decision to affirm and potentially expand same-sex marriage beyond the
borders of Mexico City represents a significant victory for relationship equality in Mexico and places both of the United States' neighbors ahead of it on
national recognition and protection of same-sex relationships. According to
one of the court's ministers, "Those of us who are in favor of this [the same-
sex marriage law] are in favor of diversity and tolerance." The court also
rejected the argument that procreation was central to the definition of marriage and that family as defined by the constitution was heterosexual-only.[78]

The Congress of Argentina, with the support of President Cristina Fernan-
dez de Kirchner, legalized same-sex marriage in 2010. However, this outcome was fueled significantly by litigation, as judges have become more
assertive policy makers in this civil law country. Several years of significant
mobilization, politically and legally, by LGBT rights groups were also crucial to this success. Events in Argentina also triggered discussion about the
legalization of same-sex marriage in neighboring Paraguay and Chile, further
accelerating the momentum for relationship equality in Latin America.

Advocacy for relationship equality began in earnest in the early 2000s,
initially through the civil association, the Argentinean Homosexual Community. At this point, the push was for civil unions, and three local jurisdictions
enacted civil union laws, largely through the influence of leftist parties:
Buenos Aires (2002), Rio Negro (2007), and Villa Carlos Paz (2007). A
schism developed among activists, as some thought that a call for same-sex

marriage was appropriate, especially after Spain legalized same-sex marriage in 2005. Eventually, advocates for same-sex marriage won the debate, and they commenced a judicial and legislative strategy. Bills legalizing same-sex marriage were introduced in Congress, and key legislators and the president were lobbied. To augment and support these efforts, activists initiated a litigation strategy to create media coverage and public awareness of the issue.[79]

The courts in Argentina have become more supportive of the rights of sexual minorities, especially the Supreme Court, but the civil law system still constrains the ability of judges to independently make policy. Like *tutelas* in Colombia, *amparos* in Argentina may be brought against government officials for violations of rights defined in statutes or the constitution. However, rulings only apply to the parties involved and do not set a general rule. Despite this limitation, activists calculated that suing on the basis of the denial of marriage licenses for same-sex couples could put pressure on the political process to the extent that judges ruled in their favor. Even if couples lost, the suits would attract media coverage. As a result, from 2007 to 2009 several same-sex couples applied for marriage licenses. While they achieved limited success, the "external" effects of the litigation were significant in shifting the political debate toward one of rights and equality and away from tradition and religion. The governor of Tierra del Fuego, the site of a successful same-sex marriage (later overturned but appealed to the Supreme Court), described the issue of same-sex marriage as "an important advance in human rights and social inclusion."[80]

Argentina's Congress passed a same-sex marriage bill in 2010 after the more conservative Senate narrowly approved the bill following approval by the House. This occurred after a committee in the Senate voted against it, but strong lobbying and the support of President Kirchner revived the bill. Kirchner took a strongly secular position, stating in a speech that the actions of the Catholic Church were in opposition to the "times of the Crusades." Indeed, the success of the bill can be partially explained by antipathy toward the church in Argentina and its history of siding with authoritarian rule. As well, public support for same-sex marriage in Argentina is the highest in Latin America. President Kirchner won reelection in a landslide in 2011, obviously strengthened by her stand in support of relationship equality.[81]

Clearly, courts have been crucial to the bulk of progress for relationship equality in Latin America, with the strongest judicialization in Colombia and Brazil, followed by Mexico and Argentina. One major exception to this trend is Costa Rica, where the Supreme Court has rejected attempts to create protections for same-sex couples. In the remaining countries, change is possible only through traditional politics, and progress has stalled. As of this writing, Chile appears to be the next nation most likely to enact relationship equality policies. Despite strong religious and cultural opposition, President

Sebastian Pinera has proposed civil union legislation, and a legal challenge to the prohibition on same-sex marriage has made it to the Supreme Court.[82] In Central America and the Caribbean, hostility to sexual minorities remains high, and they have few political or judicial allies. Cuba is an exception, with advocacy promoted by Mariela Castro, daughter of President Raul Castro, in one of the remaining authoritarian regimes in the region.[83]

GLOBAL RESISTANCE

Despite the progress in Canada, Europe, and Latin America, much of the world remains hostile toward sexual minorities, and relationship equality is a pipe dream. This is true of much of Central and Eastern Europe, the countries of the former Soviet Union, the Middle East, most of Africa, and Asia. In these regions heterosexism and homophobia are still powerful political and cultural forces, with much of this sentiment driven by religious dogma. In many of these countries, it is illegal to be lesbian or gay, and violence against sexual minorities is routine. Of course, these views are not universally held, and many of these countries possess emerging LGBT communities and activism, but this is often underground. Indeed, long-standing same-sex traditions exist in many of these countries.

The most visible example of hostility toward sexual minorities in recent years is the attempt by politicians in Uganda to enact the "kill the gays" bill. This proposed legislation appeared in 2009 after anti-gay activists from the United States highlighted the "threat" to Uganda from sexual minorities, relying on the ugliest of slurs against lesbians and gays, especially the notion that they are a threat to children and civilization itself. The bill makes being lesbian or gay punishable by death, and would prosecute individuals with knowledge of a person's illegal sexual orientation for not identifying the person to authorities. Less extreme, but still troubling, the city of St. Petersburg, Russia, has made illegal the advocacy of people with LGBT identities, reflecting the strong anti-gay sentiments in Russia and Eastern Europe. For instance, attempts to enact registered partnerships in Poland have failed repeatedly. A 2009 poll indicated that 75 percent of Poles oppose same-sex marriage, with even higher opposition to same-sex couples adopting children.[84]

Asia could be the next frontier for the expansion of relationship equality, given the large number of democracies with strong links to global human rights norms. In Nepal, the Supreme Court ordered the legislature to enact same-sex marriage, but progress has stalled as a new constitution was debated.[85] However, LGBT rights movements are not well developed in the region, and courts are not a realistic option in these civil law systems. Outside of the regions explored in this chapter, relationship equality policy expansion is unlikely in the short term, but many countries have surpassed the progress made in the United States.

NOTES

1. Charles Epp, *The Rights Revolution: Lawyers, Activists, and Supreme Courts in Comparative Perspective* (Chicago: University of Chicago Press, 1998); Ran Hirschl, "Judicialization of Politics," in *The Oxford Handbook of Law and Politics*, Keith E. Whittington, R. Daniel Kelemen, and Gregory A. Caldeira, eds. (New York: Oxford University Press, 2008), 119–41.

2. See Nancy D. Polikoff, "Raising Children: Lesbian and Gay Parents Face the Public and the Courts," in *Creating Change: Sexuality, Public Policy, and Civil Rights*, John D'Emilio, ed. (New York: St. Martin's Press, 2000).

3. Much of the information in this and following paragraphs is taken from the excellent discussion of the enactment of registered partnerships in Denmark by William N. Eskridge, Jr., and Darren R. Spedale in *Gay Marriage: For Better or Worse? What We've Learned from the Evidence* (New York: Oxford University Press, 2006).

4. Eskridge and Spedale, 58–61.

5. Martin D. DuPuis, "The Impact of Culture, Society, and History on the Legal Process: An Analysis of the Legal Status of Same-Sex Relationships in the United States and Denmark," *International Journal of Law and the Family* 9 (1995), 86–118, 106.

6. Eskridge and Spedale, 62–68.

7. Yuval Merin, *Equality for Same-Sex Couples: The Legal Recognition of Gay Partnerships in Europe and the United States* (Chicago: University of Chicago Press, 2002), 85–86.

8. Eskridge and Spedale, 68–74.

9. See Merin, 103–10.

10. Patrice Corriveau, *Judging Homosexuals: A History of Gay Persecution in Quebec and France* (Vancouver: UBC Press, 2011), 147–48.

11. "French Court Says No to Gay Marriage," *Pink News*, January 28, 2011, http://www.pinknews.co.uk/2011/01/28/french-court-says-no-to-gay-marriage.

12. Sophie Pilgrim, "French Lesbian Couple Fight for the Right to Say 'I Do,'" *France 24*, February 3, 2011, http://www.france24.com/en/20110127-lesbian-couple-parents-france-gay-marriage-ban-homosexual-rights; Joseph Bamat, "Same-Sex Marriage Reveals Cracks in Sarkozy Party," *France 24*, June 10, 2011; Stephen Gray, "French Prime Minister Promises to Implement Equal Marriage and Adoption Rights for Gays," *Pink News*, May 18, 2012, http://www.pinknews.co.uk/2012/05/18/french-prime-minister-promises-to-implement-equal-marriage-and-adoption-rights-for-gays.

13. Gert Hekma and Jan Willem Duyvendak, "The Netherlands: Depoliticization of Homosexuality and Homosexualization of Politics," in *The Lesbian and Gay Movement and the State: Comparative Insights into a Transformed Relationship*, Manon Tremblay, et al., eds. (Burlington, VT: Ashgate, 2011), 110–11; Eskridge and Spedale, 82–84; David Paternotte, "Belgium: The Paradoxical Strength of Disunion," in Tremblay, et al., 44; Merin, 148–150.

14. Kerman Calvo, "Spain: Building Reciprocal Relations between Lesbian and Gay Organizations and the State," in Tremblay, et al., 176; Sarah Rainsford, "Spain Gay Rights and Abortion Activists Fear Backlash," *BBC News*, November 24, 2011, http://www.bbc.co.uk/news/world-europe-15894536; Jose Ignacio Pichardo Galan, "Same-Sex Couples in Spain: Historical, Contextual, and Symbolic Factors," *Same-Sex Couples, Same-Sex Partnerships & Homosexual Marriages*, Marie Digoix and Patrick Festy, eds. (Paris: INED, 2004), 159–74.

15. Frank Bruni, "One Country's Big Gay Leap," *New York Times*, October 11, 2011, SR3; Barry Hattan, "Portugal Gay Marriage Ban Upheld by Court," *Associated Press*, July 31, 2009; "Same-Sex Marriage Law Backed in Portugal's Parliament," *BBC News*, January 8, 2010, http://news.bbc.co.uk/2/hi/europe/8448640.stm.

16. Merin, 142–47; "Eight E.U. Countries Back Same-Sex Marriage," *Angus-Reid Public Opinion*, December 24, 2006, http://www.angus-reid.com/polls/5787/eight_eu_countries_back_same_sex_marriage; Jessica Geen, "Germany Gives Pension Rights to Gay Civil Partners," *Pink News*, October 22, 2009, http://www.pinknews.co.uk/2009/10/22/germany-gives-pension-rights-to-gay-civil-partners; "German Court Says Gay Couples Must Have Equal Inheritance Tax Rights," *Pink News*, August 17, 2010, http://www.pinknews.co.uk/2010/08/17/german-court-says-gay-couples-must-have-equal-inheritance-tax-rights.

17. Andrew Grice, "Tory MPs Go to War over Gay Marriage," *UK Independent*, January 17, 2012, http://www.independent.co.uk/news/uk/politics/tory-mps-go-to-war-over-gay-marriage-6290679.html; Dan Littaur, "Gay Marriage Equality in Scotland 'By the End of 2013,'" *Pink News*, February 1, 2012, http://www.pinknews.co.uk/2012/02/01/gay-marriage-equality-in-scotland-by-the-end-of-2013; James Park, "David Cameron: 'The Time Has Come for Gay Couples to Marry,'" *Pink News*, May 2, 2012, http://www.pinknews.co.uk/2012/05/02/david-cameron-the-time-has-come-for-gay-couples-to-marry.

18. Edmond Broch, "Equal Marriage Moves a Step Closer in Ireland," *Pink News*, http://www.pinknews.co.uk/2012/03/31/equal-marriage-moves-a-step-closer-in-ireland; "Gay Couple in Supreme Court over Right to Wed," *Irish Times*, May 9, 2012, http://www.irishtimes.com/newspaper/ireland/2012/0509/1224315799791.html.

19. "New Family Law Allowing Gay Marriage Stirs Controversy," *Slovenia Press Agency*, September 21, 2009, http://www.sta.si/en/vest.php?s=a&id=1428986; "Ministry Confirms Changes to Gay Adoption Proposal," *Slovenia Press Agency*, January 24, 2011, http://www.sta.si/en/vest.php?s=a&id=1598682; "Italy Court Rules Gays Have Rights to 'Family Life,'" AFP, March 15, 2012, http://www.france24.com/en/20120315-italy-court-rules-gays-have-right-family-life; Christopher Brocklebank, "Gay Adoption Law Is Rejected in Slovenian Referendum," *Pink News*, March 26, 2012, http://www.pinknews.co.uk/2012/03/26/gay-adoption-law-is-rejected-in-slovenian-referendum.

20. "Hungarian Government Proposes Registered Same-Sex Partnerships," *Pink News*, February 19, 2009, http://www.pinknews.co.uk/2009/02/12/hungarian-government-proposes-registered-same-sex-partnerships; Kim Lane Sheppele, "Hungary's Constitutional Revolution," *New York Times*, December 19, 2011, http://krugman.blogs.nytimes.com/2011/12/19/hungarys-constitutional-revolution.

21. Kelly Kollman, "European Institutions, Transnational Networks, and National Same-Sex Unions Policy: When Soft Law Hits Harder," *Contemporary Politics*, 15:1 (March 2009), 37–53: 42–43; *Schalk and Kopf v. Austria,* Application no. 30141/04, Council of Europe: European Court of Human Rights, 24 June 2010; Steve Doughty, "Gay Marriage Is Not a 'Human Right': European Ruling Torpedoes Coalition Stance," *Daily Mail*, March 20, 2012, http://www.dailymail.co.uk/news/article-2117920/Gay-marriage-human-right-European-ruling-torpedoes-Coalition-stance.html.

22. *Re North et al. and Matheson* (1975), 52 D.L.R. (3d) 280 (Man. Co. Ct).

23. David Rayside, *Queer Inclusion, Continental Divisions: Public Recognition of Sexual Diversity in Canada and the United States* (Toronto: University of Toronto Press, 2008); Miriam Smith, *Political Institutions and Lesbian and Gay Rights in the United States and Canada* (New York: Routledge), 2009.

24. Rayside, *Queer Inclusion, Continental Divisions*, 123.

25. Rayside, *Queer Inclusion, Continental Divisions*, 99–100.

26. *M. v. H.*, [1999] 2 S.C.R. 3.

27. *Law v. Canada (Minister of Employment and Immigration)*, [1999] 1 SCR 497.

28. David Rayside, *On the Fringe: Gays and Lesbians in Politics* (Ithaca: Cornell University Press, 1998), 109.

29. Rayside, *Queer Inclusion, Continental Divisions*, 122–23.

30. In the Canadian legal system, these courts are housed in provinces and territories, but they are federal courts. This reflects the fact that in Canada, marriage is defined by the national government, not the provinces and territories.

31. Edited Hansard of the 36th Parliament of Canada, 2nd session, No. 49, February 15, 2000, 1005.

32. John Ibbitson, "Remaking Stephen Harper in Canada's Image," *Toronto Globe and Mail*, May 6, 2011, http://www.theglobeandmail.com/news/politics/john-ibbitson/remaking-stephen-harper-in-canadas-image/article2013255/page1.

33. Jonathan Malloy, "Canadian Evangelicals and Same-Sex Marriage," in *Faith, Politics, and Sexual Diversity in Canada and the United States* (Vancouver: UBC Press, 2011), 144–59.

34. Solange Lefebvre and Jean-Francois Breton, "Roman Catholics and Same-Sex Marriage in Quebec," in *Faith, Politics, and Sexual Diversity in Canada and the United States*, 219–33.

35. Jonathan Malloy, "Canadian Evangelicals."

36. Chapter 2, section 9: "The state may not unfairly discriminate directly or indirectly against anyone on one or more grounds, including race, gender, sex, pregnancy, marital status, ethnic or social origin, colour, sexual orientation, age, disability, religion, conscience, belief, culture, language and birth." For background, see Mai Palmberg, "Emerging Visibility of Gays and Lesbians in Southern Africa," in *The Global Emergence of Gay and Lesbian Politics: National Imprints of a Worldwide Movement*, Barry D. Adam, et al. eds. (Philadelphia: Temple University Press, 1999), 272–73.

37. Pierre de Vos, "A Judicial Revolution? The Court-Led Achievement of Same-Sex Marriage in South Africa," *Utrecht Law Review* 4:2 (June 2008), 162–74: 174.

38. See Jonathan Berger, "Getting to the Constitutional Court on Time: A Litigation History of Same-Sex Marriage," in *To Have and to Hold: The Making of Same-Sex Marriage in South Africa* (Auckland Park, South Africa: Fanele, 2008), 17–28.

39. Edwin Cameron, "Sexual Orientation and the Constitution: A Test Case for Human Rights," *South African Law Journal* 110 (1993), 450–72. At that time, Cameron advocated domestic partnerships, not same-sex marriage.

40. [2005] ZACC 19, para 17.

41. [2005] ZACC 19.

42. Fikile Vilakazi, "Lobbying for Same-Sex Marriage: An Activist's Reflections," in *To Have and to Hold*, 94.

43. David Bilchitz and Melanie Judge, "The Civil Union Act: Messy Compromise or Giant Leap Forward?" in *To Have and to Hold*. Vote counts are from *To Have and to Hold*, pages 134 and 143.

44. See Nonhlanhla Mkhize, "(Not) in My Culture: Thoughts on Same-Sex Marriage and African Practices," in *To Have and to Hold*; Mark Gevisser, "The Politics Behind Zuma's Polygamy," *Guardian*, March 4, 2010, http://www.guardian.co.uk/commentisfree/2010/mar/04/zuma-polygamy-south-africa.

45. [2005] ZACC 19, para 59.

46. Frank Bruni, "One Country's Big Gay Leap," *New York Times*, October 9, 2011, SR3.

47. See Augustus B. Cochran III, *Sexual Harassment and the Law: The Michelle Vinson Case* (Lawrence: University Press of Kansas, 2004).

48. Cameron, 463–64.

49. Carol Johnson, Sarah Maddison, and Emma Partridge, "Australia: Parties, Federalism and Rights Agendas," in *The Lesbian and Gay Movement and the State: Comparative Insights into a Transformed Relationship*, Manion Tremblay, David Paternotte, and Carol Johnson, eds. (Burlington, VT: Ashgate, 2011), 28.

50. Johnson, et al., 31–32.

51. "Same-Sex, Same Entitlements: National Inquiry into Discrimination against People in Same-Sex Relationships: Financial and Work Related Entitlements and Benefits," Human Rights and Equal Opportunity Commission, May 2001, http://www.hreoc.gov.au/human_rights/samesex/report/pdf/SSSE_Report.pdf. For the international law references, see chapter 18.

52. Johnson, et al., 33–36.

53. Angus Whitley and Jason Scott, "Gillard's Gay Marriage Vote Plan Wins over Australian Party," *Bloomberg Businessweek*, December 5, 2011, http://www.businessweek.com/news/2011-12-04/gillard-s-gay-marriage-vote-plan-wins-over-australian-party.html.

54. Paul Rishworth, "Changing Times, Changing Minds, Changing Laws—Sexual Orientation and New Zealand Law, 1960 to 2005," *International Journal of Human Rights*, 11:1–2 (March 2007), 85–107: 93.

55. Rishworth, 95–96; *Quilter v. Attorney-General* [1998] 1 NZLR 523 (NZCA).
56. *Joslin v. New Zealand*, Communication No. 902/1999, July 17, 2002. Article 23 of the Covenant reads: "The right of men and women of marriageable age to marry and to found a family shall be recognized."
57. Rishworth, 91–94.
58. See Jason Pierceson, et al., *Same-Sex Marriage in the Americas: Policy Innovation for Same-Sex Relationships* (Lanham, MD: Lexington Books, 2010).
59. See Javier Corrales and Mario Pecheny, "The Comparative Politics of Sexuality in Latin America," in *The Politics of Sexuality in Latin America: A Reader on Lesbian, Gay, Bisexual, and Transgender Rights*, Javier Corrales and Mario Pecheny, eds. (Pittsburgh: University of Pittsburgh Press), 1–30; Jason Pierceson, et al., *Same-Sex Marriage in the Americas: Policy Innovation for Same-Sex Relationships*.
60. German Lodola and Margarita Corral, "Latin America's Support for Same-Sex Marriage," *Americas Quarterly*, 2010. http://www.americasquarterly.org/node/1728.
61. Laura Saldivia, "The Argentine Supreme Court and the Construction of a Constitutional Protection for Sexual Minorities," in *Same-Sex Marriage in the Americas,* 73–92, 73.
62. Javier A. Couso, "The Transformation of Constitutional Discourse and the Judicialization of Politics in Latin America," in *Cultures of Legality: Judicialization and Political Activism in Latin America,* Javier A. Couso, Alexandra Huneeus, and Rachel Sieder, eds. (New York: Cambridge University Press, 2010), 141–60.
63. Adriana Piatti-Crocker and Jason Pierceson, "Introduction," in Pierceson, et al., *Same-Sex Marriage in the Americas: Policy Innovation for Same-Sex Relationships* (Lanham, MD: Lexington Books, 2010), 4–6; Federica Narancio, "Uruguay Will Allow Gay Adoption, A First for Latin America," *McClatchy Newspapers*, September 9, 2009; Paulo Ravecca, "'Progressive' government (2005–2009) and the LGBTTBQ Agenda: On the (Recent) Queering of Uruguay and its Limits," CERLAC Working Paper, York University, July 2010; "Por primera vez Justicia uruguay areconoce matrimonio homosexual," *El Pais Digital*, June 9, 2012, http://www.elpais.com.uy/120609/pnacio-645421/politica/por-primera-vez-justicia-uruguaya-reconoce-matrimonio-homosexual.
64. Lodola and Corral find support at only 18.4 percent.
65. Manuel Jose Cepeda Espinosa, "The Judicialization of Politics in Colombia: The Old and the New," in *The Judicialization of Politics in Latin America*, Rachel Sieder, et al., eds. (New York: Palgrave Macmillan, 2005).
66. Decision C-075/2007; Decision C-029/2009.
67. Decision C-577/11. Decision summary found at http://www.matrimonioigualitario.org/p/en-el-congreso.html.
68. According to Lodola and Corral, support for marriage equality stands at 34 percent.
69. "Colombian Court Rules in Favour of Equal Rights for Gay Couples," *Pink News*, October 6, 2007, http://www.pinknews.co.uk/news/articles/2005-5666.html.
70. Shawn Schulenberg, "Policy Stability without Policy: The Battle for Same-Sex Partnership Recognition in Brazil." In *Same-Sex Marriage in the Americas,* 93–127.
71. Schulenberg, 100–103, 112–115. The equality provisions include Article 5, "All are equal before the law, without distinction." In addition, Article 3, paragraph 4 states that the republic must "promote the well-being of all, without prejudice as to origin, race, sex, color, and any other forms of discrimination."
72. Javier Corrales, "Brazil's Recognition of Same-Sex Unions," *Americas Quarterly*, May 11, 2011, http://www.americasquarterly.org/node/2528.
73. English summary of the STF decision in ADI 4277 (*Attorney General v. National Congress*) and ADPF 132 (*Governor of the State of Rio de Janeiro v. Courts of Justice of the States*), May 5, 2011, http://www2.stf.jus.br/portalStfInternacional/cms/destaquesClipping.php?sigla=portalStfDestaque_en_us&idConteudo=179046.
74. "Brazil High Court Allows Gay Marriage," News24.com, October 26, 2011, http://www.news24.com/World/News/Brazil-high-court-allows-gay-marriage-20111026; "Decision: Fourth class admits marriage between same-sex," STJ website, October 25, 2011, http://www.stj.jus.br/portal_stj/publicacao/engine.wsp?tmp.area=398&tmp.texto=103687. This is the high-

est court of appeal for nonconstitutional challenges, and the court does not have the same sweeping power to mandate policy as does the Supreme Court. Its decisions only apply directly to the parties involved.

75. The enactment of civil unions in Coahuila was something of a fluke, and not based on a coordinated, grassroots movement. See Genaro Lozano, "Same-Sex Relationship Equality in Mexico," in *Same-Sex Marriage in the Americas*, 149–52.

76. Lozano, 136.

77. Jennifer Gonzalez, "Mexico City Approves Gay Marriage," *AFP*, December 21, 2009, http://www.google.com/hostednews/afp/article/ALeqM5h4_uOzElZivyqR7ZpWRTnJdAJ5dg. Poll results for Mexico City in 2009 are from an *El Universal* poll found at http://www.eluniversal.com.mx/graficos/pdf09/infografias/encuesta_g.html.

78. Rex Wockner, "Mexico City Gay Marriage Law Upheld," *Bay Area Reporter*, August 12, 2010, http://www.ebar.com/news/article.php?sec=news&article=4988; Karina Anasolabehere, "More Power, More Rights? The Supreme Court and Society in Mexico," in *Cultures of Legality*, 78–111.

79. Adriana Piatti-Crocker, "Constructing Policy Innovation in Argentina: From Gender Quotas to Same-Sex Marriage," in *Same-Sex Marriage in the Americas,* 37–72; Maria Gracia Andia, "Disadvantaged Groups, the Use of Courts, and Their Impact: A Study of Legal Mobilization in Argentina through the LGBT Movement," paper presented at the Annual Meeting of the American Political Science Association, Washington, D.C., 2010.

80. See Andia. Quote is from Almudena Calatrava, "Gay Marriage in Argentina is 1st in Latin America," *Associated Press,* December 29, 2009.

81. Dan Fasterberg, "A Brief History of International Gay Marriage." *Time.com*, July 22, 2010, http://www.time.com/time/world/article/0,8599,2005678,00.html; Alexei Barrionuevo, "Argentina Senate to Vote on Gay Marriage." *New York Times*, July 13, 2010, http://www.nytimes.com/2010/07/14/world/americas/14argentina.html?_r=1. According to Lodola and Corral, support in Argentina is around 57 percent.

82. Stephanie Garlow, "Chile Moves toward Legalizing Same-Sex Civil Unions," *Global Post*, July 12, 2011, http://www.globalpost.com/dispatches/globalpost-blogs/que-pasa/gay-rights-civil-unions-chile.

83. Piatti-Crocker and Pierceson, 8–10.

84. "Poles Overwhelmingly Reject Same-Sex Marriage," *Angus-Reid*, August 5, 2009, http://www.angus-reid.com/polls/36772/poles_overwhelmingly_reject_same_sex_marriage; Fred Ojambo, "Uganda Parliament Votes to Continue Anti-Homosexual Bill," *Bloomberg Businessweek*, October 25, 2011, http://www.businessweek.com/news/2011-10-25/uganda-parliament-votes-to-continue-anti-homosexual-bill.html; Stephen Gray, "St. Petersburg Governor Signs 'Gay Propaganda' Bill into Law," *Pink News*, March 13, 2012, http://www.pinknews.co.uk/2012/03/13/st-petersburg-governor-signs-gay-propaganda-bill-into-law.

85. Lisa Caputo, "Sexual Minorities in India and Nepal: Some Recent Developments," in *Equality and Justice: Sexual Orientation and Gender Identity in the XXI Century*, Alexander Schuster, ed. (Udine, Italy: Forum, 2011).

Chapter Four

The First Modern Phase of Litigation, Backlash, and Litigation's Legacy

Hawaii, Washington, D.C., Alaska, Vermont, and Massachusetts

As was discussed in chapter 2, the desire and the need for same-sex marriage persisted throughout the 1980s, and new legal avenues were beginning to open. This eventually led to a new round of same-sex marriage litigation in the early 1990s that created a mixed reaction: new relationship equality–supportive jurisprudence, with victories in Hawaii, Alaska, Vermont, and Massachusetts, new policies (reciprocal beneficiaries in Hawaii, civil unions in Vermont, and same-sex marriage in Massachusetts), but also a powerful backlash in the form of state constitutional amendments banning same-sex marriage and the federal Defense of Marriage Act (1996). Despite this, the legal and political groundwork was established to create more success for advocates of same-sex marriage in the past decade. It was the first time that high-level courts began to take the claims of same-sex couples seriously, rather than laughing them out of court, as well as the first time that elected officials beyond the city level began to take the claims seriously and grapple with the issue.

LAWYERS DISAGREE, A LEGAL STRATEGY IS REJECTED, AND
COUPLES PUSH THE ISSUE; ELITE LEGAL THINKING BEGINS TO
EVOLVE

The case of *Bowers v. Hardwick* (1986) was a devastating defeat for LGBT rights advocates. The case was the culmination of over a decade of legal strategizing to eliminate sodomy laws, seldom-enforced but consequential laws for sexual minorities, as they were often used to harass and intimidate and even deny parenting rights to LGBT individuals. While many states had repealed these laws, many remained, and they served as a source of legal stigma and a barrier to full equality for sexual minorities. In *Bowers,* the court narrowly (5-4) upheld Georgia's sodomy law, refusing to apply the court-defined right to privacy to the case, a right that had been used to protect heterosexual sexual activity.[1] The case almost went the other way, with Justice Lewis Powell changing his vote to uphold the Georgia law. Advocates had been quite optimistic about the outcome, and the decision caused many in the movement to question the use of courts on issues of sexuality.[2] This, combined with the early losses in the 1970s, made legal advocates wary of a litigation-based strategy to achieve same-sex marriage, even as the need for marriage was becoming more obvious to many. As a result, the new round of litigation would be initiated by local couples making their own rights claims, eventually joined by national litigation groups.

Ambivalence about a litigation strategy is evident in the deliberations of the Legal Roundtable, a group of leading LGBT lawyers formed by Lambda Legal Defense and Education Fund, the leading LGBT litigation organization. After contentious deliberations, the group decided against a litigation strategy, with some arguing that marriage was a patriarchal, sexist institution not worth pursuing, including Nancy Polikoff from chapter 1, while others decided against litigation purely on pragmatic grounds. Some, including Evan Wolfson, who would become a leading national advocate for same-sex marriage, supported a limited litigation strategy on the grounds that the legal environment was shifting. Also, after *Bowers*, a state-by-state strategy was appealing, especially in states without sodomy laws and with liberal judicial traditions. After all, states traditionally defined marriage, not the federal government. Choosing a hospitable legal arena is called forum shopping, and this approach was eventually utilized with great success as a more formal litigation strategy emerged.

By the late 1980s, prominent law professors published law review articles arguing for more constitutional protection for a range of LGBT rights and equality claims, as did a leading constitutional law casebook by a leading advocate of liberal constitutionalism, Lawrence Tribe of Harvard. These writings influenced judicial thinking, as they were often cited in judicial opinions. In particular, they gave ammunition for liberal judges looking for legal arguments supportive of LGBT rights claims in a legal landscape that was generally hostile or inattentive to the legal status of sexual minorities. In this literature, feminist scholars began to make the connection between gender discrimination and discrimination based on sexuality, some even arguing that prohibitions on same-sex marriage are a form of gender discrimination, an argument utilized by the Hawaii Supreme Court in 1993, discussed below. Some of this thinking was triggered by the LGBT rights loss in *Bowers v. Hardwick* in 1986 in which the Supreme Court refused to apply the constitutional right to privacy to sexual minorities. This led many scholars to turn to the promise of the Equal Protection Clause and similar clauses in state constitutions.[3] As Nan Hunter, law professor and former director of the ACLU's Lesbian and Gay Rights Project, summarized the thinking of many, "There is a rapidly developing sense that the legalization of marriage for lesbian and gay Americans is politically possible at some unknown but not unreachable point in the future, that it shimmers or lurks—depending on one's point of view—on the horizon of the law."[4]

WASHINGTON, D.C.: THE SAGA CONTINUES

A gay male couple in Washington, D.C., commenced the first major same-sex marriage litigation during this period, driven by their legal consciousness and resisted by national litigation groups. The litigation was a new phase in the story of same-sex marriage in the capital that began in the 1970s and eventually culminated in the enactment of same-sex marriage in D.C. in 2009. While the litigation was unsuccessful in its goal of immediately legalizing same-sex marriage, a domestic partnership law was enacted by the D.C. city council in 1992. Because of the federal government's oversight of D.C., this resulted in the first engagement with the issue of relationship equality for same-sex couples by the Congress, a few years before the debate over the Defense of Marriage Act in 1996. Congress eventually defunded the implementation of the law, but it remained on the books, and couples eventually registered their relationships with the District.

Craig Dean and Patrick Gill applied for a D.C. marriage license in November of 1990 after being together for four and a half years. After the license was denied, they sued in federal court, the only possible jurisdiction for a D.C. matter. Dean was a graduate of Georgetown Law School where William Eskridge, Jr., was on the faculty at the time. Eskridge, a leading authority of sexuality and the law, represented the couple in the litigation, along with Dean. The couple was not media-shy, and they were interviewed by Phil Donahue and Oprah Winfrey. Indeed, part of their goal was to raise awareness for the issue of same-sex marriage through the media. As Dean stated, "We've set a goal for ourselves to get married so it seems the media attention is a venue to reach our goal. Also, we are causing a great amount of consciousness-raising in the American public, I think." Reflecting their own high level of legal consciousness on the issue, Dean also described their motivation: "It all started because Pat and I love each other. A marriage license is important because it's going to protect our relationship within and without. By not fully asserting ourselves and trying to get the license, we would be agreeing with society that our relationship is less than other marriages. We would be giving in to our own homophobia."[5]

Gill and Dean argued that the D.C. marriage law was gender-neutral and thus not prohibitive of same-sex marriage. In addition, they argued that the denial of the license violated the District's Human Rights Act, which prohibits discrimination on the basis of gender and sexual orientation, among other categories. The couple also made constitutional arguments, mainly that they were entitled to the fundamental right of marriage and that denial of this right was a violation of equal protection. Perhaps reflective of the fact that the right to marriage had never been applied to same-sex couples at the federal level—sexual orientation had never been found by a federal court to be a suspect, or quasi-suspect, classification—and the recent *Bowers* decision, the couple and their lawyers framed their claim on statutory, rather than constitutional, arguments, trying to persuade the D.C. courts that same-sex marriage was already authorized by D.C. law. They did so mainly by putting a particular spin on the efforts of Alderman Dixon in the 1970s. Essentially, the couple argued that there is no evidence of Dixon's backing away from the desire to legalize same-sex marriage and that the gender-neutral language of the bill eventually enacted still authorized same-sex marriage.[6] This, of course, contradicts the historical record outlined in chapter 2 (Dixon clearly backed down, and gay rights advocates at the time reluctantly accepted this), and it illustrates the tight spot in which these litigants found themselves in the federal courts in the early 1990s.

Even activists supportive of a litigation-based approach in principle saw no path to same-sex marriage through the federal courts. Tom Stoddard, executive director of Lambda Legal and a litigation supporter, was highly critical of this litigation: "I feel fervent support for their goals, but their tactics are shortsighted. The District of Columbia is probably the worst jurisdiction in the country for seeking action like this. Both Congress and the Supreme Court have oversight over legal developments in the District, and neither forum has shown itself to be welcoming to lesbians and gay men in the past. Better to establish a favorable precedent in other jurisdictions and then come back to the District." Stoddard was thus expressing the great fear of social cause litigants: a negative precedent stemming from ill-considered litigation. Dean countered by viewing this caution as unprincipled timidity: "Lambda has a history of only taking on cases that are velvet-lined—clearly winnable." Eventually, however, lesbian and gay advocacy groups supported the litigation after it was under way, including Lambda and the ACLU, a dynamic that would also be seen in Hawaii.[7]

In the end, Stoddard was correct. The litigation was not successful. However, the case resulted in an interesting opinion by a judge on the D.C. Court of Appeals pointing in the direction of a constitutional mandate for same-sex marriage, but the case resulted in a two-to-one decision against Gill and Dean. While there was some judicial light at the end of the tunnel, Gill and Dean were likely asking too much of the federal courts. Indeed, they were initially trounced by D.C. Superior Court Judge Shellie Bowers, who went as far as citing the Bible in rejecting their claims.[8] The situation was less theocratic on appeal. On the typical three-judge federal appellate panel, two judges rejected the statutory and constitutional arguments of the couple, while another, the author of the bulk of the opinion, found that the exclusion of same-sex couples from marriage was a violation of the Equal Protection Clause.

While the dissenting equal protection analysis of Judge John Ferren, a Carter appointee, had no direct legal effect, it is noteworthy that a well-developed defense of same-sex marriage was expressed from the federal bench. Ferren agreed that a statutory approach did not save the same-sex marriage claim, but he viewed sexual minorities as a suspect class, deserving of heightened scrutiny when laws discriminated against them. He would have preferred to remand the case to the trial court for a hearing to ascertain whether the District could present arguments strong enough to meet the compelling interest test. His opinion suggested that he was skeptical that they would present sufficient evidence and arguments to allow the discrimination against same-sex couples. Interestingly, Ferren's speculation about the nature of these arguments did not include what would become the central rationale put forth by states to justify bans on same-sex marriage: the procreation justification, or the claim that states have an interest in human procreation and this is best facilitated by heterosexual marriage. Rather, he speculated that the most powerful justifications might be grounded in a fear of promoting homosexuality by the government. Ferren seemed to think that this would be a weak claim, but he wanted a trial to explore the issue.[9] Finally, he was clearly influenced, or already agreed with, the emerging legal liberal scholarship on LGBT rights, as his decision contains references to work by Bruce Ackerman, Cass Sunstein, and Lawrence Tribe on the topic. His colleagues rejected his equal protection analysis, asserting, in 1970s style, that marriage was inherently heterosexual, procreative, and not open to same-sex couples; discrimination simply was not an issue. According to Judge John Steadman, a Reagan appointee, "The Marriage statute is simply not the same as, say, a statute prohibiting the employment of homosexuals. . . . Rather, it is a statute of inclusion of opposite-sex couples who may wish to enter a particular legal status recognized by the state."[10]

This decision ended the litigation, and, tragically, Patrick Gill died in 1997. The case was eclipsed by the litigation in Hawaii, as an initial ruling of the Hawaii Supreme Court favorable to same-sex marriage claims was handed down in 1993, between the initial proceedings and the appeal. Whereas the *Washington Post* gave prominent coverage to the case at the start of the litigation, it buried a brief story on the appellate decision the day after the decision was announced.[11]

An effort to enact a domestic partnership law in D.C. ran parallel to this litigation, and the case helped to frame both advocacy and the positive political environment for the law's enactment as well as opposition to it, especially given congressional oversight of the District. D.C. witnessed the same push for domestic partnership frameworks as other large cities in the late 1980s. After almost two years of consideration, and five years of advocacy by LGBT rights leaders, the D.C. Council passed a domestic partnership law in 1992, despite heavy last-minute lobbying by some religious leaders. The bill was signed by Mayor Sharon Pratt Kelly.[12] During her campaign for mayor, Kelly appeared to endorse same-sex marriage (triggered by the litigation filed in 1990), but once elected, she instead changed her position to support for domestic partnerships. And her administration defended the District's ban on same-sex marriage in court.[13] The law caused a great deal of controversy in Congress, and, while not overturning the law, Congress voted to eliminate funding for the law's implementation. Many members of Congress saw the law as opening a door to same-sex marriage.[14] The vote to remove the funding occurred a few weeks before the 1992 general election, and an attempt to revive funding after the election of Bill Clinton, with Democrats still in control of Congress, was unsuccessful, deemed "too controversial" to be a part of Clinton's economic stimulus package of 1993.[15]

The election of Democrats to majorities in Congress in 2006, for the first time in the same-sex marriage era, provided an opening for activists in D.C. to expand relationship recognition. First, in May of 2009, the D.C. Council enacted a law, by a vote of 12 to 1, recognizing same-sex marriages performed in other jurisdictions. Then, in December, the council enacted a marriage equality law for the District. This passed by a margin of 11 to 2. Democrats in Congress kept the Republicans at bay, and Congress did not challenge the law. A city commission and the courts thwarted attempts, led by the anti–marriage equality bishop Harry Jackson and other religious objectors, to create a referendum on the law. The commission, narrowly affirmed by the D.C. Court of Appeals, held that a referendum could result in a discriminatory act in violation of the District's antidiscrimination law, and the Supreme Court declined to hear the case. In 2010, thirty-five years after the introduction of the Dixon bill, same-sex marriage became legal in the nation's capital. However, the future of the law under a Republican Congress and president would be uncertain, at best. [16]

HAWAII: A FLEETING, BUT CONSEQUENTIAL, VICTORY

Only weeks after Dean and Gill applied for a marriage license in D.C., Nina Baehr and Genora Dancel, along with two other same-sex couples, applied for a marriage license in Hawaii. The chain of events that followed turned out to be much more consequential in the short term for the cause of same-sex marriage. In 1993, the Hawaii Supreme Court provisionally ruled in favor of the Hawaii couples, setting off a firestorm in Hawaii and in the rest of the country. While the court was ultimately thwarted by a popular referendum enacted in 1998, its initial decision started the national conversation about same-sex marriage in the contemporary era. The defeats of the D.C. couples kept a lid on the backlash, because same-sex marriage never appeared to be a judicially mandated reality. However, the favorable Hawaii decision caught the eye of the media, politicians, and the public as the specter of same-sex couples married in Hawaii and returning to their home states seemed quite real.

The Litigation

As with the D.C. litigation, the Hawaii case was initiated by local activists and lawyers, with resistance from national groups. A local gay rights activist, Bill Woods, had identified couples willing to apply for marriage licenses during gay pride events in the summer of 1990, but delayed action to allow the state ACLU chapter to deliberate about supporting the effort. The ACLU preferred a legislative strategy focused on domestic partnerships, fearing "a long and tedious battle," if litigation were commenced. [17] Ultimately, Woods and the couples decided to proceed without them.

　　When the licenses were denied, the couples sued the state with a local attorney, Dan Foley. Foley emphasized privacy arguments in support for same-sex marriage in Hawaii, as there was a privacy provision written into the state's 1978 constitution, thus providing the claim with a textual foundation. Interestingly, the constitution also contained a gender-based equal rights amendment, but Foley did not make a gender argument, instead initially focusing on the right to privacy. (On appeal, sexual orientation–based equal protection and due process/marriage as a fundamental right argument would be presented more prominently.) Ultimately, however, the gender-based argument would be used by the state high court, outlined below. Circuit court judge Robert Klein ultimately ruled against the couples, rejecting the privacy argument and applying an equal protection analysis to reject the claim that same-sex couples in Hawaii were entitled access to marriage. He was unwilling to apply any form of heightened scrutiny, deeming sexual minorities to be politically powerful and not enduring a history of discrimination because of Hawaii's tradition of tolerance of diversity (a disputable claim, of course, especially in light of what was to come). He also denied the immutability of homosexuality. Applying rational basis review, Klein found sufficient justification in the state's "sanctioning [of] traditional man-woman family units and procreation."[18]

Judge Klein would be the first of many state trial court judges reluctant to find in favor of same-sex marriage claims. In this first phase of litigation, success came primarily from state supreme courts. Trial court judges shy away from judicial innovation, as many of them wish to rise in the judicial ranks and fear the negative career consequences of excessive reversals on appeal, particular when an area of jurisprudence is new. As we will see, however, in later years, trial court judges find in favor of same-sex marriage claims, empowered and enabled by a growing jurisprudence in support of same-sex marriage claims forged by state high courts.

The appeal of the decision to the Hawaii Supreme Court resulted in a judicial earthquake, both because of its unpredictability and the size of its potential effects. With only one dissenting vote, the court held that the state's ban on same-sex marriage violated the state constitution's equal protection provisions, specifically the prohibition of gender-based discrimination. "We conclude that the circuit court's order runs aground on the shoals of the Hawaii constitution's equal protection clause," the majority emphatically declared.[19] The invocation of gender, rather than sexual orientation, allowed the court to sidestep the question of whether sexual orientation triggers strict scrutiny, a question still not decided definitively by the federal or most state courts to this day.

The court also rejected the argument that same-sex marriage is a fundamental right, because the historical nature of this approach simply could not support same-sex marriage arguments. As Judge Levinson wrote, "We do not believe that a right to same-sex marriage is so rooted in the traditions and collective consciousness of our people. . . . Neither do we believe that a right to same-sex marriage is implicit in the concept of ordered liberty."[20] As we will see, the fundamental right argument generally will be avoided by supportive courts in favor of equal protection analysis.

However, the court even more forcefully rejected the state's analysis, and the approach of the judges in the 1970s cases, that marriage was by definition opposite-sex-only, thereby precluding an equal protection critique of the same-sex marriage ban, and the judges used *Loving v. Virginia* in their rejection. In *Loving*, defenders of miscegenation laws, including judges in Virginia courts, claimed that these laws did not run afoul of the Equal Protection Clause, because they applied equally to all races and they were divinely inspired, grounded in long-standing tradition. Speaking to the Virginia judges of the 1960s, and more importantly to Judge Klein and the state of Hawaii, Levinson declared: "We do not believe that trial judges are the ultimate authorities on the subject of Divine Will, and, as *Loving* amply demonstrates, constitutional law may mandate, like it or not, that customs change with an evolving social order."[21] Here we see not a cautious, deferential court but one willing to use the law to respond to, and potentially push, social transformation. Indeed, the court had a reputation for articulating progressive jurisprudence, with Justice Levinson seen as the most liberal member of the court.

The invocation of gender discrimination automatically triggered a more searching review of the state's reasons for discrimination under federal and state equal protection approaches. Notably, Foley never emphasized the gender argument in briefs or oral arguments. He only included it in a footnote in a brief.[22] The judges arrived at this argument mostly through their own research and deliberation, having the law review articles outlining this approach at their (and their clerks') disposal. Justice Walter Burns brought the issue up during oral argument.[23] Having invoked gender-based equal protection under the state constitution, the high court remanded the case to a lower court for a trial on the state's justification for heterosexual-only marriage, unwilling to challenge directly the legislature and the public quite yet. Jurisprudentially, the court was confident, but not quite so politically. A dissent by Walter Heen invoked the rational basis test and argued that "the statute's classification is clearly designed to promote the legislative purpose of fostering and protecting the propagation of the human race through heterosexual marriages and bears a reasonable relationship to that purpose."[24] The judges in the majority were all relatively young, liberal, and activist.[25]

The Political Reaction

The decision triggered the first serious and sustained debate on same-sex marriage in the country. A proposed constitutional amendment banning same-sex marriage *and* a domestic partnership law were part of the initial legislative response in Hawaii. Much of the early legislative debate focused on the role of the judiciary, with the judiciary committees of both legislative chambers rebuking the court for judicial activism. The chair of the House judiciary committee declared: "I believe that if same-sex marriage licenses are to be issued, that policy decision belongs to us in the Legislature. . . . I cannot stand idly by and allow our Judiciary . . . to decide on issues of such importance."[26] The specific vehicle for this sentiment was a proposed law, passed overwhelmingly in a legislature dominated by Democrats, criticizing the decision and reaffirming that marriage was solely between a woman and a man in Hawaii, "to foster and protect the propagation of the human race."[27]

The law also authorized the creation of a commission to study the issue, a typical tactic utilized by legislators trying to avoid an issue, especially with an election upcoming. Most of the votes against the law came from legislators representing urban Honolulu.

Remarkably, the initial legislative reaction was somewhat muted, given the eventual backlash in the state and in the country, likely due to the fact that opponents had not yet fully mobilized. Also, no one was expecting success from the litigation, and the decision took many people off-guard. Later litigation in other states would have a much higher profile, but this was still very new territory in 1993 and 1994. Some legislators took the court's reasoning seriously and argued for some form of recognition of same-sex couples. In the 1994 election, Democratic governor Benjamin Cayetano took the position that the state should provide domestic partnerships for same-sex and opposite-sex couples, with the definition of marriage left to churches. He was reelected. Legal scholar Andrew Koppelman wrote in 1995 that "Hawaii hasn't panicked or risen up in hostility. In fact, the response there has turned out to be remarkably mild."[28] This would prove to be the calm before the storm, both in Hawaii and nationally.

The Commission

The charge of the Commission on Sexual Orientation and the Law was to study the possibility of extending marriage to same-sex couples, with an exclusive focus on legal and economic benefits, not moral concerns. Remarkably, and foreshadowing the role that religion would come to play in the backlash against same-sex marriage in Hawaii, the membership of the commission included two members each of the Catholic and Mormon Churches, out of the eleven total members. This improper mixing of church and state was invalidated by a federal court. A new version of the commission excluded formal religious membership. Legislative opponents of same-sex marriage saw to it that two members of the commission had ties to the Religious Right: James Hochberg, a lawyer with the conservative Rutherford Institute, and antiabortion activist Marie Sheldon.[29]

However, the majority of the new seven-member commission, including former lieutenant governor and congressman Thomas Gill, was supportive of marriage equality in some form. This eventually led to a recommendation to the legislature on December 8, 1995, that same-sex marriage be enacted. The majority did not think that anything short of marriage would comport with the *Baehr* decision.[30] Of course, Hochberg and Sheldon objected and submitted a minority report recommending that the legislature enact a constitutional amendment defining marriage as between one man and one woman only. Citing fears of the effects of the legalization on children and the prospect of teaching homosexuality in public schools, Hochberg and Sheldon ultimately grounded their objections in the neoconservative argument against same-sex marriage: "The minority members of this commission understand that because there are good reasons to support the heterosexual norm, due to the fact that it has been developed with great difficulty and can be maintained only if it is cared for and supported, we cannot be indifferent to attacks upon it."[31] So far, then, the state supreme court and a government commission supported same-sex marriage. This would soon be followed by a trial on same-sex marriage in which the judge also validated same-sex marriage claims.

Judge Chang's Trial

Trials have been rare in the history of same-sex marriage in the United States. In most litigation, motions for summary judgment at the trial court level are made and decided upon by judges before a trial can begin. These summary judgment motions are the basis for appeals centering on constitutional arguments. Therefore, most same-sex marriage cases are decided without witnesses and cross-examination and the resulting factual record that results. A notable exception is the Proposition 8 federal trial under Judge Vaughn Walker in California, with its high-profile lawyers Ted Olson and David Boies, discussed in chapter 8, but this trial mandated by the Hawaii Supreme Court to determine whether the state could meet the high standard of strict scrutiny review outlined in *Baehr* preceded the Prop. 8 trial by nearly fifteen years.

Judge Kevin Chang presided over the trial, considered by most observers to be a moderate who had worked as a prosecutor and corporate lawyer. The trial was delayed pending the outcome of the commission's deliberations, explaining the over two-year gap from the supreme court remand. The state's claim that the ban on same-sex marriage was linked to the state's interest in procreation and child development was the central focus of the testimony of the trial. Witnesses included sociologists, family therapists, and psychologists, and Chang found the plaintiff's (the same-sex couples) witnesses "to be especially credible," and he ruled that the state failed to meet its burden. Chang rejected the argument that same-sex marriage would harm children: "The evidence presented by Plaintiffs and Defendant established that the single most important factor in the development of a happy, healthy and well-adjusted child is the nurturing relationship between parent and child. . . . The sexual orientation of parents is not in and of itself an indicator of parental fitness." Following the reasoning of *Baehr v. Lewin*, Chang found the "heterosexual-only" definition of marriage unconstitutional and ordered the state to begin granting marriage licenses to same-sex couples, thus becoming the third governmental entity in Hawaii to endorse same-sex marriage. However, he stayed his ruling pending an appeal of his decision.[32]

country had shifted toward strong support for civil unions by this time. The reality is that the protest that stalled the legislative process was nonmajoritarian. This instance provides another example of theocratic influences on sexuality-based policy making.

In the 2010 legislative session, both chambers approved the bill, after broadening it to include opposite-sex couples, but Governor Lingle vetoed it, setting up an election-year fight over the issue. In response, Lambda Legal and the ACLU filed a lawsuit seeking judicially mandated, but majority-supported, civil unions for same-sex couples, the strongest form of equality given the 1998 amendment. However, the courts were not needed. The election of 2010 gave impetus to the enactment of civil unions in Hawaii. Democrat Neil Abercrombie, a strong supporter of civil unions, won handily in an election where the issue was prominent, and many church-supported candidates were defeated.[39] As the head of the Hawaii Christian Coalition stated, "We failed . . . in the last election cycle. We needed to take out some people to let the Legislature know we are a powerful force to be reckoned with, and we did not do that."[40] After almost two decades of dominating the political conversation in the state, religious conservatives were on the losing side of the debate when Abercrombie signed the bill into law on February 23, 2011, to take effect on January 1, 2012, nineteen years after the decision in *Baehr*.

THE ALASKAN ODYSSEY: LIBERAL JURISPRUDENCE MEETS TRADITIONALISTIC POLITICS

Alaska constitutionally forbids same-sex marriage, but government entities in the state grant domestic partnership benefits, as a result of litigation. And litigation designed to allow for some benefits of marriage for same-sex couples has begun. In the struggle for relationship equality in the state, courts utilizing liberal constitutionalism have been central, but this has been combined with a deeply socially conservative Republican Party in the state that has successfully mobilized strong opposition to relationship equality claims in court. But activists and judges have not given up, carving out policy space to the maximum extent possible, given the constraints of politics in the state. Judges in the state have a history of liberal, activist decisions, but they have been shielded from direct backlash by a merit selection process and lack of direct election. Judges in the state face periodic retention elections, but they are seldom voted from office.[41] In particular, judges in Alaska have developed a strong individual rights and right to privacy jurisprudence that some commentators attribute to the "live and let live" ethic of the Alaskan frontier.[42] Events in Alaska clearly represent a clash between legal and political culture, with interesting, and continually evolving, results.

Obviously inspired by events in Hawaii, Jay Brause and Gene Dugan applied for a marriage license in Alaska but were denied. Reflecting the emerging consciousness of same-sex couples described in chapter 2, they participated in a religious marriage in 1979. The couple challenged the license denial in court, eventually leading to a favorable ruling from Judge Peter Michalski in 1998. Reflecting the strain of libertarian jurisprudence in Alaska, Michalski held that the right to same-sex marriage was protected by the right to privacy in the Alaska constitution and that choosing one's life partner was a fundamental right, regardless of gender, thus triggering strict scrutiny. According to the judge, "It is the decision itself that is fundamental, whether the decision results in a traditional choice or the nontraditional choice Brause and Dugan seek to have recognized."[43] Like the Hawaii court, Michalski found the license denial to be a form of gender discrimination, but this would have triggered a lower level of review in Alaskan law. Interestingly, Michalski would be alone as a trial judge finding in favor of same-sex marriage claims for several years, as most lower court judges in other states would be unwilling to rule in favor of same-sex marriage claims until more state high courts would lead the way.

The legislature responded quickly to the decision, particularly after the supreme court refused to overturn the decision of the lower court, enacting a constitutional amendment banning same-sex marriage to be approved by the state's voters. The amendment was approved by a legislative committee a mere five days after Judge Michalski's decision. The legislature had already enacted a statute defining marriage as between a man and a woman in 1996 in response to the lawsuit and in response to litigation attempting to grant domestic partnership benefits at the University of Alaska. The latter suit was ultimately successful with both the superior court and the supreme court finding that same-sex domestic partner benefits were required, as the denial of benefits was discrimination on the basis of marital status, a category protected in the state's antidiscrimination law. The trial court judge even hinted that the state's gender-neutral marriage law might not prohibit same-sex marriage.[44] The litigation was supported by national litigation groups, including Lambda Legal, demonstrating that these groups saw promise in the legal culture of Alaska.[45]

Despite a supportive legal environment, the political environment of Alaska was quite hostile to LGBT rights claims, particularly because of the strong role played by religious conservatives in the state's politics in this mostly Republican state. Unlike Hawaii, there was little progressive political capital from which supporters of same-sex marriage could draw, especially in the legislature, and events moved much more quickly, with no positive policy results for same-sex couples. The Mormon Church again played a prominent role in the campaign for the amendment, donating $500,000 to the effort. The amendment was approved that fall by a 2 to 1 margin.[46]

In a challenge to the amendment before it was enacted, the supreme court struck a sentence from the language approved by the legislature. It allowed "To be valid in this state, a marriage may exist only between one man and one woman." It removed "No provision of this constitution may be interpreted to require the State to recognize or permit marriage between individuals of the same-sex." The court reasoned that it wanted to avoid the "possibility that the sentence in question might be construed at some future time in an unintended fashion which could seriously interfere with important rights."[47] Clearly, as we will see below, the court tried to limit the damage to same-sex couples from the amendment, keeping the door open to litigation granting rights outside of the state's (heterosexual-only) marriage framework.

Litigation for relationship equality did not stop with the enactment of the amendment, however. The amendment banned only same-sex marriage, and this provided an opening for the Alaska Civil Liberties Union to file a suit on behalf of municipal employees, arguing that the denial of benefits to same-sex partners of employees violated the state's equal protection provision. A trial court rejected this claim, but the Alaska Supreme Court accepted the argument in a unanimous decision in 2005, six years after the initial litigation in *Alaska Civil Liberties Union Ex Rel. Carter v. Alaska*. In a nod to the divide between the legal and political cultures in Alaska, the court began its discussion with a statement of the need to keep religion and morality out of the legal discussion: "Irrelevant to our analysis must be personal, moral, or religious beliefs—deeply held by many—about whether persons should enter into intimate same-sex relationships or whether same-sex domestic partners should be permitted to marry."[48] In its analysis, the court found that the denial of benefits was facially discriminatory and a violation of equal protection under the Alaska constitution, even under the most minimal level of review.[49] The court also made a clear distinction between the amendment barring same-sex marriage and domestic partner benefits, because "the amendment does not address the topic of employment at all,"[50] thanks in large part to the court's limiting of the amendment's language several years earlier. The court, however, did not propose a remedy, leaving it up to the government to decide how to create a benefits framework, thereby creating an opening for opponents to undermine the decision.

And attempt to undermine it they did. After all, this was a significant decision in the direction of relationship equality. While it applied only to government employees, the reasoning could be, and later was, applied to Alaska citizens in general. Opponents saw is as the backdoor legalization of same-sex marriage. Republican governor Frank Murkowski was not subtle in his condemnation of the decision. He declared, "I'm absolutely outraged by this shameful court ruling. This is a clear example of how out of touch the state Supreme Court is with mainstream Alaskans who overwhelmingly believe that marriage is a union between a man and a woman." He vowed to introduce a constitutional amendment in the legislature to overturn the decision and ordered the attorney general to work to undermine the decision.[51] However, the amendment never got out of the legislature, continually failing to achieve the two-thirds support necessary for sending it to voters. Republicans attempted other tactics, including proposing a law making it a crime to comply with the decision (it failed) and the refusal by the lieutenant governor to sign the regulations establishing benefits. Eventually, the legislature passed a symbolic bill prohibiting the government from granting the benefits and providing for an advisory public referendum on the question.[52] After a series of delays, same-sex partners were given the benefits mandated by the court. Interestingly, it was Governor Sarah Palin who stopped the opposition to the ruling by vetoing the bill forbidding the government from granting the benefits. She opposed the supreme court decision but felt compelled by its mandates.[53] An underwhelming 53 percent support for a constitutional amendment in the referendum further stalled the opposition, even after intense mobilization by religious conservatives in the state, who framed the issue as being "not about health benefits. It's about public affirmation of homosexuality," according to the Alaska Family Council.[54]

The stalled backlash allowed for continuing court expansion of relationship equality policy in the state. Relying squarely on the high court decision in *ACLU v. Alaska*, a trial court judge found the denial of a property tax benefit open to married couples, but not same-sex couples, to be an unconstitutional violation of equal protection. This, of course, implicates other provisions in state law open only to married couples and denied same-sex couples who cannot marry.[55] It seems likely that the supreme court would affirm this decision, taking the conflict over same-sex rights in Alaska to a new level.

Sixteen years of litigation in the state by Alaska civil liberties unions and other groups have resulted in policy change, despite the constitutional amendment. The courts in Alaska aggressively asserted liberal constitutionalism in the face of deep religious conservatism in the state, demonstrating the power of legal culture. Had the court not been an ally for relationship equality advocates, the political process clearly would not have produced the limited change seen in the state, and it remains to be seen just how far this clash between legal and political culture will allow relationship equality policy to evolve. However, the courts appear to have the upper hand, short of requiring full marriage equality.

VERMONT: THE FIRST FULL VICTORY FOR SAME-SEX COUPLES

Same-sex marriage advocates achieved a significant victory in Vermont in the late 1990s, having learned a great deal from events in Hawaii and Washington, D.C. Unlike these previous efforts, this litigation was carefully planned, and a grassroots campaign designed to support the litigation was orchestrated in tandem with the legal efforts. This resulted in a unanimous decision from the Vermont Supreme Court that same-sex couples were entitled to equal protection under Vermont's constitution, and, under court mandate, the legislature enacted a civil union law that replicated the Vermont marriage statute. A decade later, the legislature went beyond the civil union approach and legalized same-sex marriage in 2009.

The Litigation and Grassroots Campaign

Vermont lawyers Beth Robinson and Susan Murray decided to initiate litigation for same-sex marriage in the mid-1990s, motivated by events in Hawaii and by the legal and political climate in their own state. Vermont possesses a strong progressive political tradition, combined with a vocal but politically outnumbered contingent of social conservatives, not unexpected in this mostly rural state. In the state's fight over same-sex marriage, these voices would be loud but, in the end, not persuasive. Robinson and Murray saw promise in the progressive tradition. The state had recently enacted antidiscrimination and hate crime laws protective of sexual orientation, and litigation and legislation authorized same-sex adoption. The state thus already recognized lesbian and gay families. In addition, the Vermont constitution was very difficult to amend, potentially undermining a potential backlash to a pro–marriage equality decision from the state high court. Legally and politically, the timing seemed right.

They created a grassroots organization as the first step in the process, the Freedom to Marry Taskforce, with chapters around the state. A video of same-sex couples describing their relationships and their desire for marriage was created in an attempt to humanize the issue by focusing on real families. Telling personal stories also became a central thrust of the public relations effort once the litigation was commenced. The press release announcing the litigation stated that the couples in the lawsuit "want to marry for the same mix of reasons that other couples choose to marry: they love each other, they want to make a public commitment to one another, and they seek the legal protections and obligations of civil marriage."[56] Rather than directly advocate for same-sex marriage through the legislative process, however, this group was designed to shore up support for equal treatment for same-sex couples should the Vermont courts rule in their favor. In other words, it was an attempt to soften the backlash. Indeed, when the issue of same-sex marriage indirectly arose in the legislature just prior to the initiation of the litigation, Murray urged legislators to avoid the issue. Theirs was clearly a litigation-centered, not a legislative, strategy. To assist with these efforts, Robinson and Murray teamed with Boston-based Gay and Lesbian Advocates and Defenders (GLAD), an LGBT litigation organization, and their crusading lesbian and gay rights lawyer, Mary Bonauto. By this point (1997), national litigation groups were more supportive of litigation strategies to achieve same-sex marriage.

They lost in the trial court, where Judge Linda Levitt rejected the couples' claims, citing the state's interest in procreation under rational basis review and citing the 1970s cases as justification for her decision.[57] On appeal to the state supreme court, however, the outcome was much different. At oral argument, the justices appeared to be quite receptive to the couples' arguments and were skeptical of the state's procreation argument. For instance, one justice asked the state's lawyer if the state could be allowed to prohibit infertile couples from marrying, under the state's logic that the purpose of marriage was for procreation. Two justices focused on possible remedies to the claimed discrimination, indicating that they largely agreed with the plaintiff's assessment of the constitutional problem.

The decision of the high court was a sweeping affirmation of the liberal constitutional arguments supporting same-sex marriage that were first articulated in the legal academy. While the court only applied rational basis review under the state constitution's equal protection provision, the Common Benefits Clause,[58] to reject the state's procreation defense, the language used by Chief Justice Jeffrey Amestoy fully affirmed same-sex couples: "The extension of the Common Benefits Clause to acknowledge plaintiffs as Vermonters who seek nothing more, nor less, than legal protection and security for their avowed commitment to an intimate and lasting human relationship is simply, when all is said and done, a recognition of our common humanity."[59]

The justices disagreed about the remedy, however. The majority of the five justices chose to leave the remedy up to the legislature, with the proviso that the remedy must not violate the court's equality analysis. Essentially, the court understood the potential political backlash, and gave the legislature some wiggle room, particularly noting that creating domestic partnerships for same-sex couples would be a constitutionally sound approach. This approach was likely influenced by Amestoy's past as an elected official—he was a seven-term state attorney general, with a reputation for consensus building.[60] The decision can also be fairly described as reflecting the jurisprudential approach of "judicial minimalism," or ruling in a manner that is less confrontational toward legislatures. Indeed, Amestoy quoted a leading advocate of this approach, Cass Sunstein, in the section of the decision discussing a remedy.[61] However, this approach may have been less minimalist than it at first appeared—the court retained the prerogative to revisit the remedy if the legislature did not act according to the court's mandate. Learning from the mistake of the Hawaii court, the justices did not allow the political process to be played out without the court's oversight. Justice Denise Johnson dissented from this remedy, arguing for a court mandate for equal treatment for same-sex couples. She adopted the gender-based analysis of the *Baehr* court and applied a higher level of scrutiny, requiring a more aggressive remedy. While legally more pure, Amestoy's approach would prove to be more politically sound.

Thus, Robinson and Murray were successful forum shoppers, having found a very receptive court. As noted previously, the court ruled in favor of same-sex adoption in 1993. The court also ruled in 1996, under the Common Benefits Clause, that the state's system of public school financing was un-constitutional. With much less to fear than judges in other states, with a difficult-to-amend constitution and an appointment process that fosters judicial independence, the Vermont Supreme Court was an active policy maker.

The Political Reaction: Civil Unions

In assessing the political reaction, it is important to separate activity within the legislature, where respect for the court's decision was reasonably high, and the grassroots, especially among conservatives who consistently viewed same-sex marriage and the court's decision as a threat to society. While the latter was able to stridently (perhaps too stridently in this liberal state) campaign against same-sex marriage and the supreme court, opponents could not derail the legislative process favoring equal treatment, nor could they mount an effective campaign to repeal the eventual civil union legislation or the *Baker* decision. Unlike Hawaii, there was no well-funded campaign from powerful and wealthy religious organizations, and proponents of same-sex marriage had worked effectively to support the positive outcome from the litigation.

The most important legislative activity occurred in the House of Representatives, where the Judiciary Committee quickly got to work on the court's mandate. The process was driven by the Republican chair of the committee, Thomas Little. He took the court's mandate and reasoning seriously, telling the committee, "My goal is not only to keep the Committee's 'eye' on the Constitutional principles, but also to build consensus and avoid divisiveness within the General Assembly and throughout the state."[62] All committee members of all three parties in the state (Democrat, Republican, and Progressive) supported some type of legislation extending rights to same-sex couples. Consensus emerged to author a bill mirroring the rights and benefits of the state's marriage statute that does not use the word "marriage." This came to be called a civil union instead of a marriage. As a Republican member of the committee from a remote part of the state declared: "Somehow, when you listen to the compelling stories of gay and lesbian people, it demystifies who they are, what they stand for and how valuable they are for our communities."[63]

What a difference a few years make. In Hawaii, another overwhelmingly Democratic state, few legislators, including Democrats, were willing to affirm the equality of same-sex couples, but this approach found bipartisan (or tripartisan) support in Vermont. The state's governor, Democrat Howard Dean, supported a domestic partnership approach. Clearly, the grassroots efforts of Freedom to Marry Vermont paid dividends, assisted by the lack of a coordinated and well-funded opposition from religious groups like the Mormon and Catholic Churches. Neither denomination has a strong presence in Vermont.

Opposition came from the group Take Back Vermont. The organization worked to generate grassroots opposition to *Baker* in rural areas, proposed unsuccessful impeachment and popular referendum efforts in the legislature, and worked with the most conservative Republican legislators to stop the civil union bill. These efforts temporarily postponed full consideration in the House, as members tried to gauge public sentiment. Polls indicated that a slight majority of the public opposed the *Baker* decision, but there appeared to be more support among lawmakers. When the bill made it to the floor, an emotional speech by openly gay House member William Lippert clearly swayed some members on the fence, while legislators in opposition may have taken their rhetoric a bit too far. Republican Nancy Sheltra argued on the floor that the creation of civil unions would be legalizing sodomy (this was legalized in Vermont in 1977), leading to more cases of HIV, and that Vermont was provoking the wrath of God.[64]

The bill was passed in the House, 79 to 68, and passed in the Senate by nearly a 2 to 1 margin, as the momentum had shifted in favor of civil unions by the time of the Senate's consideration. Governor Dean signed the bill in a private ceremony, seeming fearful of excessive public support with an election pending and a majority of citizens, according to one poll, opposing the law 52 percent to 43 percent. Dean was reelected in 2000, but Republicans gained a majority of seats in the House for the first time in almost two decades. Opponents of same-sex marriage hoped for more of a backlash, but there was no groundswell of opposition. An exit poll found 49 percent of voters in support of the law, with 48 percent opposed.

Subsequent efforts to weaken or repeal the law were defeated. By 2002, most of the opposition had subsided, constrained by the lack of a popular referendum mechanism and a difficult-to-amend constitution.[65] While falling short of the goal of full marriage equality, as civil unions were seen as a "separate but equal" category and they were not portable to other states, the litigation in Vermont was remarkably successful for its contribution to the evolving, pro-marriage equality jurisprudence and the concrete policy result it created.

Separate but equal was ended in Vermont family law in 2009 when the state enacted a same-sex marriage law. Spurred by the Iowa Supreme Court decision mandating same-sex marriage in that state, the legislature passed the same-sex marriage law in a dramatic vote to override the veto of Republican governor Jim Douglas. The goal of Robinson and Murray was finally realized. This was another first for Vermont—the first state to enact same-sex marriage through the legislative process, not judicial mandate, and the law's enactment set off a wave of legislative activity in New England, as will be discussed in chapter 6. That same day, the D.C. City Council voted to recognize same-sex marriages performed in other jurisdictions, creating a small explosion of progress for same-sex marriage advocates. According to Jennifer Pizer of Lambda Legal, "This is a week we all will remember: first Iowa, then Vermont, then D.C. We have turned another critical corner in this equal rights movement."[66]

MASSACHUSETTS: THE FIRST SAME-SEX MARRIAGE STATE

In 2003, the Massachusetts Supreme Judicial Court ruled that marriage equality was required under the state's constitution, and ordered the legislature to equalize the marriage law. This decision resulted in the first same-sex marriage policy in any U.S. state, and, coming only a year before a presidential election year, triggered a new wave of the national debate about marriage equality. The high point of the backlash against marriage equality came in 2004, with the popular enactment of thirteen state constitutional amendments banning same-sex marriage (and often similar legal frameworks). However, a supportive political environment prevented a backlash in Massachusetts, and the decision inspired pro–marriage equality activity in other states.

Talk of an Amendment Triggers Litigation

Litigation in Massachusetts was considered following the Hawaii decision, but no action was taken. The GLAD-sponsored litigation was ultimately triggered by a proposed constitutional amendment banning same-sex marriage. Advocates wished to take the initiative and not let the issue be defined by opponents of marriage equality. As Mary Bonauto of GLAD described the situation: "We knew our opponents wanted to change the constitution. We knew we'd be talking about marriage anyway. Hawaii ensured that, and Vermont double-ensured that. We didn't want to lose this opportunity."[67] The Massachusetts courts, like the Vermont courts, were seen as a favorable forum, and this assessment turned out to be quite true.

Conservative activists moved ahead with the amendment, eventually obtaining enough signatures to send it to the legislature for consideration. Interestingly, the amendment was a "super-DOMA," as it banned same-sex marriage or any benefits for same-sex couples. Opponents of same-sex marriage often argue that court imposition of marriage equality is inconsistent with majority rule and, thus, illegitimate. At the same time, they are willing to support policies, often enshrined in constitutions, that only have minority support. While same-sex marriage was not supported by a majority of citizens at the time (but this majority was quickly forming), the public supported some form of recognition and protection for same-sex couples. Conservative activists were hoping to have their policy preferences enshrined into the constitution, riding the wave of opposition to same-sex marriage. As we will see, marriage equality opponents would try this in other states with majority support for relationship recognition. In Massachusetts, they were not successful. Of course, same-sex marriage advocates were willing to use the courts to push public opinion in their direction. The reality is that activists use all the tools at their disposal to achieve policy goals. Many of these approaches, not just litigation, are countermajoritarian.

Unsurprisingly, given the role of trial court judges in Hawaii and Vermont, Judge Thomas Connolly dismissed the claims of the plaintiffs, seven Massachusetts same-sex couples, ultimately arguing that the issue should be handled by the legislature, not courts.[68] Overall, Connolly's approach reflected the approach of the 1970s precedents, with an emphasis on a facial "heterosexual-only" definition of the state's marriage statute, tradition, and procreation as a legitimate policy rationale for discriminating against same-sex couples. Despite this decision, opponents of same-sex marriage still feared a favorable decision from a higher court and submitted the amendment to the legislature, after gathering the sufficient amount of signatures. However, the legislature, controlled by Democrats, killed the amendment on a procedural vote in July of 2002 (the legislative constitutional convention was adjourned before a direct vote), a crucial victory for marriage equality advocates.[69] Only 25 percent of legislators were required to approve the amendment before it was given to the voters. Without the procedural maneuver, the amendment would have been on the ballot. While public opinion was quickly moving in the direction of marriage equality support, a defeat of the amendment was not guaranteed, potentially nullifying any favorable ruling from the courts.

The Decision: *Goodridge v. Department of Public Health*

The case was granted an expedited appeal to the Supreme Judicial Court. GLAD lawyers learned an important lesson from the Vermont litigation where they focused excessively on the benefits of marriage, rather than its cultural status. In this round of litigation, according to Mary Bonauto, "We spent more time . . . talking about how marriage is a basic human and civil right. . . . We talked about what marriage is in our culture."[70] In keeping with GLAD's careful litigation strategy, the couples were strategically chosen to engender sympathy from judges and the public.[71]

The Supreme Judicial Court of Massachusetts overruled Connolly in a 4 to 3 decision. While the voting margin was narrow, the language of the majority opinion of Chief Justice Margaret Marshall was notable for its thorough endorsement of liberal constitutional arguments in favor of same-sex marriage. Indeed, Marshall emphasized the requirements for positive notions of freedom in the Massachusetts constitution. As she stated,

> The individual liberty and equality safeguards of the Massachusetts Constitution protect both "freedom from" unwarranted government intrusion into protected spheres of life and "freedom to" partake in benefits created by the state for the common good. . . . Both freedoms are involved here. Whether and whom to marry, how to express sexual intimacy, and whether and how to establish a family—these are among the most basic of every individual's liberty and due process rights.[72]

Furthermore, Marshall declared that "the decision whether and whom to marry is among life's momentous acts of self-definition."[73] However, this approach did not include a holding that sexual orientation triggered heightened scrutiny under Massachusetts jurisprudence. Marshall rejected the state's procreation argument under rational basis review and consequently redefined marriage in Massachusetts to include same-sex couples. For her, marriage was defined as an "exclusive commitment of two individuals to each other [that] nurtures love and mutual support."[74] This aggressiveness under rational basis review, which is traditionally a deferential standard, was compelled, according to Marshall, by the fact that the Massachusetts constitution "affirms the dignity and equality of all individuals. It forbids the creation of second-class citizens."[75]

Marshall placed her decision in the emerging stream of jurisprudence supporting marriage equality claims, directly or indirectly. She cited *Baker v. State of Vermont, Lawrence v. Texas* (the U.S. Supreme Court decision decided mere months before *Goodridge*) and its language supportive of sexual minorities (discussed in greater detail in chapter 8), and recent Canadian court decisions finding in favor of same-sex marriage claims.[76] Marshall also discussed *Loving*, and noted the role of another state supreme court in laying the foundation for that decision, the California high court in *Perez v. Sharp* in 1948.[77] Marshall clearly placed her court in the tradition of liberal constitutional innovation. This came as a surprise to few. Marshall was a progressive civil rights activist who actively followed human rights innovations around the world, especially in her home country of South Africa. Liberal Republican William Weld appointed her to the court largely on the basis of this civil rights perspective. Indeed, Weld noted her "passion for justice." After the decision, philosopher Martha Minow noted the link between Marshall's opinion and the new South African constitutional tradition explored in chapter 3: "It is like a South African decision. Beginning with the use of the word 'scar' there's a directedness about injury and the emotional dimensions of injury. . . . And there is her attention to dignity, which comes right from the South African constitution."[78]

Interestingly, the fourth vote creating the majority came from Justice Judith Cowin, who was generally considered to be a conservative and who was skeptical of the couples' claims during oral argument, asking, "Why should we do something that virtually no other state has done?"[79] In a concurring opinion, Justice John Greaney argued for the application of gender-based equal protection analysis, thus triggering heightened scrutiny. As he stated, "This case calls for a higher level of legal analysis. Precisely, the case requires that we confront ingrained assumptions with respect to historically accepted roles of men and women within the institution of marriage."[80] More broadly, however, he agreed with the general liberal constitutional approach of Marshall: "Simple principles of decency dictate that we extend to the plaintiffs, and to their new status, full acceptance, tolerance, and respect."[81]

The court's conservatives other than Cowin dissented and created an alternative narrative to Marshall's crusading liberalism. Using formal, deferential reasoning, the dissenters argued that the rational basis test was a deferential test, and they would have preferred a legislative solution. They viewed *Baehr* and *Baker* as jurisprudential outliers, thus refusing to be part of the emerging judicial arguments for relationship equality. However, their support for legislative protection of same-sex couples was undermined by their use of an 1810 marriage case, *Milford v. Worcester*. In that case, marriage was viewed as an institution "intended to regulate, chasten, and refine, the intercourse between the sexes; and to multiply, preserve, and improve the species."[82] Beyond the narrow arguments about jurisprudential standards, the debate between the majority and dissenters in this case reflects the larger political and philosophical debate over same-sex marriage. As I have noted elsewhere, "This was a fight between modern liberals who emphasize autonomy, liberation, and freedom and neoconservatives who value social institutions that impose limits on individuals and structure social intercourse."[83]

The Political Reaction

The decision was consistent with emerging majority sentiment for same-sex marriage in the state. A poll conducted a few months before the decision found 50 percent of respondents in favor of same-sex marriage. Polls immediately following the decision reflected similar levels of support of around 50 percent. The decision softened opposition in the state, with those opposed to marriage equality dropping to 38 from 44 percent in a poll conducted before and after the decision. However, the strong criticism of the opinion by elected officials, led by Republican governor Mitt Romney, led to a short-term dip in support by early 2004. All during the period, however, strong majorities in the state favored some form of equal treatment for same-sex couples. Thus, both the court and its critics were able to affect public opinion at the margins, but the overall trend of increasing support continued. By 2012, support for same-sex marriage measured as high as 62 percent. [84]

The first reaction to the decision was one of confusion by elected officials or, more likely, wishful thinking that they had a more politically palatable option. The court stayed its decision for 180 days to allow the legislature to change statutes to comply with the ruling, but many officials, including Romney, thought that this was a Vermont-style mandate allowing for civil unions as a remedy. State officials went back to the court for clarification, hoping for a civil union option, but the majority reaffirmed its holding that marriage equality was required. [85] The state began granting same-sex marriage licenses on May 17, 2004.

However, a Republican governor with a bully pulpit and presidential ambitions (Romney), combined with the low legislative threshold to put a constitutional amendment banning same-sex marriage before the voters, kept the backlash against marriage equality alive. First, Romney began enforcing a 1913 law intended to allow the state to not recognize interracial marriages by limiting Massachusetts marriage to residents of the state. As a result, couples from outside of Massachusetts could not get married. Second, opponents of same-sex marriage were more than happy to go to court, arguably to further their nonmajoritarian agenda, by suing to compel the legislature to take a vote on an amendment banning same-sex marriage initiated when 170,000 signatures were gathered for the amendment process in 2006. The legislative constitutional convention adjourned in November of that year without taking a vote on the initiated amendment. Supporters of same-sex marriage were unsure that they had the votes to defeat the amendment. (In 2004, an amendment banning marriage but providing for civil unions narrowly passed the 25 percent threshold, but this was defeated on the second vote in 2005 as the legislative backlash waned in the face of the reality of marriage equality in the state.) [86] This maneuver appeared to kill the amendment, but Romney and others sued to force a vote. While the Supreme Judicial Court ruled that it lacked the authority to compel legislative action even though they felt that a vote was required, the justices shamed legislators for their lack of action. Justice Greaney stated: "The members of the General Court [the legislature] are the people's elected representatives, and each one of them has taken an oath to uphold the Constitution of the Commonwealth. Those members who now seek to avoid their lawful obligations, by a vote to recess without a roll call vote by yeas and nays on the merits of the initiative amendment (or by other procedural vote of similar consequence), ultimately will have to answer to the people who elected them."[87]

Needless to say, this language shifted the debate and led to a vote in which sixty-one legislators voted to approve the amendment. The vote also triggered the required second vote in the new session. However, more marriage equality supporters were elected to the legislature in the prior fall elections, in addition to the election of the first Democratic governor in sixteen years, Deval Patrick, a strong supporter of same-sex marriage. In the new session, the amendment only received forty-five votes after intensive lobbying by marriage equality supporters, including the new governor. This effectively killed the backlash in the state, as marriage equality opponents would need several more years to get a new amendment before voters. And the trends in public opinion were clearly working against them. In addition, the legislature repealed the 1913 law, thus allowing for marriages of out-of-state couples.[88]

CONCLUSION

Thus, from legal consciousness–driven rights claiming, a sophisticated litigation strategy evolved within a decade to achieve important jurisprudential and policy results. The argument that same-sex couples deserved constitutional recognition and state protection was no longer a fringe argument, especially in the legal academy and on the bench. However, the entrenched connection between religion and the state on family policy was still potent, resulting in a significant backlash to this litigation. By 2004, the fight between liberal constitutionalism and religious traditionalism was fully engaged. In the next several chapters, these themes will be examined further, as marriage equality litigation continued in states where legal activists saw potential for success.

NOTES

1. As Marc Stein argues, this right was clearly created with heterosexuals in mind. See Stein, *Sexual Injustice: Supreme Court Decisions from* Griswold *to* Roe (Chapel Hill: the University of North Carolina Press, 2010).

2. For more on sodomy law litigation before and after *Bowers*, see Pierceson, *Courts, Liberalism, and Rights: Gay Law and Politics in the United States and Canada* (Philadelphia: Temple University Press, 2005), chs. 5 and 6.

3. According to Tribe, "The history of homosexuality has been largely history of opprobrium; indeed, it would not be implausible to find on this basis that homosexuals constitute a discrete and insular minority entitled to heightened protection under the equal protection clause." Lawrence H. Tribe, *American Constitutional Law*, 2nd ed. (Mineola, NY: The Foundation Press, 1988), 1427. See also Sylvia A. Law, "Homosexuality and the Social Meaning of Gender," *Wisconsin Law Review*, (March/April 1988), 187; "Note: The Constitutional Status of

Sexual Orientation: Homosexuality as a Suspect Classification," *Harvard Law Review* 98:6 (April 1985), 1285–1309; Cass R. Sunstein, "Sexual Orientation and the Constitution: A Note on the Relationship between Due Process and Equal Protection," *Harvard Law Review*, 55:4 (Autumn 1988), 1161–79; Claudia A. Lewis, "From this Day Forward: A Feminine Moral Discourse on Homosexual Marriage," *Yale Law Journal* 97:8 (July 1988), 1783–1803.

4. Nan D. Hunter, "Marriage, Law, and Gender: A Feminist Inquiry," *Law & Sexuality Review* 1 (1991), 10.

5. Both quotes are from Elizabeth Kastor, "The Marriage Proposal: Two Men and Their Crusade for the Right to a Legal Union," *Washington Post*, January 28, 1991, B1.

6. "Plaintiff's Post-Hearing Submission on the Passage of Amendments to the District of Columbia Marriage and Divorce Act," *Dean v. The District of Columbia*, Civil Action No. 90 CA 13892, submitted by Craig Dean, William Eskridge, Jr., and Robert Teir. Franklin Kameny Papers, Manuscript Division, Library of Congress.

7. Quotes taken from Kastor, "The Marriage Proposal."

8. Patrice Gaines-Carter, "D.C. Judge Rejects Suit Seeking Gay Marriage; Bible, Legal Definition Cited in Ruling," *Washington Post*, January 2, 1992, D2.

9. *Dean v. District of Columbia*, 653 A.2d 307 (D.C. App. 1995), 355.

10. *Dean v. District of Columbia*, 362. The third judge in the case, John Terry, was also a Reagan appointee.

11. "D.C. Court of Appeals Upholds Superior Court Judge's Ruling Against Gay Couple's Marriage," *Washington Post*, January 20, 1995, C6.

12. Rene Sanchez, "D.C. Council Approves Partners Bill; Ministers' Opposition Fails to Kill Measure," *Washington Post*, April 8, 1992, B1.

13. Karlyn Barker, "D.C. Gay Couple to Press Fight for Marriage License; Kelly Assailed for Alleged Reversal on Issue," *Washington Post*, January 7, 1992, D1.

14. Rene Sanchez and James Ragland, "Council Members Not Giving Up on Domestic-Partners Law," *Washington Post*, October 1, 1992, J3.

15. Kent Jenkins, Jr., "D.C. Officials Seek to Revive Domestic Partners Initiative," *Washington Post*, March 1, 1993, D5.

16. Tim Craig, "D.C. Council Votes to Recognize Same-Sex Marriages Performed Elsewhere," *Washington Post*, May 6, 2009, http://www.washingtonpost.com/wp-dyn/content/article/2009/05/05/AR2009050501618.html; Ian Urbina, "D.C. Council Approves Gay Marriage," *New York Times*, December 16, 2009, A28; Robert Barnes, "Supreme Court Refused to Revive Effort to Put D.C. Same-Sex Marriage Law to Vote," *Washington Post*, January 18, 2011, http://www.washingtonpost.com/wp-dyn/content/article/2011/01/18/AR2011011802214.html.

17. Walter Wright, "Same-Sex Marriage Ban May Be Tested," *Honolulu Advertiser*, November 25, 1990, A1.

18. *Baehr v. Lewin*, slip opinion, Circuit Court of the First Circuit, State of Hawaii, Civil No. 91-1394-05, October 1, 1991.

19. *Baehr v. Lewin*, 852 P.2d 44 (Hawaii 1993), 54.

20. *Baehr*, 57.

21. *Baehr*, 63.

22. Martin D. DuPuis, "The Impact of Culture, Society, and History on the Legal Process: An Analysis of the Legal Status of Same-Sex Relationships in the United States and Denmark," *International Journal of Law and the Family* 9 (1995), 86–118, 97.

23. Linda Hosek, "Homosexuals Ask Court for Right to Marry," *Honolulu Star-Bulletin*, October 14, 1992, A3.

24. *Baehr*, 74.

25. See Pierceson, *Courts, Liberalism, and Rights*, 111–12.

26. *Journal of the House of Representatives of the Seventeenth Legislature, State of Hawaii*. Regular Session of 1994, 135–36.

27. Act 217, Session Laws of Hawaii, 1994, Section 1.

28. Andrew Koppelman, "No Fantasy Island," *New Republic*, August 7, 1995, 22.

29. The discussion of the political response in Hawaii draws from Pierceson, *Courts, Liberalism, and Rights*, 112–125.

30. "Report of the Commission of Sexual Orientation and the Law," State of Hawaii, December 8, 1995, 40.

31. "Report," 46.

32. *Baehr v. Miike*, Circuit Court of Hawaii, First Circuit, Civil No. 91-1394, December 3, 1996.

33. The constitutional amendment was passed by the House by a margin of 38 to 14, while the domestic partnership law was passed by the Senate by a margin of 14 to 11.

34. Ronald T. Y. Moon, Supreme Court of Hawaii, State of the Judiciary Address, January 22, 1997.

35. The relevant parts of the act are those relating to states and federal policy. States: "No State, territory, or possession of the United States, or Indian tribe, shall be required to give effect to any public act, record, or judicial proceeding of any other State, territory, possession, or tribe respecting a relationship between persons of the same sex that is treated as a marriage under the laws of such other State, territory, possession, or tribe, or a right or claim arising from such relationship." For federal policy: "In determining the meaning of any Act of Congress, or of any ruling, regulation, or interpretation of the various administrative bureaus and agencies of the United States, the word 'marriage' means only a legal union between one man and one woman as husband and wife, and the word 'spouse' refers only to a person of the opposite sex who is a husband or a wife." Public Law 104-199, 104th Congress.

36. Mark Niesse, "Lawmakers Mull Civil Unions Bill," *Associated Press*, January 31, 2007.

37. Mark Niesse, "Analysis: Cast of Characters Downs Civil Unions," *Associated Press*, March 27, 2009.

38. Mark Niesse, "Hawaii Steps Closer to Civil Union for Gay Couples," *Associated Press*, February 13, 2009.

39. Mark Niesse, "Hawaii Positioned to Pass Same-Sex Civil Unions," *Associated Press*, November 6, 2010.

40. Mark Niesse, "Civil Unions in Hawaii Head toward Final Vote," February 15, 2011.

41. Tillman J. Finley, "Note: Judicial Selection in Alaska: Justification and Proposed Courses of Reform," *Alaska Law Review* 20:49 (June 2003).

42. Susan Orlansky and Jeffrey M. Feldman, "Justice Rabinowitz and Personal Freedom: Evolving a Constitutional Framework," *Alaska Law Review* 15:1 (1998), 2.

43. *Brause v. Bureau of Vital Statistics*, 1998 WL 88743 (Alaska Super. Ct. Feb. 27, 1998).

44. Kevin G. Clarkson, et al., "The Alaska Marriage Amendment: The People's Choice on the Last Frontier," *Alaska Law Review* 16:2, 213–67 (1999).

45. *University of Alaska v. Tumeo*, 933 P.2d 1147 (Alaska 1997).

46. Liz Rushkin, "Limits on Marriage Passes in Landslide," *Anchorage Daily News*, November 4, 1998, 1A.

47. *Bess v. Ulmer*, 985 P.2d 979 (Alaska 1999), 995.

48. *Alaska Civil Liberties Union Ex Rel. Carter v. Alaska*, 122 P.3d 781 (Alaska 2005), 783.

49. *Carter*, 788.

50. *Carter*, 787.

51. "Alaska Governor, Outraged by Supreme Court Same-Sex Marriage Ruling, Directs AG to Draft Legislation to Correct the Ruling," *States News Service*, October 28, 2005.

52. Anne Sutton, "House Votes to Challenge Courts on Same-Sex Benefits and Adjourns," *Associated Press*, November 18, 2006.

53. Kyle Hopkins, "Same-Sex Benefits Plan Gets Palin Veto," *Anchorage Daily News*, December 9, 2006, A1.

54. Mary Pemberton, "Gay Benefits Issue in Alaska Galvanizes Groups," *Associated Press*, April 2, 2007; Anne Sutton, "Both Sides Claim Victory in Same-Sex Benefits Advisory Vote," *Associated Press*, April 4, 2007.

55. *Schmidt v. State of Alaska*, Case No. 3AN-10-9519 CI, Superior Court of Alaska, Third Judicial Circuit at Anchorage, September 19, 2011.

56. "Plaintiff's Press Release of July 22, 1997," Vermont Freedom to Marry.

57. *Baker v. State,* slip opinion, Chittenden (VT) Superior Court S1009-97CnC (1997).

58. The clause reads: "Government is, or ought to be, instituted for the common benefit, protection, and security of the people, nation, or community, and not for the particular emolument or advantage of any single person, family, or set of persons, who are a part only of that community." Chapter 1, Article 7 of the Vermont constitution.

59. *Baker v. State of Vermont*, 744 A.2d 864 (VT 1999), 889.

60. David Moats, *Civil Wars: A Battle for Gay Marriage* (New York: Harcourt, 2004), 140.

61. *Baker v. State of Vermont*, 888.

62. "Memorandum from Thomas A. Little to the House Judiciary Committee Members," January 4, 2000.

63. Adam Lisberg, "Panel Backs Gay Partnerships," *Burlington Free Press*, February 10, 2000, 1A.

64. Audio recording of the Vermont House of Representatives, March 15, 2000 (copy on file with the author).

65. Legislative votes and polls are from Pierceson, *Courts, Liberalism, and Rights*, 141–42.

66. Jessica Garrison, "Vermont Legislature Gives Final OK to Gay Marriage," *Los Angeles Times*, April 8, 2009, http://articles.latimes.com/2009/apr/08/nation/na-gay-marriage8.

67. Yvonne Abraham, "10 Years' Work Led to Historic Win in Court," *Boston Globe*, November 23, 2002, A1.

68. *Goodridge v. Department of Public Health*, slip opinion, Massachusetts Superior Court, Suffolk County, No. 2001-1647-A.

69. Jennifer Peter, "Legislature Kills Proposed Amendment to Ban Gay Marriage," *Associated Press*, July 17, 2002.

70. Emily Bazelon, "A Bold Stroke," *Legal Affairs*, May/June 2004, http://www.legalaffairs.org/issues/May-June-2004/feature_bazelon_mayjun04.html.

71. Abraham, "10 Years' Work."

72. *Goodridge v. Dept. of Public Health*, 798 N.E.2d 941 (Mass. 2003), 959.

73. *Goodridge*, 955.

74. *Goodridge*, 948.

75. *Goodridge*, 948.

76. Thanassis Cambanis, "Ruling Extends 20 Years of Cases," *Boston Globe*, November 19, 2003.

77. *Goodridge*, 966–67.

78. Bazelon, "A Bold Stroke."

79. Kathleen Burge, "SJC Peppers Lawyers on Same-Sex Marriage," *Boston Globe*, March 5, 2003, A1.

80. *Goodridge*, 973.

81. *Goodridge*, 973.

82. *Goodridge*, 985. The case citation is 7 Mass. 48 (1810).

83. Pierceson, *Courts, Liberalism, and Rights*, 148.

84. "New Survey Shows Massachusetts Residents Approve of Same-Sex Marriages," *Associated Press*, April 8, 2003; Frank Phillips and Rick Klein, "50% in Poll Back Ruling on Gay Marriage," *Boston Globe,* November 23, 2003, A1; "Poll Shows Public Split on Question Of Gay Marriage," *Associated Press*, February 23, 2004; Tom Jensen, "MA Okay with Gay Marriage, Socks Fans with Bobby V," Public Policy Polling, June 29, 2012, http://www.publicpolicypolling.com/pdf/2011/PPP_Release_MA_062812.pdf.

85. Raphael Lewis, "SJC Affirms Gay Marriage," *Boston Globe*, February 5, 2004, http://www.boston.com/news/local/massachusetts/articles/2004/02/05/sjc_affirms_gay_marriage; Steve LeBlanc, "Mass. Legislature Rejects Proposed Amendment Banning Gay Marriage," *Associate Press*, September 14, 2005.

86. Rick Klein, "Vote Ties Civil Unions to Gay Marriage Ban," *Boston Globe*, March 30, 2004, http://www.boston.com/news/specials/gay_marriage/articles/2004/03/30/vote_ties_civil_unions_to_gay_marriage_ban.

87. Pam Belluck, "Same-Sex Marriage Setback in Massachusetts," *New York Times*, January 3, 2007, http://www.nytimes.com/2007/01/03/us/03gay.html; *Doyle v. Secretary of the Commonwealth*, 858 N.E.2d 1090 (Mass. 2006), 1096.

88. Pam Belluck, "Bid to Ban Gay Marriage Fails in Massachusetts," *New York Times*, June 14, 2007, http://www.nytimes.com/2007/06/14/us/154cnd-gay.html; David Filipov, "5 Years Later, Views Shift Subtly on Gay Marriage," *Boston Globe*, November 17, 2008,http://www.boston.com/news/globe/city_region/breaking_news/2007/06/foes_of_samesex.html.

Chapter Five

Same-Sex Marriage in the Midwest

Until the end of the 2000s, much of the progress on relationship equality occurred on the East and West coasts of the United States. However, with the unexpected decision by the Iowa Supreme Court to legalize same-sex marriage in 2009, the politics of relationship equality emerged in the region with a new vigor. This resulted in the enactment of civil unions in Illinois in 2011 and a domestic partnership law in Wisconsin in 2009. Many states in the Midwest possess progressive political traditions along with more conservative political traditions. Indeed, Wisconsin's domestic partnership law stands alongside a super-DOMA enacted by voters in 2006, and Minnesota voters voted down a constitutional amendment banning same-sex marriage in 2012. Other midwestern states, Ohio and Michigan, have enacted state constitutional DOMAs or super-DOMAs. The Midwest, then, is a microcosm of the relationship equality debate in the entire country. This chapter will focus primarily on the four most progressive midwestern states, Illinois, Iowa, Minnesota, and Wisconsin, to illustrate what happens when the struggle for same-sex marriage leaves the coasts to tap into pockets of progressive politics in the middle of the country. The use of litigation varied greatly from state to state, from an aggressive litigation strategy in Iowa to the avoidance of litigation in Illinois, reflecting a political sophistication on behalf of relationship equality activists and litigators.

RELATIONSHIP EQUALITY LITIGATION AND POLICY IN WISCONSIN

Wisconsin has been a state of contradictions concerning LGBT rights policy. It was the first U.S. state to adopt a sexual orientation antidiscrimination law in 1982, but it also enacted, by popular referendum, a sweeping anti–relationship equality constitutional amendment in 2006. It is a state with a storied progressive tradition alongside deep-seated cultural conservatism (reflective of a strong urban/rural split) and a politically active Catholic Church. In terms of partisanship, the state was trending slightly Democratic until Republicans took complete control of the government in the election of 2010. Republican legislative control facilitated the passage of the constitutional amendment in 2006. The Republican Party in the state has mirrored the national trend toward conservatism, away from the state party's more moderate history.[1] Democrats took control of the state senate in the 2006 elections, ironically in the same election where the amendment was enacted, and won a majority of seats in the state assembly in 2008.[2] Democratic governor James Doyle, in office from 2003 to 2011, was a strong supporter of LGBT rights, as demonstrated by his opposition to the amendment and push for domestic partnership benefits, chronicled below. Despite the passage of the amendment, the Democrats were not wary of enacting LGBT rights–protective policies, as reflected by the domestic partnership law. Public opinion in Wisconsin is generally on their side. According to political scientists Jeffrey Lax and Justin Phillips, mean public opinion support for gay rights is 57 percent, with 42 percent support for same-sex marriage and 50 percent support for civil unions.[3] However, the 2010 election put a stop to progress on LGBT rights in the state.

ACLU Litigation and the Amendment

A lawsuit filed in 2005 by the ACLU of Wisconsin on behalf of state employees was designed to force the state to grant domestic partner benefits to same-sex couples. This suit is notable both because a similar lawsuit failed to achieve the same results several years earlier, and because the lawsuit was commenced in the middle of a highly visible and contested fight over a proposed constitutional amendment banning same-sex marriage or its equivalent in the state.

The amendment was approved in 2006 with 59 percent of the vote, more than most observers had predicted.[4] Because it was potentially harmful to efforts to defeat the amendment, initiating litigation during this amendment fight was controversial, but the ACLU and activists in the state saw it as an opportunity to add to their communication efforts during the campaign against the amendment by highlighting the discriminatory treatment of same-sex couples.[5]

The earlier case was decided against the claims of a same-sex couple seeking family health insurance coverage from the state. This litigation was also supported by the ACLU. Interestingly, the suit was initiated before the Hawaii Supreme Court decision in 1993 brought same-sex marriage litigation to prominence and such suits began to be coordinated nationally. However, the issue of same-sex marriage was directly implicated by the Wisconsin suit. As the appellate court wrote, "Understandably, most of [plaintiff] Phillips's arguments on gender and sexual orientation discrimination/classification are grounded on the fact that Wisconsin does not recognize same-sex marriages."[6] Thus, the issue was broached in the Wisconsin courts in the early 1990s. Nonetheless, the court rejected the statutory and constitutional claims, broadly deferring to the agency's definition of "spouse," which did not include same-sex partners. The court was somewhat sympathetic toward the couple involved, describing their relationship as "a committed relationship that partakes of many of the attributes of marriage in the traditional sense,"[7] but the judges were not willing to defy the legislature and executive branch by creating a new right for same-sex partners to receive state employee benefits.[8] The court acted formally and deferentially, refusing to make new policy for the state.

Notably, the court cited a California decision from 1985 denying same-sex partners dental benefits for state employees to bolster its decision.[9] These cases indicate that lawsuits concerning state employees in same-sex relationships were, in some ways, the second phase of relationship equality litigation, the first having been commenced in the early 1970s in the wake of the Stonewall Riots and increased gay and lesbian visibility and activism.[10]

The negative precedent from 1992 makes the filing of the 2005 case in Wisconsin empirically interesting and strategically problematic. The ACLU apparently felt that a change in legal and political conditions had taken place and would allow more active court policy making. The filing of the suit in April 2005 was accompanied by a public relations campaign carried out by the ACLU and Action Wisconsin, the leading LGBT advocacy organization in the state. A lead ACLU attorney on the case, Larry Dupuis, appealed to citizens' sense of basic fairness with a bit of Clintonesque political rhetoric: "Wisconsin has a long tradition of fairness: If you work hard, and play by the rules, you should be able to support your family. It's unfair that these people who work as hard as their neighbor in the next cubicle, the teacher in the next classroom, are not able to share in the kinds of benefits that their co-workers share in."[11] Indeed, the suit included a broad range of state employees, from teachers and researchers to corrections employees.[12] Chris Ott, the executive director of Action Wisconsin, emphasized that "[t]his is not the issue that it once was. It's really becoming mainstream."[13] While advocates of the litigation emphasized equality, fairness, and lack of novelty, opponents saw the lawsuit as an activist attempt to change policy through the courts. Referencing cost and utilizing a common conservative narrative about liberal judicial activism, a leading anti-gay politician, Assembly Speaker John Gard, stated, "It is disappointing that when Wisconsin can least afford it, the ACLU is trying to legislate their liberal social agenda through the court system."[14]

The litigation was initiated largely in response to legislative inaction on the issue of relationship equality, particularly under Republican control. Domestic partnership insurance benefits legislation was consistently rejected by the legislature.[15] At the same time, the years preceding the lawsuit witnessed highly visible legislative deliberations over the issue of relationship equality, mostly centered on the marriage and civil unions amendment eventually approved in 2006. Given that this amendment required legislative approval in two consecutive sessions, it remained on the political agenda in the state for some time.

Predicating the denial of benefits on the lack of recourse to same-sex marriage in the state, the lawsuit centered on a state equal protection claim on the basis of sexual orientation, gender, and marital status, and described the couples bringing the suit as identical to heterosexual married couples.[16] According to the complaint, "Plaintiff couples view themselves and hold themselves out to their families and communities as committed, loving intimate couples, who are as committed to one another as spouses in a marital relationship."[17] Thus, even though the relief sought in the suit is substantially less than the full rights and benefits of marriage, the suit utilized the language of same-sex marriage litigation. This particularly makes sense if part of the goal of the lawsuit was to shape public perception about same-sex couples. Indeed, much of the complaint described the couples, their lives together, and the challenges they faced without legal protections for their relationships.

However, if the goal of the lawsuit was to assist in the defeat of the constitutional amendment, advocates were not successful. In fact, the strategy may have backfired. The amendment passed with 59 percent support, surprising many, including the gay activist community in the state. Polling had indicated a much closer vote, especially during the months preceding the elections.[18] The Catholic Church was actively involved, leveraging the power of the state's 1.7 million Catholics, along with conservative evangelical churches in the state. Opponents of the amendment tried to emphasize the sweeping nature of the amendment, but arguments about marriage traditionalism and the threat to society claimed by supporters of the amendment trumped the opponents' arguments. Madison bishop Robert Morlino asserted that same-sex marriage would cause the collapse of "society in due time" in a recorded homily that he mandated to be played in every parish.[19] Amendment supporters engaged in a relatively low-profile public campaign, with much of the focus on organizing in churches, with the Catholic Church especially active. All five Catholic bishops in Wisconsin sent a letter to parishioners opposing same-sex marriage and urging support for the amendment. At an information session sponsored by the Diocese of Green Bay, a deacon declared: "At the center of the holy family is God. That's what Christian marriage is. We believe men and women are called by God to be married." Outside of the churches, opponents of relationship equality did not want to jeopardize the amendment by causing more moderate voters to question the second sentence also banning "substantially similar" legal arrangements to marriage.[20]

Thus, a policy not supported by a majority of Wisconsin citizens (majority support existed in the state for recognition short of marriage) was enshrined in the state constitution, thereby impeding future efforts to give same-sex couples more than a handful of rights. The amendment states: "Only a marriage between one man and one woman shall be valid or recognized as a marriage in this state. A legal status identical or substantially similar to that of marriage for unmarried individuals shall not be valid or recognized in this state."

After the amendment passed, a consensus emerged that the amendment, while it banned marriage and civil unions, may still allow for minimal domestic partnership protections, such as health insurance coverage. The outgoing attorney general, Peggy Lautenschlager, asserted exactly this point in a letter to the city attorney of Madison, a municipal government that provides domestic partner benefits. Also, Governor Jim Doyle continued to propose benefits for domestic partners of state employees.[21] At the same time, the amendment provided a powerful resource for conservative groups to challenge existing domestic partner benefits at the local government level.[22]

Nearly three years after the passage of the Wisconsin amendment, a trial court judge ruled against the ACLU and the plaintiffs. In the end, the negative precedent of the *Phillips* case prevailed, with the judge indicating sympathy for the arguments about discrimination but ultimately feeling bound by precedent, not an unusual act for a trial court judge. The court applied *Phillips*'s holding that the statutes in question categorize on the basis of marital status, not gender or sexual orientation.[23]

However, the judge made a clear finding that the 2006 amendment did not prohibit domestic partner benefits, based on the legislative history of the amendment and public debate about the amendment, and ruled that the amendment had no bearing on the case.[24] In fact, the court used the amendment as evidence of the powerlessness of sexual minorities and used this to justify categorizing sexual orientation as a suspect classification, also relying on recent high court decisions from Iowa, California, and Connecticut that did precisely this.[25] Thus, it was the early-1990s *Phillips* lawsuit that was the truly unwise litigation. The negative precedent in this case clearly complicated more recent litigation efforts. Given this fact, the decision to initiate the 2005 litigation may not have been as productive as litigation in other states without similar legal and political barriers.

While the lawsuit was not sufficiently visible in 2006 to negatively affect the outcome of the amendment fight, it certainly did not add to the efforts of advocates. The fight in Wisconsin became a typical contest over the morality of same-sex marriage, and progressives were overwhelmed by conservative rhetoric and were not able to successfully frame the issue as one of equal rights and fairness.

Domestic Partnership Law

By the time the trial court ruling was handed down in late May 2009, it was eclipsed by activity in the legislature to enact a domestic partnership law for all state citizens, not simply the state employees that the lawsuit envisioned. Governor Doyle included a provision in the state budget to grant about forty rights to same-sex couples who register with the state as domestic partners. The policy was enacted and took effect on August 3, 2009, making Wisconsin the first state to enact such a law after the passage of an anti–relationship equality state constitutional amendment. Legislators were careful to not ask for too much, given the debate over the amendment, such as adoption rights. According to Mark Pocan, an openly gay Democratic legislator, "We tried to find out what things were the most needed immediately. Most of the benefits (afforded by the registry) are probate- or health-care-related. What we do in the future will be based on where we see the need and what we feel can be accomplished."[26] This represents the first legislative enactment aimed at relationship equality in the Midwest and is a remarkably positive turnaround given the policy landscape immediately following passage of the amendment in 2006.

The Law Is Challenged

Even this minimal policy has triggered a lawsuit from conservative opponents who claim that it is a violation of the 2006 amendment, indicating that opponents are not simply protecting heterosexual marriage but are, contrary to public opinion in the state, out to oppose any pro-gay policies.[27] In addition, gay rights groups were reluctant to sign on to a lawsuit challenging the amendment, especially as the state high court has become more conservative.[28] The state high court unanimously upheld the amendment, rejecting arguments that it unconstitutionally dealt with more than one issue.[29] The lawsuit challenging the domestic partners law was brought by the leading anti-gay activist in the state, Julaine Appling. As president of Wisconsin Family Action (formerly executive director of the Family Research Institute of Wisconsin), a conservative Christian advocacy group, she was at the center of the legislative efforts to enact the amendment and its passage in 2006. Interestingly, in 2005 she negatively characterized litigation to achieve policy goals, the ACLU lawsuit in particular. According to an op-ed penned by Appling, "The most egregious part of the lawsuit is the blatant attempt by homosexuals to again use the court system to get their way. Like petulant children who have repeatedly been told no, they look for ways to circumvent the groups that have blocked them: citizens and state legislatures."[30] Whether or not she considered herself a petulant child, she filed a lawsuit challenging the action of Wisconsin legislators, supported by public opinion, in August of 2010. She was supported by the right-wing, Christian-based litigation group, the Alliance Defense Fund (ADF).[31] The ADF describes itself as "a servant organization that provides the resources that will keep the door open for the spread of the Gospel through the legal defense of religious freedom, the sanctity of life, marriage and the family."[32] Their position was that the domestic partnership law was "substantially similar" to marriage and unconstitutional.

About nine months later, Circuit Judge Daniel Moeser ruled against Appling and the ADF, strongly rejecting the argument that domestic partnerships were substantially similar to marriage. His finding relied upon abundant evidence from legislative and interest group supporters of the amendment that domestic partnerships were permitted. Only a policy mirroring marriage, such as civil unions copying a state's marriage rights, was prohibited according to this record of statements. These statements were a political necessity to facilitate passage by emphasizing that the amendment was about protecting marriage, not eliminating potential rights for Wisconsin citizens. In a memo to fellow legislators, amendment sponsors wrote: "[T]his proposal does not prohibit the state, local governments or private entities from setting up their own legal construct to provide particular privileges or benefits, such as health insurance benefits, pension benefits, joint tax return filing, hospital visitation, etc."[33] Moeser also referenced public statements made by amendment supporters during the campaign, including Julaine Appling countering the argument by opponents of the amendment that it was too broad. "It's just inflammatory rhetoric. This amendment isn't going to change benefit structures that exist."[34]

Of course, the discrepancy between these statements and the lawsuit's goals is glaring. In retrospect, these statements appear to be a duplicitous tactic, as the real goal of the amendment's primary Republican and conservative Christian supporters was the complete nonrecognition of same-sex relationships. This is confirmed by the fact that the administration of Republican governor Scott Walker has withdrawn from defending the domestic partnership law after he took over from Jim Doyle.

Initial examination of the litigation in Wisconsin points to an overreliance on this litigation and its role in the broader fight for relationship equality in Wisconsin. Given that the political process was already pushing the domestic partnership issue, particularly through the governor's office, the ACLU and Action Wisconsin might have been better off not filing the lawsuit. There is little evidence that the litigation assisted in the fight over the amendment, and the domestic partnership policy recently enacted was not driven by the lawsuit. However, activists in Wisconsin thought the lawsuit was going to be a net benefit in their broader fight. This indicates a continued reliance on the legal framework among cause lawyers and their allies.

SAME-SEX MARRIAGE LITIGATION IN IOWA: A REMARKABLE LEGAL SUCCESS

Iowa is the site of perhaps the most successful litigation strategy for same-sex marriage to date, given the sweeping nature of the unanimous 2009 decision and the fact that the decision was not expected in many quarters. The outcome was the result of an extremely careful and thoughtful litigation strategy.

Iowa's politics are similar to those in Wisconsin, with a recent window of Democratic Party control of the governorship and the legislature after a period of more divided control. In the 2010 election, Republicans gained a majority in the House and the governorship; however, these party dynamics have significantly affected the politics over relationship in the state, as will be discussed. According to Gallup, Iowa is the twenty-third most Democratic state, with similar party identification as Wisconsin.[35] Lax and Phillips give Iowa a mean public opinion support for gay rights of 56 percent, with 38 percent for marriage and 51 percent for civil unions.[36]

The Litigation

The same-sex-marriage lawsuit filed in Iowa in December 2005 was in line with similar litigation from national litigation groups in the past decade. Lambda Legal filed the suit in Polk County, Iowa, in a determined effort to affect relationship equality policy in the state. The lawsuit argued that the prohibition of same-sex marriage in Iowa violated due process and equal protection provisions of the Iowa constitution. Lambda Legal attorneys believed that the Iowa constitution and due process and equal protection jurisprudence in the state created a highly favorable forum for the suit. According to Lambda Legal lawyer Camilla Taylor, Iowa was chosen as the venue for its litigation because of favorable legal and political factors. In an interview, Taylor noted that Iowa citizens are highly educated as a result of the Iowa caucuses, and they observe a custom of respect for the views of others. She also noted the "live and let live" ethic in Iowa political culture, particularly in the Iowa courts.[37] In their public messages about the litigation, Lambda drew upon these traditions, while also using language common to public description of litigation efforts. In a press release Taylor declared, "This is a question of fairness and equality for same-sex couples across Iowa, and we are asking the court to decide based on clear Iowa legal principles."[38] Lambda also wanted to initiate litigation in the Midwest to propel the movement for same-sex marriage. According to Kevin Cathcart, Lambda Legal's executive director, "We thought that it would be important from a public-education point of view and from a law-reform point of view to show people that progress can be made not just in New England, the mid-Atlantic states, and not just on the West Coast. It would give gay people and our allies in the middle of the country a shot in the arm that victory and change is possible where they live."[39]

Lambda Legal was likely encouraged by a related case recently handled by the Iowa courts, an "accidental" case concerning relationship equality. In 2003, a district court judge in western Iowa dissolved a civil union between two women that had been performed in Vermont in 2002. Judge Jeffrey Neary claims that he did not recognize that the parties were both women but later stood by his decision to approve the dissolution after he was aware that he was dissolving a same-sex relationship, citing the full faith and credit clause of the U.S. Constitution.[40] Neary was a newly appointed judge; Governor Tom Vilsak, a Democrat, appointed him to the district court in 2002.[41] In response to considerable attention drawn by the case, particularly from conservatives in the state, Neary emphasized that his decision was legally routine. "I'm not here crusading for anything or anybody. I'm dealing with legal problems," he stated in defense of his decision.[42] Neary eventually amended his order, replacing the word "marriage" with "civil union."[43]

This did not quiet the controversy in the state, however. A conservative public policy group, the Iowa Family Policy Center, campaigned to defeat Neary in a retention election. They, along with legislators and a church from northwestern Iowa, also filed a lawsuit with the state supreme court attempting to invalidate Neary's ruling. They viewed his decision as an attempt to legalize same-sex marriage in the state. According to the center's president, Chuck Hurley, the decision was a "nuclear missile [aimed] at the nuclear family."[44] The retention election became a high-profile campaign, which was quite unusual for retention elections in the state. In the end, Neary was retained, but 41 percent of voters in the rural, Republican district voted to remove him, despite a clear statement by Neary that he opposed same-sex marriage.[45] The case also contributed to a decision by Republican lawmakers to propose an anti-same-sex-marriage constitutional amendment in early 2005, but split partisan control of the state senate and the eventual Democratic takeover of both chambers has neutralized these efforts.[46] Clearly, though, the "lesbian divorce" case was highly salient in the state.

The legal attempt to challenge the ruling failed when the Iowa Supreme Court ruled that those challenging Neary's decision lacked standing.[47] And by not overturning Neary, the unanimous court appeared to downplay the rhetoric of conservatives in the state about the threat to marriage posed by the decision and seemingly left the door open to the idea of legal space for civil unions in the state. As Chief Justice Lewis Lavorato wrote: "We fail to see how the district court's action in dissolving a civil union of another couple harmed in any specific way these plaintiffs' marriages. . . . We therefore agree with amicus that these plaintiffs have claimed an interest in Iowa and federal marriage laws that has nothing to do with the district court's decision."[48]

In this case, amicus was none other than Camilla Taylor of Lambda Legal. Indeed, Taylor was substantially involved in the litigation after the initial decision on an amicus basis, as well as by making public statements about the case. She characterized the attempt to challenge Neary in court and in his election as an attempt at judicial intimidation. Taylor also viewed the controversy as an opportunity for Lambda and other gay rights groups to portray conservative opponents of same-sex marriage as extremists while defending the privacy and integrity of same-sex, and opposite-sex, relationships. "Iowans want to know that they can go to court and have their private legal matters resolved, without having their issues hijacked by extremist groups and used as a vehicle to further their political agendas," Taylor declared after the supreme court decision.[49] Roughly six months after the decision, Lambda Legal filed its same-sex marriage suit. The fact that Neary's decision held up most certainly was taken as a cue from the Iowa courts that some form of relationship equality was possible in the jurisprudence of the state.

Lambda's summary judgment brief created a strong narrative that emphasized the rights and dignity of same-sex couples. It also argued that Iowa jurisprudence fully supports claims for same-sex marriage on the basis of equal protection and fundamental rights analysis with its "strong jurisprudence in defense of rights of personhood" and "storied tradition of protecting personal liberty and equality against majority tyranny."[50] Thus, while Lambda's involvement in the lesbian civil union dissolution emphasized libertarian concerns and the right to be left alone, this litigation relied on a much richer notion of rights and argued that Iowa jurisprudence could sustain this richer view.[51]

In their legal arguments, but especially in their public statements about the litigation, Lambda emphasized the importance of same-sex marriage for children. Nearly half of the press release announcing Lambda's brief is devoted to a discussion of issues relating to children, emphasizing the large numbers of same-sex couples raising children and the positive child development literature on same-sex parenting.[52] This is increasingly a common theme and tactic for same-sex marriage advocates and litigants, and it was used successfully, both legally and politically, in the Massachusetts litigation.[53]

Lambda's filings for the case included extensive affidavits from family law and LGBT legal and history scholars, indicating an attempt to educate both the courts and the public about misperceptions concerning gay history and family issues.[54] However, the emphasis was clearly on the litigation. Unlike the Vermont case, where grassroots political organizing preceded the litigation, the litigation came first in Iowa. Lambda was aware of the educational effects of litigation and developed grassroots efforts to supplement and broaden the process, but this was secondary to the litigation efforts. Lambda and supportive groups in Iowa hired a grassroots political coordinator, but this, again, was initiated after the litigation was commenced.[55] The tool for policy change being used in Iowa was a lawsuit, not a well organized and orchestrated grassroots political campaign.

Judge Hanson's Decision

The litigation strategy, of course, was highly effective. Following the trend of trial court judges ruling in favor of same-sex marriage,[56] a Polk county judge ruled in late August 2007 that same-sex couples were entitled to the state's marriage framework and that the state's 1998 Defense of Marriage Act was unconstitutional. Beyond its relative aggressiveness, this decision is noteworthy for several reasons. Judge Hanson was highly skeptical of religious and policy arguments against same-sex marriage, finding that the exclusion of same-sex couples from the array of rights and benefits under the state's marriage laws was arbitrary and most likely based on animus, rather than legitimate policy concerns.[57] While the level of review invoked was the generally deferential rational basis test, the decision was sweeping, in both substance and tone, in its support for same-sex marriage arguments. Hanson declared:

> As a result of their exclusion from the civil institution of marriage, Plaintiffs, their relationships and their families are stigmatized. . . . Through the marriage exclusion the State devalues and delegitimizes relationships at the very core of the adult Plaintiff's sexual orientation and expresses, compounds, and perpetuates the stigma historically attached to homosexuality, for them and all gay persons.[58]

Lambda certainly found a sympathetic judge.

The decision also highlights a crucial element of comparative institutional policy analysis. Judge Hanson was quite skeptical of several of the defendant's witnesses who proposed to testify to the religious and historical underpinnings of traditional, heterosexual marriage and ruled that these witnesses would likely be inadmissible at trial.[59] In doing so, Hanson noted that "[t]he views espoused by these individuals appear to be largely personal and not based on observation supported by scientific methodology or based on empirical research in any sense."[60] This reflects a phenomenon noted by Evan Gerstmann, whereby state courts are increasingly rejecting arguments based on tradition and religion in favor of more "rational" approaches that support egalitarian outcomes in the same-sex marriage debate.[61] This role is important, especially given the way that morality politics occurs outside of the courts. According to Christopher Mooney, "morality-policy politics" are defined by several factors, which he identifies as "conflicts of first principle, technically simple policy, potential for high salience, and high levels of citizen participation."[62] LGBT rights policies generally fare poorly in the arena of majoritarianism because opponents are able to mobilize clear, focused opposition—sometimes based on majoritarian sentiment, sometimes not, but always visible to policy makers.[63] In this arena, all arguments, including those based on religion and tradition, have standing. However, in litigation, the range of argument can be limited, which can enhance the standing of pro-LGBT arguments.

Reaction from conservatives to the decision was predictable, but opponents of the ruling were limited in their ability to respond through policy, given the Democratic control of the state government. Calls for a constitutional amendment or the impeachment of Judge Hanson went largely unheeded. However, the decision caused discussion of the issue of same-sex marriage during the lead-up to the 2008 Iowa caucuses.[64]

The Iowa Supreme Court Issues a Sweeping Opinion

On April 3, 2009, the Iowa Supreme Court ruled unanimously that same-sex marriage was required by the state constitution.[65] The court viewed the issue as a civil rights issue, not an issue of traditional morality and religion. Indeed, the court went out of its way to recognize, but ultimately fence out, religious objections to same-sex marriage, arguments that are front and center in nonlegal debates.[66] According to the court, "Civil marriage must be judged under our constitutional standards of equal protection and not under religious doctrines or the religious views of individuals. This approach does not disrespect or denigrate the religious views of many Iowans who may strongly believe in marriage as a dual-gender union, but considers, as we must, only the constitutional rights of all people, as expressed by the promise of equal protection for all."[67] Instead, the court, following Judge Hanson, framed its discussion on the expert opinion of medical and professional groups on the worth of, and obstacles faced by, families with same-sex parents, and the policy discrimination faced by same-sex couples.[68] The court also heavily referenced its role as an innovator in the area of civil rights and equality, particularly its role in the early elimination of slavery and segregation in the state and its leading role concerning the rights of women.[69] The justices saw themselves as the defenders of an egalitarian jurisprudential tradition in the state.

Following that tradition, the court found sexual orientation to trigger more than traditional rational basis review, given the history of discrimination against sexual minorities, the immutability of sexuality, and the political powerlessness of sexual minorities. This allowed the justices to directly engage, and reject, the procreation/welfare of children argument:

> If the statute was truly about the best interest of children, some benefit to children derived from the ban on same-sex civil marriages would be observable. Yet, the germane analysis does not show how the best interests of children of gay and lesbian parents, who are denied an environment supported by the benefits of marriage under the statute, are served by the ban. Likewise, the exclusion of gays and lesbians from marriage does not benefit the interests of those children of heterosexual parents, who are able to enjoy the environment supported by marriage with or without the inclusion of same-sex couples. . . . Consequently, a classification that limits civil marriage to opposite-sex couples is simply not substantially related to the objective of promoting the optimal environment to raise children. This conclusion suggests stereotype and prejudice, or some other unarticulated reason, could be present to explain the real objectives of the statute.[70]

The court also noted that same-sex couples were capable of procreation, further undermining the government's main objective for discrimination.

The justices were fully aware of the aggressiveness of their decision and its potential consequences, although it is doubtful that they could have foreseen the successful recall effort the following year. They knew that their opinion was inconsistent with public opinion on same-sex marriage at the time. As Justice Mark Cady declared in the opinion, invoking U.S. Supreme Court Justices John Marshall and Robert H. Jackson, "Our responsibility, however, is to protect constitutional rights of individuals from legislative enactments that have denied those rights, even when the rights have not yet been broadly accepted, were at one time unimagined, or challenge a deeply ingrained practice or law viewed to be impervious to the passage of time."[71] Consequently, the justices saw no need to soften the political impact of their decision by opening the door to civil unions; instead, they ordered the marriage statute changed to include same-sex couples.

The Political Reaction: A Stalled Amendment, Justices Are Voted off the Court, and Vander Plaats's Pledge Gets Negative National Attention

The decision received a great deal of attention nationwide and signaled a new turning point in the debate about same-sex marriage, particularly because it was the first positive news for same-sex marriage advocates since the passage of Proposition 8 in California five months earlier. It was followed by legislative enactments of same-sex marriage in Vermont, New Hampshire, and Maine and spurred activity in other states, such as New York.

Discussion immediately focused on a constitutional amendment to overturn the decision, particularly from the state's conservative and Republican leaders and citizens; however, the Democrats mostly have opposed this. Indeed, the state party platform endorses same-sex marriage. Soon after the decision, Democratic legislative leaders issued a statement in support of the decision, echoing the court's logic and emphasis on civil rights leadership in the state, and they have resisted calls to take up a constitutional amendment.[72] However, it should be noted that Democratic governor Chet Culver publicly opposed same-sex marriage and exhibited more ambivalence about the litigation.[73]

At any rate, the Iowa constitution is not as easily amended as other state constitutions. Rather than a simple referendum, an amendment needs approval from two consecutive sessions of the Iowa legislature before it is put to voters. Alternatively, a state constitutional convention can be called by a majority vote of the state's voters in a constitutionally required vote that takes place every ten years. This would be followed by a popular vote to ratify the results of the convention.[74] This lag time in the amendment process is one of the main reasons that the state was chosen as a venue for litigation. In the 2010 election, Republicans captured a majority in the House and the governorship. They tried to revive the amendment process, but the Democrats in the Senate continued to block the amendment. As Senate Majority Leader Michael Gronstal stated, "I am not going to put discrimination in the constitution."[75] In a shrewd, but clearly anti-same-sex marriage, political move, Governor Branstad appointed a Democratic state senator to a state board, creating a vacancy in a Republican-leaning district.[76] His effort was unsuccessful, and Democrats retained control of the Senate in the 2012 election, thereby keeping same-sex marriage as the state's policy.

The supreme court faced the brunt of the backlash with the loss of three of its justices in retention elections in 2010. This vote was unprecedented, the first time that a high court justice was not retained since Iowa adopted the Missouri Plan in the 1960s.[77] The campaign against the justices was coordinated by Republican gubernatorial candidate and extreme social conservative Bob Vander Plaats. Religious conservatives spent over $1,000,000 on the campaign against the justices, split between the National Organization for Marriage, the Family Research Council, and the American Family Association (labeled a hate group by the Southern Poverty Law Center for its virulently anti-gay rhetoric).[78] This overshadowed spending by the group supporting retention, Fair Courts for Us, which raised $366,000.[79] In addition, the justices were part of the Republican and anti-incumbent wave in 2010 nationally, and they did not aggressively campaign for their jobs, as is often the norm in retention elections. Clearly, however, many voters in Iowa, especially those who turned out, were upset by the decision. After the election, Cady defended his decision, despite the backlash, and demonstrated the power of the mindset of the court's justices. As he stated, "That decision was crafted with all of the energy, all of the strength. Everything that we do as judges was in that opinion. Everything that Iowa is about is in that opinion."[80]

Trying to maintain his momentum as a conservative player in Iowa, and potentially national, politics, Vander Plaats authored a socially conservative pledge for Republican presidential candidates in advance of the 2012 Iowa caucuses. The pledge, a crude version of the Manhattan Declaration, caused controversy when it came to light that it appeared to praise family structure during slavery, comparing it favorably to contemporary family culture. However, its language about same-sex marriage, including footnotes invoking the "gays are diseased" narrative, was par for the course in Republican Party politics and did not receive quite the same level of media disapproval.[81] It was yet another glimpse into the persistent religious and LGBT-marginalizing opposition to same-sex marriage in the United States.

Same-sex marriage was thus legalized in Iowa through judicial policy making, with acquiescence from the other political branches after the initiation of a carefully planned and orchestrated litigation strategy. This reflects a policy outcome that goes beyond the parameters of public opinion in that civil unions, which do have public support, were not allowed by the state high court. This, of course, engendered a significant backlash at the polls for the state supreme court in 2010, but same-sex marriage will likely remain legal in Iowa for the foreseeable future.

ILLINOIS: AVOIDANCE OF LITIGATION LEADS TO SUCCESS

From the perspective of relationship equality policy advocates, until 2010, Illinois was the worst of both worlds—it had both an unsympathetic judiciary and legislature, neither reflective of public opinion in this blue state. Based upon Democratic Party dominance and strong public opinion support for LGBT rights, Illinois should have easily enacted relationship equality legislation. The state is solidly Democratic, with large party majorities in the legislature. According to Gallup, the state is the seventh most Democratic state.[82] Lax and Phillips measure mean public opinion support for gay rights in Illinois at 60 percent, with 53 percent support for civil unions and 42 percent support for same-sex marriage.[83] As measured by public opinion, Illinois is the most supportive of LGBT rights in the Midwest.

However, a bill legalizing civil unions was stalled in the legislature for several years. It was enacted only after it appeared that a conservative governor would be elected in the fall of 2010, thereby putting the issue off the table for at least another four years. Advocates in Illinois intentionally focused on a legislative, rather than judicial, strategy to enact relationship equality policy. In fact, the courts have been actively avoided as potential policy makers. This dynamic does not only apply to LGBT rights issues; progressive policy advocates in the state have generally been wary of the courts. According to Samuel Gove and James Nowlan, "The Illinois political system and culture seem to discourage the state from being a national leader in progressive causes, and the courts are generally conservative and nonactivist."[84]

The avoidance of social activism describes not only the Illinois courts but also the other branches of state government, which tend to focus more on "bread and butter" issues like taxes, spending, and so on. In a state where political patronage has a long history, "who gets what" has long been the focal point of politics. As one of the leading commentators on Illinois politics, Kent Redfield states, "In a system like Illinois that's very pragmatic and job-oriented, we tend to not work on the social issues. If I vote pro-life and abortion is not criminalized, the people that voted for me are not going to throw me out of office. But if I don't get a road paved like I promised, watch out."[85] As a result, LGBT rights issues struggled to gain a foothold on the policy agenda, and enactment of policy has lagged far behind generally supportive public opinion until recently.

Before working to enact civil unions, activists in Illinois worked for years on adding sexual orientation and gender identity to the state's antidiscrimination law. The bill was able to get through the Democratic House, but had failed repeatedly in the Republican Senate. In 2002, Democrats took control of the legislature and the governorship, opening up the stalemate. However, even the Democrats acted slowly, finally enacting the law early in 2005.

This history indicates that partisan control is important in Illinois, but it is not a guarantee of LGBT rights successes. Legislation enacting civil unions languished for two consecutive legislative sessions. A same-sex marriage bill was introduced, but it lacked support, forcing advocates to focus on the civil union approach. In fact, in an attempt to broaden the appeal of the bill, the proposed and eventually enacted civil union legislation applied to unmarried heterosexual couples as well, and advocates argued that the legislation would assist elderly heterosexual couples in particular—a kind of European cohabitation model.

In 2010, indications were that the law could pass in the Senate, but that sufficient votes for passage did not exist in the House. The House Speaker, Michael Madigan, is a fairly conservative Democrat, and he wields tremendous power in the chamber. His primary focus was the reelection of Democrats to the House in 2010, and he is notoriously risk averse, particularly in a climate where Democrats could have been vulnerable given a lingering budget crisis and the ethical cloud caused by former Democratic governor Rod Blagojevich.

After falling short of securing enough House votes in May of 2010, activists and legislators engaged in a renewed push to enact civil unions in the fall of 2010 as polls showed the conservative Republican Bill Brady ahead of the incumbent, Democrat Pat Quinn. It appeared that Illinois would follow the national trend of a Republican wave. Brady was a strong opponent of relationship equality, but he signaled that he would not work to overturn civil unions if they were enacted before he took office, if elected, in a nod to clear public support for civil unions in a close election. This created a window for activists, who feared at least four years of a potential Brady veto of the law. Activists were also motivated by activity in Iowa and Wisconsin, not wanting to be outdone by their less progressive neighbors. House Democrats were lobbied heavily to get to the sixty-vote threshold for passage. Especially after the narrow reelection of Pat Quinn as governor and the preservation of the Democratic majorities in the legislature, the political downside to supporting civil unions was lessened significantly. By then, all Democratic leaders, including Madigan, were strongly supportive of civil unions. In addition, political insiders viewed the much stronger showing of socially moderate Republican Mark Kirk in the Senate race over Brady in the crucial Chicago suburbs as an indication that social conservatism, while still strong in rural areas, was rapidly declining as a force in statewide politics. The bill passed in the House by a vote of 61 to 52 and in the Senate by 32 to 24. Thus civil unions were enacted in Illinois when the controlling Democrats finally found it "safe" to do so, finally following public opinion.[86]

Advocates of civil unions in Illinois actively attempted to neutralize traditional religious opposition to relationship equality by working with progressive religious organizations to undercut conservative religious voices in the debate. In addition, the bill was entitled "The Illinois Religious Freedom Protection and Civil Union Act" and included language exempting religious organizations from performing civil unions: "Nothing in this Act shall interfere with or regulate the religious practice of any religious body. Any religious body, Indian Nation or Tribe or Native Group is free to choose whether or not to solemnize or officiate a civil union."[87] It did not, however, include an exemption for the complete nonrecognition of civil unions by religious organizations, according to leading LGBT advocates. This language, especially the first sentence, has been interpreted by religious conservatives as granting a broad exemption to ignore civil unions.

After Quinn signed the bill into law in January of 2011, the conflict shifted to equality versus religious freedom on two fronts, in the legislature and in the courts, triggered by the issue of parenting rights under the new law. In the wake of the enactment of the civil union law, the Illinois Department of Children and Family Services did not renew the adoption and foster parenting contracts of religious organizations refusing to place children in same-sex households. One group, Catholic Charities, sued the state, citing a violation of religious freedom.[88] This action was also instigated by an investigation by the Civil Rights Bureau of the Office of the Illinois Attorney General. In a letter to Catholic Charities of Springfield, Assistant Attorney General Polly A. Hayes alleged that Catholic Charities "has requirements for potential foster or adoptive parents that are not required by Illinois law—for example requirements about religious beliefs—or refused to provide services to potential foster or adoptive parents in violation of Illinois law—for example refused to provide services based on the marital status or sexual orientation of a potential foster or adoptive parent."[89] Clearly, the state was, through its enforcement power, siding with equality for same-sex couples against broad religious freedom claims—not a surprise coming from Attorney General Lisa Madigan, a Democrat and more progressive daughter of Speaker Madigan.

Rather than tackle the larger question of religious freedom, the judge instead focused his inquiry narrowly, like many trial court judges confronting a highly controversial case. He focused on the more mundane question of whether Catholic Charities had a vested right to the contract with DCFS, given that it had been in place for forty years. Judge Schmidt converted the case from constitutional to administrative law, from a question of religious freedom to a due process question relating to government contracts. Ruling against Catholic Charities, Schmidt asserted: "No citizen has a recognized legal right to contract with the government."[90] Arguably, Schmidt was taking a personal and political risk with the decision. He is a Catholic who is active in the Springfield Diocese and was facing an election in 2012 in a heavily Catholic region.[91]

In the legislature, relationship equality advocates successfully lobbied in 2011 to defeat proposed legislation to make this religious-based discrimination state policy, trumping the determination of the agency. Such legislation was supported by the Senate sponsor of the civil union law, Democrat Dave Koehler of Peoria. As he explained his position, "I gave my word that I would come back and try to clarify this. I'm very proud to have been the sponsor of the civil unions bill, and I want to see that work. This is an issue that is not so much a political issue for me, as really an issue of conscience and one of personal conviction."[92] Having taken such a political risk for a downstate (outside of urban Chicago) legislator, Koehler was likely attempting to limit the damage with this push for the religious exemption. During the debate on the civil union bill, Koehler argued that the law provided for a broad exemption, beyond the right to not perform civil unions. This also likely facilitated enactment of the law by defusing some opposition, but most advocates for relationship equality have since taken a narrower view of the religious exemption. The issue will not go away. Koehler and others have vowed to keep trying to clarify the religious exemption through the legislative process, alongside the litigation.

Thus, the question of religion played prominently in the debate over, and reaction to, civil unions. The ultimate answer to the question of the relationship between civil unions and religious freedom broadly defined likely will be decided by the Illinois courts, not exactly a leader in the realm of equality. While repeal of the law is unlikely, opponents clearly wish to use the litigation and the political process to portray themselves as victims of religious persecution, consistent with the emerging critique of relationship equality, and to set the stage for a more robust religious challenge to the inevitable debate over same-sex marriage in the state.

In a clear reversal of the litigation avoidance strategy, Lambda Legal and the ACLU filed same-sex marriage lawsuits in Chicago in late May 2012. The most likely reason for the shift is the fact that no legal actors in the state will defend the state's statutory ban on same-sex marriage. Democratic attorney general Lisa Madigan requested to intervene in the case on the side of the plaintiffs, neither defending the law nor staying neutral. Governor Quinn came out in support of marriage equality in the state just before the lawsuits were filed, and it is highly unlikely that the Democrat-controlled legislature would intervene to defend the law.[93] Two downstate county clerks were granted permission to defend the law, and the litigation is proceeding.

MINNESOTA: FAVORABLE OPINION, BUT CONSERVATIVES GAIN A FOOTHOLD AND PUSH AN AMENDMENT

Developments in Minnesota demonstrate that public opinion does not always drive policy outcomes on relationship equality. According to Lax and Phillips, mean public opinion support for pro-gay policies is 58 percent, slightly lower than Illinois (60 percent) and slightly higher than Iowa (56 percent) and Wisconsin (57 percent). Mean public opinion support for health benefits for same-sex couples is 60 percent and for civil unions is 51 percent.[94] This would seem to point in the direction of the enactment of policies granting rights to same-sex couples in Minnesota. However, policy in the state lags behind Iowa, Illinois, and Wisconsin, its upper midwestern peers. Indeed, following a Republican takeover of the legislature in 2010, voters faced a proposed constitutional amendment banning same-sex marriage in 2012. This followed several years of conservative opposition to same-sex marriage in the state, led by then–state legislator Michele Bachmann, who built her early political career substantially on opposition to same-sex marriage.

Bills to enact civil unions and same-sex marriage failed to get a hearing in the legislature. An attempt by the legislature to provide same-sex couples with death benefits was vetoed by Republican governor Tim Pawlenty in 2010.[95] This decision was clearly connected to the governor's presidential aspirations. It was not public opinion in Minnesota the governor heeded with this veto but the much more conservative voters in national Republican primaries. The governor's approach is frustrating for advocates in the state, because, like activists in Illinois, they have pursued a mostly legislative strategy. This tactic is the result of the negative precedent of *Baker v. Nelson*,[96] the early same-sex marriage challenge that went against same-sex marriage advocates.[97] As a result, leading activists in Minnesota have actively discouraged any litigation in the state and have criticized a recent lawsuit initiated by rival activists.

Same-sex marriage activists were optimistic about the potential for change before the 2010 election. The legislature had moved in the direction of relationship equality with the death benefits bill, and the prospect of a Democrat (DFL)[98] replacing Pawlenty diminished the veto threat. Indeed, openly gay state senator Scott Dibble planned to introduce a same-sex marriage bill in 2011 in an effort to "start moving on these ideas a little more tangibly, to see real progress happen."[99] However, Republicans won a sweeping and unexpected victory in the election that fall, gaining control of the legislature for the first time in thirty-eight years.[100] While same-sex marriage was not a defining issue of the election, the results created an opportunity for a conservative wish list of policy priorities. The amendment process is relatively easy in Minnesota—only a majority vote in each legislative chamber is required. Given the election of a DFL governor, Republicans saw the amendment process as a way to enact policies without the threat of a veto.

Interestingly, in a nod to evolving public opinion, the Republicans' proposed amendment only banned same-sex marriage, not civil unions and domestic partnerships. Conservative activists and party leaders clearly saw a broader amendment as more difficult to approve, a clear shift from Wisconsin in 2006 and that state's super-DOMA amendment. The amendment passed through both chambers, largely along party lines. However, a prayer by a controversial and virulently anti-gay preacher, Bradlee Dean, nearly derailed the Republicans' efforts. Dean strongly implied that President Obama was not a Christian, causing the House Speaker to reset the session and denounce Dean.[101] In the aftermath of the episode, the media highlighted Dean's distasteful statements on sexual minorities, including advocating imprisonment and even death for those who practice sodomy. He also plays heavily on the discredited notion of gay men as pedophiles. The fact that such a religious leader could so casually and easily get to start a session of the Minnesota House of Representatives reflects the strong connections between religious extremists and the Republican Party. Dean's ministry had developed close ties to the state party.[102]

Indeed, conservative religious mobilization for the amendment was significant in the state, as was the case in Wisconsin, with a coalition between the National Organization for Marriage, the Minnesota Family Council (a conservative evangelical Protestant group), and the Minnesota Catholic Conference. Like Bradlee Dean, the Minnesota Family Council pushed the pedophilia claim on its website, and a leading Catholic priest referred to homosexuality as a "condition," thus signaling that the campaign for the amendment will be as much about religiously defined sexual morality as the "sanctity of marriage," as much theological as neoconservative.[103] A DVD sent to four hundred thousand homes by the Archdiocese of St. Paul and Minneapolis reflected the emerging themes of anti–marriage equality campaigns. Threats to civilization, threats to children from non–male/female homes, threats to religious freedom, and forced indoctrination in public schools were all themes emphasized in the video. In addition, the video invoked Martin Luther King, Jr., as being opposed to same-sex marriage, tying him to the Catholic natural law tradition, and it advocated celibacy for persons with same-sex attraction.[104]

On the opposite side of the debate, a DFL legislator became a YouTube sensation with a speech before a committee considering the amendment. Directly challenging conservative religious perspectives, Representative Steve Simon asked, "How many more gay people does God have to create before we ask ourselves whether or not God actually wants them around?"[105] In a preview of the primary argument of amendment opponents, Governor Mark Dayton symbolically vetoed the amendment and declared: "I urge Minnesotans to reject this mean-spirited, divisive, un-Minnesotan and un-American amendment. Minnesotans are better than this."[106] Public opinion and a quirk of the amendment process were on Dayton's side. Early polls showed a lack of support for the amendment, well below 50 percent, and any blank votes on a ballot are counted as "no" votes, making the mobilization of energized conservative and religious voters key to the passage of the amendment, but the trend was moving away from them.[107] The amendment failed with only 47 percent support.

Because of the *Baker* decision from the early 1970s, most advocates have avoided litigation as a path to relationship equality in Minnesota, as was the case in Illinois with its nonactivist courts. However, the lure of litigation stemming from the legal consciousness of same-sex couples in the state has trumped this legal-political calculation, and a group was formed in 2008 to litigate for same-sex marriage in the state, Marry Me Minnesota. The organization has been shunned by the more established LGBT advocacy organizations in the state. OutFront Minnesota declared that "the road to Marriage

Equality [sic] in Minnesota runs through the legislature, not the courts."[108] Deflecting the argument that the amendment is needed to prevent activist judges from bringing same-sex marriage to Minnesota is one of the central elements of the campaign against the amendment, and OutFront Minnesota uses the *Baker* decisions in its public relations efforts.[109]

The lawsuit claimed several ways in which the state's ban on same-sex marriage was unconstitutional: it was a violation of the state's due process and equal protection provisions (and distinguished from *Baker* because that case was based on federal constitutional law), it ran afoul of the state constitution's single subject rule for statutes, and it violated religious freedom and freedom of association provisions of the state constitution. Reflecting conventional wisdom in the state, the lawsuit was dismissed by a trial court judge, largely relying on *Baker*, indicating that she was powerless to act in the wake of this clear precedent that marriage in Minnesota was heterosexual-only. She also speculated that the finding of the Minnesota Supreme Court in *Baker* would have been the same under the Minnesota constitution. In sum, according to Judge Mary DuFresne, "Times may have changed, but the law has not. . . . Same-sex marriage will not exist in this state unless the Minnesota Supreme Court overrules its own decision in *Baker*, or the State Legislature repeals the State DOMA."[110] The same-sex couples have appealed but are unlikely to achieve their goals, leaving the political process as the best avenue for success.

THE REST OF THE MIDWEST

Outside of the more progressive Upper Midwest, legal or policy change in the direction of relationship equality is nonexistent, while anti-same-sex-marriage policies are present. Activists have struggled legally and politically in several midwestern states, largely constrained by Republican Party control of whole or parts of state governments, negative public opinion, and uncooperative judiciaries.

Indiana

In Indiana, a super-DOMA constitutional amendment was provisionally approved by the legislature in 2011 but must be approved again in the next legislative session, after Republicans took over full control of the legislature. Democrats had been successful in blocking an amendment by controlling the House from 2006 to 2010, again demonstrating the importance of party for relationship equality. If ultimately approved, it could go before voters in 2014. Unless the Democrats regain control of a chamber, this appears to be likely. A few months after the 2011 vote, a state newspaper printed e-mails outlining the efforts of a Republican representative, Phillip Hinkle, who voted for the amendment, to secure the companionship of a young man for up to $140 through a Craigslist advertisement.[111] While Barack Obama carried the state in 2008, it leans Republican. Support for same-sex marriage is low for the Midwest, 35 percent, while support for civil unions is higher, 45 percent.[112]

Indiana was also the site of same-sex marriage litigation. In 2002, three couples who had obtained Vermont civil unions requested marriage licenses from county clerks in Indiana but were denied. They sued the clerks and the state, with the assistance of the Indiana Civil Liberties Union (ICLU). The ICLU was a reluctant partner to the litigation, assessing the chances of success as slim, and no other pro-same-sex-marriage groups signed on to the effort, reflected by the absence of friend of the court briefs in the litigation from potential allies.[113] All of the amicus briefs in the case were submitted by conservative opponents of same-sex marriage. Legally, the deck was stacked against the plaintiffs, particularly on the crucial question of equal protection. Unlike Iowa, with its strong jurisprudential tradition of equality activism, Indiana jurisprudence concerning equal protection claims only invokes a rational basis test, with no heightened scrutiny, and is highly deferential to legislative assessments of acceptable discrimination. A trial judge's dismissal of the couples' suit in 2003 reflected this state of affairs.[114]

The Indiana Court of Appeals confirmed this approach, but the court's majority did so by making a curious argument about the state's interest in preserving heterosexual marriage. With an argument that would also be invoked by New York's highest court in rejecting a challenge to that state's prohibition of same-sex marriage, the court held that the need to protect children from the consequences of "accidental" procreation by heterosexuals was a legitimate state interest justifying discrimination against same-sex couples. The court noted that same-sex couples are required to engage in a great deal of planning to have children through adoption or artificial insemination and they must bring a significant amount of resources to the effort, thereby creating a relatively stable environment for their child or children.

> By contrast, procreation by "natural" reproduction may occur without any thought for the future. The State, first of all, may legitimately create the institution of opposite-sex marriage, and all the benefits accruing to it, in order to encourage male-female couples to procreate within the legitimacy and stability of a state-sanctioned relationship and to discourage unplanned, out-of-wedlock births resulting from "casual" intercourse. Second, even where an opposite-sex couple enters into a marriage with no intention of having children, "accidents" do happen, or persons often change their minds about wanting to have children. The institution of marriage not only encourages opposite-sex couples to form a relatively stable environment for the "natural" procreation of children in the first place, but it also encourages them to stay together and raise a child or children together if there is a "change in plans."[115]

This line of reasoning was emphasized by the state during oral argument, and it appears to have greatly influenced at least two members of the three-judge panel.[116] However, in a concurring opinion, Judge Ezra Friedlander noted the weakness of this argument, particularly the negative implication for infertile heterosexual couples. He also noted that it ignored the actual discrimination faced by same-sex couples and their families.[117] Nonetheless, he felt bound by the low level of review in Indiana equal protection jurisprudence, or the "low bar of constitutionality" set by precedents.

Perhaps reflecting the lack of pro-same-sex-marriage amicus briefs, the majority opinion relied heavily on conservative legal and other sources, including Maggie Gallagher of the National Organization for Marriage. While Judge Friedlander could envision a potential positive right to marriage for same-sex couples (coming from the legislature, as his hands were tied in his view), the majority opinion envisioned the rights of same-sex couples as falling exclusively in the private realm, even parental rights. Judge Michael Barnes justified the discrimination against same-sex couples by noting the extensive (negative) freedoms available to them: "The Plaintiffs' intimate relationships are not illegal under the laws of this State and they enjoy extensive freedom to organize their personal affairs in a manner that suits them, which encompasses the freedom to create a family unit that includes children."[118] This libertarian, conservative, and deferential jurisprudence left same-sex couples with no legal options in Indiana, combined with a hostile political environment. Ultimately, the litigation was counterproductive by adding credence to the argument that a constitutional amendment was needed in the state to prevent activist judges from imposing same-sex marriage. While the state's judges proved themselves to be distinctly nonactivist, the very presence of the litigation, sponsored by the ICLU, aided this argument in the political arena.

Michigan

Given the more conservative political climate in Michigan, the legal and political conversation concerning relationship equality has primarily focused on domestic partnerships for state employees. Indeed, Michigan voters enacted a super-DOMA in 2004, and the state supreme court ruled that government same-sex domestic partnership benefits were banned by the amendment. This led government agencies, primarily universities, to allow benefits for another adult in the household in order to remove the same-sex requirement. However, a decision to apply this approach to all state employees by a state board in 2011 met strong resistance from the Republican-controlled government. In 2010, Republicans took complete control of the government and have pursued a highly conservative policy agenda, including opposition to any form of recognition or benefits for same-sex couples, a position inconsistent with public opinion in the state.

The Michigan Supreme Court decision declaring domestic partnerships inconsistent with the amendment is notable for its lack of anything but a facile form of interpretation. As the dissent in the case notes, the majority ignored the fact that the organization behind the amendment, the Citizens for the Protection of Marriage (CPM), strongly emphasized that the amendment would not affect domestic partnership arrangements, largely because public opinion supported such arrangements. The dissent cited a poll showing 70 percent opposition to making civil unions and domestic partnerships illegal.[119] While this type of analysis has been more influential in the Wisconsin courts, the majority of the Michigan Supreme Court allowed opponents of relationship equality to have their cake and eat it, too by letting them play the game of denying the sweep of the amendment while also letting its sweeping nature be enshrined in the state constitution and backed up by the courts.

After the decision, jurisdictions in the state began granting benefits to same-sex and opposite-sex domestic partners as a way around the decision, an approach validated by the Michigan Civil Service Commission in 2011, but Republicans in the legislature tried to undo this decision through legislation attempting to overturn the legislation. However, the effect of this legislation in unclear, given the commission's clear authority to make such decisions and the fact that the legislature has not blocked the rule by a two-thirds vote, as required, likely triggering a new round of litigation. At any rate, it is clear that the political and legal dynamics in Michigan are limiting recognition and protections for same-sex couples in a manner inconsistent with public sentiment in the state.

Ohio

The situation in Ohio mirrors that of Wisconsin. A super-DOMA was enacted in 2004, but domestic partnerships for same-sex couples have escaped the reach of the amendment. Immediately after the amendment was passed, judges invalidated the state's domestic violence law as it applied to unmarried couples, but the state supreme court overruled this approach.[120] State courts have also rejected challenges to public employee same-sex domestic partnership benefits.[121] Like Wisconsin, Minnesota, and Indiana, complete Republican Party control of the government after the 2010 election makes further advancement for relationship equality unlikely until the partisan dynamic changes.

CONCLUSION

Given its position geographically and politically in the center of American politics, a variety of approaches to relationship equality have played out in the Midwest. Republicans in the region, allied with conservative religious activists, have worked diligently to see that no form of relationship recognition exists, undermining the argument that the debate is simply about the preservation of "traditional" marriage. Hostility toward sexual minorities is still a large part of the opposition to relationship equality. Control of whole or part of state government by Democrats has led to policies recognizing and granting rights to same-sex couples, or the forestalling, often only temporarily, of constitutional bans on same-sex marriage or similar arrangements. Given Republican gains in the 2010 election, prospects for further change in the region are dim, and the climate may worsen for relationship equality in some states.

In the legal arena, events in the Midwest highlight the crucial role played by variations in legal culture, a dynamic made obvious by contrasting the approaches of courts in Iowa and Indiana. In Iowa, a robust tradition of equal protection jurisprudence resulted in the judiciary's support for same-sex marriage, despite a lack of public support for full marriage equality. But in Indiana, a legacy of minimal equal protection analysis and great deference to legislative categorization of, and discrimination against, groups resulted in the lack of a legal challenge to the relatively conservative political approach to relationship equality in the state. The lack of a tradition of civil rights activism by the courts in Illinois channeled the debate to the political arena. In Minnesota, a negative precedent from the 1970s has created, thus far, an insurmountable barrier to judicial policy making. Outside of Iowa (and arguably Wisconsin and Ohio by leaving the door open for limited domestic partnerships), courts have not been strong allies for relationship equality advocates and have generally strengthened the hand of conservative opponents.

This variation in legal and political outcomes exists in a region with broadly similar levels of support for LGBT rights, demonstrating the importance of institutional/cultural and partisan differences as forces driving or prohibiting change. If public opinion alone drove outcomes, most states in the Midwest would adopt a domestic partnership framework for same-sex couples. However, some have done more, and most have done much less. This further reinforces the fact that the movement for same-sex marriage in the United States faces the unique challenge presented by federalism and the great variation in state approaches to the issue.

NOTES

1. Patricia Simms, "Legislature Is like the Hatfields and the McCoys," *Wisconsin State Journal*, February 1, 2005, A1.

2. Indeed, there was speculation that turnout by young voters against the amendment helped to elect Democrats to the legislature.

3. Jeffrey R. Lax and Justin H. Phillips, "Gay Rights in the States: Public Opinion and Policy Responsiveness," *American Political Science Review* 103:3 (August 2009), 367–86: 373.

4. http://www.cnn.com/ELECTION/2006/pages/results/ballot.measures/.

5. I was on the board of directors of Action Wisconsin from 2003–2005, then the leading LGBT rights advocacy organization in the state. This information is derived from participation in conversations about the litigation and its relationship to the amendment fight.

6. *Phillips v. Wisconsin Personnel Commission*, 167 Wis. 2d 205 (Ct. App. 1992), 213, note 1.

7. *Phillips v. Wisconsin Personnel Commission*, 219.

8. *Phillips v. Wisconsin Personnel Commission*, 227.

9. *Hinman v. Department of Personnel Administration*, 213 Cal. Rptr. 410 (Cal. App. 1985). Cited in *Phillips* at 221.

10. For a discussion of the early litigation, see Jason Pierceson, *Courts, Liberalism, and Rights: Gay Law and Politics in the United States and Canada* (Philadelphia: Temple University Press, 2005), 104–7.

11. Phil Brinkman, "Same-sex couples file benefits lawsuit; State plans discriminate, suit alleges," *Wisconsin State Journal*, April 21, 2005, A1.

12. Plaintiff's amended complaint, *Helgeland v. Dept. of Employee Trust Funds*, Dane County, Wis. Circuit Court, Case Number 05-CV-1265, June 8, 2005.

13. Brinkman, A1.

14. Brinkman, A1.

15. "Domestic partner legislation re-introduced," *Capitol Times*, November 19, 2001, 3A.

16. Amended complaint, 30.

17. Amended complaint, 29.

18. Bill Glauber, "State voters say 'I do' to marriage amendment; Civil unions may be banned; lawsuits could follow," *Milwaukee Journal Sentinel*, November 8, 2006, A9; Judith Davidoff, "Conflicted state; outside Madison, voters wrestle with gay marriage and civil unions question; backers mostly quiet," *Capitol Times*, October 26, 2006, A1. As the story notes, a St. Norbert College poll found 51 percent support for the amendment, with 44 percent opposed in October.

19. Robert Imrie, "Churches Reach Out to Faithful to Turn Vote on Gay Marriage," *Associated Press*, November 2, 2006.

20. Judith Davidoff, "Conflicted State," *Capitol Times*, October 26, 2006, A1.

21. Letter from Peggy A. Lautenschlager, attorney general of Wisconsin, to Michael P. May, city attorney, Madison, Wisconsin, December 27, 2006.

22. Ryan J. Foley, "Marriage ban creates uncertainty for gay couples," *The Associated Press State & Local Wire*, November 8, 2006.

23. *Dunnum v. Dept. of Employee Trust Funds*, Dane Co. Wisconsin Circuit Court, May 29, 2009, slip opinion, 46. For a criticism of this aspect of *Phillips*, see William B. Turner, "The Gay Rights State: Wisconsin's Pioneering Legislation to Prohibit Discrimination Based on Sexual Orientation," *Wisconsin Women's Law Journal*, 22:91 (2007).

24. *Dunnum*, 28.

25. *Dunnum*, 39.

26. Jessica Van Egeren, "Wisconsin's domestic partnership registry is open for business," Madison.com, August 3, 2009, http://www.madison.com/tct/news/stories/460603.

27. Ryan Foley, "Lawsuit challenges Wis. domestic partnership law," *Associated Press*, July 23, 2009.

28. The lawsuit was brought by an individual citizen and not as yet joined by Fair Wisconsin and Lambda Legal, but Fair Wisconsin has voiced support. See Judith Davidoff, "Citizen McConkey: A one-man battle against state's gay marriage ban," *Capitol Times*, July 15, 2009, http://www.madison.com/tct/news/458312.

29. Ryan J. Foley, "Wisconsin Gay Marriage Ban Upheld by State Supreme Court," *Associated Press*, June 30, 2010.

30. Julaine Appling, "Court Is Wrong Place to Make Law on Benefits," *Wisconsin State Journal*, May 26, 2005, A14.

31. Complaint, *Appling v. Doyle*, Dane County (WI) Circuit Court, Case no. 10CV4434.

32. ADF website, http://www.alliancedefensefund.org/About.

33. *Appling v. Doyle*, Decision of the Dane County (WI) Circuit Court, Branch 11, Case No. 10-CV-4434, June 20, 2011, 20.

34. *Appling v. Doyle*, 23.

35. Jeffrey M. Jones, "Political Party Affiliation: 30 States Blue, 4 Red in '09 So Far," *Gallup.com*, August 3, 2009, http://www.gallup.com/poll/122003/Political-Party-Affiliation-States-Blue-Red-Far.aspx.

36. Lax and Phillips, 373.

37. Phone interview with Camilla Taylor, Lambda Legal Midwest Office, January 5, 2007.

38. "Lambda Legal Asks Iowa Court Today to Rule for Same-Sex Couples Seeking Marriage," Lambda Legal Press Release, January 30, 2007.

39. Patrick Caldwell, "Disorder in the Court: How an Anti-Gay-Marriage Campaign Upended Iowa's Model Judiciary," *American Prospect*, September 19, 2011, http://prospect.org/cs/articles?article=disorder_in_the_court2.

40. David Pitt, "Same-sex divorce fuels argument over effect on marriage law," *Associated Press State & Local Wire*, December 12, 2003.

41. "Group forms to oust judge who approved lesbian divorce," *Associated Press State & Local Wire*, August 14, 2004.

42. "Judge who signed divorce for lesbians said issue needs solution," *Associated Press State & Local Wire*, December 22, 2003.

43. Mike Wilson, "Judge amends order in lesbian divorce case," *Associated Press State & Local Wire*, December 30, 2003.

44. "Judge denies he's promoting homosexual agenda," *Associated Press State & Local Wire*, October 12, 2004.

45. "Political battle over judge draws cash contributions," *Associated Press State & Local Wire*, October 20, 2004; Amy Lorentzen, "Chief justice calls lesbian divorce a 'thorny' issue," *Associated Press State & Local Wire*, January 14, 2005.

46. "Gay marriage amendment filed in Iowa," 365Gay.com, January 27, 2005, http://www.365gay.com/newscon05/01/012705iowa.htm.

47. *Alons v. Iowa Dist. Court for Woodbury County*, 698 N.W.2d 859 (Iowa 2005).

48. *Alons*, 870, 873.

49. Mike Glover, "Supreme Court refuses to tamper with termination of civil ruling," *Associated Press State & Local Wire*, June 17, 2005.

50. Plaintiff's brief for summary judgment, January 30, 2007, *Varnum v. Brien*, Polk County, Iowa District Court, Case no. CV5965, 13–14.

51. I develop the issue of positive rights and same-sex marriage claims extensively in my book, *Courts, Liberalism, and Rights*.

52. Lambda press release, January 30, 2007.

53. Pierceson, *Courts, Liberalism, and Rights*, 145.

54. See affidavit from leading experts, http://data.lambdalegal.org/pdf/794.pdf.

55. Interview with Camilla Taylor.

56. Trial court judges have ruled in favor of relationship equality claims in Oregon, Washington, California, Maryland, New York, and Iowa. This is noteworthy given that trial court judges tend not to be policy innovators.

57. *Varnum v. Brien*, Iowa District Court for Polk County, Case No. CV5963, slip opinion, August 31, 2007, 60.

58. *Varnum*, 22.

59. The case never proceeded to trial but was decided on a motion for summary judgment.

60. *Varnum*, 7.

61. Evan Gerstmann, "Litigating Same-Sex Marriage: Might the Courts Actually Be Bastions of Rationality?" *Political Science and Politics* 38:2 (2005), 217–20.

62. Christopher Z. Mooney, "The Decline of Federalism and the Rise of Morality-Policy Conflict in the United States," *Publius* 30:1 (Winter 2000), 171–88, 174.

63. Donald P. Haider-Markel and Kenneth J. Meier, "The Politics of Gay and Lesbian Rights: Expanding the Scope of the Conflict," *Journal of Politics* 58 (May 1996), 332–49.

64. Bob von Sternberg, "Gay marriage in Iowa gets wary reception," *Minneapolis Star Tribune*, September 1, 2007, 1A.

65. *Varnum v. Brien*, 763 N.W.2d 862 (Iowa 2009).

66. *Varnum*, 904–6.

67. *Varnum*, 905.

68. *Varnum*, 874.

69. *Varnum*, 877–78.

70. *Varnum*, 901.

71. *Varnum*, 876.

72. "Lawmakers React to Same-Sex Ruling," KCCI.com, April 3, 2009, http://www.kcci.com/news/19077529/detail.html; Jason Hancock, "State Legislative Leaders Vow No Action on Gay Marriage," *The Iowa Independent*, May 29, 2009, http://iowaindependent.com/15568/state-legislative-leaders-vow-no-action-on-gay-marriage.

73. Monica Davey, "Iowa Court Voids Gay Marriage Ban," *New York Times*, April 4, 2009, http://www.nytimes.com/2009/04/04/us/04iowa.html.

74. Iowa constitution, http://www.legis.state.ia.us/Constitution.html#a10s1.

75. Mike Glover, "Iowa House Passes Bill Seeking Gay Marriage Vote," *Associated Press*, February 1, 2011.

76. Jason Clayworth, "Senator Resigns, Leaving Slim Democratic Majority in Jeopardy," *DesMoinesRegister.com*, September 16, 2011, http://blogs.desmoinesregister.com/dmr/index.php/2011/09/16/democratic-senator-to-resign-leaving-slim-majority-in-jeopardy-gay-marriage-vote-possible/.

77. The Missouri Plan involves appointment of judges by the governor with periodic retention elections for judges. It is a hybrid of the approaches of appointment for life and direct, competitive (and potentially partisan) election.

78. Evelyn Schlatter, "18 Anti-Gay Groups and Their Propaganda," Intelligence Report, Winter 2010, Issue 140, Southern Poverty Law Center, http://www.splcenter.org/get-informed/intelligence-report/browse-all-issues/2010/winter/the-hard-liners.

79. Grant Schulte, "Iowans Dismiss Three Justices," *DesMoinesRegister.com*, November 3, 2010, http://www.desmoinesregister.com/article/20101103/NEWS09/11030390/Iowans-dismiss-three-justices; Caldwell, "Disorder in the Court."

80. Mike Glover, "Cady Says He Doesn't Regret Gay Marriage Ruling," *Associated Press*, January 14, 2011.

81. "The Marriage Vow: A Declaration of Dependence upon Marriage and Family," The Family Leader, copy archived at http://www.politico.com/static/PPM187_marriage.html.

82. Jones, "Political Party Affiliation."

83. Lax and Phillips, 373.

84. Samuel K. Gove and James D. Nowlan, *Illinois Politics and Government: The Expanding Metropolitan Frontier* (Lincoln: University of Nebraska Press, 1996), 148.

85. Quoted in Mary Massingale, "House Passes Gay Rights Bill," *State Journal-Register*, January 12, 2005, 9.

86. Dave McKinney, "Vote for Civil Unions in Illinois?" *Chicago Sun Times*, November 10, 2010, 3.

87. Section 15, Illinois Public Act 096-1513.

88. Plaintiff's Complaint, *Catholic Charities of the Diocese of Springfield v. State of Illinois*, Case No. 2011-MR-254, Circuit Court for the Seventh Judicial Circuit, Sangamon County, Illinois.

89. Letter to Steven E. Roach, Catholic Charities of the Diocese of Springfield-in-Illinois from Polly A. Hayes, Office of the Illinois Attorney General, March 8, 2011.

90. *Catholic Charities of the Diocese of Springfield v. Illinois*, Decision by Judge John Schmidt, Circuit Court for the Seventh Judicial Circuit, Sangamon County, Illinois, Case no. 2011-MR-254, August 18, 2011, 3.

91. Rich Miller, "Judge Schmidt: No citizen has a recognized legal right to contract with the government," capitolfax.com, August 18, 2011, http://capitolfax.com/2011/08/19/judge-schmidt-no-citizen-has-a-recognized-legal-right-to-a-contract-with-the-government/.

92. Doug Finke, "Panel Turns Down Bill to Let Faith-based Adoption Groups Reject Gay Couples," *State Journal-Register*, April 13, 2001, http://www.sj-r.com/top-stories/x250639801/Panel-turns-down-bill-to-let-faith-based-adoption-groups-reject-gay-couples.

93. Chris Geidner, "Illinois AG Supports Marriage Equality Lawsuits, Raising Question of Who Will Defend Civil Unions," *Metro Weekly*, June 2, 2012, http://www.metroweekly.com/poliglot/2012/06/illinois-attorney-general-to-support-lawsuits-seek.html.

94. Lax and Phillips, 373.

95. Jason Hoppin, "Pawlenty vows veto of same-sex measure," *St. Paul Pioneer Press*, May 13, 2010, http://www.twincities.com/politics/ci_15073921?nclick_check=1.

96. 191 N.W.2d 185 (Minn. 1971)

97. Rochelle Olson, "Same-sex couples file action against marriage law," *Minneapolis Star Tribune*, May 12, 2010, http://www.startribune.com/local/93410259.html.

98. The Democratic Party in Minnesota is the Democratic-Farmer-Labor Party (DFL).

99. Patrick Condon, "Gay Marriage Foes Boosted by Minn. GOP Takeover," *Associated Press*, November 5, 2010.

100. Martiga Lohn, "GOP Takes Over Minn. Legislature after 38 Years," *Associated Press*, November 3, 2010.

101. Rachel E. Stassen-Berger and Bob von Sternberg, "Opening Prayer Causes Disorder in House," *Minneapolis Star-Tribune*, May 21, 2011, 1A.

102. Andy Birkey, "GOP-linked Punk Rock Ministry Says Executing Gays Is 'Moral,'" *Minnesota Independent*, May 25, 2010, http://minnesotaindependent.com/58393/gop-linked-punk-rock-ministry-says-executing-gays-is-moral.

103. Eric Roper, "Marriage Vote Sparring Begins," *Minneapolis Star Tribune*, June 12, 2011, 1B; Editorial, "Build Voter Support in Gay Marriage Fight," *Minneapolis Star Tribune*, June 29, 2011, 10A.

104. Archdiocese of St. Paul and Minneapolis "Marriage DVD," http://www.youtube.com/watch?v=23nmWEhfmGo.

105. Patrick Condon, "Minn. Democrat's Pro-Gay Speech a YouTube Hit," *Associated Press*, May 5, 2011.

106. Rachel E. Stassen-Berger, "Dayton Adds Vetoes Real and Symbolic," *Minneapolis Star Tribune*, May 26, 2011, 1B.

107. Poll citation.

108. "OutFront Minnesota Does Not Support Gay Marriage Lawsuit," The Colu.mn, May 12, 2010, http://thecolu.mn/3484/outfront-minnesota-does-not-support-gay-marriage-lawsuit.

109. Dale Carpenter, "Top 3 Myths about the Marriage Amendment," OutFront Minnesota, http://www.outfront.org/marriage/myths.

110. *Benson v. Alverson*, Hennepin County District Court, Fourth Judicial District, Case No. 27 CV 10-11697, March 7, 2011, 8, 15.

111. Alex Campbell, "Email Rendezvous Entangles State Rep. Hinkle," *Indystar.com*, August 12, 2011, http://www.indystar.com/article/20110812/LOCAL1804/108120333/Email-rendezvous-entangles-state-Rep-Phillip-Hinkle?odyssey=tab%7Ctopnews%7Ctext%7CIndyStar.com.

112. Lax and Phillips, 373.

113. "Gay Couples Plan to Sue for Right to Same-Sex Unions," *Associated Press*, August 22, 2002; *Morrison v. Sadler*, 821 NE 2d 15 (Ind.Ct. App. 2005).

114. "Indiana Judge Dismisses Lawsuit Challenging Ban on Same-Sex Unions," *Associated Press*, May 8, 2003.

115. *Morrison v. Sadler*, 24–25.

116. Deanna Wrenn, "Court Hears Challenge to Indiana Same-Sex Marriage Ban," *Associated Press*, January 13, 2004.

117. "I must admit that I am somewhat troubled by this reasoning. Pursuant to this rationale, the State presumably could also prohibit sterile individuals or women past their child-bearing years from marrying. In fact, I would assume the State may place any restrictions on the right to marry that do not negatively impact the State's interest in encouraging fertile, opposite-sex couples to marry. Yet, I.C. § 31-11-1-1's [the statute defining marriage as heterosexual] narrow focus is to prohibit marriage among only one subset of consenting adults that is incapable of conceiving in the traditional manner—same-sex couples. Such laser-like aim suggests to me that the real motivation behind I.C. § 31-11-1-1 might be discriminatory." *Morrison v. Sadler*, 36–37.

118. *Morrison v. Sadler*, 34.

119. Dissenting opinion, *National Pride at Work v. Granholm*, Case No. 133429, Michigan Supreme Court, May 7, 2008, 12.

120. *State v. Carswell*, 114 Ohio St.3d 210 (Ohio 2007).

121. *Brinkman v. Miami University*, 2007 Ohio 4372 (Ohio Ct. App., Butler County, Aug. 27, 2007).

Chapter Six

Continued Progress and Backlash, 2004–2012

The East and South

After the judicially mandated legalization of same-sex marriage in Massachusetts in 2004, the legal and political movement for marriage equality received new momentum, as did the movement's opposition, reflected in the thirteen successful ballot measures against same-sex marriage, and often other similar arrangements, in 2004. Litigation continued in progressive venues with significant success in New Jersey, Connecticut, California, and Iowa (discussed in chapter 5) but notable failures as well in Oregon, Washington, Maryland, and New York. Even where litigation failed to directly achieve results, however, policy change, or significant policy efforts, ensued. The political process was also engaged in new ways with mayors marrying same-sex couples, actions against state policy and outside of their authority, in 2004. By the end of the period of 2004 to 2012, relationship equality policies in more progressive states were more likely to be enacted without the cover of courts as with judicial mandates. This, of course, took the judicial activism charge away from opponents, but they were no more pleased at the legislative enactment of relationship equality, citing threats to religious freedom and the decline of civilization, in addition to a more cloaked (at least by conservative elites) homophobia and heterosexism. This chapter explores the continuing fight in the states in the eastern part of the country and New York's high-profile and consequential legislative enactment of same-sex marriage in 2011.

Table 6.1.   State Relationship Equality Policies

State	Year Enacted	Type of Policy	Litigation?	Court Mandate?
Wash., D.C.	1992	Domestic partnerships (limited)	Yes	No
Hawaii	1997	Reciprocal beneficiaries (limited)	Yes	No
Vermont	2000	Civil unions	Yes	Yes
Maine	2004	D. p. (limited)	No	No
Mass.	2004	Marriage	Yes	Yes
New Jersey	2004	D. p. (limited)	Yes	No
California	2005	D. p. (broad)	Yes	No
Connecticut	2005	Civil unions	Yes	No
New Jersey	*2006*	*Civil unions*	*Yes*	*Yes*
New Hampshire	2007	Civil unions	No	No
Oregon	2007	D. p. (broad)	Yes	No
Washington	2007	D. p. (broad)	Yes	No
Connecticut	*2008*	*Marriage*	*Yes*	*Yes*
California	*2008*	*Marriage*	*Yes*	*Yes**
Wisconsin	2009	D. p. (limited)	Yes	No
Colorado	2009	D. p. (limited)	No	No
Iowa	2009	Marriage	Yes	Yes
Maine	*2009*	*Marriage*	*No*	*No**
Nevada	2009	D. p. (broad)	No	No
Wash., D.C.	*2009*	*Marriage*	*Yes*	*No*
Vermont	*2009*	*Marriage*	*Yes*	*No*
New Hampshire	*2010*	*Marriage*	*No*	*No*
Illinois	2011	Civil unions	No	No
New York	2011	Marriage	Yes	No
Hawaii	*2011*	*Civil unions*	*Yes*	*No*
Rhode Island	2011	Civil unions	No	No
Delaware	2012	Civil unions	No	No
Washington	*2012*	*Marriage*	*Yes*	*No*
Maine	*2012*	*Marriage*	*No*	*No*
Maryland	2012	Marriage	Yes	No

*Overturned by popular referendum.
Italics indicate an expanded policy.

Table 6.2.   Votes on State Constitutional Amendments Banning Same-Sex Marriage

State	Year	Percent Support	Marriage Only	Super-DOMA
Hawaii*	1998	71	X	
Alaska	1998	68	X	
Nebraska	2000	70		X
Nevada	2002	67	X	
Arkansas	2004	75		X
Georgia	2004	76		X
Kentucky	2004	75		X
Louisiana	2004	78		X
Michigan	2004	59		X
Mississippi	2004	86	X	
Missouri	2004	71	X	
Montana	2004	67	X	
North Dakota	2004	73		X
Ohio	2004	62		X
Oklahoma	2004	76		X
Oregon	2004	57	X	
Utah	2004	66		X
Kansas	2005	70		X
Texas	2005	76		X
Alabama	2006	81		X
Arizona	2006	48 (failed)		X
Colorado	2006	56	X	
Idaho	2006	63		X
South Carolina	2006	78		X
South Dakota	2006	52		X
Tennessee	2006	81	X	
Virginia	2006	57		X
Wisconsin	2006	59		X
Arizona	2008	56	X	
California	2008	52	X	
Florida	2008	62		X
North Carolina	2012	61		X
Minnesota	2012	47 (failed)	X	

*The amendment did not define marriage, but it gave the sole authority to define marriage to the legislature, thus eliminating a potential court mandate of same-sex marriage.

SUCCESS IN VERMONT AND MASSACHUSETTS TRIGGERS CHANGE IN NEW ENGLAND AND THE NORTHEAST

Due to litigation, strong grassroots activism, supportive public opinion, a regionally weak Republican Party, and a weak Religious Right, the region from Maine down to Maryland and Delaware has seen the most uniform progress on relationship equality. Outside of Iowa, it is the only region where same-sex marriage is legal: Maine, Vermont, New Hampshire, Massachusetts, New York, Connecticut, Maryland, and Washington, D.C. Civil unions are legal in New Jersey, Delaware, and Rhode Island. Few of these states possess fully citizen-controlled constitutional amendment processes, thereby eliminating the common tool used by opponents of marriage equality.

NEW JERSEY

Given its progressive political and legal climate, and timed to highlight the struggles faced by same-sex couples directly affected by 9/11, New Jersey was selected by Lambda Legal as the site of a same-sex marriage lawsuit in 2002.[1] The Supreme Court of New Jersey was a leader on LGBT equality, having ruled in favor of James Dale, an Eagle Scout kicked out of the Boy Scouts after he came out as a gay man. The court ruled that the state's antidiscrimination law (inclusive of sexual orientation) trumped the right of association of the Boy Scouts.[2] This decision was reversed by the more conservative U.S. Supreme Court,[3] but the case demonstrated the presence of a strong equality jurisprudence in the state. In addition, like many northeastern states, New Jersey is dominated by the Democratic Party, with moderate, pro-LGBT rights, Republican governors often elected. Support for LGBT rights in public opinion is at one of the highest levels of any state.[4]

Lambda grounded its challenge to the state's prohibition on same-sex marriage in fundamental rights and equal protection claims stemming from the New Jersey constitution. Both trial and appellate courts rejected these arguments, but a significant victory was achieved in the supreme court in 2006, in a virtual repeat of the Vermont high court decision, in *Lewis v. Harris*. The court rejected the fundamental rights claim, asserting that the right to same-sex marriage was too new to be deemed "fundamental." However, the court unanimously held that the denial of state benefits to same-sex couples was a denial of equal protection. The court especially emphasized the harm to children caused by the discrimination and found no legitimate governmental interest for the denial of equal treatment. Interestingly, the state did not offer the typical "procreation justification," instead presenting an argument about the need to keep marriage laws uniform among states. This was easily dismissed by the court under a minimal standard of review.[5]

The court divided on the question of a remedy. While three of the seven justices would have mandated the legislative enactment of same-sex marriage, similar to the Massachusetts court, the majority gave the option of a civil union approach to the legislature. Because of the majority's perception that marriage was fundamentally heterosexually defined, the redefinition of the institution should only come from the legislature. According to the majority opinion, "To alter that meaning [the heterosexist definition of marriage] would render a profound change in the public consciousness of a social institution of ancient origin. When such a change is not compelled by a constitutional imperative, it must come about through civil dialogue and reasoned discourse, and the considered judgment of the people in whom we place ultimate trust in our republican form of government."[6] Of course, the legislature was not completely free to follow the outcome of their reasoned debate. The court gave them one hundred and eighty days to act in a manner to provide equal treatment for same-sex couples, in terms of state rights and benefits.[7] In fact, the most recent preference of the legislature was for a minimal set of rights for same-sex couples and opposite-sex couples aged sixty-two or older, as expressed by a domestic partnership law enacted in 2004. This was a political response to the lawsuit and events in Massachusetts, but the legislative process, without a direct mandate, resulted in less than full equality in terms of benefits and rights and a de-gaying of the issue, with the benefits for straight seniors.[8] The law was pushed through in a lame-duck session by Democrats after they gained full control of the government in the election of 2003.[9] Reflecting the complicated interplay between law and politics, the legislative efforts were cited by the trial court judge in dismissing the suit, thereby lessening the need for judicial intervention, according to the judge.[10]

Responding to the court, the legislature passed a civil union law late in 2006, but this did not end the political and legal debate over same-sex marriage in the state. One provision of the law created a commission to study the new civil unions and their impact on the equality of same-sex couples in the state. In late 2008, the commission submitted a report calling on the legislature and governor to enact same-sex marriage, as civil unions were an inadequate framework for equal treatment for same-sex couples. They caused confusion for employers and hospitals, created a stigma of inferiority and psychological harm for same-sex couples, and generally did not result in the same rights and protection enjoyed by married couples in New Jersey law. This spurred a new round of legislative activity in 2009, especially as it appeared likely that Republican Chris Christie would defeat Democrat Jon Corzine (a same-sex marriage supporter) for governor in that fall's election and potentially veto a same-sex marriage bill (recall a similar dynamic in Illinois discussed in the previous chapter). A marriage bill was defeated in the Senate by a vote of 20 to 14 early in 2010 after a several-week period of intense mobilization by both sides, thereby ending this last-minute effort. Christie's election caused prominent Democrats to lose interest in aggressive support for same-sex marriage, fearing a backlash from voters concerned with economic issues and social conservatives, despite polls showing majority support for same-sex marriage. As in other states with large Catholic populations, the church was highly mobilized in opposition.[11] Not even an endorsement by New Jersey's own Bruce Springsteen could unclog the process and ensure the enactment of same-sex marriage at that political moment.[12]

Shamed by their timidity in 2010, Democrats in the legislature renewed their push for marriage equality in 2012, hoping to force Christie's hand. Christie continued to voice opposition to same-sex marriage (but support for the civil unions law already in place) and called for a public referendum on the issue. This was a shrewd political move: Christie was caught between his desire for a stronger role in national Republican politics (he flirted with a run for the presidency in 2011 and was on the short list of names for the party's vice presidential candidate in 2012) and marriage equality supportive public opinion in his liberal state. The Democrats passed a same-sex marriage bill in February of 2012, but Christie vetoed it. However, the Democrats have two years to find the votes to override the veto, leaving the legislative situation in continued limbo.[13]

Given the political uncertainty, Lambda returned to the supreme court asking for the legalization of same-sex marriage on the grounds that the legislature's civil union solution did not meet the court's equality mandate in *Lewis v. Harris*. However, the court refused this request, holding that a trial was needed to fully develop a factual record. Clearly, the court was not yet willing to mandate same-sex marriage on its own, although three of the seven justices were willing to hear the case directly and potentially make a decision.[14] Given the favorable legal and political climate in the state, Lambda aggressively condemned civil unions in their complaint in the case, more aggressively than would a litigation group in a state where civil unions were the best possible option:

> The denial of access to the legal status of "marriage" and "spouse" has caused the Plaintiff couples . . . and their children concrete harms. Because of the novel legal construct to which they have been consigned, they face a persistent and widespread lack of recognition of the rights in civil and commercial dealings. They are denied workplace benefits equal to those accorded to married couples. They are blocked from seeing loved ones during medical emergencies. Their exclusion from marriage deprives them of certainty in their legal rights and status, and burdens them and their families with the resulting finan-

cial consequences. Their separate status is a badge that requires that they reveal their sexual orientation whether they wish to or not, in situations such as job interviews and jury service, invading their privacy and exposing them to additional discrimination. The segregation of lesbian and gay couples into a novel legal status, like other classifications unrelated to a person's ability to perform or contribute to society, also wrongly enshrines the view that lesbian and gay individuals are not as worthy or deserving as others, causing dignitary and psychic harm.[15]

Reflecting the increased confidence of similar groups in federal equal protection jurisprudence as a source of legal support (discussed more extensively in chapter 8), Lambda is making both state and federal equal protection and due process arguments in the litigation, thus opening the door to potential U.S. Supreme Court review. This would have been unthinkable just a few years ago, especially given the negative federal precedent of *Baker v. Nelson* (discussed in chapter 2) and the general conservatism of the federal courts. The case is proceeding to a trial, and, in an initial ruling, the judge agreed that federal equal protection law was shifting in a positive direction for Lambda. According to Republican-appointed judge Linda Feinberg in an opinion written a few weeks before retiring from the bench, "While in *Baker* the Supreme Court dismissed the appeal for want of a substantial federal question . . . subsequent developments support the conclusion that the issues raised in *Baker* would no longer be considered unsubstantial. Accordingly, in today's legal arena, *Baker* is not controlling."[16]

Thus, significant progress has been made toward full relationship equality in New Jersey, but hesitancy from the high court and the political process, especially the election of a Republican governor who supports civil unions but not full marriage equality, has prevented the state from matching the progress of Massachusetts and other states in the region. It remains to be seen how the high court will view the constitutionality of the civil union approach.

CONNECTICUT

In 2008, the Supreme Court of Connecticut joined its neighboring court in Massachusetts in mandating same-sex marriage, despite the fact that civil unions for same-sex couples were enacted by the legislature in 2005. The political process was clearly triggered by events in neighboring states and the strong level of support for LGBT rights in the state.[17] Given these factors, political and legal activists viewed marriage equality as a realistic goal, and commenced a strategy of lobbying and litigation. The lobbying resulted in civil unions (the first such policy enacted without a judicial mandate), while the litigation resulted in marriage equality.

Efforts to recognize and protect same-sex couples began in 2001, after the success in Vermont and after Connecticut activists successfully lobbied the legislature on a law to expand rights for same-sex parents. However, early efforts stalled due to legislative resistance. Civil union and marriage bills were introduced in 2002 in the Democratically controlled legislature but went nowhere. The legislature enacted weak domestic partnership legislation in 2002 as a compromise, but the dynamic shifted dramatically after the Massachusetts decision in November of that year. Activists, including the group Love Makes a Family (formed to lobby for the adoption rights), viewed marriage equality as a realistic option. This caused a split in the activist community, as many saw civil unions as more realistic. For instance, the state's Republican governor, Jodi Rell, supported civil unions but not same-sex marriage. Indeed, the civil union law enacted in 2005 was initially opposed by Love Makes a Family. Given the governor's support and polls showing a clear majority in favor of the policy, the civil union bill sailed through the legislature with significant support from Republicans, aided by an amendment defining marriage as heterosexual-only. [18]

The Massachusetts decision and the apparent stalling of the political process motivated GLAD to file a lawsuit seeking full marriage equality in 2004. As Mary Bonauto stated, "It is about treating people fairly. And from everything we see, Connecticut is ready for that." [19] She, of course, turned out to be correct, but not before an initial loss. Superior Court Judge Patty Jenkins Pittman dismissed the suit on the grounds that the civil union law equalized treatment for same-sex couples. She rejected the "separate but equal" arguments presented by the plaintiffs in an opinion that is almost mocking in tone. She dismissed the stigma claimed by the plaintiffs as hurt feelings that do not rise to the level of a constitutional violation. It was all in their heads. As Pittman declared, "Though the plaintiffs may feel themselves to be relegated to a second class status, there is nothing in the text of the Connecticut statutes that can be read to place the plaintiffs there." When she addressed the argument about the lack of portability of civil unions, she declared, "This, alas, is a real injury." But this, Pittman argued, is the fault of other states for not enacting a similar policy. In the end, for Pittman, the redefinition of marriage was a job for the legislature, not the courts. [20]

When the case reached the Connecticut Supreme Court, a narrow, but sweeping, reversal resulted. A narrow 4 to 3 majority ruled that the lack of same-sex marriage violated the equality provision of the state constitution, holding that sexual orientation triggered heightened scrutiny, like gender, under the state's jurisprudence. According to the majority, tradition alone was the justification for discrimination against same-sex couples, and this rationale, of course, fell under the higher level of scrutiny. The existence of the civil union law was not sufficient to demonstrate the state's compliance with the constitution; indeed, the law made the constitutional violation worse by creating a "separate but equal" status, especially in light of the history of discrimination faced by sexual minorities—a stunning turnaround from the approach of the trial judge, who saw the civil union law as the state's constitutional remedy for unequal treatment. In every way, the high court opinion was a stark contrast to the dismissive tone of Judge Pittman. Justice Richard Palmer clearly articulated the majority's application of a more robust liberalism in their examination of same-sex marriage: "In view of the role that sexual orientation plays in a person's fundamental right to self-determination, we fully agree with the plaintiffs that their sexual orientation represents the kind of distinguishing characteristic that defines them as a discrete group" necessary for constitutional protection.[21] The majority viewed sexual orientation as almost identical to gender, in terms of its political and constitutional treatment, thus further demonstrating the long-standing connection between gender and sexuality in the law. The majority opinion concludes with a strong statement of legal liberalism: "[O]ur conventional understanding of marriage must yield to a more contemporary appreciation of the rights entitled to constitutional protection. Interpreting our state constitutional provisions in accordance with firmly established equal protection principles leads inevitably to the conclusion that gay persons are entitled to marry the otherwise qualified same sex partner of their choice."[22] Finally, the court rejected the argument that the recognition of same-sex marriage violates a right to religious freedom, rejecting any influence of theological arguments on the state's stance toward sexual minorities and noting that religious institutions were free to not perform same-sex marriages.[23] In other words, theirs was a purely secular approach, in no way influenced by the new natural law. It should be noted that this decision was handed down after the California Supreme Court ruled in favor of same-sex marriage that same year, and the opinion relied heavily on that opinion, especially in support of moving beyond rational basis review for same-sex marriage cases. The California case is discussed in chapter 7.

The dissenting justices would have reviewed the case using the rational basis test, and they felt that the state's interest in procreation was sufficient to justify discrimination against same-sex couples concerning marriage. The remedy was the democratic process, not the courts, and the political activity surrounding civil unions indicated that a process was engaged to make this change down the road, in their view. Thus, this was a truly divided court. The dissenters likely would not have mandated civil unions if they had not already existed, given that they disputed the constitutional violation claimed by the majority.

MAINE, NEW HAMPSHIRE, AND RHODE ISLAND: MARRIAGE EQUALITY POLITICS WITHOUT LITIGATION

As the only other state in New England outside of Massachusetts that allows popular referendums, in this case the "people's veto," Maine was the site of a notable popular rejection of a same-sex marriage law in 2009. Maine voters changed their minds in the fall of 2012, approving same-sex marriage. Spurred by activity in neighboring states and Democratic majorities in the legislature, activists and legislators pushed for, and achieved, a same-sex marriage law, signed by Democratic governor James Baldacci after a change of heart. He previously opposed full marriage equality, opting for civil unions. When signing the law, he cited his obligation to protect the state constitutional rights of same-sex couples.

For the campaign to eliminate the law, conservative activists, funded significantly by the Catholic Church and the National Organization for Marriage, hired the same consulting firm behind the Prop. 8 campaign in California the previous year (this is discussed in greater detail in chapter 7). That firm's approach in California was to stay away from direct opposition to LGBT equality in a progressive state, instead creating the specter of harm to children, especially stemming from "indoctrination" of public school children about same-sex marriage. As Lisa Leff and David Sharp of the Associated Press described the campaign to repeal the law, "Voters . . . were besieged with images of what would supposedly happen if same-sex marriage were legal: Students on a field trip to a lesbian wedding, elementary kids gobbling up books featuring gay couples, kindergartners learning about homosexuality from their teachers." The measure passed with 53 percent of the vote. Marriage equality activists hoped that the referendum to create same-sex marriage would be more successful in 2012. This represented their only realistic option, given the Republican advances in the state in 2010. The 2012 vote was the first instance of the popular creation of a same-sex marriage law in the country.[24]

Sandwiched between Vermont and Massachusetts, relationship equality policy in New Hampshire reacted to developments in these states (as well as neighboring Maine) and developed in response to political changes in the state, particularly the takeover of the legislature in 2006 by the Democrats for the first time in a century. Indeed, while under Republican control, the state resisted efforts to expand relationship equality in the wake of the judicial legalization of same-sex marriage in Massachusetts. In 2004, the legislature passed a law specifically prohibiting the recognition of out-of-state same-sex marriages, while also calling for a commission to study the issue of possible legal protections and benefits for same-sex couples. However, this commission was stacked with the leading politicians opposed to same-sex marriage in the state, and the majority report eventually recommended the enactment of a constitutional amendment banning same-sex marriage. The report also denied that the issue of relationship equality was a civil rights issue, asserting that sexual orientation was a choice. In other words, the ruling Republicans in New Hampshire were not about to follow the lead of their neighboring states. They mostly ignored what had taken place in Vermont and defensively reacted to the threat of same-sex marriage on their southern border in Massachusetts to keep New Hampshire a relationship equality–free zone. This stance ignored public opinion in the state. A University of New Hampshire poll indicated support for same-sex marriage at 54 percent in 2003 and 55 percent in 2004. The Republican constitutional amendment was defeated by a wide margin (207 to 125 in the House) in 2006. Such an amendment would have required a 60 percent majority in the legislature and approval from two-thirds of voters.[25]

This dynamic, however, changed significantly with the elections of Democrats to legislative majorities in 2006. Democrat John Lynch was also reelected as governor. The legislature passed, and Lynch signed, after being noncommittal about civil unions throughout the process (he opposed same-sex marriage), a civil unions bill with significant Republican support in the large House (twenty-seven Republican votes), but no support in the much smaller Senate.[26]

Within a year, Democratic legislators were pushing for marriage equality, as neighboring Vermont was engaging in its upgrade from civil unions, and as legislators in Maine were approving a same-sex marriage bill. After significant legislative maneuvering, mostly over exemptions to same-sex marriage recognition for religiously based charitable and educational institutions, a bill was passed in 2009. The law did not exempt businesses simply owned by religious individuals, as some legislators had desired. Lynch changed his mind on marriage equality and signed the law. He emphasized his desire for religious protections, even though his recommended changes did not offer any significantly new protections.[27]

In 2010, Republicans won large, veto-proof majorities in the legislature. The Republican tide of that year was strengthened considerably in the state due to a quirk in the state's electoral process. Representatives were elected in multimember legislative districts, which tend to magnify electoral shifts. Repeal of the same-sex marriage law was on the agenda for many of the Republican legislators, but legislative leaders were much more reluctant to repeal. The party, after all, had won in 2010 on a platform of economic libertarianism, not social conservatism, and support for same-sex marriage only increased after its enactment. In addition, many Republican legislators strongly opposed repeal, utilizing libertarian arguments about personal freedom, making an override of a promised Lynch veto more difficult to sustain. The leaders' first reaction was to put off consideration of repeal for year. When Republican members pushed more aggressively for repeal in 2012, a vote backfired, with a repeal measure failing by a vote of 211 to 116. This was clearly connected to public opinion. The public wanted to keep the law. In a 2011 poll, only 27 percent of respondents supported repeal. In New England, then, the mostly unanimous opposition to same-sex marriage from Republican elected officials and candidates is not a certainty, especially given strong public support for marriage equality throughout the region. [28]

Rhode Island was the last state in New England to enact a relationship recognition policy (counting Maine's marriage law subsequently repealed by voters). Given its proximity to Massachusetts, serious conversations and activism commenced in the wake of *Goodridge* in 2003, although legislators held a hearing on a marriage equality bill as early as 2000. [29] GLAD has avoided litigation in the state, citing the "extremely risky" tactic of using state courts to mandate marriage equality. [30] Indeed, the Rhode Island Supreme Court narrowly ruled in 2007 that state courts lacked jurisdiction to hear a divorce case of a same-sex couple from Rhode Island married in Massachusetts, thus reflecting a lack of innovation on the part of courts in the state. [31] Despite being a heavily Democratic state, Rhode Island politics have exhibited a high level of traditionalist attitudes toward sexual minorities, with particularly strong influence from the Catholic Church. Indeed, while courts in much more conservative states were invalidating anti-sodomy statutes in the 1990s, the Rhode Island Supreme Court upheld its law in *State v. Lopes* (another example of GLAD's reluctance to litigate in the state). [32] Legislative repeal was achieved in 1998, long after repeals by most of the state's neighbors, by surprisingly narrow margins. [33] Obviously, efforts to achieve marriage equality would face barriers, given this traditionalist strain of politics and a lack of legal allies.

In the divorce case, GLAD was clearly trying to expand the law in the state. The case was sufficiently consequential as to trigger amicus briefs from GLAD and the ACLU, as well as opposing briefs from the Family Research Council and the Becket Fund for Religious Liberty. The court ruled that the term "marriage" in the divorce statute referred only to heterosexual marriage, arguing that this was the intent of the legislature. The majority was explicitly unwilling to make new policy. On the contrary, GLAD urged the court to construe the divorce statute "liberally . . . to assist and protect families," and the two dissenting justices would have done exactly this. But GLAD came up one vote short. [34] In addition, in the same year, 2007, the state attorney general issued a nonbinding opinion that out-of-state same-sex marriages should be recognized in Rhode Island. [35] Thus, activists leveraged the legal system to the maximum extent possible, but this was not enough to change policy.

Republican control of the governor's office from 1995 to 2010 constrained relationship equality–related legislative efforts. The election of liberal Republican senator Lincoln Chaffee in 2010 (he officially ran for the office as an independent after leaving the Republican Party) created an opening for activists, because Chaffee supported same-sex marriage. However, the openly gay Speaker of the House, Gordon Fox, calculated that a same-sex marriage bill lacked support in the Senate, so legislative efforts were focused on a civil union bill. The bill became law in 2011, but marriage equality activists opposed it and discouraged same-sex couples from obtaining civil unions. They felt that full marriage equality should be the only policy option and that it was possible, given the existence of marriage equality in other New England states. Activists also objected to the strong religious exemptions in the law. Not only were religious institutions exempted from performing civil unions, they were also given the right to not recognize the unions while providing services, such as faith-based social services or religiously affiliated hospitals. Thus, in contrast to civil unions in Illinois (enacted a few months prior to Rhode Island's law), where activists viewed this policy as the best option given the political environment in the state, activists in Rhode Island viewed civil unions as too politically expedient and suboptimal (several polls showed majority support for marriage equality by 2011), even dangerous with the broad religious exemptions, exemptions not existing in Illinois or other state recognition policies. Because of the stance of advocates, far fewer civil unions have been performed in Rhode Island than in Illinois. As of December 2011 Illinois granted more than 3,700 unions, while Rhode Island had granted only thirty-nine during roughly the same period of time. In 2012, Chaffee signed an executive order mandating the recognition of out-of-state same-sex marriages, putting into effect the earlier attorney general opinion.[36]

NEW YORK

In New York, same-sex marriage was legalized in 2011 by the legislature. Indeed, the New York courts were generally quite hostile to same-sex marriage claims, thus forcing advocates, inclined to use the courts, into the legislative arena. However, despite the state's liberal political culture and supportive public opinion, Republican control of the Senate, combined with opposition from some conservative Democrats in the legislature, stymied legislative efforts until a breakthrough came in 2011, driven significantly by the new Democratic governor, Andrew Cuomo.

Events in New York accelerated in response to the court decisions legalizing same-sex marriage in neighboring Massachusetts and Ontario, Canada (think Niagara Falls and weddings), and a decision in early 2004 when Mayor Jason West of New Paltz (aged twenty-six and a member of the Green Party) and local Unitarian ministers began granting marriage licenses to same-sex couples, inspired by a similar tactic of Mayor Gavin Newsom in

San Francisco. After a local prosecutor charged them with several misdemeanors, they stopped, but this civil disobedience inspired same-sex couples across the state to apply for marriage licenses, thus triggering a slew of lawsuits challenging the denial of the licenses.[37]

Unexpected Litigation Failure: New York Courts Bend Over Backward to Defer to the Legislature

At the trial court level, same-sex marriage advocates achieved only one victory out of five cases filed. This lone victory came in a Lambda-sponsored suit in New York City. Advocates hoped that by bringing a variety of suits throughout the state (not just in New York City) they would facilitate the ultimate sanction of same-sex marriage by the New York Court of Appeals, the state's highest court. This appeared to be the only option for advocates, given the strong control of the state senate by Republicans. Senate Republicans had just recently approved adding sexual orientation to the state's antidiscrimination law. Same-sex marriage bills were proposed in 2003, but they stalled.[38] Indeed, in future years the Democratic House would repeatedly pass bills creating marriage equality, but the Senate repeatedly balked. Unfortunately for marriage equality advocates, for most trial court judges in New York, same-sex marriage law had not changed since the 1970s. Most of the decisions assumed that marriage was heterosexual-only (at least as defined by the 1909 Domestic Relations Act), and they applied federal standards to claims of equal protection and fundamental rights, invoking the rational basis test to uphold the ban on same-sex marriage and ruling that same-sex marriage was not sufficiently historically rooted to justify categorization as a fundamental right.

New York City trial court judge Doris Ling-Cohan was a significant exception. In a strongly worded decision, Judge Ling-Cohan made much use of the analogy to bans on interracial marriage and found same-sex marriage to be a fundamental right (or the right to choose one's life partner, regardless of gender) and its prohibition by the state a violation of equal protection. Interestingly, she also cited other strong trial court decisions, especially those in Alaska and Washington State. She viewed families of lesbian and gay couples as equal to heterosexual families, while most New York judges viewed these types of families differently, thus allowing for different treatment by the legislature. Ling-Cohan also noted the evolving nature of the institution of marriage, citing bans on interracial marriage and the poor legal status of married women until the last several decades. And, citing cases like *Braschi* (1989) (discussed in chapter 2), Ling-Cohan argued that New York courts, as well as the political branches, were trending in the direction of same-sex relationship recognition, although she did not engage in equal protection analysis, nor did she rule that sexual minorities were a suspect class.

In other words, marriage has changed, so the fundamental right to marriage required a judicially mandated update if the legislature was unwilling to respond to the changes. As she stated, "There has been a steady evolution of the institution of marriage throughout history which belies the concept of a static traditional definition. Marriage, as it is understood today, is both a partnership of two loving individuals . . . and a state institution designed to promote stability for the couples and their children."[39] Ling-Cohan mandated the issuance of marriage licenses to same-sex couples in thirty days.

Ling-Cohan's decision was overturned on appeal, and this was affirmed by the state's highest court, the Court of Appeals. Four of the cases were consolidated for the appellate process under the name *Hernandez v. Robles*, Ling-Cohan's case. A four-to-one majority of the judges on the appellate court took a much more traditional view of parenting as ideally heterosexual-only and asserted that marriage "systematically regulates heterosexual behavior" by channeling male sexual desires into an appropriate and procreative form.[40] According to the *New York Times*, the "decision offered a ringing defense of heterosexual marriage, which the court portrayed as an important way of ensuring child welfare and stability."[41] The majority also scolded Ling-Cohan, as she "usurped the Legislature's mandated role to make policy decisions as to which type of family unit works best for society," thus promoting a deferential judicial role and a neoconservative approach to marriage law and policy.[42] Notably, the lone dissenting judge found the state's ban on same-sex marriage to be a form of gender discrimination, as well as sexual orientation discrimination, in addition to violating the fundamental right emphasized by Ling-Cohan.

The theme of marriage as constraining wanton heterosexual sexuality was central to the four-to-two holding of the Court of Appeals affirming the appellate court. Like the Indiana court discussed in chapter 5, the New York high court justified the ban on same-sex marriage under rational basis review as a reasonable assumption that lesbian and gay parents are more intentional parents and less requiring of benefits to assist in parenting. As the plurality opinion authored by Judge Robert Smith argued: "The Legislature could find that unstable relationship between people of the opposite sex present a greater danger that children will be born into or grow up in unstable homes than is the case with same-sex couples, and thus that promoting stability in opposite-sex relationships will help children more."[43] Obviously, then, not all courts are bastions of rationality on the question of same-sex marriage. In fact, Judge Victoria Graffeo distanced her vote from this claim in a concurring opinion, placing more emphasis on the need to defer to legislative judgment, and she invited the legislature to update the state's marriage laws.[44]

The high level of formalism and deference from most New York judges encountering this litigation was puzzling to many commentators who noted the state's progressive legal tradition.[45] Jurisprudential norms dictate that judges in the state are allowed to interpret rights and equality provisions in the state constitution more broadly than federal jurisprudence might allow, and New York courts have innovated in other areas of the law. Indeed, Chief Judge Judith Kaye accused the majority of abandoning this tradition of innovation in her dissent, which echoed the fundamental rights arguments made by Ling-Cohan. She found the ban to be a form of sex-based discrimination, requiring heightened scrutiny. Kaye asserted that the state's position was faulty even under a rational basis standard, arguing, contrary to the majority, that excluding same-sex couples undermined the state's interest in protecting children.[46]

The shift on the Court of Appeals from a liberal, activist court toward a more deferential stance reflects one of the goals of New York's three-term Republican governor, George Pataki. While his predecessor, liberal Democrat Mario Cuomo, was able to fill the court with his (mostly liberal) appointees, Pataki used his appointments to counter the court's activism for liberal causes. Judges on the Court of Appeals are appointed to fourteen-year terms by the governor with the consent of the Senate. (Trial court judges are elected, however. This likely explains the reluctance of trial court judges to find in favor of same-sex marriage outside of New York City.) Three of Pataki's four appointees voted with the majority in *Hernandez v. Robles*, while the fourth, Albert Rosenblatt, recused himself because his daughter was a legal advocate for marriage equality. The marriage equality lawyers targeted him as a potential vote in favor of their side.[47] Of the three Cuomo appointees still on the court, two dissented and one voted with the majority. This judge, George Bundy Smith, regarded as being very liberal (he authored an opinion overturning the state's death penalty, for example), was striving to be reappointed by Pataki, despite being close to the mandatory retirement age of seventy. His reappointment, however, would make it likely that a Democrat would choose his successor (Democrats were poised to win the governor's race in 2006, and they did exactly that with Eliot Spitzer). As a result, Pataki chose not to reappoint him, choosing a Republican judge instead.[48] Thus, it was reasonable for marriage equality litigants to assume a potential majority of Cuomo appointees and Rosenblatt, but events were not on their side.

Legislative Failure, Then Consequential Success

As efforts shifted to the legislative arena, the Senate became the sticking point, either because of Republican control of the chamber or the resistance from conservative (and theologically driven) Democrats when their party controlled the chamber. The Democratic Assembly passed a same-sex marriage bill on several occasions (2007, 2009, and 2011), and Democratic governors Eliot Spitzer (2007–2008), David Patterson (2008–2010), and Andrew Cuomo (2011–present), strongly supported marriage equality and actively lobbied for its enactment, as did liberal Republican New York City mayor Michael Bloomberg. The impasse in the Senate resulted in a methodical and focused campaign by advocates to convince conservative Democrats and liberal Republicans to support a marriage bill. However, an effort to pass a bill failed in late 2009, while the Senate was under Democratic control, with no Republican votes and Democratic defections from the party's support for marriage equality. Senator Ruben Diaz, a socially conservative Pentecostal minister, was the leader of the Democratic opposition, and he was joined by eight other Democrats (four of them serving in their first term) in voting against the bill—a level of party defections that surprised advocates and made the future prospects for marriage equality appear quite dim. A mix of direct theological opposition and electoral timidity by Democrats scuttled the bill. A few Republicans who signaled support wanted the cover of more Democratic votes, and these were obviously not forthcoming. The deal collapsed at the last minute, facilitated by a very weak and scandal-ridden Governor Patterson. This occurred while public support for same-sex marriage was growing into a solid majority.[49]

A new, more powerful governor, an off-guard Catholic Church, and Wall Street money, all supported by favorable public opinion, resulted in a reversal of fortunes in 2011. After his election, Andrew Cuomo (son of former governor, and liberal hero, Mario Cuomo) used his political capital to push a marriage equality bill through the legislature, likely out of principle but also with an eye toward the 2016 Democratic nomination for president. Cuomo lobbied legislators aggressively, and his office coordinated efforts with state LGBT advocacy groups, including a $3 million media campaign targeted at the districts of reluctant Senate Democrats and moderate Senate Republicans. Given that Republicans controlled the Senate, the bill reached a crucial turning point when the Republican majority leader, Dean Skelos, allowed a floor vote as a part of a compromise on a range of issues facing the legislature and the governor, even though he voted against the bill. After activists applied extensive constituent pressure, most of the Democrats previously opposed voted in favor this time, except for Diaz, and four Republicans joined them. One of these Republicans, Mark Grisanti, was elected to office on a platform of opposing marriage equality. He apologized to those constituents who felt betrayed by his reversal, but, as Grisanti stated, "I cannot deny a person, a human being, a taxpayer, a worker, the people of my district and across this state . . . the same rights that I have with my wife." Cuomo and his aides were able to secure large contributions from wealthy Wall Street Republicans who supported same-sex marriage to be used to protect supportive Republicans from potential electoral backlash, thus making their support easier to gain.

Finally, Archbishop Timothy Dolan and the Catholic Church were not fully engaged in opposition, perhaps not contemplating that a Republican-controlled Senate would approve the bill.[50]

The fact that one of the largest states enacted marriage equality through the legislature, not the courts, was viewed by many, on both sides of the debate, as a significant turning point in the movement for marriage equality. It clearly motivated marriage equality activists in Maryland and Washington to enact same-sex marriage and helped to discourage New Hampshire Republicans from repealing that state's same-sex marriage law, in addition to sparking the renewed efforts in New Jersey.

THE D.C. EFFECT IN THE MID-ATLANTIC: MARYLAND, DELAWARE

The legalization of same-sex marriage in the District of Columbia (discussed in chapter 4) gave new impetus to legislative activity in Maryland and Delaware. The conversation in Delaware, which resulted in a civil union law, was newer, whereas in Maryland activists pursued a narrowly unsuccessful litigation strategy for marriage equality for several years prior to the legislative success. In many ways, the events in Maryland mirror those in New York: unsuccessful litigation for same-sex marriage, followed by a surprising political stalemate, finally pushed by an engaged governor with national ambitions. The major difference is that conservative opponents possessed an additional tool in Maryland—the popular referendum. The law enacted by the legislature in 2012 was put to the voters in November of 2012.

Advocates First Go to Court in Maryland

Advocates in Maryland first tried a legal strategy, hoping to build on the successes in Vermont and Massachusetts and tapping into the state's progressive legal culture.[51] The ACLU filed a same-sex marriage lawsuit in 2004. According to Dan Furmansky, then the executive director of Equality Maryland, "Courts play an important role in creating social change for civil rights issues."[52] While he also noted that advocates were working on public education and legislative strategies, litigation was the central thrust of their efforts. Their strategy initially achieved success nearly two years later when Judge M. Brooke Murdock, in one of the aggressive trial court opinions of this period, ruled that the state's ban on same-sex marriage was unconstitutional. The ACLU presented the usual range of constitutional violations in their complaint, but Murdock held that the denial of marriage licenses for same-sex couples was a form of gender discrimination, violating the equal rights amendment of the Maryland constitution. Indeed, Murdock made note of the interesting timeline relating to same-sex marriage and gender stemming from the 1970s D.C. area activism, discussed in chapter 2. Couples applied for licenses in 1972, leading to a clarification in the law enacted by the legislature in 1973. While this was occurring, the state ERA was enacted in 1972. While the political system at the time separated the issues, Murdock brought them back together. Murdock aligned herself with Justice Johnson's dissent in *Baker v. State*, which also found a sex-based constitutional violation. Of course, invoking gender discrimination required a heightened level of review, strict scrutiny under Maryland jurisprudence. Murdock rejected the state's interest in procreation under this test, as well as the argument that tradition justified the law. "When tradition is the guise under which prejudice or animosity hides, it is not a legitimate state interest," asserted Murdock.[53] It is perhaps no surprise that Murdock viewed the issue through the prism of gender discrimination. She had long been active in women's issues in the state, serving on the board and president of the Women's Law Center of Maryland in the 1980s and 1990s.[54] Murdock's opinion triggered both an unsuccessful impeachment attempt and a failed attempt by Republicans to amend the constitution to overturn the decision. Democratic control of the legislature prevented this backlash.

Instead, the backlash came from a divided Maryland Court of Appeals, the state's highest court. Only two of the seven judges agreed with Murdock's reasoning, while another would have achieved the same result with different reasoning. This left four judges in the majority overruling Murdock. The majority argued that the state ERA was not intended to apply to same-sex marriage and that sexual minorities, while suffering from a clear history of discrimination, are not politically powerless, nor did the judges think that sexuality was an immutable characteristic. As a result, they applied rational basis review and deferred to the state's reasons for discriminatory treatment rejected by Murdock. The majority also invoked the rhetoric of negative liberty and privacy when describing same-sex relationships, relegating these relationships to a clearly subordinate position. As Judge Glenn Harrell, Jr., wrote: "We are not unmindful of the fact that the relationships gay, lesbian, and bisexual persons seek to enter involve intimate and private decisions that extend to the core of the right to personal autonomy. Those decisions do not necessarily require us or the State to recognize formally those relationships in the form of State-sanctioned marriage."[55] In other words, you have the constitutional right to exist but not to be seen by the state, a right to negative not positive liberty. The role of *Loving* was also disputed in the litigation, with the case playing a central role in Murdock's analysis, while the Court of Appeals majority found little connection between interracial and same-sex marriage.

Given the close vote, it is likely that a decision coming a bit later would have gone the other way, as two of the most conservative judges on the court, and in the majority in this case, retired while the case was under consideration. They were, as is the custom, allowed to participate until the governor named their replacements. Democrat Martin O'Malley would have named their replacements, most certainly making those seats more liberal.[56]

Legislative Reluctance Gives Way to Success after D.C.

After the defeat, activists shifted their efforts to the legislature, but prospects there were dim, despite Democratic control. Equality Maryland decided to pursue a gradualist strategy of enacting law extending some rights to same-sex couples, but the ground shifted when the D.C. Council passed the same-sex marriage law in 2009. Crucially, the state's Democratic attorney general, Douglas Gansler, issued an opinion asserting that D.C.'s, and other jurisdiction's, same-sex marriages would be treated as legally valid in Maryland, effectively legalizing same-sex marriage in the state, especially given the proximity to D.C.[57] This elevated the debate in the legislature, leaving "less-than-marriage" approaches off the agenda, and activists expected legislative success in the 2011 session. However, after passage in the Senate, an expected successful vote in the House of Delegates failed as socially conservative Democrats defected from the party.[58]

During this debate, Governor O'Malley was mostly on the sidelines. However, after the defeat, he committed to working aggressively to enact a same-sex marriage law, as his potential rival for a future Democratic presidential nomination, Andrew Cuomo, had done in New York.[59] The bill narrowly passed in both chambers in 2012, after intense lobbying of a few individual legislators who previously withheld support, most notably delegate Tiffany Allston. She switched from support to opposition in the 2011 vote. The votes of two Republican delegates also created the margin of victory in the House.[60] Opponents gathered the requisite signatures to place a referendum on the law on the November 2012 election ballot, but a majority of voters approved the law.

Particularly after the failure in 2011, much was made of the role of religiously conservative African American activists and legislators for the relative lack of success, particularly because Maryland is a state with a significant African American population. However, it should be noted that many African Americans supported marriage equality in Maryland, including the Baltimore chapter of the NAACP. And religious conservatism also came from the significant Catholic population and church hierarchy. Catholic Martin O'Malley came quite late to supporting marriage equality, and only after support was more politically useful, with strong criticism from the state's Catholic leaders. After President Obama's endorsement of marriage equality in 2012, as well as the endorsement of the national arm of the NAACP (discussed in chapter 8), African American support for same-sex marriage rose significantly.[61]

A few days after the marriage equality bill passed in Maryland, the Democratic governor of neighboring Delaware declared that the enactment of same-sex marriage in the state was inevitable. As governor, Jack Markell signed a civil union bill into law in 2011, after it rather uneventfully passed the legislature by nearly 2-to-1 margins in this strongly Democratic state. This followed the addition of sexual orientation to the state's antidiscrimination law in 2009 after Democrats took control of the House in the 2008 election. The contrasting notions of freedom held by opponents and supporters of civil unions in the state were reflected in statements made by an Alliance Defense Fund lawyer and Markell. "Nothing in Delaware prevents people from living as they want or having intimate relationships with whom they want," the ADF lawyer Austin Nimocks stated before the law was passed. After signing the bill into law, Markell declared, "Tonight we say to loving and committed couples across the state who want the law to endorse the promise that they made so long ago in their hearts, 'Your love is equally valid and deserving, your family is now equal under the law.'" Or at least as equal as was possible in Delaware at that political moment.[62]

THE 2012 NORTH CAROLINA INITIATIVE AND SAME-SEX MARRIAGE IN THE SOUTH

In 2012, North Carolina became the last state in the South (with the exception of West Virginia, where Democrats still have political clout) to enact a constitutional ban on same-sex marriage. The process started in the 2004 wave of amendments, with Arkansas (75 percent), Georgia (76 percent), Kentucky (75 percent), Louisiana (78 percent), and Mississippi (86 percent), followed quickly in 2005–2006 by Alabama (81 percent), South Carolina (78 percent), Tennessee (81 percent), Texas (76 percent), and Virginia (57 percent). Florida lagged with its amendment in 2008, approved with 62 percent support. This represents remarkably quick and thorough regional policy coordination. In Mississippi, only 13 percent of the public supports the legalization of same-sex marriage, according to a 2011 poll, reflecting little progress since the vote.[63] The deep, religiously based opposition in the South illustrates the difficulty of a near-term national solution to the issue of marriage equality, an example of the downside of American federalism for marriage equality. The South has been especially receptive to the Religious Right's coordinated attempt, dating to the 1970s, to repeal or prevent LGBT rights at the ballot box. According to Amy Stone, "The Religious Right is far more successful at the ballot box, where it can rely on voters' homophobia, than in the legislative or judicial arenas."[64]

The 2012 Texas Republican Party Platform provides a window into the official views of Republican elected officials and candidates in that state and demonstrates the very high level of hostility toward sexual minorities that persists in the region, as well as other parts of the country:

> We support the definition of marriage as a God-ordained, legal and moral commitment only between a natural man and a natural woman, which is the foundational unit of a healthy society, and we oppose the assault on marriage by judicial activists. . . . We support the enforcement of the State and Federal Defense of Marriage Act by state and federal officials respectively, and oppose creation, recognition and benefits for partnerships outside of marriage that are being provided by some political subdivisions. . . . We believe in the sanctity of marriage and that the integrity of this institution should be protected at all levels of government. We urge the Legislature to rescind no-fault divorce laws. We support Covenant Marriage. . . . We affirm that the practice of homosexuality tears at the fabric of society and contributes to the breakdown of the family unit. Homosexual behavior is contrary to the fundamental, unchanging truths that have been ordained by God, recognized by our country's founders, and shared by the majority of Texans. Homosexuality must not be presented as an acceptable "alternative" lifestyle, in public policy, nor should "family" be redefined to include homosexual "couples." We believe there should be no granting of special legal entitlements or creation of special status for homosexual behavior, regardless of state of origin. Additionally, we oppose any criminal or civil penalties against those who oppose homosexuality out of faith, conviction or belief in traditional values. [65]

Here, theology, explicit hostility toward sexual minorities, gender rigidity, religious freedom, judicial activism, and opposition to divorce under most circumstances are tied together with ease, indicating the historically strong interrelationship between these factors. In other words, opposition to same-sex marriage is not merely an objection to redefining a particular institution. It stems primarily from anti-gay animus, driven by a particular theological position on homosexuality, both factors that reinforce heterosexual supremacy. Remarkably, this platform reflected progress in the Texas Republican Party. In the 2010 platform, the party called for the recriminalization of sodomy, but this was removed in 2012. The platform also called for a law making it a felony to grant a marriage license to same-sex couples. Language describing the health dangers of nonheterosexuality was also removed. [66]

The South was the site of important litigation to eliminate sodomy laws in the years preceding *Lawrence v. Texas*. The state high courts of Arkansas, Georgia, Kentucky, and Tennessee responded positively to litigation strategies focused on the negative right to privacy; however, organized LGBT rights advocates have not touched the issue of marriage equality and its demand for positive freedom and full equality for same-sex couples until quite recently. [67]

For years, Democrats in control of the North Carolina legislature blocked proposed amendments. However, as in many states, Republicans gained control in 2010 (the first time they took complete control in 140 years), and an amendment banning all same-sex relationship recognition became a priority for Republicans. The amendment sailed through the legislature with significant Democratic support. Democrats in opposition tried to make the argument that the amendment would hurt North Carolina businesses who provide benefits to same-sex employees or prevent businesses from relocating to the state, but these arguments gained little traction, given the close relationship between the Religious Right and the now-in-control Republicans. During the amendment campaign, the Republican House Speaker admitted that same-sex marriage was coming to the state in within a generation, but he placed much more emphasis on the current political dynamics in the state for him and his party, thus cynically shepherding the sweeping amendment through the legislative process.[68]

The amendment was sweeping: "Marriage between one man and one woman is the only domestic legal union that shall be valid or recognized in this state." The language triggered legal speculation that it could prevent the enforcement of local domestic partnership laws or even prohibit legal protections for unmarried heterosexuals, such as domestic violence orders of protections. The sweeping language did not substantially diminish support for the amendment. It passed with 61 percent of the vote.[69]

The campaign to enact the amendment was a clear instance of Goldberg-Hiller's description of the amendment in Hawaii—an attempt to purify the state for heterosexual supremacy. Indeed, the proposed amendment set off a wave of religious condemnation of sexual minorities. One pastor's sermon advocated physical violence toward a male child exhibiting physical actions not consistent with hypermasculinity. In response to President Obama's endorsement of marriage equality soon after the passage of Amendment One, pastor Charles Worley of Providence Road Baptist Church called for lesbians and gays to be put into concentration camps (an electrified pen) where they would die, ridding society of homosexuality.[70] More "mainstream" religious voices also argued stridently, though not so violently, for the amendment. North Carolina native Billy Graham, in a full-page advertisement in fourteen newspapers in the state, declared: "At 93, I never thought we would have to debate the definition of marriage. The Bible is clear—God's definition of marriage is between one man and one woman."[71] He framed the issue in terms of moral decline, with the strong implication that sexual minorities were responsible for the decline with their demands for political equality.

The umbrella organization spearheading the campaign to enact the amendment emphasized several themes, among them the neoconservative argument about the dangers of "redefining marriage" and the resulting civilizational chaos, threats to religious freedom and businesses, and threats to children. According to the group, same-sex marriage "proclaims the false notion that a man can be a mother and a woman can be a father—that men and women are exactly the same in rearing children."[72] Thus the campaign was a successful mix of theocracy, neoconservative social decline arguments, and rigid gender essentialism in the service of protecting children.

NOTES

1. Elizabeth Kennedy, "Gay Couples File Suit over Denial of Marriage Licenses," *Associated Press*, June 26, 2002.

2. *Boy Scouts of America v. Dale*, 734 A.2d 1196 (N.J. 1999).

3. *Boy Scouts of America v. Dale*, 530 U.S. 640 (2000).

4. Lax and Phillips estimate mean opinion on LGBT rights at 64 percent.

5. *Lewis v. Harris*, 908 A.2d 196 (N.J. 2006).

6. *Lewis v. Harris*, 222.

7. *Lewis v. Harris*, 224.

8. Domestic Partnership Act, P.L.2003, c.246.

9. Robert Moran, "Democrats Will Stay the Course, While Quietly Addressing Two Issues," *Philadelphia Inquirer*, November 6, 2005, B01.

10. *Lewis v. Harris*, Docket #15-03, Mercer County Superior Court (NJ), November 5, 2003.

11. David Kocieniewski, "Some Democrats Back Off Bid to Legalize Gay Marriage in New Jersey," *New York Times*, November 23, 2009, A29; David Kocieniewski, "New Jersey Senate Defeats Gay Marriage Bill," *New York Times*, January 7, 2010, A14.

12. Diego Ribadeneira, "Springsteen Says No to Christie and Yes to Same-Sex Marriage," *New York Times*, December 9, 2009, http://cityroom.blogs.nytimes.com/2009/12/09/springsteen-says-no-to-christie-and-yes-to-same-sex-marriage/.

13. Kate Zernike, "Gay Marriage, Passed, Awaits Veto by Christie," *New York Times*, February 17, 2012, A1; Kate Zernike, "Christie Keeps His Promise to Veto Gay Marriage Bill," *New York Times*, February 18, 2012, A19.

14. *Lewis v. Harris*, 997 A.2d 227 (N.J. 2010).

15. Lambda Legal Complaint, *Garden State Equality v. Dow*, Mercer County (NJ) Superior Court, June 29, 2011, http://lambdalegal.org/sites/default/files/legal-docs/downloads/gse_nj_20110629_complaint-for-declaratory-and-injunctive-relief.pdf, 3.

16. *Garden State Equality v. Dow*, Mercer County (NJ) Superior Court, Civil Action Opinion, Docket No. MER-L-1729-11, February 21, 2012, 18; Lisa Coryell, "Feinberg to Retire from the Bench," *Trenton Times*, January 31, 2012, http://www.nj.com/mercer/index.ssf/2012/01/feinberg_to_retire_from_bench.html.

17. Lax and Phillips estimate mean public opinion supporting LGBT rights at 65 percent.

18. Kathryn Masterson, "Senate Gives Final Approval to Expanded Rights for Gay Couples," *Associated Press*, May 7, 2002; Avi Salzman, "Tying Half the Knot," *New York Times*, April 17, 2005, www.nytimes.com/2005/04/17/nyregion/17CONN.html; William Yardley, "Connecticut House Backs Gay Civil Unions," *New York Times*, April 14, 2005, www.nytimes.com/2005/04/14/nyregion/14hartford.html.

19. William Yardley, "Move Is Made in Connecticut Courts to Legalize Gay Marriage," *New York Times*, August 26, 2004, www.nytimes.com/2004/08/26/nyregion/move-is-made-in-connecticut-courts-to-legalize-gay-marriage.html.

20. *Kerrigan v. State of Connecticut*, slip opinion, New Haven Superior Court, NNH CV 04 4001813, July 12, 2006, 22.

21. *Kerrigan v. Commissioner of Public Health*, 957 A.2d 407 (Conn. 2008), 438.

22. *Kerrigan*, 482.

23. *Kerrigan*, 475.

24. Glenn Adams and Holly Ramer, "Gay Marriage Leaps Ahead in Maine, New Hampshire," *Associated Press*, May 6, 2009; Glenn Adams, "Maine Governor Defends Gay Marriage Action," *Associated Press*, May 9, 2009; Glenn Adams, "Catholic Donations to Fight Gay Marriage Top $550K," *Associated Press*, October 23, 2009; Lisa Leff and David Sharp, "Schools Emerge as New Tactic in Gay Marriage Votes," *Associated Press*, November 6, 2009; Clarke Canfield, "Changes Seen in Maine on Gay Marriage Since Vote," *Associated Press*, February 25, 2012.

25. "UNH Poll Shows Support for Gay Marriage," *Associated Press*, February 25, 2004; Norma Love, "New Hampshire Governor Signs Bill Blocking Gay Marriage," *Associated Press*, May 14, 2004; Beverly Wang, "Gay Marriage Panel Sharply Divided," *Associated Press*, December 1, 2005; Beverly Wang, "House Votes Down Proposed Amendment to Ban Gay Marriage," *Associated Press*, March 22, 2006.

26. Beverly Wang, "Senate Committee Hears Civil Unions Bill," *Associated Press*, April 10, 2007; Beverly Wang, "N.H. Senate Approves Civil Unions," *Associated Press*, April 26, 2007.

27. Norma Love, "New Hampshire Legislature Approves Gay Marriage," *Associated Press*, June 3, 2009.

28. Norma Love, "Republicans Win Large Majorities in NH Legislature," *Associated Press*, November 3, 2010; "Poll: Little Support for Gay Marriage Repeal in NH," *Associated Press*, October 14, 2011; Norma Love, "NH House Kills Gay Marriage Repeal Bill," *Associated Press*, March 21, 2012.

29. "Rhode Island Lawmaker Says State Not Ready for Gay Marriages," *Associated Press*, March 18, 2000.

30. "Marriage Guide for Rhode Island Same-Sex Couples," Gay and Lesbian Advocates and Defenders, December 10, 2010, http://www.glad.org/uploads/docs/publications/ri-marriage-guide.pdf.

31. *Chambers v. Ormiston*, 935 A.2d 956 (R.I. 2007).

32. 660 A.2d 707 (R.I. 1995).

33. See Jason Pierceson, *Courts, Liberalism, and Rights: Gay Law and Politics in the United States and Canada* (Philadelphia: Temple University Press, 2005), 96–97.

34. GLAD Amicus Brief, *Chambers v. Ormiston*, http://www.glad.org/uploads/docs/cases/chambers-v-ormiston/Chambers-GLAD.pdf; *Chambers v. Ormiston* (R.I. 2007).

35. Katie Zezima, "Rhode Island Steps toward Recognizing Same-Sex Marriage," *New York Times*, April 21, 2007, http://www.nytimes.com/2007/02/22/us/22rhode.html.

36. David Klepper, "Gay RI House Speaker Takes Heat for Gay Marriage Vote," *Associated Press*, May 18, 2011; Ian MacDougall, "RI Senate Passes Civil Unions Bill," *Associated Press*, June 29, 2011; "RI, IL See Different Results with Civil Unions," *Associated Press*, December 9, 2011; PolitiFact labeled the statement by NOM-Rhode Island that the state's residents opposed same-sex marriage as a "Pants on Fire" lie based on recent poll data, with support in polls as high as 60 percent. "Executive director of marriage group says most Rhode Islanders oppose gay marriage," PolitiFact Rhode Island, May 11, 2011, http://www.politifact.com/rhode-island/statements/2011/may/11/christopher-plante/executive-director-marriage-group-says-most-rhode-/; Erika Niedowski, "Gov.: RI Recognizing Out-of-State Gay Marriages," *Associated Press*, May 14, 2012.

37. Robert D. McFadden, "Bloomberg Is Said to Want State to Legalize Same-Sex Marriages," *New York Times*, March 6, 2004, http://www.nytimes.com/2004/03/06/nyregion/bloomberg-is-said-to-want-state-to-legalize-same-sex-marriages.html.

38. James McKinley, Jr., "Gay Marriages Are Still Far from Approval by Albany," *New York Times*, September 24, 2003, http://www.nytimes.com/2003/09/25/nyregion/25GAY.html.

39. *Hernandez v. Robles*, 7 Misc 3d 459 (Sup Ct, New York County 2005), 24.

40. Joanna Grossman, "New Developments in the Same-Sex Marriage Wars," Findlaw.com, December 13, 2005, http://writ.findlaw.com/grossman/20051213.html.

41. Anemona Hartocollis, "Appeals Court Voids Ruling In Favor of Gay Marriage," *New York Times*, December 9, 2005.

42. *Hernandez v. Robles*, 805 N.Y.S.2d 354 (N.Y. App. Div. 2005), 362.

43. *Hernandez v. Robles*, slip op., New York Court of Appeals, July 6, 2006, 6. The formal citation for the case is 855 N.E.2d 1 (N.Y. 2006).

44. Anemona Hartocollis, "New York Judges Reject Any Right to Gay Marriage," *New York Times*, July 7, 2006, http://www.nytimes.com/2006/07/07/nyregion/07marriage.html.

45. Anemona Hartocollis, "Top State Court's Ruling on Gay and Lesbian Marriage is Awaited," *New York Times*, July 5, 2006, http://www.nytimes.com/2006/07/05/nyregion/05marriage.html.

46. "This State has a proud tradition of affording equal rights to all New Yorkers. Sadly, the Court today retreats from the proud tradition." *Hernandez*, slip op., dissent, 2.

47. Richard Perez-Pena, "The Pataki Court Speaks," *New York Times*, July 6, 2006, http://empirezone.blogs.nytimes.com/2006/07/06/patakis-court-legacy/.

48. Richard Perez-Pena, "Pataki Gets a Decision He Wanted on the State's Highest Court," *New York Times*, July 7, 2006, http://www.nytimes.com/2006/07/07/nyregion/07justices.html; Michael Cooper, "Pataki Appoints Fifth Republican to Highest Court," *New York Times*, August 18, 2006, http://www.nytimes.com/2006/08/19/nyregion/19judge.html.

49. Jeremy W. Peters, "New York Senators Hedge on Gay Marriage," *New York Times*, May 10, 2009, http://www.nytimes.com/2009/05/10/nyregion/10gays.html; Jeremy W. Peters, "New York State Senate Votes Down Gay Marriage Bill," *New York Times*, December 2, 2009, http://nytimes.com/2009/12/03/nyregion/03marriage.html.

50. Nicholas Confessore and Michael Barbaro, "New York Allows Same-Sex Marriage, Becoming the Largest State to Pass Law," *New York Times*, June 25, 2011, A1; Michael Barbaro, "Behind Gay Marriage, an Unlikely Mix of Forces," *New York Times*, June 26, 2011, A1.

51. Tim Craig, "Suit Challenges Gay Marriage Ban," *Washington Post*, July 8, 2004, B1.

52. Dan Furmansky, "Maryland: Same-Sex Marriage," *Washingtonpost.com*, July 8, 2004, http://www.washingtonpost.com/wp-dyn/articles/A34721-2004Jul7.html.

53. *Deane v. Conaway*, slip opinion, Circuit Court for Baltimore County (Md.), Case No.: 24-C-04-005390, January 20, 2006, 19.

54. Profile of Judge M. Brooke Murdock, Maryland State Archives, http://www.msa.md.gov/msa/mdmanual/31cc/html/msa02642.html.

55. *Conaway v. Deane*, 932 A.2d 571 (Md. 2007), 628.

56. Lisa Rein and Mary Otto, "Md.'s Highest Court Upholds Ban on Same-Sex Marriage," *Washington Post*, September 19, 2007, A1.

57. Aaron C. Davis and John Wagner, "Md. to Recognize Same-Sex Marriages from Other Places," *Washington Post*, February 25, 2010, A1.

58. John Wagner, "Md. House Turns Back Same-Sex Marriage," *Washington Post*, March 12, 2011, A4.

59. John Wagner, "Stepping Up for Gay Marriage," *Washington Post*, July 23, 2011, B1.

60. John Wagner, "Gay Marriage Vote Nearly Failed Again in Md. House," *Washington Post*, February 19, 2012, C5; Aaron Davis, "Gay Marriage Bill approved by Md. Senate," *Washington Post*, February 24, 2012, A1.

61. According to Public Policy Polling, African American support for the law increased from 39 percent to 55 percent, mirroring shifts in other states like Pennsylvania and nationally. "Maryland Polling Memo," Public Policy Polling, May 24, 2012, http://www.publicpolicypolling.com/main/2012/05/maryland-polling-memo.html.

62. Randall Chase, "Civil Union Bill Clears Del. Senate Panel," *Associated Press*, March 31, 2011; Beth Miller, "Governor Signs Del. Civil Unions Bill," *Gannett News Service*, May 12, 2011; Randall Chase, "New Year Brings Same-Sex Civil Unions in Delaware," *Associated Press*, December 29, 2011; Fred Katayama and Edith Honan, "Delaware Governor Says Gay Marriage is 'Inevitable' in His State," Reuters, March 12, 2012.

63. "Mississippi Voters on a Variety of Topics," Public Policy Polling, November 18, 2011, http://www.publicpolicypolling.com/pdf/2011/PPP_Release_MS_1118.pdf. In the poll 38 percent of respondents supported same-sex marriage or civil unions, with 60 percent opposed to any form of legal recognition.

64. Amy L. Stone, *Gay Rights at the Ballot Box* (Minneapolis: University of Minnesota Press, 2012), xv.

65. Texas Republican Party Platform 2012, http://s3.amazonaws.com/texasgop_pre/assets/original/2012-Platform-Final.pdf.

66. Texas Republican Party Platform 2010, http://static.texastribune.org/media/documents/FINAL_2010_STATE_REPUBLICAN_PARTY_PLATFORM.pdf.

67. Pierceson, *Courts, Liberalism, and Rights*, 72–95.

68. Gary D. Robertson, "NC House Oks Marriage Ballot Question for 2012," *Associated Press*, September 13, 2011; "North Carolina Will Put Same-Sex Marriage Amendment on 2012 Ballot," *CNN Wire*, September 13, 2011; Michael Biesecker, "Tillis Stands by Prediction on NC Gay Marriage Ban," *Associated Press*, March 27, 2012.

69. Tom Breen, "Marriage Proposal's Broader Effects Debated in NC," *Associated Press*, February 18, 2012.

70. "Charles L. Worley, North Carolina Pastor: Put Gays and Lesbians in Electrified Pen to Kill Them Off," *Huffington Post*, May 21, 2012, http://www.huffingtonpost.com/2012/05/21/north-carolina-pastor-gay-rant-starvation_n_1533463.html.

71. Campbell Robertson, "Issue of Gay Rights, But Not a Simple One," *New York Times*, May 12, 2012, A1.

72. "The Threat to Marriage," Vote for Marriage NC, http://www.voteformarriagenc.com/threat/.

Chapter Seven

Continued Progress and Backlash, 2004–2012

The West

Arguably, the most consequential fight over same-sex marriage has occurred in California, the largest state, with the state supreme court's mandating same-sex marriage in 2008, the approval by votes of Proposition 8 banning same-sex marriage in the state constitution, and the subsequent federal legal challenge resulting in the overturning of Prop. 8 by Judge Vaughn Walker in 2010. This case made its way to the U.S. Supreme Court in the 2012–2013 term. This chapter will explore the developments in California, as well as the creation of relationship equality policies in Oregon and Washington after (ultimately unsuccessful) litigation was initiated in those states after the success in Massachusetts and the civil disobedience campaign of mayors in 2004. Further inland, a domestic partnership law was enacted in Nevada in 2009, and serious attempts have been made to enact civil unions in Colorado and New Mexico. In Montana, activists are trying to achieve civil unions through litigation, despite the state's conservative political climate. Litigation concerning domestic partnership benefits for state employees in Arizona has been appealed to the U.S. Supreme Court.

OREGON AND WASHINGTON: TRIAL COURT SUCCESS, HIGH COURT LOSSES, AND PARTNERSHIPS ARE RECOGNIZED

Mayor Gavin Newsom's granting of marriage licenses in 2004 seemingly triggered similar action in Portland, Oregon, when Multnomah County officials began granting same-sex marriage licenses. However, activists from

Basic Rights Oregon had been lobbying county officials to begin granting licenses as a way to blunt the impact of a coming constitutional amendment referendum banning same-sex marriage. BRO was a sophisticated organization, having spent the previous decade fighting anti-gay initiatives in the state. They were hoping to gain some forward momentum in the face of the inevitable backlash to the idea of same-sex marriage. As the group's executive director, Rochella Thorpe, stated, "We could see the backlash coming no matter what we did."[1]

The lobbying triggered a confidential memo from the county attorney to the county commissioners stating that same-sex marriages were required under the Oregon constitution. The opinion was based upon a state appeals court decision, *Tanner v. OHSU*, in which the court found that sexual orientation was a suspect classification under the state constitution.[2] Using the authority of the memo, the commissioners authorized the granting of licenses to same-sex couples.

Tanner was a fairly remarkable decision for 1998, and it provides a window into Oregon legal culture and its strong egalitarianism. The appeals court easily found that the denial of benefits to same-sex state employees was a form of sexual orientation discrimination prohibited by the Oregon constitution. A more flexible approach to equal protection analysis created by the state supreme court facilitated the outcome. Rather than a three-tiered framework with a several-point test to find where a form of discrimination fits in the tiers, Oregon courts asked whether a distinct characteristic has triggered societal discrimination and stereotyping. *Tanner* led many state legal officials, including the attorney general of Oregon and the legislature's chief counsel, to conclude that the denial of recognition and benefits to same-sex couples was likely constitutionally suspect.[3]

Two trial court judges agreed. One judge refused a request by conservative groups for an injunction against the county's issuance of licenses to same-sex couples because they stood little chance of proving that the licenses were unconstitutional. Another, Frank Bearden, stopped the county's actions but ruled that the lack of recognition of same-sex couples was unconstitutional under the Oregon constitution. He, too, relied heavily on *Tanner*, as well as *Goodridge* and *Baker*, and he ordered the legislature to remedy the situation by enacting civil unions or a similar remedy. This was no timid trial court judge. As he ordered: "This court will allow the legislature until ninety days after the commencement of the next regular or special session, whichever comes first, to produce legislation that would balance the substantive rights of same-sex domestic partners with those of opposite-sex marriage couples or Multnomah County will be required to issued marriage licenses to same-sex couples to avoid further violating Article I, Section 20," the equality provision.[4]

However, before the state supreme court could rule (the appeal was expedited to the high court), opponents of same-sex marriage successfully placed a constitutional amendment referendum banning same-sex marriage on the ballot in the fall of 2004. The amendment passed with 57 percent support, the relatively low support likely due to a strong campaign by marriage equality advocates and a strong turnout of younger voters.[5] A few months later, the supreme court unanimously ruled that the amendment prohibited the recognition of same-sex marriage in the state and that county officials lacked the power to issue marriage licenses, thereby nullifying the 3,000 marriages granted by Multnomah County.[6] The court refused to let the case convert to one mandating civil unions, despite the trial court decision, because the original filing of the plaintiffs called for same-sex marriage. Indeed, at oral argument, the author of the opinion, Justice Michael Gillette, ridiculed their attempts to do so.[7] Because of the amendment, the court did not address the applicability of *Tanner*, and it is difficult to say how the court would have ruled without the amendment. The court had a reputation for civil rights innovation, often expanding rights and protections beyond federal constitutional standards.[8] Given the emerging legal consensus, there was strong legal ammunition for a favorable ruling for same-sex couples. But the high court had a more narrow view of judicial power than did Judge Bearden, perhaps as a result of the popular vote.

The issue then shifted to the legislature, but Republicans in control of the House refused to consider a civil union bill supported by Democratic governor Ted Kulongoski, despite strong support in the Democrat-controlled Senate, which passed the bill by a vote of 19 to 10. In addition, the supreme court decision undermined efforts of advocates to protect same-sex couples, as many legislators argued that the court gave them permission to do nothing. And while supporters of the amendment argued during the campaign that civil unions were not banned by the amendment, conservatives opposed civil unions as being identical to marriage after the vote, a convenient bait-and-switch for opponents of relationship equality.[9] Given the lack of Republican support, the effort stalled. However, the election of Democrats to the House majority in 2006 opened the door to policy change. Advocates shifted from "civil unions" to "domestic partnerships" (only a semantic change). In 2007, the domestic partnership law was approved by wide margins, and with a few Republican votes, and it granted all of the rights of marriage under Oregon law.[10] Thus, what started as a form of legally inspired civil disobedience by Multnomah County officials in 2004 resulted in a substantial shift in policy in the state three years later.

Strong statements of liberal constitutionalism by trial courts reversed by a high court describe the dynamic present in Oregon's neighboring state of Washington, too. A mere couple of days after the issuing of same-sex marriage licenses by Multnomah County, same-sex couples applied for marriage

licenses in Seattle and filed suit after King County officials refused to grant
the licenses, with the support of Lambda Legal and the Northwest Women's
Law Center. A few weeks later, the ACLU filed a similar suit.[11] Judge
William Downing decided the first case in favor of the same-sex couples in a
ringing judicial defense of same-sex marriage. Judge Downing declined to
apply an equal protection analysis, unwilling "to announce a potentially far-
reaching new rule that homosexuality defines a suspect class for purposes of
constitutional analysis."[12] He also held that the plaintiff's argument that the
state's ERA compelled same-sex marriage was undone by *Singer v. Hara*,
discussed in chapter 2.[13] Instead, he anchored his decision in the claim that
same-sex marriage was a fundamental right, relying on U.S. Supreme Court
cases such as *Loving*, *Lawrence*, and *Turner v. Safley*. As he declared: "That,
then, is the right being asserted by the plaintiffs here—the autonomous right
to have such a 'most important relation' in their lives and, in that relationship, to be able to make their own unique contribution to the foundation of
society. That right—a right unquestionably burdened by the statutes in question—is the fundamental right to marry."[14] As a result, Downing rejected
morality (because of separation of church and state), tradition, and the procreation rationale as compelling interests to justify the denial of this fundamental right. Interestingly, Downing did not devise a remedy, leaving this
role for the state supreme court. He was fearful of weakening the institution
of marriage through the creation of "quasi-marriage." In his mind, it was all
or nothing, and he seemed to trust that the supreme court would grant it all to
the plaintiffs.

Finally, while he noted that judges should tread carefully when challenging legislative enactments, Downing was not shy about an aggressive judicial
role, asserting that "constitutions empower the courts to ensure both that no
group is singled out for special privileges and also that no minority is de-
prived of rights to which its members should be entitled."[15] A jurist known
for a strong sense of empathy, Downing was aware of the stakes involved in
the case, especially if he ruled aggressively, as he did, but he felt obligated to
follow the law as he saw it, rather than duck the issues. As one commentator
familiar with the judge stated, "A lot of trial judges are afraid of any controversial issues so they'll do the least controversial thing. But Judge Downing
will do what he thinks is right based on the law."[16] A conscientious objector
during the Vietnam War, he certainly had experience with principled arguments and the consequences of social stigma. But he was surprised by the
ferociousness of the response to his decision: "I know this is an emotional
volatile issue. I never thought I would be hearing from people directly," a
statement reflecting the political insularity of many judges.[17] On a daily
basis, they are not injected into politics and generally operate in obscurity.

A few months later in a quirky opinion, Judge Richard Hicks ruled that same-sex marriage was required by the Washington constitution. Hicks relied on the Oregon *Tanner* decision to find that sexual minorities were a suspect class and also found same-sex marriage to be a fundamental right, thus rejecting the procreation defense of the state. [18] In fact, both states have a similar equality provision, their privileges and immunities clauses. Washington took the clause from the Oregon constitution. However, whereas the Oregon courts have generally adopted a method of interpretation distinct from the federal Equal Protection Clause, Washington judges have resisted this, as will be seen shortly in the discussion of the Washington Supreme Court decision. Hicks, unlike Downing, incorporated the Oregon approach. He closed the opinion with an invocation of secular, communitarian values:

> For the government, this is not a moral issue. It is a legal issue. Though these issues are often the same, they are also quite different. The conscience of the community is not the same as the morality of any particular class. Conscience is what we feel together as a community. Conscience makes us one people. What fails strict scrutiny here is a government approved civil contract for one class of the community not given to another class of the community. Democracy means people with different values living together as one people. . . . This is the democracy of conscience. [19]

Clearly, this was another aggressive decision coming from a trial court judge in the Pacific Northwest. In response to these decisions, one legislator called for a constitutional amendment banning same-sex marriage, but an amendment would have required two-thirds of the legislature to support it before it was sent for popular ratification—a nearly impossible threshold in the body controlled by Democrats. [20] Like Vermont and Iowa, and other states with high constitutional amendment thresholds, marriage equality advocates in Washington operated without the prospect of an easy amendment process used by opponents.

The 5 to 4 supreme court decision in 2006 reflected the sixteen-month time frame utilized by the court for its decision: six separate opinions and acrimonious language. It was a muddled mess, but it preserved the ban on same-sex marriage in the state. Two justices strongly opposed same-sex marriage, three found no constitutional basis for it but invited the legislature to remedy what they saw as the unequal treatment of same-sex couples, and four dissenters agreed with the lower court judges that same-sex marriage was required by the state constitution. The majority was unwilling to apply the more supportive Oregon jurisprudence, instead applying federal equal protection analysis and finding that the procreation argument was sufficient to justify unequal treatment. The dissenters applied an aggressive liberal constitutionalism of equal protection and fundamental rights analysis and accused the majority of ducking their judicial duty, cowering to public opinion.[21] According to one justice, "It was a difficult issue, something the citizenry is split on. I don't know why our court should be any different. Our diverse court reflects our diverse society's views."[22]

One dissenting justice viewed the state DOMA as driven primarily by religious factors, and, thus, creating a "shadow establishment" of religion as described by Gordon Babst. Citing a brief in the case from the Libertarian Party of Washington State calling the DOMA an unconstitutional establishment of religion, Justice Bobbe Bridge stated: "If the DOMA is really about the 'sanctity' of marriage, as its title implies, then it is clearly an unconstitutional foray into state-sanctioned religious belief."[23] Justice Bridge was an outlier. Judges have been generally unwilling to identify the explicit theological arguments against same-sex marriage, instead relying on neoconservative arguments about family structure when defending bans on same-sex marriage, or, if in support, invoking liberal constitutionalism to trump any consideration of the motivations behind the bans.

The decision also surprised most of the parties and commentators involved, as most expected some kind of challenge to the status quo, either through a mandate for marriage or civil unions. The fact that some of the justices were up for reelection may have influenced the outcome, but the justices facing election were on both sides of the decision.[24] Notably, all high courts ruling in favor of relationship equality claims through 2011 were appointed, some with retention elections, but none with partisan or nonpartisan elections like Washington State. In other words, Washington State justices are more exposed to electoral politics, and their opinions are more visible in the public arena than trial court decisions.

The loss in the supreme court and long-standing Democratic control of the legislature, where change was possible without Republican opposition, shifted relationship equality advocacy efforts to the legislative arena, where activists and lawmakers pursued a gradualist strategy that resulted in the eventual identical treatment of same-sex couples under state law for marriage. Starting in 2007, the legislature established a domestic partnership framework and added rights until all of the state rights of marriage were attained in 2009. This approach was even confirmed by voters after opponents of relationship equality placed a veto of the law on the ballot. It was defeated by a margin of 53 to 47 percent,[25] marking the first time that a relationship equality policy had been ratified by a popular vote. Notably, Microsoft Corporation donated $100,000 to the campaign to keep the law.[26] During the campaign, opponents of the law argued that it was same-sex marriage with a different name. The fact that the referendum passed with this argument in the public arena encouraged advocates of same-sex marriage that the state was ready, or nearly ready, for marriage equality. In 2011, one poll found plurality support for same-sex marriage (46 percent) while another found stronger support for legislation, with 55 percent of respondents indicating that they would vote to uphold a same-sex marriage law enacted by the legislature.[27]

In 2012, Democratic governor Christine Gregoire, who had been in office since 2004 and supported domestic partnerships, endorsed a marriage equality bill in the legislature.[28] According to Gregoire, "It's time, it's the right thing to do, and I will introduce a bill to do it. I say that as a wife, a mother, a student of the law, and above all as a Washingtonian with a lifelong commitment to equality and freedom. Some say domestic partnerships are the same as marriage. That's a version of the discriminatory 'separate but equal' argument."[29] A leading opponent, emphasizing the neoconservative (rather than religious, sin-based argument) stated, "Marriage has never existed for the purpose of affirming relationships involving adults. The primary function of marriage is to create the greatest likelihood that children will be raised by their mother and father."[30] The bill was also supported by Washington-based corporations Nike, Starbucks, and Microsoft. Thus, by 2012, Washington State appeared to be the next state ready to "upgrade" to same-sex marriage, after a narrow loss in the courts, arguably contrary to the state's legal culture. For instance, in addition to the two lower court decisions, the state bar association declared its support for same-sex marriage in 2008.[31] The legislative process was also facilitated by a relatively large number of openly lesbian or gay lawmakers who kept the issue on the agenda. One journalistic tally early in 2012 indicated that advocates were only two votes shy of passage in the Senate, with much stronger support in the House. Commitments were gained from senators on the fence, and the bill eventually passed the Senate by a vote of 28 to 21 with four Republican votes.[32] The law was put on hold pending the outcome of another popular veto, but the voters approved the law.

Events in Washington State also led to a U.S. Supreme Court decision, *Doe v. Reed* (2010). Conservative opponents of domestic partnerships sued to block the state from releasing the name of those who signed the petitions to place the referendum on the 2009 law on the ballot. They argued that signatories faced potential harassment. They were supported by a federal district court judge, but the Ninth Circuit Court of Appeals ruled that the names must be made public, according to state law. In an 8 to 1 decision, the U.S. Supreme Court largely agreed. Arguing that the harassment had not been proven, Chief Justice John Roberts and the court majority sided with openness and transparency. The desire to keep the signatures a secret reflects the larger cultural shift in favor of LGBT rights. It is unlikely that conservative opponents would have advocated secrecy a decade ago, more confident in their position.[33]

CALIFORNIA: THE BIGGEST BATTLE YET

The conflict over Prop. 8 has been the most visible and ongoing state battle over same-sex marriage. It has involved incremental legislative action, state litigation, federal litigation, and popular referenda. It has also taken place in the largest state, arguably a leader in the creation of new public policies. While the federal challenge to Prop. 8 will be examined in chapter 8, along with other federal cases, this section will examine the prelude to the federal court challenge filed in 2009. The case was the end result of a long legal and political battle begun, in contemporary terms, soon after the Hawaii decision in 1993.

As was discussed in chapter 2, California was the primary home to the 1980s movement toward domestic partnerships, particularly in its most progressive jurisdictions. Religious conservatives stymied translating this to the state level in the early 1990s, but events in Hawaii triggered activity that would eventually lead to the enactment of statewide domestic partnerships. A bill creating a limited set of rights for same-sex couples, and opposite-sex couples over the age of sixty-two, narrowly passed the Democratic legislature in 1994, but Republican governor Pete Wilson vetoed the bill. Proponents of the bill framed their advocacy in terms of the reality of changing relationships, an extension of the move away from traditional marriage, a path followed by many European nations through the creation of cohabitation frameworks. As the lead sponsor stated, "There are thousands of couples who live together and for one reason or another choose not to be married. It's about time the state of California recognized these relationships."[34] At the time, polls indicated emerging majority support for the law, and this support increased over the next several years. This shift, combined with the persistent, but purposefully incremental, efforts of Assemblywoman Carole Midgen ultimately led to the enactment of the law in 1999. This time, the bill was signed into law (though reluctantly and after he lobbied for a more limited set of rights) by a Democrat, Grey Davis. A series of expansions of the law led to the inclusion of all rights and benefits under California marriage law for registered domestic partners by 2003.[35]

At the same time, however, conservatives pushed for a popular initiative (Proposition 22) to guarantee that same-sex marriages performed in other states would not be recognized in California. Recall that California clarified its marriage law in 1977 as heterosexual-only after the applications for marriage licenses by same-sex couples. In other words, state law was already clear, but conservatives in California, like those in many other states by 2000, wanted to create a public policy exemption to full faith and credit clause requirements. According to a spokesperson for the organization supporting the amendment, "This simply closes a loophole so that we don't have to recognize marriage from another state with a definition different from our own. It's a way we can protect the right to determine for ourselves how we will define the institution of marriage in our state, which we feel should be between men and women."[36] Like conservatives in other states, California activists declared a minimalist interpretation during the campaign, but, after the vote (the amendment was approved with 61 percent of the vote), they argued that the amendment also prevented the legislature from creating same-sex marriage in the state. Indeed, the relationship between Prop. 22 and a same-sex marriage bill twice enacted by the legislature and vetoed by Republican governor Arnold Schwarzenegger would become a source of political and legal controversy, only ended by Prop. 8's constitutional ban on same-sex marriage.

Democratic San Francisco mayor Gavin Newsom changed the political and legal landscape in California when he ordered the city to begin granting marriage licenses to same-sex couples in 2004. "It's just the last great civil rights struggle. It's bigger than just gay marriage: It's about human dignity, it's about freedom," Newsom stated in a liberal constitutionalist justification of his actions.[37] Leading litigation groups were not pleased with Newsom. In 2003, lawyers from the ACLU, Lambda, and the National Center for Lesbian Rights agreed to avoid litigation in the state, given the ease of amending the constitution through a referendum.[38]

The California Supreme Court eventually stopped Newsom, while leaving the constitutional issues surrounding same-sex marriage unaddressed,[39] but his actions of civil disobedience (he did not have the authority to grant licenses) inspired similar tactics in Multnomah County, Oregon; Sandoval County, New Mexico; and New Paltz, New York. Newsom's actions also spurred legislative activity in his state. For the first time in history, a legislative committee in California approved a same-sex marriage bill in 2004, and, the following year, the Democratic legislature passed a same-sex marriage bill that was vetoed by Schwarzenegger, citing Prop. 22.[40] The bill was revived on a procedural maneuver, after first failing to gain enough votes in the House, reflecting the tenacity of the bill's sponsor, openly gay Democrat Mark Leno.[41] This scenario played out again in 2007.[42] In both cases, the bills were opposed by all Republicans and a few Democrats.

Litigation: Both Sides Go to Court, but Liberal Supporters Win in the California Supreme Court

Newsom's actions also triggered litigation related to the state's prohibition of same-sex marriage. Conservative groups challenging Newsom's actions initiated some of the suits, while others were from same-sex couples desiring to be married. These suits were consolidated into one lawsuit under Judge Richard Kramer of the San Francisco County Superior Court. In a forceful decision (by yet another trial court judge), Kramer ruled that the 1977 law banning same-sex marriage and Prop. 22 were unconstitutional. He deemed the provisions to discriminate on the basis of gender and to violate the fundamental right to marry, in his words, "the basic human right to marry a person of one's choice."[43] As a result, he applied strict scrutiny. Kramer also relied heavily on *Perez v. Sharp* (a California Supreme Court case from 1948 that was a precursor to *Loving v. Virginia*) and *Lawrence v. Texas*, using both cases to justify a liberal constitutional approach to the issue of same-sex marriage. In particular, Kramer used these cases to attack the state's assertion that the ban on same-sex marriage was justified by tradition. He also viewed the domestic partnership law as an insufficient remedy to the unequal treatment for same-sex couples and even possibly unconstitutional itself, a "separate but equal" status certainly not sufficient to save the state's ban on same-sex marriage. Interestingly, Kramer was a Roman Catholic and a Republican, but he was known for having a "social worker attitude."[44]

However, an appellate court reversed this decision by a 2-to-1 vote. The judges in the majority were unwilling to challenge the legislature, more concerned about the appropriate limits on judicial power than on the rights of same-sex couples. They were fearful of "policy making" by judges. The majority rejected both the fundamental rights and equal protection (whether gender or sexual orientation) arguments. "Under the highly deferential standard of judicial review that applies [the rational basis test], we believe it is rational for the Legislature to preserve the opposite-sex definition of marriage, which has existed throughout history and which continues to represent the common understanding of marriage in most other countries and most states of our union," the majority declared.[45] They were especially confident in this statement, given the domestic partnership law and its attempt to achieve some form of equality.

Accused by the majority of being too emotional, the dissent by Judge J. Anthony Kline agreed with Judge Kramer that state marriage policy violated the fundamental right to marry and was also an equal protection violation, although on the basis of sexual orientation, not gender. Judge Kline asserted that sexual minorities were a suspect class and chastised his colleagues: "Judicial opinions upholding blanket denial of the right of lesbians and gay men to enter into society's most fundamental and sacred institution are as incompatible with liberty and equality, and as inhumane, as the many opinions that upheld the denial of that right to interracial couples. Like them, such opinions will not stand the test of time."[46] Judge Kline also noted the theological underpinnings of arguments against same-sex marriage, even in arguments about tradition invoked by the state.

In the fight over relationship equality in California, conservatives were as willing to use litigation for policy goals as liberal supporters of marriage equality. For instance, the conservative Proposition 22 Legal Defense and Education Fund challenged Newsom's licenses and challenged the state's recognition of domestic partnerships for violating Prop. 22. While the courts rebuffed this latter effort, it demonstrates, as has been illustrated in previous chapters, that conservatives are not concerned with challenging majorities when it suits their purposes and policy preferences.[47] Despite popular and legislative support for domestic partnerships, they wished to use Prop. 22 as a ban on all forms of relationship recognition, despite its reference to marriage only. Clearly, a theologically driven desire to prevent the state from affirming sexual minorities animates a significant part of the opposition to same-sex marriage beyond a concern for a certain definition of the institution. Conservatives also responded to these events (in the courts and in the legislature) by beginning the process for a voter-approved constitutional ban on same-sex marriage, but early efforts were undermined by a conflict over whether the amendment should ban recognition beyond marriage. The decision was eventually made by one camp of conservative and religious organizations to go beyond marriage, but advocates of this approach failed to achieve the requisite number of signatures, by a significant margin.[48] Overall, this series of events reflects the fact that issues of relationship equality in California involved a complex interplay of legislative, judicial, and popular politics that would continue to play out in coming years.

Roughly two years later, a divided California Supreme Court handed down a sweeping decision invalidating the state's prohibition on same-sex marriage and declaring sexual orientation to be a suspect classification under California law. The seven-member court was composed of six Republican appointees, and while the court had a decades-old reputation as a judicial innovator, it was more recently viewed as a cautious court under Chief Justice Ronald George, a Pete Wilson appointee. Indeed, many experts predicted that the court would not challenge state policy, especially given the vote on Prop. 22. However, the court had become increasingly supportive of LGBT rights claims, with decisions expanding parenting rights and prohibiting discrimination against same-sex families. In other words, the court was becoming an advocate for LGBT families. For instance, the court ruled in 2005 that a lesbian couple was entitled to a family membership from a private country club, and the court granted full parenting status to nonbiological parents in a same-sex relationship after a relationship ends.[49]

For the justices in the majority, liberal constitutionalism trumped any concern about an inappropriate judicial role. The majority rejected the appeals court's deference and its argument that the domestic partnership scheme was sufficient equal treatment for same-sex couples. The decision by Chief Justice George repeatedly discussed the "respect and dignity" required for same-sex couples under the California constitution, a strong, not merely libertarian, liberalism. As he stated, "The California Constitution cannot properly be interpreted to withhold from gay individuals that same basic civil right of personal autonomy and liberty (including the right to establish, with the person of one's choice, an officially recognized and sanctioned family) that the California Constitution affords to heterosexual individuals" as a part of due process.[50] Like the trial court decision, the majority invoked *Perez v. Sharp* and *Lawrence v. Texas* in its argument for a richer liberalism and the need to ignore tradition that leads to discrimination and a withholding of fundamental rights. Unlike that court, however, the majority rejected the argument that this was an instance of gender discrimination. Instead, the majority held that the state's policy was a form of sexual orientation discrimination and declared that sexual orientation was a suspect classification. Arguably, this was a more difficult path for a trial court, given the lack of precedent in federal and state constitutional jurisprudence. The approach of the majority also marked a significant shift in state equal protection jurisprudence on marriage equality, because it was the first time that a state high court ruled that sexual orientation was a suspect classification (the Connecticut high court did so soon after, followed by Iowa in 2009), a clear judicial innovation. Recall that previous courts used the rational basis test to strike down same-sex marriage bans. In defense of this judicial activism, George cited law professor Jesse Choper on the need for courts to uphold individual rights, even if the decision will be "subject to criticism, hostility, or disobedience."[51]

Predictably, a dissent by Justice Marvin Baxter criticized the majority decision on majoritarian grounds. "A bare majority of this court, not satisfied with the pace of democratic change, now abruptly forestalls that process and substitutes, by judicial fiat, its own social policy view for those expressed by the people themselves," Baxter scolded.[52] In fact, the majority held that Prop. 22 was both a prohibition on out-of-state same-sex marriages and a ban on internally authorized same-sex marriages. The dissenting viewed this as clear evidence for the need for judicial restraint, while the majority found it to be an unconstitutional limitation on individual rights. Baxter also rejected the claim of a fundamental right to same-sex marriage and argued that the increased political power of the lesbian and gay community undermined the majority's holding that sexual minorities were a suspect class.

In an interview after the decision, Chief Justice George made clear his inspiration for the opinion—a strong dislike toward unequal treatment of groups. He admired the courage of the *Perez* court in 1948 when it challenged the legal, and public opinion–supported, prohibition on interracial marriage. George also indicated that his views on discrimination were forged as a young man on a visit to the segregated South. "It sensitized me to the fact that there are minorities of all sorts of types who can be victimized by the majority," and the role of courts is to remedy this problem by protecting minorities, according to George. He wanted to author the majority opinion, because of his belief that it is the role of the chief justice to be the object of any potential backlash.[53]

Proposition 8: Religious Forces Strike Back

And the backlash came in the form of Prop. 8 ("Only a marriage between a man and a woman is valid or recognized in California"), passed by a relatively narrow margin on November 4, 2008, 52 to 48 percent, but the effect was significant: overturning the decision of the supreme court from just months earlier and calling into question the validity of the roughly 18,000 same-sex marriages performed since that decision, *In re Marriage Cases*. This was a huge setback for marriage equality advocates, as it came from the largest and one of the most progressive states in the country. It also triggered federal litigation explored in the next chapter. In the end, Prop. 8 was successful largely due to the money and influence of religious organizations, or organizations with strong connections to religion, especially the Mormon Church, a replay of events in Hawaii a decade earlier. Arguments that same-sex marriage threatens religious freedom, especially the freedom of parents and teachers forced to teach, or accept, the teaching about same-sex marriage in the public schools, played prominently in the public relations efforts of Prop. 8 supporters.

Founded in 2007, the National Organization for Marriage (NOM) played a significant financial and issue-framing role in supporting Prop. 8, as it has done in most state debates over same-sex marriage since its founding. While the organization plays down anti-gay rhetoric and takes a more neoconservative approach to the defense of heterosexual-only marriage, its position is grounded in Catholic natural law approaches. Robert George is the organization's leading intellectual influence and was chair of its board of directors. NOM's founder and first president, Maggie Gallagher, became a visible spokesperson for the organization through the campaign for Prop. 8 and beyond, before stepping down in 2010, replaced by Massachusetts anti–marriage equality activist Brian Brown. Gallagher's opposition to same-sex marriage is rooted in her general political conservatism and her experience as an unwed mother. She argues that the heterosexual nuclear family is the only family form that should be supported in law and policy. Before becoming a leading anti-same-sex-marriage advocate, she was a critic of feminism and its challenges to traditional gender and family norms for prominent conservative publications and think tanks.[54]

Of course, more secular groups like NOM gladly form alliances with religious groups to fight the movement for marriage equality. In California, this ally was the Mormon Church, relying on its worldwide donor base and its political ties to the western United States. While NOM did not officially partner with the Mormon Church, it created an organization, ProtectMarriage.com and its official ballot measure political arm, Yes on 8, with the

American Family Association and Focus on the Family, both virulently anti-gay groups.[55] Recall that the American Family Association was categorized as an anti-gay hate group by the Southern Poverty Law Center in 2010.[56]

Through the summer of 2008, polls indicated that Prop. 8 would be defeated. The legal framing of same-sex marriage as a right required by the California constitution appeared to hold sway over a majority of prospective voters. In fact, a change in the language describing the amendment by Attorney General Jerry Brown, triggered by the supreme court decision, caused support for the amendment to drop to 38 percent (from 42 percent several months earlier) in the Field Poll. Brown changed the language from "Limit on Marriage" to "Eliminates the right of same-sex couples to marry."[57] However, during the fall, conservative and religious opponents of marriage equality orchestrated a campaign, significantly funded by the Mormon Church, to emphasize the threat to religious freedom and to children in schools posed by now-legal same-sex marriage.[58] The focus on schools and children, developed by the consulting firm Schubert Flint Public Affairs, proved to be highly successful. After the commercial "Princes," in which a young Latina comes home from school and shares, "Guess what I learned in school today. I learned how a prince married a prince, and I can marry a princess," began airing in October, support for Prop. 8 began to rapidly rise in the polls.[59]

Despite being only 2 percent of the state's population, Mormons in California and around the country contributed half of the $40 million spent to pass Prop. 8. This led to a backlash against the church and a level of visibility not generally welcomed by church leaders. The strong role of the Mormon Church in these battles, especially in western states where the church is strongest politically, stems from a particular point of Mormon theology, beyond the traditional, but disputed, Christian claims about the sinfulness of homosexuality. For Mormons, the afterlife is strongly tied to the heterosexual family, in which families reunite in celestial unity. Challenges to this family structure threaten the Mormon notion of heaven. As Elizabeth Ellen Gordon and William L. Gillespie note, "Mormons believe in the eternal nature of gender and the family, so earthly changes loosening the bond of marriage and weakening the patriarchal structure of family and church represents very substantial losses."[60] They also chronicle the extensive role played by Mormons in the fight against the ERA in the 1970s and 1980s. The church is also extremely hierarchical, with dictates from the Prophet in Salt Lake City given tremendous authority. This allows for highly effective political organizing. According to a *Time* magazine account,

> Prop 8 constituted a kind of perfect political storm of theology, demographics and organization. At the Alameda [California] Meeting House last June (as at other Mormon churches statewide), a letter from [Prophet Thomas] Monson and his counselors advised believers to "do all you can to support the proposed

constitutional amendment by donating of your means and time." A string of Protect Marriage coalition meetings followed. They never occurred on LDS property, but they were overwhelmingly Mormon in attendance and sought Mormon support. Alaina Stewart, a church member, was asked to employ a list of "who in the ward we thought could contribute. We'd call and say, 'We're asking you to give such and such an amount,'" she says.[61]

After the vote on Prop. 8, much was made of an exit poll showing very high levels of support coming from the African American community. Given the community's strong support for Barack Obama in the election for president, many commentators asserted that the African American community put Prop. 8 over the top in a close election. However, subsequent analysis by public opinion experts demonstrated that this poll was inaccurate and that slightly stronger levels of support for banning same-sex marriage in the African American community stem from the community's higher levels of religiosity. Like many communities in the United States, religion affects public opinion on same-sex marriage, but this influence is waning over time. However, as discussed in chapter 3, this phenomenon continues to play a significant role in the U.S. debate.[62]

Marriage equality advocates went back to court to challenge the validity of Prop. 8, but the California Supreme Court was unwilling to challenge the outcome of the vote.[63] Interestingly, however, Jerry Brown, rather than defend Prop. 8 as would be customary for an attorney general, asked the court to overturn the initiative, because it was "inconsistent with the guarantees of individual liberty" in the state constitution.[64] The California Supreme Court's validation of Prop. 8 shifted the legal fight to the federal courts, where it was struck down at the district and appellate court levels, a dynamic examined in the next chapter.

ARIZONA, COLORADO, NEVADA, AND NEW MEXICO

A conservative state, Arizona has nonetheless been the site of some interesting relationship equality developments. The urban areas of Tucson and Phoenix and the presence of very large state universities (University of Arizona and Arizona State University) have fostered political and legal activism for relationship equality. The state has witnessed unsuccessful same-sex marriage litigation, the (only to-date) defeat of a super-DOMA amendment in 2006, and the enactment of both statutory and constitutional bans on same-sex marriage. Currently, litigation challenging the withdrawal of domestic partner benefits for state employees is working its way through the federal courts.

194   *Chapter 7*

Efforts to enact domestic partner benefits began in major cities in the late 1990s, and a local gay couple brought a legal challenge to the ban on same-sex marriage in the wake of the *Lawrence* decision in 2003. National groups did not support the litigation, and it was unsuccessful. However, it contributed to backlash efforts. Legislators approved a ballot initiative banning marriage and similar legal statuses in 2006, but this was defeated by a margin of 52 to 48 percent, marking the first time that an anti–marriage equality initiative was defeated. Arizona voters objected to the expansive nature of the amendment, a fact emphasized in the campaign against the amendment. A marriage-only amendment passed in 2008 by a margin of 56 to 44 percent. Given Arizona's conservatism, both of these votes reflect relatively low levels of support for banning the recognition of same-sex relationships.[65]

In 2008, just before she left the governor's office to serve as secretary of homeland security in the Obama administration, Janet Napolitano ordered that all state employees be eligible for domestic partner health insurance benefits, including same-sex couples. This decision was reversed in 2009 by the conservative legislature and Napolitano's conservative successor, Jan Brewer. Indeed, in the past several years, the Arizona political system has produced some of the most right-wing legislation in the country, on immigration and women's rights in particular, and Brewer has become a conservative icon. Lambda Legal sponsored litigation challenging this reversal, and a federal district court judge and the Ninth Circuit have ruled that the state's actions are unconstitutional under the Equal Protection Clause, failing rational basis review, as the costs of the coverage are minimal.[66] The case has been appealed to the U.S. Supreme Court. Thus, the federal courts have been allies in supporting this minimal relationship recognition policy. Politically, however, it is unlikely that policy will extend beyond the status quo in the near future, leaving this policy and the domestic partnership ordinances in some larger cities and in Pima County.

The election of a Democratic majority in the state senate in 2008, joining with an already Democratic state assembly majority, facilitated the enactment of a domestic partnership law in Nevada in 2009. This required an override of a veto by Republican governor Jim Gibbons, however, with some Republicans joining in the override. While the recognition of same-sex relationships requires a fuller liberalism than libertarianism embraces, advocates of the law framed it in libertarian terms, hoping to tap into a strong strain of political culture in Nevada, and in the West generally. According to Democratic assemblywoman Sheila Leslie, the law fit with "the great tradition of Nevada libertarianism. . . . Since when do we want government deciding where we live, who we live with, and who we should love?"[67] The law also included opposite-sex couples, and this, too, was emphasized by advocates.

Strong support from the gaming industry in the state also facilitated enactment of the law.[68] The law was as far as policy could extend in the state, because voters approved a constitutional ban on same-sex marriage in 2002.

In spite of supportive public opinion, efforts to enact domestic partnership legislation in New Mexico have stalled, especially with the election of a Republican governor in 2010. Democrat Bill Richardson, governor from 2003–2011, was a strong supporter of a domestic partnership law, but conservative Democrats in the legislature scuttled the legislation. At the same time, however, the state possesses neither a statute nor a constitutional amendment banning same-sex marriage. The political conversation over relationship equality accelerated in 2004 when, in response to inquiries triggered by Gavin Newsom's actions, a Republican county clerk in Sandoval County, Victoria Dunlap, granted marriage licenses for a day before being stopped by higher legal authorities. She was bolstered by the opinion of the county attorney that denying licenses may violate the state's ban on sex discrimination. More recently, the state attorney general promulgated an opinion asserting that out-of-state same-sex marriages could be recognized by the state. Thus, New Mexico has been the site of activity surrounding relationship equality, but little tangible policy change with a reluctant political system and no serious court activity to date.[69]

New Mexico is also the site of a notable case exploring the claimed tension between religious liberty and relationship equality. A New Mexico photography business's refusal to photograph a same-sex commitment ceremony has become a cause célèbre for the Religious Right, because the business was found to have violated the state's sexual orientation–inclusive antidiscrimination law by the New Mexico Human Rights Commission and forced to pay around $7,000 in attorney fees and other costs related to the complaint. This has been portrayed by opponents of LGBT equality, including the Alliance Defense Fund supporting the photographer, as an example of the threat to religious liberty posed by marriage equality. The decision was affirmed by a trial court, and this decision was upheld on appeal. Of course, the case was not about marriage equality (same-sex marriage is not legal in New Mexico); rather, it dealt with a violation of an antidiscrimination law. Carving out a religious exemption to such laws easily could create a backdoor approach to undermining these laws, potentially for categories other than sexual orientation. Under a religious freedom exemption, one could claim a religious reason for discriminating on the basis of religion, gender, or race, for example. As the New Mexico Court of Appeals stated: "This does not deny Elaine Photography the right to express religious opinion. The owners are free to express their religious beliefs and tell . . . anyone . . . what they think about same-sex relationships and same-sex ceremonies. However, like the . . . owners of all other public accommodations, Elaine Photography may not discriminate in its commercial activities against protected classes as the basis for expressing its religious opinion."[70] Thus, the argument about the threats to religious freedom from LGBT equality is more sweeping than a concern about relationship equality. It attempts to privilege not just religious expression but all religiously motivated activity above all other rights and claims to equality. Thus far, courts have been unwilling to create such a sweeping right, as evidenced by this case and the Catholic Charities litigation in Illinois.

In Colorado, a law with limited benefits for same-sex couples is in place. This law, the Designated Beneficiaries Act, mirrors the reciprocal beneficiaries law in Hawaii and was the result of complete Democratic Party control of the levers of powers in the state in 2009. This came after a referendum calling for the creation of same-sex domestic partnerships was defeated by a vote of 47 to 53 percent in 2006, representing the first serious attempt to enact such a policy though the popular referendum process in the nation. The legislature coupled this potential amendment with a marriage definition amendment that passed in the same election with 56 percent support.[71]

Attempts to expand this policy were undermined by the election of a Republican House majority in 2010. For example, in 2011, a civil union bill was defeated in the House judiciary committee by one vote, the margin of Republican control of the committee, after passing the Senate with all Democrats and three Republicans (all women) in support. As Republican senator Jean White, who has a gay niece and a gay nephew, stated: "My vote today is for love and respect and commitment. My vote today is for my niece and nephew." Thus, for White, family ties were the vehicle that transformed traditional Republican opposition into positive freedom recognition of same-sex relationships. However, her Republican Senate colleague, Scott Renfroe, had a decidedly more theological take on the issue when he stated, "I'm a follower of Jesus. And I believe following Jesus is the way through which we can run the race and finish strong. Marriage is the fundamental institution that holds our society together and my Christian beliefs."[72] Republicans also used the failed referendum vote from 2006 as evidence of a lack of public support, despite the five-year gap in time and likely increase in public support. In fact, a poll from late 2011 showed significant support for civil unions and plurality support for same-sex marriage, though not yet a majority.[73] With this dramatic shift in public opinion, it would seem that relationship equality policy would continue to advance. However, a renewed push to enact civil unions in 2012 failed when the Republican Speaker of the House, Frank McNulty, effectively killed a bill twice, once in regular session (where he sacrificed thirty other pending bills in order to derail the civil union bill) and once in a special session called by pro–civil unions governor and Democrat John Hickenlooper, despite the fact that the bill had the votes to pass in the Republican-controlled House (some Republicans would have supported the bill) after passing the Democratic Senate. Republican representative Don

Koram cast the deciding committee vote in the special session, after McNulty assigned it to a "kill" committee, despite his stated support for civil unions and having a gay son. He weakly claimed that the bill contained the word "spouse" too many times.[74]

Thus, public opinion could not change the Republican Party's strong opposition to relationship recognition, despite the support of some Republican lawmakers not running for reelection. This episode further undermines the assumption that legislatures are more majoritarian than courts. Had the Colorado courts mandated civil unions, opponents would have cried "judicial activism." Instead, procedural moves to deny a legislative majority (supported by public opinion) vote are viewed as a normal part of the democratic process.

THE REST OF THE WEST AND THE GREAT PLAINS: THE WYOMING MYSTERY AND LITIGATION IN MONTANA

Elsewhere in the West and the Great Plains, the situation is bleak for relationship equality. Most states possess super-DOMA amendments that passed with significant majorities: North Dakota (73 percent), South Dakota (52 percent), Nebraska (70 percent), Kansas (70 percent), Utah (66 percent), Oklahoma (76 percent), Texas (76 percent), and Idaho (63 percent). Montana's marriage-only ban was passed with 67 percent support. Republican Party dominance in these states prevents the enactment of supportive policies. The dominance of the Mormon Church in Utah's politics creates a virtual theocracy in that state. While the church has signaled that it would consider supporting antidiscrimination protections based on sexual orientation, it is nearly inconceivable that it would support relationship equality policies, given its participation in events in Hawaii and California. Nebraska's amendment was the nation's first super-DOMA in 2000. South Dakota's amendment almost failed in 2006, likely the result of strong Democratic mobilization in this low-population state. Also on the ballot was a measure that would have outlawed most abortions. This was defeated, and the mobilization against it likely spilled over into votes against the marriage amendment. Also, as in Arizona, opponents emphasized the potential negative consequences for heterosexuals, especially elderly, unmarried couples. The presence of the abortion issue also distracted conservative activists, as the abortion question was their top priority. Interestingly, polling indicated that support for the ban increased as Election Day neared. Arguably, the amendment would have failed had the voting taken place a few months earlier, given the narrow margin in the end.[75]

By all measures, Wyoming should have a constitutional amendment banning same-sex relationship recognition, but it does not. It is a thoroughly Republican state. In 2012, Republicans outnumbered Democrats in the legislature by 50 to 10 in the House and 26 to 4 in the Senate. Barack Obama only received 38 percent support in the 2008 election. However, attempts to enact constitutional amendments barring the recognition of same-sex marriage have consistently failed. Notably, even an attempt to enact a statute banning recognition of out-of-state same-sex marriages failed when the Senate failed to agree to an amendment also banning the recognition of civil unions, and this has created a potential opening for advocates to enact civil unions. Recent attempts to ban recognition stem from a request by a lesbian couple married in Canada in 2008 to get a divorce in Wyoming. After being denied by a trial court, the state high court ruled that the couple could obtain a divorce in the state. Some politicians viewed this as an open door to judicial recognition of foreign jurisdiction same-sex marriages, despite the fact that the court limited its ruling only to divorce.[76]

Several factors explain Wyoming's lack of an amendment. First, no popular route exists for constitutional amendments. These must start by a two-thirds vote of the legislature. Second, many Republicans take libertarian arguments seriously, and many Republicans have opposed attempts to negatively change the law. While successfully running for governor in 2010, Matt Mead, a former U.S. attorney, stated not only that he supported the "traditional" marriage, but also that "we need to make sure people in Wyoming are treated fairly, they're treated honestly, that they have worth, and we do not treat them as a lesser class of citizens."[77] Given his legal experience, Mead also opposed the conservative reaction to the lesbian divorce case, stating that the courts should be open to same-sex couples.[78] In other words, he viewed the issue through a legalistic lens, not only a moralistic one. Playing to the libertarian leaning of many Republicans, a Democratic House member stated: "We don't do this in Wyoming. We don't interfere in neighbors' lives."[79] Here, libertarian arguments were deployed to counter a ban on relationship recognition, not to create positive policies, although Mead's comments arguably pointed in this direction. In addition, the Wyoming legislature has very short general sessions every other year. In 2011, the session only lasted from January 11 to March 3.[80] Thus, activists on either side of the relationship equality issue have relatively infrequent and short windows in which to plead their case. Finally, because Wyoming was the site of the horrific hate crime against Matthew Shepard in 1998, a desire to avoid the vilification of sexual minorities pervaded the public discussion about relationship equality, as evidenced by Mead's statement. Perhaps these unique circumstances could lead to same-sex relationship recognition in Wyoming.

In 2011, a civil union bill failed by only one vote in the House judiciary committee, and advocates have vowed to keep trying. Governor Mead has expressed a willingness to consider civil unions.[81]

For the most part, activists in the West have avoided litigation, not at all confident in success in courts with conservative judges and with clear constitutional prohibitions on a range of relationship recognition laws. However, the marriage-only ban in Montana created an opening for the Montana ACLU to sue for the recognition of same-sex domestic partnerships in 2010. Additionally, the Montana Supreme Court struck down the state's sodomy law in 1997 and, more importantly, ruled in 2004 that state employees were entitled to same-sex domestic partner benefits.[82] In other words, a potential legal path existed for the ACLU to force the state to recognize same-sex couples short of marriage. A trial court judge ruled against the ACLU. Judge Jeffrey Sherlock did not analyze the constitutional arguments presented; he simply asserted that he lacked the power to compel the legislature to pass a domestic partnership or civil union law, the requested remedy.[83] In 2012, the Supreme Court ruled against the plaintiffs on procedural grounds, leaving the constitutional questions for future litigation.

In new litigation, the Montana court could prove to be a wild card, particularly when the 2004 decision is analyzed with an eye toward the current controversy. The ruling that state university employees were entitled to domestic partner insurance benefits was connected to the fact that common law marriages are recognized in Montana. The court ruled that an affidavit affirming a common law marriage allowed for in the insurance policy unconstitutionally disallowed same-sex couples to sign and thus be eligible for spousal insurance benefits. The dissenting judges saw this as appropriately recognizing heterosexual-only common law marriage, but the majority applied rational basis review and found no legitimate reason for the denial of benefits for same-sex couples. In a strongly worded concurring opinion, Justice James Nelson (the longest-serving member of the current court, elected three times by the voters in nonpartisan elections) wished to create a jurisprudence strongly protective of sexual minorities under the Montana constitution through the judicial establishment of "a stronger bulwark against the majoritarian oppression that gays and lesbians suffer daily. . . . I believe that this is the appropriate case in which we should begin to develop the law of equal protection based on Montana's unique Constitutional guarantee of the inviolability of human dignity coupled with the right to equal protection of the law and the prohibition against private and State discrimination."[84] Seldom is a judge so explicit about a desire to change the law through interpretation, but the opinion provides a window into a strain of rights protection for sexual minorities in Montana jurisprudence first seen in the 1997 case striking down the state's sodomy law, a law that had strong political support when it was invalidated.[85] The current litigation represents the first potential example of judicial aggressiveness in the inland West. It remains to be seen whether the court follows the path of this jurisprudence or whether it feels that the judicial mandating of relationship equality policies pushes this jurisprudence too far.

CONCLUSION

Clearly, jurisprudentially and politically, the progressive East has been more favorable to arguments for marriage equality than the progressive West, especially given the prevalence of voter initiatives in the West. However, after the legalization of same-sex marriage in Massachusetts in 2004, it was inevitable that legal and political activists would use all of the tools at their disposal in the country's most progressive states. This resulted in a complicated interplay of legal and political forces creating genuine policy change, particularly where Democrats controlled the levers of power. The shift of litigation from the state to the federal level after Prop. 8 and the reality of same-sex marriage in the Northeast created a new arena for the fight over marriage equality, although state battles continue to play out. For all of the progress, however, the backlash in conservative states is powerful, and poses strong legal and political barriers to the legalization of marriage equality throughout the country. The Supreme Court will consider the question of whether, and precisely how, these barriers can be overcome in the 2012–2013 term, an issue explored in the next chapter. *Groundhog Day* in the states is mostly over, but a new chapter has begun. As usual, the U.S. Supreme Court will play a large role in how the story unfolds.

NOTES

1. Ashbel S. Green and Brent Walth, "Tenacity, Timing Prove Pivotal in Push for Same-Sex Marriage," *Oregonian*, March 11, 2004.

2. Agnes Sowle, Memorandum to the Multnomah County Commission, March 2, 2004 (copy on file with the author); *Tanner v. OHSU*, 971 P.2d 435 (Ore. App. 1998).

3. Letter from Hardy Myers, Attorney General of Oregon to Governor Ted Kulongoski, March 12, 2004 (copy on file with the author); Jeff Mapes, "Legislators' Top Lawyer Backs Gay Marriage," *Oregonian*, March 10, 2004.

4. Ashbel S. Green, et al., "Judge Declines to Halt Licenses to Gay Couples," *Oregonian*, March 9, 2004; *Li v. State of Oregon*, slip opinion, Multnomah Circuit Court, no. 0403-03057, April 20, 2004, 16.

5. Bill Graves, "Oregonians Vote against Land Rules, Gay Marriage," *Oregonian*, November 3, 2004.

6. *Li v. State of Oregon*, 110 P.3d 91 (Ore. 2005).

7. The following summary of Gillette's questioning is from Ashbel S. Green, "Fight Shifts to Civil Unions," *Oregonian*, December 16, 2004: "Justice Michael Gillette asked whether gay-rights advocates think the Supreme court had authority to create civil unions. 'If there is doubt in my voice, it's intentional,' Gillette added. [ACLU lawyer Kenneth] Choe replied that the court could make it clear that the Legislature has to create civil unions in order to comply with

the Oregon Constitution's equal privileges clause. But that clause no longer applies to marriage, Gillette shot back. 'You can read. You should be able to figure that out,' Gillette said. Choe disagreed. 'Measure 36 has not affected the ability of unmarried plaintiff couples to seek the privilege of an automatic entitlement to the complete package of protections that married couples enjoy under the law,' he said. Gillette hammered on. 'But you have to bring a lawsuit seeking that, and there's nothing about that, I would submit, in your complaint,' he said."

8. Ashbel S. Green, "High Court History Favors Gay Marriage," *Oregonian*, March 14, 2004.

9. Ashbel S. Green and Michelle Cole, "Court Annuls Gay Marriages," *Oregonian*, April 15, 2005; Charles E. Beggs, "Senate Oks Civil Union Bill," *Associated Press*, July 8, 2005.

10. Brad Cain, "Domestic Partners Bill Wins Final OK from Oregon Lawmakers," *Associated Press*, May 2, 2007. The vote in the Senate was 21 to 9 after a narrower 34 to 26 vote in the House.

11. "Gay Marriage Ruling: How Issue Evolved in State, Nation," *Seattle Times*, August 5, 2004, A15.

12. *Andersen v. King County*, slip opinion, King County Superior Court, No. 04-2-04964-4 SEA, August 4, 2004, 10.

13. *Andersen*, 23.

14. *Andersen*, 14.

15. *Andersen*, 9.

16. Janet I. Tu, "Judge No Stranger to Famous Cases," *Seattle Times*, August 5, 2004, A14.

17. Lornett Turnbull and Sanjay Bhatt, "Gay-Marriage Fight Heats Up after Ruling," *Seattle Times*, August 8, 2004, A1.

18. *Castle v. State of Washington*, slip opinion, Thurston County Superior Court, No. 04-2-00614-4, September 7, 2004, 30, 35.

19. *Castle*, 37–38.

20. Lornett Thurnbull and Sanjay Bhatt, "Gay Marriage Fight Heats Up after Ruling," *Seattle Times*, August 8, 2004, A1.

21. *Andersen v. State of Washington*, 138 P.3d 963 (Wash. 2006).

22. David Postman, "Gay Marriage in Washington State: Nine Justices, Six Opinions, No Consensus," *Seattle Times*, July 27, 2006.

23. *Andersen*, 1028.

24. Curt Woodward, "State Supreme Court Upholds Washington Gay Marriage Ban," *Associated Press*, July 26, 2006; David Ammons, "Gay Marriage Ruling Could Rock Supreme Court Races," *Associated Press*, July 27, 2006. All justices up for reelection retained their seats.

25. "New Domestic Partnership Law Goes into Effect on Dec. 3," *US State News*, December 3, 2009.

26. "Microsoft Gives $100K to Washington Gay-Partners Effort," *Associated Press*, October 6, 2009.

27. "WA Voters Done with Rossi, Not Open to Kucinich Bid," *Public Policy Polling*, May 23, 2011, http://www.publicpolicypolling.com/pdf/PPP_Release_WA_0523.pdf; "The Washington Poll," University of Washington Center for Survey Research, October 31, 2011, http://www.washingtonpoll.org/results/103111.pdf. In this poll, 43 percent supported same-sex marriage, 22 percent supported the same legal rights without the name "marriage," 15 percent supported a limited set of rights, and only 17 percent supported no legal recognition for same-sex couples.

28. Rachel La Corte and Mike Baker, "Wash. Lawmakers Diverge on Gay Marriage Debate," *Associated Press*, January 5, 2012.

29. Press release, "Gov. Gregoire Announces Historic Legislation for Marriage Equality in Washington State," January 4, 2012, http://www.governor.wa.gov/news/news-view.asp?pressRelease=1828&newsType=1.

30. Rene Lynch, "Wash. Gov. Chris Gregoire to Champion Same-Sex Marriage," *latimes.com*, January 4, 2012, http://latimesblogs.latimes.com/nationnow/2012/01/washington-gov-chris-gregoire-to-champion-same-sex-marriage.html.

31. "State Bar Association Supports Same-Sex Marriages," *Associated Press*, September 28, 2008.

32. Tom Watkins, "Washington State Legislature Votes to Approve Same-Sex Marriage," CNN.com, February 8, 2012, http://articles.cnn.com/2012-02-08/us/us_washington-same-sex-marriage_1_lesbian-couples-marriage-washington-state?_s=PM:US.

33. *Doe v. Reed*, 561 U.S. __ (2010).

34. Jerry Gilliam, "Bill Would Recognize Rights of Unmarried Domestic Partners," *Los Angeles Times*, February 17, 1994.

35. For more on the process and the shift in public opinion, see Jason Pierceson, *Courts, Liberalism, and Rights: Gay Law and Politics in the United States and Canada* (Philadelphia: Temple University Press, 2005), 153–54.

36. Evelyn Nieves, "Ballot Initiative That Would Thwart Gay Marriage Is Embroiling California," *New York Times*, February 25, 2000, A12.

37. Anna Bedkhen, "The Battle over Same-Sex Marriage: Mayor Argues Case at Harvard," *San Francisco Chronicle*, February 9, 2005, B4.

38. Linda Hirshman, *Victory: The Triumphant Gay Revolution* (New York: Harper Collins, 2012), 302.

39. *Lockyer v. City and County of San Francisco*, 95 P.3d 459 (Cal. 2004).

40. Robert Salladay, "Gay, Lesbian Marriage Bill Advances," *Los Angeles Times*, April 20, 2004; John Wildermouth and Lynda Gledhill, "A Day After Assembly's OK, Schwarzenegger Pledges to Kill Same-Sex Marriage Bill," *San Francisco Chronicle*, September 8, 2005, A1.

41. Lynda Gledhill, "Gay Marriage Now Up to Governor," *San Francisco Chronicle*, September 7, 2005, A1.

42. Jill Tucker, "Governor Cites Prop. 22 as He Vetoes Leno Bill," *San Francisco Chronicle*, October 13, 2007, B2.

43. *Marriage Cases*, slip opinion, San Francisco County Superior Court, March 14, 2005, 21.

44. Stacey Finz and Jaxon Van Derbeken, "Judge Is Catholic and Republican—'A Brilliant Guy,'" *San Francisco Chronicle*, March 15, 2005, A12.

45. *In re Marriage Cases*, 143 Cal App. 4th 873 (2006), 931. The reference to policy making is found at 928.

46. *In re Marriage Cases*, 983.

47. Bob Egelko, "Domestic Partner Law Upheld," *San Francisco Chronicle*, April 5, 2005, B8; *Knight v. Superior Court*, 128 Cal. App. 4th 14 (2005).

48. Wyatt Buchanan, "Measures Mark Split for Conservatives," *San Francisco Chronicle*, August 12, 2005, B1; "Gay Marriage Ban Won't Be on Ballot," *San Francisco Chronicle*, December 28, 2005, B3. They fell roughly 200,000 signatures short out of nearly 600,000 needed.

49. Bob Egelko, "California's Highest Court Taking Up Gay Marriage," *San Francisco Chronicle*, March 3, 2008, A1; Bob Egelko, "Firms Must Treat Domestic Partners like Married Pairs, Top State Court Says," *San Francisco Chronicle*, August 2, 2005, A1; Bob Egelko, "Court Grants Equal Rights to Same-Sex Parents," *San Francisco Chronicle*, August 23, 2005, A1.

50. *In re Marriage Cases*, 183 P.3d 384 (Cal. 2008), 429.

51. *In re Marriage Cases*, 448.

52. *In re Marriage Cases*, 457.

53. Bob Egelko, "George Sees Eventual Equal Rights for Gays and Lesbians, Compares Situation to Ruling on California's Ban on Interracial Marriage," *San Francisco Chronicle*, June 15, 2008, A13.

54. Mark Oppenheimer, "The Making of Gay Marriage's Top Foe," Salon.com, February 8, 2012, http://www.salon.com/2012/02/08/the_making_of_gay_marriages_top_foe/singleton/. Website of the National Organization for Marriage, http://www.nationformarriage.org/site/c.omL2KeN0LzH/b.3836955/k.BEC6/Home.htm.

55. http://www.protectmarriage.com.

56. Evelyn Schlatter, "18 Anti-Gay Groups and their Propaganda," Southern Poverty Law Center *Intelligence Report*, Issue No. 40 (Winter 2010).

57. Carrie Sturrock, "Move to Ban Same-Sex Marriage Trails in Poll: Amended Ballot Language after Court Ruling Seen as a Factor," *San Francisco Chronicle*, September 18, 2008, B1.

58. John Wildermuth, "Harsh, Emotional Campaign on Prop. 8," *San Francisco Chronicle*, November 1, 2008, A7.

59. Hirshman, 306.

60. Elizabeth Ellen Gordon and William L. Gillespie, "The Culture of Obedience and the Politics of Stealth: Mormon Mobilization against ERA and Same-Sex Marriage," *Politics and Religion* 5 (2102), 343–66: 347.

61. David Van Biema, "The Church and Gay Marriage: Are Mormons Misunderstood?" *Time.com*, June 22, 2009, http://www.time.com/time/magazine/article/0,9171,1904146,00. html.

62. Patrick Egan and Ken Sherrill, "California's Proposition 8: What Happened, and What Does the Future Hold?" National Gay and Lesbian Task Force Policy Institute, January 2009, http://www.thetaskforce.org/downloads/issues/egan_sherrill_prop8_1_6_09.pdf.

63. *Strauss v. Horton*, 207 P.3d 48 (Cal. 2009).

64. Bob Egelko, "Brown Asks Court to Toss Out Prop. 8," *San Francisco Chronicle*, December 20, 2008, A1.

65. Paul Davenport, "Same-Sex Marriage Issue before Arizona High Court," *Associated Press*, April 8, 2004; Amanda Lee Myers, "Anti-Gay Marriage Initiative Loses in Arizona," *Associated Press*, November 8, 2006; Paul Davenport, "Age, Religion Factors in Ariz. Vote on Marriage," *Associated Press*, November 5, 2008.

66. *Diaz v. Brewer*, 656 F.3d 1008 (9th Cir. 2012).

67. Brendan Riley, "Domestic Partner Bill Endorsed," *Associated Press*, May 15, 2009.

68. "Big Casinos Back Domestic Partnership Law Change," *Associated Press*, May 22, 2009.

69. A poll from 2011 indicated that 45 percent of respondents supported same-sex marriage with 67 percent supporting marriage or another form of recognition. "New Mexico for Gay Marriage," Public Policy Polling News Release, December 20, 2011, http://www. publicpolicypolling.com/pdf/2011/PPP_Release_NM_1219424.pdf; Susan Montoya Bryan, "Same-Sex Couples Line Up in Sandoval County to Get Married," *Associated Press*, February 20, 2004; Deborah Baker, "Domestic Partnership Bill Fails in the Senate," *Associated Press*, February 27, 2009; Barry Massey, "AG: Out-of-State Gay Marriages Likely Valid in NM," *Associated Press*, January 5, 2011.

70. *Elaine Photography v. Willock*, slip op., New Mexico Court of Appeals, Docket No. 30, 203, May 31, 2012, 16.

71. Kevin Simpson, "Amend. 43 Supporters Revel in Double Victory," *Denver Post*, November 9, 2006, B6.

72. Ivan Moreno, "Colo. Civil Unions Bill Clears Sen., Goes to House," *Associated Press*, March 24, 2011; Ivan Moreno, "Republicans Reject Colorado Civil Unions Bill," *Associated Press*, April 1, 2011.

73. "Colorado Favors Gay Marriage, Marijuana Use, Loves Tebow," Public Policy Polling, December 9, 2011, http://www.publicpolicypolling.com/pdf/2011/PPP_Release_CO_12091205.pdf. In the poll, 76 percent of respondents favored civil unions, while 47 percent supported same-sex marriage.

74. "Colorado Lawmakers Reach Impasse on Civil Unions," *Associated Press*, May 1, 2012; Dan Frosch, "Colorado Rejects Same-Sex Civil Unions," *New York Times*, May 15, 2012, A19; Kevin Torres, "Gay Son Upset with Father Over Killing of Civil Unions Bill," 9News.com, May 15, 2012, http://www.9news.com/rss/story.aspx?storyid=268203.

75. Terry Woster, State Not United on Marriage Question," *Sioux Falls Argus Leader*, August 4, 2006, A1; Megan Myers, "Argus Leader Poll: Gay Marriage," *Sioux Falls Argus Leader*, November 3, 2006, A1; John Walker, "Narrow Vote on C Raises Questions," *Sioux Falls Argus Leader*, November 10, 2006, A1.

76. *Christiansen v. Christiansen*, 253 P.3d 153 (Wyo. 2011).

77. Ben Neary, "Wyoming Governor Candidates Split on Gay Issues," *Associated Press*, October 13, 2010.

78. Ben Neary, "Same-Sex Marriage Bill Stalls in Committee," *Associated Press*, March 1, 2011.

79. Marjorie Korn, "Emotions High in Wyoming over Marriage Bill," *Associated Press*, February 4, 2009.

80. "2011 Legislative Sessions Calendar," National Conference of State Legislatures, http://www.ncsl.org/legislatures-elections/legislatures/2011-legislative-session-calendar.aspx.

81. Jeremy Pelzer, "Civil Unions Fight Looms in Wyoming," *Casper Star Tribune*, May 9, 2012, http://trib.com/news/opinion/blogs/capitol/civil-unions-fight-looms-in-wyoming/article_72a307ca-9a18-11e1-a634-001a4bcf887a.html.

82. *Snetsinger v. Montana University System*, 104 P.3d 445 (Mont. 2004); *Gryczan v. State of Montana*, 942 P.2d 112 (Mont. 1997).

83. *Donaldson v. State of Montana*, slip op., Cause No. BDV-2010-702, April 2011.

84. *Snetsinger* (Mont. 2004), 454, 459–60.

85. For more on the sodomy case, see Pierceson, *Courts, Liberalism, and Rights*, 83–85.

Chapter Eight

Same-Sex Marriage and the Supreme Court

Because of the conservatism of the federal constitution, activists consciously avoided the federal courts for many years out of a fear of creating negative precedents. However, this approach recently changed, with a spate of federal litigation initiated by activists, most of it being an attempt to strike down the Defense of Marriage Act. This litigation reached the Supreme Court in the October 2012 term. The federal challenge to California's Proposition 8 reached the high court, but this case is more controversial and would ask the court to engage in more sweeping judicial activism than did the DOMA challenges. Indeed, the court routinely takes on Congress,[1] but taking on the thirty-one states with constitutional bans on same-sex marriage would be an ambitious undertaking, and the court may lack the resolve or desire to do so. This chapter will explore the federal jurisprudence relating to marriage and LGBT rights as a preview of the cases and issues the court will grapple with as it engages the issue of same-sex marriage. It will then examine the current federal litigation on marriage equality, with an eye toward predicting how the court may rule. In doing so, the chapter also explores the Supreme Court as a policy maker and how it is embedded in the legal and political system of the nation.

THE SUPREME COURT AS A POLICY MAKER

Given its exalted status in the American political mind, the Supreme Court is often reflexively seen as an institution focused on achieving justice and equality. *Brown v. Board of Education* (1954) is often cited as evidence of this role. However, *Brown* did very little in the short term to change attitudes or policy about racial segregation. In fact, in the short term, it empowered southern white supremacists and the politicians who supported them. Not until Congress passed the Civil Rights Act of 1964 and lower federal courts began enforcing *Brown* more aggressively did the politics of segregation permanently change.[2]

Now imagine this dynamic combined with a history of hostility from the Supreme Court, and you capture the legal reality regarding the rights of sexual minorities. As was discussed in chapter 4, the crushing defeat in *Bowers* left LGBT activists wary of the Supreme Court. Bowers was a manifestation of the conservative turn of the federal courts that began in the 1970s with the election of mostly Republican presidents. Liberals were forced into state courts, as many of these jurisdictions continued or expanded liberal constitutional jurisprudence, a phenomenon referred to by scholars as the "new judicial federalism." However, this strategy could only hold for so long for marriage equality advocates, especially given the hostility to their claims in a majority of states, and with the lack of federal recognition for legal same-sex marriages. By 2009, the fear of federal litigation had subsided, or was ignored out of wishful thinking, as activists brought a range of federal constitutional challenges to the denial states to recognize marriage equality in the law and to the Defense of Marriage Act. Public opinion was shifting in their favor, and increasingly, some legal scholars and activists began to see jurisprudential promise in two Supreme Court opinions authored by Justice Anthony Kennedy, *Romer v. Evans* (1996) and *Lawrence v. Texas* (2003), and a possible vote from the conservative Kennedy, combined with the votes of the four most liberal justices, to support marriage equality claims on the court. So far, federal courts have quite uniformly accepted the arguments of marriage equality activists that California's Proposition 8 and the federal Defense of Marriage Act are unconstitutional, thus initially justifying the gamble.

This jurisprudential success should not be taken as predicting Supreme Court success. Decision making on the court is fickle and difficult to predict. It is a mix of political and legal forces and calculations, as well as a mix of the personalities and agendas of the individual justices. Take the recent court ruling on the Affordable Care Act: Few commentators and experts predicted the outcome of an alliance upholding the individual mandate between conservative Chief Justice John Roberts and the four liberals, Ruth Bader Ginsburg, Stephen Breyer, Sonya Sotomayor, and Elena Kagan. Nor, frankly, did many experts predict that two of the liberals, Breyer and Kagan, would join with the conservatives (Roberts, Kennedy, Antonin Scalia, Clarence Thomas, and Samuel Alito) in invalidating Congress's attempts to expand Medicare by withdrawing all funding if states refused to expand coverage to new beneficiaries. On the individual mandate, the conventional wisdom predicted either a 5 to 4 conservative invalidation or a 6 to 3 vote to uphold the mandate, with

Roberts and Kennedy joining the liberals. The fact that Roberts solely joined the liberals, for the first time in his tenure on the court, stunned most everyone.[3]

MODELS OF DECISION MAKING ON THE COURT

Supreme Court scholars fall into four broad camps for explaining court decision making. Under one of these models, the attitudinal model, justices vote primarily based on their ideological predisposition. In other words, they vote either as a liberal or a conservative. In any given case, once you identify the liberal or conservative position, you can predict the outcome of the case. Attitudinalists attempt to do exactly that, and are able to accurately predict votes in a majority of cases. After all, presidents try to appoint justices who share their ideological viewpoint in order to create political allies on the court. Under this theory, law is used instrumentally to achieve the justices' ideologically based policy goals, rather than imposing an obligation to rule in a particular manner, as required by precedent, for instance. In other words, law matters very little. The legal analysis in an opinion is nothing more than a rationalization for the judge's ideological preference.[4] This theory gives great credence to the phrase "politics by other means" in that politics on the court mirrors politics, though not exactly, in the electoral arena, with its clash of ideologies. Evidence for the theory is also seen in the phenomenon of forum shopping often discussed in earlier chapters—LGBT legal activists did not just sue in any court but generally tried to find the court, or court system, most favorable to their claims, an assessment largely based on the perceived ideology of the judge or judges.

Another theory asserts the political nature of judging on the court, but in a different way. For advocates of the strategic model, justices are constrained by external political forces. This perspective is connected to an argument made by Alexander Hamilton in *The Federalist*. Hamilton asserted that the Supreme Court, feared by the anti-federalists as a source of federal tyranny over the states, would be the weakest of the new national branches of government: "The Judiciary . . . has no influence over either the sword or the purse. . . . It may truly be said to have neither FORCE nor WILL, but merely judgment; and must ultimately depend upon the aid of the executive arm even for the efficacy of its judgments."[5] In other words, the court requires a reservoir of good will stemming from the soundness of its decisions and is constrained by what is politically acceptable. If it rules aggressively, and contrary to the political status quo, it will lose support from the public and the other branches of government. It is the other branches that are the most potentially dangerous for the court, according to the strategic model, because the president can use the bully pulpit to criticize the court, and Congress can change its funding (just not reduce justices' salaries) and alter its jurisdiction, or ability to hear certain cases. As a result, justices must make calculations about what is politically acceptable while considering a case, and this will influence their vote. This is why public opinion may influence the court, despite being shielded directly from electoral politics. In addition, individual justices are constrained by other justices and must calculate what it will take, especially in terms of legal language, to win the vote of a justice on the fence, leading to a lot of bargaining and compromise inside the court. These dynamics lead scholars in this camp to conclude that the court seldom strays beyond the boundaries of politics defined by public opinion and the policy preference of the other federal branches. Rather than being a crusader for justice, the court merely reinforces the status quo, and true change comes only from the political arena.[6]

The legal model, against which the first two camps react, holds that judges make decisions exclusively on the basis of legal doctrine. In other words, judges follow the law and put aside their own preferences. This approach is also called legal formalism, reflecting the notion that the law in every case is clearly knowable, and judges scientifically apply the law to the case at hand. And, in routine cases, this is often an accurate description of judicial decision making. However, in instances when the law is not clear or is in flux, discretion may come into play. This view tends to be more prominent among law professors, unlike the attitudinal and strategic models that dominate thinking among social scientists who study the courts.[7] Therefore, a great deal of legal scholarship focuses on tracing the evolution of judicial doctrine as a way to understand judicial outcomes or the creation of innovative and more "correct" legal interpretations for judges to follow.

A final approach asserts that law matters for judicial decision making, but not as strongly as the legal model suggests. New institutionalism asserts that the perspective held by both attitudinalist and strategic theorists mistakenly emphasizes only the effect politics has on law. Instead, new institutionalist scholars argue that legal outcomes may be shaped by institutional rules and practices, as expressed by judges. A respect for precedent may trump a judge's ideological commitment, for example. Some scholars take this approach a step further and argue that legal language can shape, or change, the political dynamics of an issue. To use the issue addressed in this book, once courts began defining same-sex marriage as a constitutional right, some citizens and political actors began to view the issue in a new way, not simply as an issue of majoritarian morality. Of course, this is not an automatic or guaranteed process, but it may alter the terms of a political debate. In addition, simply filing a lawsuit provides advocates with a public forum not guaranteed in the political arena. Legislators can laugh you out of their office, but courts must take legal claims, deemed laughable in the political arena (as marriage equality claims were for quite some time), more seriously, at least initially. We will return to this approach when the issue of courts and social change is discussed in the next chapter. Indeed, I will use new institutionalist perspectives to argue that litigation has achieved important change for marriage equality.[8]

At the very least, from considering these theories, we can see that the Supreme Court is a political institution and does not simply rule based on what the law requires. In fact, because of its visibility, it may be the most politically exposed court in the nation. When considering same-sex marriage, the justice will consider all of the following to varying degrees: their own views on the issue, what they think the law requires or allows, and what they assess to be the political reaction to a particular outcome, thus creating a complex interplay of factors. For instance, a justice may think that Prop. 8 violates the Equal Protection Clause but be wary of the consequences for the court's legitimacy and reputation of challenging similar amendments in the majority of states, as would be the case with a broad decision striking down Prop. 8. (Thus, as we will see, some federal judges overturning Prop. 8 have limited their rulings to California.)

FEDERAL JURISPRUDENCE ON EQUAL PROTECTION AND THE RIGHT TO MARRY

As was discussed in chapter 2, *Loving v. Virginia* (1967) triggered activism for same-sex marriage, because it confirmed marriage to be a fundamental right. Indeed, over the course of the twentieth century the court created a jurisprudence of privacy in family matters that was highly skeptical of attempts by governments to regulate family decisions, such as whom to marry and decisions about having children—or not having children. *Griswold v. Connecticut* (1965) created a right to privacy for heterosexual married couples' decisions to use contraceptives, and subsequent decisions broadened this beyond married couples. This right to privacy in the family realm supported the absolute right of a woman to terminate a pregnancy in the first trimester in *Roe v. Wade* (1973). The court's treatment of marriage is best summarized by Justice Thurgood Marshall in *Zablocki v. Redhail* (1978):

> Although *Loving* arose in the context of racial discrimination, prior and subsequent decisions of this Court confirm that the right to marry is of fundamental importance for all individuals. Long ago, in *Maynard v. Hill* (1888), the Court characterized marriage as "the most important relation in life," and as "the foundation of the family and of society, without which there would be neither civilization nor progress." In *Meyer v. Nebraska* (1923), the Court recognized that the right "to marry, establish a home and bring up children" is a central part of the liberty protected by the Due Process Clause, and in *Skinner v. Oklahoma ex rel. Williamson* [1942], marriage was described as "fundamental to the very existence and survival of the race."

More recent decisions have established that the right to marry is part of the fundamental "right of privacy" implicit in the Fourteenth Amendment's Due Process Clause. In *Griswold v. Connecticut* (1965), the Court observed: "We deal with a right of privacy older than the Bill of Rights—older than our political parties, older than our school system. Marriage is a coming together for better or for worse, hopefully enduring, and intimate to the degree of being sacred. It is an association that promotes a way of life, not causes; a harmony in living, not political faiths; a bilateral loyalty, not commercial or social projects. Yet it is an association for as noble a purpose as any involved in our prior decisions."[9]

Demonstrating the depth of this right in the minds of the justices, the right to marry was even extended to prisoners in *Turner v. Safley* (1987). Of course, as was previously discussed, this line of jurisprudence was deeply heterosexist. The court did not conceive that same-sex families were included, and reflected the refusal of a narrow court majority in *Bowers v. Hardwick* (1986) to apply the right to privacy to same-sex intimacy. Additionally, as discussed in chapter 1, fundamental rights analysis is inherently conservative, as it is focused on the judicial definition of long-standing rights. As Marshall's summary makes clear, the court linked procreation to marriage, and, as we have seen, this has proven to be a barrier for litigation at the state level and could serve as a convenient jurisprudential excuse for justices reluctant to declare a fundamental right to marriage regardless of the gender of the parties. While in the abstract, this line of jurisprudence could support a right to same-sex marriage, in practice it has not been successful at either the state or federal court levels. However, for activists, hope may lie in the pro–gay rights decision of *Lawrence v. Texas* (2003), discussed below, in which the court included same-sex intimacy in the right to privacy, despite the court's clear statement that the decision did not directly apply to the question of marriage equality.

The equal protection route is more promising for marriage equality advocates. Indeed, recent federal court decisions have extensively invoked the reasoning of *Romer v. Evans* (1996). In that case, the court invalidated, on a vote of 6 to 3, Colorado's Amendment 2, a voter-approved constitutional amendment enacted in 1992 barring local governments from including protections on the basis of sexual orientation in their antidiscrimination laws, as some had already done. In the majority opinion, Justice Anthony Kennedy ruled the amendment unconstitutional under the usually deferential rational basis test, stating that laws may not be motivated by animus toward a group, and that Amendment 2 was driven solely by animus toward sexual minorities and lacked a legitimate policy purpose. Noting that "it is not in our constitutional tradition to enact laws of this sort,"[10] Kennedy began his unlikely role, given his conservatism, as an advocate for the rights of sexual minorities. For Kennedy, Amendment 2 was a vindictive act, an attempt to erase sexual minorities from the public sphere and constitutional protection: "We must conclude that Amendment 2 classifies homosexuals not to further a proper legislative end but to make them unequal to everyone else. This Colorado cannot do. A State cannot so deem a class of persons a stranger to its laws."[11] Applying this to marriage equality litigation, the court's determination of the constitutionality of Prop. 8, and potentially other state bans, will involve an assessment of the reasons for the amendment.

Put another way, Kennedy's approach disfavors purely moralistic arguments as the basis for laws. It is not enough to assert that a majority's moral beliefs may justify a law, and this assertion led to a vigorous dissent from Antonin Scalia in which Scalia both criticizes Kennedy's approach and demonstrates his dislike for sexual minorities. For Scalia, moral disapproval alone was a sufficient basis on which to ground a law, and he accused Kennedy of taking the side of elite legal liberals, clearly demonstrating that he (Scalia) had problems with the societal trend toward acceptance of sexual diversity. He objected to Kennedy's "verbally disparaging as bigotry adherence to traditional attitudes." Indeed, his tirade against the majority opinion deserves to be extensively quoted:

> When the Court takes sides in the culture wars, it tends to be with the knights rather than the villains—and more specifically with the Templars, reflecting the views and values of the lawyer class from which the Court's Members are drawn. How that class feels about homosexuality will be evident to anyone who wishes to interview job applicants at virtually any of the Nation's law schools. The interviewer may refuse to offer a job because the applicant is a Republican; because he is an adulterer; because he went to the wrong prep school or belongs to the wrong country club; because he eats snails; because he is a womanizer; because she wears real-animal fur; or even because he hates the Chicago Cubs. But if the interviewer should wish not to be an associate or partner of an applicant because he disapproves of the applicant's homosexuality, then he will have violated the pledge which the Association of American Law Schools requires all its member schools to exact from job interviewers: "assurance of the employer's willingness" to hire homosexuals.[12]

It is unusual to see the politics of resentment so clearly on display in a Supreme Court opinion. Applying the attitudinal model, we can safely predict that Scalia will not vote in favor in marriage equality in any form.

Kennedy also authored the majority opinion in *Lawrence v. Texas* (2003), a case that overruled *Bowers v. Hardwick* (1986) by finally extending the right to privacy to same-sex intimacy. Most notable for the discussion of marriage equality, Kennedy's language was strong and supportive when describing same-sex couples. He did more than simply overrule *Bowers*; he created a rhetorical framework on which to base future expansions of jurisprudence, despite the holding relating to sodomy laws. Indeed, while the case dealt with the negative right to be left alone in the bedroom by the state, Kennedy's language was distinctly positive. The majority opinion in the Massachusetts same-sex marriage case of *Goodridge* was decided a few months after *Lawrence*. As Kennedy stated, "When sexuality finds overt expression in intimate conduct with another person, the conduct can be but one element in a personal bond that is more enduring. . . . Persons in a homosexual relationship may seek autonomy [to define their lives] . . . just as heterosexual persons do."[13]

This language, combined with a concurring opinion from Justice Sandra Day O'Connor invalidating the law using equal protection analysis, provoked the accusation from Justice Scalia in dissent that the decision opened the door to same-sex marriage, despite Kennedy's clear statement to the contrary ("The present case does not involve . . . whether the government must give formal recognition to any relationship that homosexual persons seek to enter.").[14] He noted that O'Connor's "reasoning leaves on pretty shaky grounds state laws limiting marriage to opposite-sex couples."[15] After all, for Scalia, if moral condemnation or tradition was not sufficient to save a statute under due process or equal protection analysis, laws banning sodomy and same-sex marriage were two sides of the same coin, especially if a federal judge saw both as reflecting only moral disapproval of sexual minorities. However, the fact that Scalia was in the minority in both *Romer* and *Lawrence* provided some hope for legal activists that the federal courts were not as hostile toward LGBT rights claims as they had been.

FEDERAL LITIGATION AFTER *ROMER* AND *LAWRENCE*: THE FIRST ORGANIZED FEDERAL MARRIAGE EQUALITY CHALLENGE

Romer was central to an ACLU and Lambda case filed in 2003 (before the *Lawrence* decision) challenging the sweeping nature of Nebraska's first-enacted super-DOMA. The suit responded to the political movement for maximalist approaches to opposing marriage equality from social conservatives by leveraging the new federal gay rights jurisprudence. In the litigation and in public statements, the ACLU and Lambda carefully emphasized that their suit was not designed to mandate marriage equality, only "a level playing field on which to lobby elected officials for family protections." The organizations argued that the amendment violated the Equal Protection Clause under *Romer* and was an unconstitutional bill of attainder, or a law targeting a specific individual or group for punishment.[16]

Federal district judge Joseph Batallion, a Clinton appointee, accepted the arguments of the plaintiffs and added to them. It also violated the First Amendment rights of same-sex couples, because they could not realistically lobby for legal protections short of marriage. And, citing *Lawrence*, the amendment violated the right to intimate association by banning all forms of same-sex relationship recognition, according to Batallion. In the opinion, Batallion also noted that "between fifty percent and seventy-five percent of those petitions [to place the amendment on the ballot] were gathered by volunteers associated with the Church of Jesus Christ of Latter Day Saints."[17] The opinion was a forceful example of legal liberalism, viewing the amendment as the manipulation of the popular amendment process by a religious group to fence out, and punish, a group disfavored by that religion, or at least by the voters who approved of the amendment and who shared the views of the religion.

However, the decision of the Eighth Circuit Court of Appeals signaled to marriage equality litigators that the federal courts were not yet full allies on the project of challenging state amendments through legal liberalism, despite the recent jurisprudential shifts. The three-judge panel, all Republican appointees, ruled unanimously that the Nebraska amendment was constitutionally sound, unwilling to break new legal ground. Interestingly, the judges, in a rather brief opinion, completely rejected the framing relating to the amendment's expansiveness; rather, they viewed the amendment as a ratification of the traditional definition of marriage, justified under rational basis review by the state's interest in promoting procreation. The court cited the "wanton and accidental heterosexual procreation" reasoning of the New York and Indiana cases previously discussed.[18] After a rehearing by the full Eighth Circuit was denied, the ACLU and Lambda decided not to appeal the case to the Supreme Court. In response to the decision, the executive director of the ACLU of Arkansas (under the jurisdiction of the Eighth Circuit) declared, "With the current climate in the courts, I think it's a very bad time to attack this problem [of state constitutional bans on marriage equality]."[19]

Federal litigation not sponsored by the national groups also achieved no results other than creating negative precedent. For instance, a lesbian couple married in Massachusetts challenged the constitutionality of DOMA in a federal district court in Florida, but the judge dismissed the case.[20] Litigation challenging DOMA from a couple in California who sued after being denied a marriage license in Orange County in 2004 was dismissed by the Ninth Circuit Court of Appeals for a lack of standing because they were not yet married by a state.[21] The suit was strongly opposed by litigation groups, but the couple's lawyer criticized this opposition by saying, "You'd never say to a victim of civil rights abuse that this isn't a convenient time to address your rights."[22] Once again, a couple's legal consciousness and what the federal courts were willing to deliver were in conflict. Another "orphan" suit out of Oklahoma, challenging DOMA and the state's constitutional amendment banning same-sex marriage, is still pending in the federal courts after many years of legal wrangling.[23]

PROPOSITION 8 FEDERAL LITIGATION: HOLLYWOOD CASTS A
PERFECT DUO TO CHALLENGE THE AMENDMENT

As we saw in the last chapter, Prop. 8 was challenged, unsuccessfully, in the California courts. Given the negative results with the Nebraska amendment, marriage equality litigators were not sanguine about a federal challenge to Prop. 8. A challenge to California's amendment, unlike the more narrow Nebraska challenge, would potentially ask the federal courts to dismantle the constitutionally entrenched backlash against same-sex marriage. After all, if California's amendment were a violation of equal protection, then all state amendments might be. The general consensus was that this would be asking too much of the conservative majority on the Supreme Court, or even the court's liberals.

While the traditional litigators were wary, other activists saw a federal challenge as a realistic way to eliminate Prop. 8, especially because a political strategy to ask voters to repeal the amendment in a near-future election divided activists in the state. Many did not want to take the chance of another loss at the polls, despite that narrow margin in 2008 and the fact that public opinion was trending in their favor. Other liberal activists, especially the director Rob Reiner and Democratic consultant Chad Griffin, eventually decided on a federal legal challenge. After interning in the Clinton White House, Griffin worked for Reiner for several years as head of a charitable foundation. (In 2012, Griffin was selected to lead the Human Rights Campaign, a leading LGBT political advocacy group.) At lunch one day, Reiner and Griffin encountered Kate Moulene, who suggested the next day that they contact her former brother-in-law, conservative lawyer Theodore (Ted) Olson. Olson was a conservative activist lawyer who argued the case of George W. Bush in *Bush v. Gore* in 2000 and was appointed by Bush to be solicitor general, the federal government's lawyer before the Supreme Court. Eventually, Olson agreed to take the case, along with his foe in *Bush v. Gore*, David Boies, a powerful combination on many levels: skills, bipartisanship, and overall flashiness. Of course, none of this is a guarantee of success, as indicated by criticism of the Hollywood-based litigation from leading litigation groups.[24]

Indeed, despite the star power, many activists were initially skeptical and quite critical, especially with the Supreme Court at the end of the line. Leading gay rights organizations (Lambda Legal, ACLU, Human Rights Campaign, National Center for Lesbian Rights) publicly criticized the lawsuit. Longtime LGBT activist and law professor Nan Hunter described her reservations: "As a purely formal matter, one could argue that Olson and Boies are correct. But invalidating roughly forty state laws that define marriage as between a man and a woman is an awfully heavy lift for the Supreme

Court. . . . I fear that their strategy is: Ted Olson will speak, Anthony Kennedy will listen, and the earth will move," noting that "there's more ego than analysis in that."[25]

However, the prospect of a televised trial, the intention of Northern District of California Chief Judge Vaughn Walker, was eventually viewed by marriage equality litigators as a tremendous educational opportunity. According to Jennifer Pizer of Lambda Legal, "It has the potential to be an extraordinarily powerful teaching moment because it's going to be televised. This is usually just bandied about on attack TV shows. But this promises to be a serious examination of the arguments in a trial setting, with evidence and cross-examination."[26] However, the Supreme Court quashed Walker's attempt to televise the trial.

Prop. 8 Trial and Judge Walker's Opinion

Roughly a decade-and-a-half after Judge Chang's trial in Hawaii, another complete same-sex marriage trial began in January of 2010 (recall that most legal proceedings in same-sex marriage cases revolve around motions for summary judgment, not full-blown trials), this time in federal court. Whereas Chang's trial was relatively untouched by the national media, the trial in Chief Judge Vaughn Walker's courtroom received heavy media attention. In the end, the trial was a significant public relations victory for Olson, Boies, and their supporters, formalized in the organization the American Foundation for Equal Rights. In fact, the trial was a catastrophe for Prop. 8's legal defenders. Their witnesses were few and their testimony was either strongly undermined on cross-examination or directly supported the claims of the plaintiffs. This state of affairs was reflected in Walker's strong opinion invalidating Prop. 8, a decision upheld, more narrowly, on appeal by the Ninth Circuit Court of Appeals.

Beyond the technical legal questions involving fundamental rights and equal protection, Olson and Boies put supporters of Prop. 8 on trial by highlighting the harm to sexual minorities stemming from their tactics and rhetoric, especially the tactic, explored in the last chapter, of emphasizing the harm to children from same-sex marriage and the legal validation of sexual minorities. Or, as Boises characterized the campaign, "characterizing gay people as a threat,"[27] an example of the moralistic condemnation of outsiders identified by James Morone. Indeed, this was the theme of the testimony of Olson and Boies's first several witnesses, themselves plaintiffs in the case. Witness Paul Katami effectively articulated this approach: "We're not a country about us and them. We're supposed to be a country about us, all of us, working in concert, doing things together. That's why we have these [constitutional] protections. My state is supposed to protect me. It's not supposed to discriminate against me."[28] Other themes from the plaintiffs' first witnesses emphasized their coming-out stories, especially the innateness of their sexuality, their traditional desires to get married and have children, and the stigma and humiliation stemming from being relegated to second-class status by the law.

After the plaintiff witnesses, the plaintiffs' lawyers called to the stand a long line of experts—historians, political scientists, psychologists, economists—all designed to demonstrate the negative effects from the exclusion and stigma stemming from laws such as Prop. 8 and to illustrate the many positive effects stemming from the legalization of same-sex marriage, including positive health effects for same-sex married couples and economic benefits associated with new marriages. On cross-examination, the defendants' lawyers attempted to undermine these claims, often by trafficking in stereotypes about sexual minorities, repeatedly noting how lesbians and gay men are different from heterosexuals, or by turning the tables and painting supporters of Prop. 8 as victims of bias and intimidation from marriage equality advocates.

For instance, plaintiffs' witness historian Nancy Cott was used to emphasize that marriage has evolved over time. Her testimony explored the regulation of marriage by the state, largely for economic purposes, explored the reasons for bans on interracial marriage (connecting this to contemporary bans on same-sex marriage), and noted how changing gender roles lead to a rethinking of marriage as more gender-neutral, thus opening the door to consideration of same-sex marriage. Her conclusion?

> I do think there has been an overall direction of change in the way marriage has been defined and understood, and regulated through the states. And that is toward a greater symmetrical understanding of the two partners' roles in the marriage, greater equality of those two partners, and fewer restrictions on the choice of marital partner. Therefore, . . . the shift has been toward reemphasizing the extent to which marriage choice and the zone of privacy and intimacy and familial harmony that marriage ideally should create has been the emphasis on that as a zone of liberty that it should be available to citizens has been more greatly emphasized.[29]

In other words, legal liberalism best responds to changes in the institution over time.

On cross-examination, the defendants portrayed her as an enemy of "traditional" marriage, driven by feminist and queer critiques of the institution, through real or asserted connection to other scholars like Nancy Polikoff. David Thompson also tried to get Cott to agree, unsuccessfully, with an originalist argument—that the founders thought of marriage in Christian monogamous terms, thus locking this definition in stone. Clearly, the narrative created by Prop. 8 supporters at trial was that marriage between a man and a woman, living monogamously with the explicit purpose of raising children, is the recent historical standard, at least as defined by U.S. law. Historian George Chauncy was used to explore the history of discrimination against sexual minorities, based on crude stereotypes of lesbians and gays as mentally ill sexual predators, and the links between this discrimination and the use of popular referenda to restrict the rights of sexual minorities, including Prop. 8. Thus, the narrative being created by this testimony was that Prop. 8 was primarily not about marriage but about fear of sexual minorities, especially with the campaign's strong emphasis on children. On cross-examination David Thompson coaxed Chauncey to admit that anti-gay discrimination was a thing of the past. Chauncey noted societal changes in recent years, but also noted that significant barriers remained for the achievement of full equality for sexual minorities. Thompson's desired narrative was that people opposed same-sex marriage in California out of a concern for "traditional" marriage, not anti-gay animus. If anything, according to Thompson's questions of Chauncey, supporters of Prop. 8 faced animus after the vote from supporters of same-sex marriage, in the form of harassment and protests.

Social psychologist Letitia Peplau testified that marriage generally increases the mental and physical health of individuals in marriages and that, according to the psychological literature, same-sex couples shared similar traits to opposite-sex couples. As a result, Peplau supported same-sex marriage and testified that marriage equality will not diminish opposite-sex marriage. On cross-examination Nicole Moss emphasized that no studies have compared married same-sex couples with married opposite-sex couples and tried to make the argument that gay men were not fit for "traditional" marriage, given what she determined to be higher rates of promiscuity. And, channeling the rationale of the New York Court of Appeals, Moss confirmed with Peplau that child rearing in lesbian and gay relationships is not accidental, in an attempt to undermine the assertion about the similarity of same- and opposite-sex couples, the general thrust of her cross-examination. In other words, lesbians and gay men (especially gay men) don't appreciate monogamous marriage, and they don't need it because they plan for children. They are simply too different from heterosexuals, and the risks are too high to let them have access to the institution of marriage.[30]

Another tactic of the defendants was to attack the motivation of the experts. When Dr. Michael Lamb testified, reflecting the view of all mainstream professional groups dealing with child development and welfare, that "children who are raised by gay and lesbian parents are just as likely to be well-adjusted as children raised by heterosexual parents," he was challenged by the defendants' lawyer for his contribution to liberal political organizations.[31] Indeed, the lawyer attacked scientific knowledge itself as being in no way neutral, all being driven by an agenda—in this case, a liberal, pro-gay agenda. This, of course, is a popular conservative tactic seen in the political fight over policy responses to climate change, for instance.

   In an attempt to counter the defendants' argument that Prop. 8 was merely
the reflection of neoconservative concerns about the decline of an important
social institution, not anti-gay animus, the plaintiffs called as a witness an
activist who worked on encouraging Asian Americans to support Prop. 8,
William Hak-Shing Tam. Under withering questions from David Boies, Tam
admitted that he feared that same-sex marriage would lead to increases in
pedophilia and that he was driven by purely religious motivations and un-
founded facts about homosexuality. Boies also highlighted the coordination
between Tam's organization, the Traditional Family Coalition, and other
organizations behind Prop. 8, such as the National Organization for Marriage, thus attempting to undermine the "we are not anti-gay claims" of Prop.
8 supporters. Tam was chosen as a witness because of a letter to Asian
American Christians in which he claimed that marriage equality activists
wanted to legalize sex with children and stated: "Same-Sex marriage will be
a permanent law in California. One by one, other states would fall into
Satan's hand." Tam was one of the original defendants in the case, stepping
forward to defend Prop. 8 when the state of California refused to defend the
law.[32]
   The defendants' witnesses were far fewer in number (only two), and their
testimony often seemed to undermine the defendants' narrative about Prop.
8. Political scientist Kenneth Miller was used by the defendants to make the
case that gays and lesbians were politically powerful and had strong access to
the legislative process in particular. Interestingly, however, Miller's scholarly work focuses primarily on the initiative process, and he is a critic of
popular initiatives, arguing that they undermine the constitutional system of
representative democracy, are subject to manipulation by powerful groups,
and often are used to the detriment of political minorities—an argument
seemingly tailor-made for the opponents of Prop. 8. After questions demonstrating that Miller lacked familiarity with the scholarship of LGBT rights,
thus attempting to undermine his claims about politically powerful sexual
minorities, David Boies noted Miller's extensive and repeated critiques of
the initiative process. On redirect, Miller indicated that his views had
evolved and that he now viewed initiatives as an appropriate check on judicial activism. Under Boies's questioning, Miller asserted that the right to
same-sex marriage in California was a purely judicial creation with no true
constitutional grounding, while the decision in *Brown v. Board of Education*
(1954), the groundbreaking desegregation case, was simply the application of
a right already existing in the Fourteenth Amendment, but just not discovered
by the Supreme Court until 1954. The role of religion was also central to
Boies's cross-examination. He challenged Miller's assertion that many religious groups strongly opposed Prop. 8, emphasizing the fact that the majority
of religious support (financial and mobilization support) came from churches

opposed to same-sex marriage and supportive of Prop. 8. Boies also coaxed an admission from Miller that most political scientists would view negatively an attempt by a religious majority to impose its views on a minority.[33]

The defendants' second, and last, witness was David Blankenhorn, an activist and author who emphasizes the neoconservative critiques of same-sex marriage. Blankenhorn began his marriage activism out of a concern about the social ills he felt were connected to a decline of fatherhood in the 1980s and 1990s. During direct examination, he, guided by Charles Cooper, emphasized the notion that the legalization of same-sex marriage could lead to the "deinstitutionalization" of marriage, or a fundamental change in the institution. He noted that this process began before the rise of same-sex marriage, with increasing divorce rates and increased single parenting. He testified that same-sex marriage would be the last step in this process of deinstitutionalization. Blankenhorn also repeatedly referenced the need for children to be raised by biological parents, one man and one woman. His testimony was almost excluded by Judge Walker on the grounds that he lacked proper qualifications, such as peer-reviewed publications, after Boies objected to his role as an expert witness.

On cross-examination, Boies picked apart the claim about biological parents, for instance noting (with Blankenhorn agreeing) that this was not consistent with studies on parenting. In fact, there were two narratives presented by Blankenhorn. During direct questioning, marriage was a fragile institution that required a man and a woman in order to properly raise children. This institution would fall apart if same-sex marriage were legalized. On cross-examination, Boies's questions drew from Blankenhorn a defense of same-sex marriage. According to Blankenhorn, same-sex couples and their children would benefit from being married.[34] These differing narratives reflect the fact that Blankenhorn was in the process of changing his mind on same-sex marriage. Indeed, in 2012, he published an op-ed in the *New York Times* declaring his support for marriage equality, reluctantly. While he was still concerned about moving away from purely heterosexual definitions of marriage, he was convinced that the "civil rights" arguments were more powerful. As he wrote,

> I had hoped that the gay marriage debate would be mostly about marriage's relationship to parenthood. But it hasn't been. Or perhaps it's fairer to say that I and others have made that argument, and that we have largely failed to persuade. In the mind of today's public, gay marriage is almost entirely about accepting lesbians and gay men as equal citizens. And to my deep regret, much of the opposition to gay marriage seems to stem, at least in part, from an underlying anti-gay animus. To me, a Southerner by birth whose formative moral experience was the civil rights movement, this fact is profoundly disturbing.[35]

Blankenhorn's epiphany reflects the main narrative of the trial: legal liberalism and expert opinion favor marriage (and parenting) equality, while opposition is driven by theologically supported animus.

Indeed, the trial was a rout, and this was reflected in Judge Walker's sweeping opinion invalidating Prop. 8. Walker completely rejected Blankenhorn's testimony as not credible, and partially rejected the testimony of Professor Miller. He embraced the testimony of the plaintiffs' experts and used it as the foundation for his decision. A methodical statement of facts based on plaintiffs' witnesses' testimony took up most of the opinion's pages. Like Judge Chang, he found arguments against same-sex marriage to be utterly lacking in an empirical foundation. Once again, a legal process rejected purely moralistic or theological claims, claims that continue to resonate significantly in the political arena.

The empirical claims strongly informed Walker's legal analysis. In finding that Prop. 8 violated the fundamental right to marriage, he got around the usual jurisprudential problem associated with arguing that same-sex marriage was a fundamental right by emphasizing the link between gender and marriage. As Walker declared,

> The evidence shows that the movement of marriage away from a gendered institution and toward an institution free from state-mandated gender roles reflects an evolution in the understanding of gender rather than a change in marriage. The evidence did not show any historical purpose for excluding same-sex couples from marriage, as states have never required spouses to have an ability or willingness to procreate in order to marry. Rather, the exclusion exists as an artifact of a time when the genders were seen as having distinct roles in society and in marriage. That time has passed.

Consequently, Walker put forth a gender-neutral version of the historical definition of marriage: "the right to choose a spouse and, with mutual consent, join together and form a household."[36]

Gender also played a role in Walker's equal protection analysis. While he invoked strict scrutiny in his fundamental rights analysis, he relied on rational basis review to find an equal protection violation on the basis of sexual orientation and gender, neither ruling that sexual orientation required a higher standard of review nor involving heightened scrutiny linked to gender-based classifications. He likely judged that his fundamental rights analysis was unlikely to be adopted and provided a more palatable roadmap for higher courts on the equal protection question. Walker argued that none of the arguments presented by the defendants satisfied even rational basis review, thus negating the need for more assertive equal protection analysis. Ultimately, for Walker, Prop. 8 was purely an expression of morality, an unconstitutional motivation under *Romer*: "The evidence at trial regarding the campaign to pass Proposition 8 uncloaks the most likely explanation for its passage: a desire to advance the belief that opposite-sex couples are morally superior to same-sex couples."[37]

This sweeping defeat led the defendants to legally challenge Walker's objectivity, because he came out as a gay man after the trial, by filing a motion to vacate the judgment. Ultimately, this challenge was dismissed, because, if upheld, it would potentially eliminate female judges from hearing cases about gender discrimination or judges of color from hearing racial discrimination cases. It is also problematic to formally ask judges to identify identity-based judicial bias, as this challenges their closely held norm of judicial objectivity, whether true or not. According to the judge who took over the case after Walker retired, "It is not reasonable to presume that a judge is incapable of making an impartial decision about the constitutionality of a law, solely because, as a citizen, the judge could be affected by the proceedings."[38]

The Ninth Circuit's Careful Opinion: Kennedy Is Targeted

On appeal to the liberal Ninth Circuit Court of Appeals, two broad legal questions were argued. Of course, the constitutionality of Prop. 8 was considered, but the question of whether the defendants in the trial possessed standing to appeal the decision was also considered. Recall that the state of California declined to defend the law, thus triggering motions to intervene and defend the law from the leading individuals behind the political campaign for Prop. 8. If they lacked standing, Judge Walker's decision would stand and could not be appealed, thus relegalizing same-sex marriage in California (Walker stayed his decision pending the appeals). In fact, a Supreme Court decision appeared to indicate that citizens cannot defend initiatives and that this could only be done by state officials.[39] Rather than invoke this precedent, however, the three-judge panel remanded the question of standing to the California Supreme Court. Given the prominent role of the initiative process in California, that court ruled that the citizen advocates of Prop. 8 possessed standing, and the Ninth Circuit accepted this determination.[40]

This unusual move was likely a delaying tactic by the Ninth Circuit panel, given that their preference (in retrospect) was to overturn Prop. 8, but their superiors, the Supreme Court, might not be so enthusiastic about doing the same. The concern about the high court was also reflected in the narrowly framed majority opinion of Judge Stephen Reinhardt, considered to be one of the most liberal judges on the Ninth Circuit. Reinhardt focused his analysis on the fact that same-sex marriage was legal in California before Prop. 8 was enacted. The fact that marriage equality existed made the amendment unconstitutional because it took a right away, according to Reinhardt. This is not necessarily the case with a law banning same-sex marriage before a right to it was granted. Of course, this seemingly arbitrary distinction lessens the conflict with state amendments banning same-sex marriage, because only Prop. 8 banned an existing right. Clearly, this was a strategic calculation aimed at making it easier for the Supreme Court to invalidate Prop. 8.

Targeting Anthony Kennedy, Reinhardt noted that Colorado's Amendment 2, invalidated in *Romer*, also took away existing rights, since antidiscrimination laws inclusive of sexual orientation existed in some Colorado jurisdictions before Amendment 2 was enacted. According to Reinhardt, "*Romer* . . . controls where a privilege or protections is withdrawn without a legitimate reason from a class of disfavored individuals."[41] Like Walker, he found no legitimate defense for Prop. 8 and that moral disapproval was the actual motivation for the law. "Under *Romer*, we must infer from Proposition 8's effect on California law that the People took away from Gays and lesbians the right to use the official designation of 'marriage'—and the societal status that accompanies it—because they disapproved of these individuals *as a class* and did not wish them to receive the same official recognition and societal approval . . . that the State makes available to opposite-sex couples."[42] In the dissent in this 2-to-1 decision, Judge Randy Smith, George W. Bush appointee, argued that Prop. 8's narrow goal about marriage made *Romer* inapplicable (Amendment 2 was a more sweeping enactment, in his estimation), and he held that the state's interest in procreation, expressed by the voters in November of 2008, was legitimate enough to sustain the amendment under rational basis review, citing the Nebraska case. Tellingly, the last word of his opinion was "restraint."[43]

It is unlikely that a majority of Supreme Court justices will embrace Walker's approach. The case will be a contest between Reinhardt's minimalism and Smith's restraint.

DOMA LITIGATION AND OTHER FEDERAL LITIGATION

As was noted above, legal activists were far less reluctant to pursue federal challenges relating to marriage equality, especially those attacking the Defense of Marriage Act, specifically section 3 that prohibits federal recognition of same-sex marriage. These challenges were initiated in ideologically favorable federal circuits (First, Second, and Ninth) by GLAD, the ACLU, and Lambda Legal with the goal of applying recently favorable federal jurisprudence to the clear discrimination faced by married same-sex couples from states such as Massachusetts, California, and Connecticut. To date, these suits have met with remarkable success from federal judges. This positive outcome was bolstered by the decision of the Obama administration to cease defending DOMA in court, arguing that sexual orientation classification should be subjected to heightened scrutiny review. Now that the executive branch and many federal judges agree that DOMA is unconstitutional, Supreme Court justices may have an easier task in also striking down DOMA, especially the liberals and Anthony Kennedy, because of this jurisprudential momentum.

THE HOLDER/OBAMA SHIFT AND THE HOUSE BIPARTISAN LEGAL ADVISORY GROUP (BLAG)

The DOMA challenges began in earnest after Democrat Barack Obama took office as president in 2009. He inherited a Justice Department that held the position that DOMA was constitutional, and this remained the policy for the first two years of his administration. The LGBT community and other elements of the Democratic coalition were highly critical of the administration's decision to continue to defend DOMA in court. Ultimately, this stance was reversed. On February 23, 2011, Attorney General Eric Holder wrote to House Speaker (Republican) John Boehner indicating that the president had decided not to defend DOMA. According to Holder, "The President and I have concluded that classifications based on sexual orientation warrant heightened scrutiny and that, as applied to same-sex couples legally married under state law, Section 3 of DOMA is unconstitutional."[44] Using standard equal protection analysis, Holder asserted that sexual minorities faced a history of discrimination, that sexuality was largely immutable, that sexual minorities were politically powerless, and that sexuality was not linked to any legitimate governmental interest. He stated that the administration would continue to enforce DOMA but not defend it in court. Such a decision is rare but not unprecedented. The decision would prove to be enormously consequential. Now the executive branch was on the side of DOMA opposition, and this fact could only make it easier for federal judges to also be skeptical of its constitutionality.

In response, Boehner turned to the House Bipartisan Legal Advisory Group (BLAG) to request that that body defend DOMA, as Republicans obviously disagreed with Obama's decision. The group exists to authorize the House's lawyers to take legal action and is composed of the top three Republican leaders in the House (including Boehner) and the top two Democrats.[45] Obviously, the Democrats were outvoted. Of course, had the Democrats been in the majority, the opposite decision would have been made. Thus, we see further consequential partisan decision making relating to marriage equality.

Once the BLAG lawyers engaged the litigation, they made two broad arguments in defending DOMA. First, *Baker v. Nelson* (1972) was still a binding precedent, thus precluding federal consideration of same-sex marriage cases. Second, sexual orientation fell under rational basis review, and DOMA could be defended with several legitimate rationales:

> In enacting DOMA, Congress rationally was concerned with employing proper caution when facing a possible redefinition of a fundamental social institution. Congress also had rational interests in protecting the public fisc [or treasury], preserving previous legislative judgments and bargains, and in maintaining the uniformity of federal benefits. Congress further had a rational basis in avoiding the administrative difficulties created when same-sex couples move from one state to another or seek recognition of a marriage certificate obtained abroad. Additionally, Congress rationally could have concluded that the traditional definition satisfactorily subsidized and supported stable relationships for the conception and rearing of children and should not be altered. Likewise, Congress rationally could have sought to encourage the rearing of children by parents of both sexes. [46]

However, most federal judges would reject the argument that *Baker* is a controlling precedent and reject the stated rationales either under rational basis review or by applying heightened scrutiny after finding that sexual orientation classifications warranted a higher level of review.

On equal protection analysis, BLAG lawyers denied a history of discrimination against sexual minorities, argued that sexuality was not immutable, and asserted that sexual minorities were powerful, not powerless. According to BLAG, discrimination against sexual minorities was short-lived (mostly in the mid-twentieth century), sexuality is highly fluid and changeable, and lesbians and gay men possess tremendous political clout in the political system. They are nothing like "real" minorities in constitutional jurisprudence. For example, according to BLAG, "what distinguishes sexual orientation from the characteristics that give rise to judicially-recognized suspect classes is that sexual orientation is not an obvious physical characteristic. A person's sexual orientation is often communicated by self-identification—as opposed to readily-identifiable immutable characteristics." [47]

THE GLAD CASES

Given that no previous federal cases involved couples who were legally married in the United States, the question of equal protection as applied to DOMA presented a "fresh" litigation opportunity, and legal activists saw a clear opening. In coordinated litigation GLAD and the Commonwealth of Massachusetts challenged DOMA, arguing that the invisibility of married same-sex couples in Massachusetts constituted unconstitutional discrimination and, in the case of the Commonwealth, violated constitutional principles of federalism.

Federal district judge Joseph L. Tauro, a Richard Nixon appointee, agreed on both counts. Under rational basis review, he found no legitimate rationale for DOMA's enactment, only "irrational prejudice." According to Tauro, "Congress undertook this classification for the one purpose that lies entirely outside of legislative bounds, to disadvantage a group of which it disapproves."[48] More interesting was Tauro's use of federalism arguments. He clearly viewed Congress as stepping on the authority of states to define marriage, and he noted that DOMA represented the first instance of Congress attempting to define marriage for the entire nation. Indeed, in the Commonwealth case, he found DOMA to be a violation of the Tenth Amendment. DOMA requires that states discriminate against married same-sex couples in using federal dollars when states administer state/federal programs, such as Medicaid. As Tauro declared, "That DOMA plainly intrudes on a core area of state sovereignty—the ability to define the marital status of its citizens—also convinces the court that the statute violates the Tenth Amendment."[49] Of course, many commentators noted the irony of a liberal outcome dictated by state's rights arguments usually embraced by conservatives, especially the Tea Party.

The Massachusetts cases were consolidated on appeal to the First Circuit Court of Appeals, and that court's decision to also invalidate DOMA reflected an attempt, like the Ninth Circuit, to soften the edges of a lower court decision for the Supreme Court. The unanimous decision, by one Democratic and two Republican appointees,[50] represented the first invalidation of DOMA by a federal appellate court. The opinion by Michael Boudin toned down Tauro's federalism analysis by noting that the issue of marriage is connected to many federal policies, thus giving Congress a legitimate interest in the definition of marriage. For Boudin, state and federal governments shared jurisdiction over marriage. As he noted, "Supreme Court interpretations of the Tenth Amendment have varied over the years but those in force today have struck down statutes only where Congress sought to commandeer state governments or otherwise dictate the *internal operations* of state government."[51]

However, this assessment of federalism jurisprudence may have been changed by the strong state's rights analysis in the 2012 Supreme Court decision on the Affordable Care Act, *National Federation of Independent Business v. Sibelius*, just a few weeks later. While the First Circuit panel may have been trying to soften Tauro's analysis, he may actually be more in line with views of the Supreme Court's conservative majority. In *Sibelius*, a Supreme Court majority of the five conservatives and two liberals, Elena Kagan and Stephen Breyer, ruled that Congress exceeded its authority at the expense of the states by requiring that states comply with the Affordable Care Act's expansion of Medicaid with a penalty of the elimination of all federal Medicaid funding for noncompliance, not simply the new funding for the expansion. The court viewed this as excessively coercive and violating state autonomy. Judge Tauro was similarly concerned with a threat from the Department of Veterans Affairs to rescind $19 million from Massachusetts if the state authorized the burial of a same-sex spouse in a federally funded cemetery. In fact, U.S. Solicitor General Donald Verrilli cited *Sibelius* in a brief urging the court to take the First Circuit case and strike down DOMA. Ironically, the lead lawyer for BLAG is Paul Clement, who also argued against the Affordable Care Act (and for state's rights) before the Supreme Court while Verrilli defended the law before the court. The DOMA litigation is a rematch for the two lawyers, but their views on federalism have switched from *Sibelius*.[52]

Boudin also left *Baker* intact, but went around the precedent, because same-sex marriage was already legal in Massachusetts. He then applied a nondeferential rational basis review warranted by the fact that DOMA classified on the basis of sexual orientation and that states traditionally regulated marriage. Relying on cases like *Romer*, Boudin asserted that Supreme Court precedents "have both intensified scrutiny of purported justifications where minorities are subject to discrepant treatment and have limited the permissible justifications. And . . . , in areas where state regulation has traditionally governed, the Court may require that the federal government interest in intervention be shown with special clarity."[53] Under this standard, the court rejected BLAG's rationales for DOMA, thus falling short under the court's heightened rational basis review. Interestingly, the court rejected the lower court's finding that DOMA was motivated by animus or Tauro's "irrational prejudice"; rather, it was merely an attempt to preserve tradition—not enough to survive rational basis review but not mean-spirited. Of course, following this approach would allow the Supreme Court to challenge Congress without calling members of Congress prejudiced.

In a similar GLAD-sponsored challenge to DOMA in Connecticut, District Judge Vanessa Bryant, a George W. Bush appointee, found Section 3 of DOMA unconstitutional. Bryant ruled that sexual orientation merited the application of heightened scrutiny but found that this was not needed. She rejected all of BLAG's arguments under rational basis review. She was particularly critical of an argument made by BLAG lawyers in a motion to dismiss the case: respect for self-government calls for judicial timidity in the realm of same-sex marriage. Calling this argument "curiously misguided and unavailing" and citing *Marbury v. Madison* (1803) and the "bedrock principle of our system of government [judicial review]," Bryant noted that the "argument evinces a fundamental misunderstanding of the role of judicial review and ignores the resounding voices of the Connecticut, New Hampshire, and Vermont constituencies who have, through the democratic process, afforded same-sex couples the right to marry."[54] By the time of this ruling, Bryant had the benefit of the Massachusetts cases invalidating Section 3, as well as other district court invalidations, discussed below, not to mention the new stance of the Justice Department, to undergird her judicial assertiveness. The GLAD litigation was clearly well planned and well timed.

OTHER COORDINATED FEDERAL CHALLENGES

Golinski v. OPM, Windsor v. U.S., and *Dragovich v. Department of Treasury*

Karen Golinski worked as a staff attorney for the Ninth Circuit Court of Appeals. After marrying her partner of twenty years in 2008 in California, she requested spousal coverage in her insurance plan as a federal court employee. This created an interbranch fight between the Ninth Circuit and the executive branch's Office of Personnel Management. Acting in his capacity of the highest administrator of the court, Chief Judge Alex Kozinski, a Ronald Reagan appointee, ordered the Administrative Office of the United States Courts to complete the process of authorizing coverage. He argued that the courts could provide coverage beyond the limitations of DOMA, particularly given that the Ninth Circuit Court prohibits discrimination on the basis of sexual orientation. Indeed, Kozinski invoked the separation of powers in asserting that he was not bound by the executive's determination of who was entitled to spousal insurance coverage. The process essentially ended in a stalemate, with each side asserting the authority to define federal benefit coverage in this administrative law dispute.[55]

Constitutional issues were engaged when Golinski, supported by Lambda Legal, sued the Office of Personnel Management to change its DOMA-driven decision and award coverage. Judge Jeffrey White, a George W. Bush appointee, applied heightened scrutiny and found BLAG's justifications of DOMA to be invalid. As a result, he found in favor of Golinski. In doing so, White overruled an important precedent from the Ninth Circuit, *High Tech Gays v. Defense Industrial Security Clearance Office* (1990). In that case, the court ruled that sexual orientation falls under rational basis review, especially given the Supreme Court's condemnation of homosexuality in *Bowers v. Hardwick* and the Supreme Court's holding that same-sex sexual conduct could be criminalized. However, according to White, *Lawrence* rendered *High Tech Gays* impotent as a precedent. In finding for the application of heightened scrutiny, White relied heavily on Golinski's expert testimony proffered in briefs (rather than testimony in open court, as in the Prop. 8 trial). He was quite dismissive of BLAG's attempts to undermine this testimony. Particularly regarding a source cited by BLAG criticizing studies about same-sex parenting, White declared: "This is a three-page, non-scientific article by an author with no professional expertise in child development, published by a popular online magazine without peer review."[56] Perhaps anticipating higher levels of review, White ruled that DOMA fell also under rational basis review and downplayed anti-gay statements of congressional supporters of DOMA.

Thea Spayer and Edith "Edie" Windsor had been a couple since shortly after meeting in the mid-1960s. In 2007, they were married in Canada. Spayer died in 2009, leaving her estate to Windsor. Of course, had one of them been a man, Windsor would have paid no taxes on the estate. But because both were women, Windsor paid $363,053 in federal taxes. With the assistance of the ACLU, she sued to get the money back, arguing that DOMA was a violation of equal protection. Given her grandmotherly demeanor and charm, Windsor is a sympathetic challenger to DOMA. U.S. District Judge Barbara Jones, a Bill Clinton appointee, agreed and awarded Windsor the amount she paid in taxes plus interest and court costs.[57]

Jones declined to apply heightened scrutiny, as requested by Windsor's lawyers, but she, like her colleagues in the other recent DOMA challenges (she became the fifth district court judge to invalidate DOMA),[58] found that DOMA was unconstitutional under rational basis review. She also declined to apply *Baker*, declaring: "The case before the Court does not present the same issue as that presented in *Baker*," given that DOMA does not forbid the right to same-sex marriage, only the federal recognition of such marriages.[59] Citing Tauro's decision, she asserted that DOMA "does not square with our federalist system of government" in its interference with state autonomy over family policy.[60]

In yet another example of the legal tension created by the legalization of same-sex marriage in some states and the lack of federal recognition of those marriages, California state employees sued over the denial of long-term-care benefits for their same-sex spouses and domestic partners. A law enacted by Congress the same year as DOMA incentivized the offering of long-term-care insurance through tax subsidies, but the law specifically excluded unrelated (by birth, adoption, or opposite-sex marriage) members of the same household. Applying rational basis review, federal district judge Claudia Wilkin, a Bill Clinton appointee, again found BLAG's rationale lacking and held that DOMA was based on animus, and, notably, she applied this animus finding to both married couples and those in domestic partnerships. Like White in *Golinski*, Wilkin sidestepped *Baker* and found that *High Tech Gays* was essentially overruled by *Lawrence*. She also rebuffed BLAG's attempts to apply *Adams v. Howerton* (discussed in chapter 2) by citing *Lawrence* and changes in social reality. She declared, for instance, that "*Adams'* rationale that same-sex couples never produce children has been proven false. . . . The ability of same-sex couples to have children is recognized in the Ninth Circuit," through cases such as *Perry v. Schwarzenegger*.[61]

Immigration, Bankruptcy, and Military Benefits

Federal law does not recognize the same-sex spouses of military personnel, despite the ending of the ban on open military service in 2011. Lesbians and gay men may serve openly, but, if married, their spouses are not entitled to benefits offered to opposite-sex couples. This is being challenged in federal court in several cases. As of this writing, none have been decided. In addition, same-sex spouses are not recognized fully for immigration purposes. Indeed, the status of married same-sex couples was placed in a confusing situation after President Obama announced that his administration would not defend, but would continue enforcing, DOMA. Immigration officials initially appeared to indicate that the pending deportations of any such couples would be halted. Officials later clarified that this halting was only temporary as government lawyers analyzed this issue.[62] Individuals in opposite-sex marriage can sponsor their noncitizen spouse for a green card and permanent resident status, but this does not apply to same-sex couples under DOMA. This litigation is another element of the strategy to overturn DOMA, given that federal law and policy is extensively tied to marital status.[63] On the question of immigration, however, *Adams v. Howerton* may prove to be a significant barrier to success. U.S. District Court judge Stephen Wilson, a Ronald Reagan appointee, threw out a challenge to DOMA as applied to immigration policy by citing *Adams*.[64]

NEVADA AND HAWAII

From the most recent round of federal litigation, it appears to be an easier job to ask judges to strike down DOMA than to ask them to find a right to same-sex marriage in the Constitution. To date, only Judge Walker has ruled in favor of a general federal constitutional right to same-sex marriage, but the Ninth Circuit narrowed Walker's ruling.

Another judge in the Ninth Circuit strongly rejected claims made by same-sex couples, later joined by Governor Neil Abercrombie, in Hawaii that Hawaii's ban on same-sex marriage should be struck down like Prop. 8, given that it withdrew a right that the Hawaii courts were in the process of establishing and that had been provisionally declared in *Baehr v. Lewin* and affirmed by Judge Chang's decision. Notably, this litigation is not supported by national litigation groups, only a local law firm and Equality Hawaii. Citing nearly every marriage equality–negative precedent from federal and state litigation (including the controversial "accidental heterosexual procreation" decision in *Hernandez v. Robles*), Reagan appointee Alan Kay affirmed *Baker* and *High Tech Gays* as controlling precedents, applied rational basis review (after thoroughly rejecting the plaintiffs' due process claim asserting a fundamental right to same-sex marriage and their claim of gender discrimination) to the couple's equal protection claims, and asserted that the state could legitimately limit marriage to opposite-sex couples, largely to preserve procreation. He accepted the more conservative narrative that only heterosexuals are true parents. "Same-sex couples cannot naturally procreate," Kay emphasized.[65] He also disagreed that the situation in Hawaii was similar to California, given that no same-sex couples were ever married in the state and the Hawaii amendment did not directly ban same-sex marriage. Interestingly, on the question of expert evidence, Kay asserted that "[t]he legislature could rationally conclude that other things being equal, it is best for children to be raised by a parent of each sex."[66] Unlike Walker and other federal judges siding with the strong consensus of family experts, he asserted that the worth of same-sex parents was "debatable,"[67] primarily by citing the conservative intervenor's (the Hawaii Family Forum) use of a controversial study by University of Texas sociologist Mark Regnerus. A subsequent review of the study by the journal in which it appeared, *Social Science Research*, noted serious flaws in the study's methodology and the journal's review process, but Kay used it to undermine all of the other studies pointing in the other direction.[68] Judge Kay also rejected the plaintiffs' "separate but equal arguments," viewing the state's civil union law not as a signal of inferiority but of genuine concern for the status of same-sex couples. A judicially imposed finding for marriage equality "would 'short-circuit' the legislative actions that have been taking place in Hawaii."[69]

While this high-minded defense of judicial restraint is perhaps laudable, Arthur Leonard has noted that Kay also discussed, in a footnote, laws banning incest in the context of deferring to legislative judgments about preserving procreation. While this comparison is often made in the political arena, it is less commonly seen in judicial opinions. Leonard also noted Kay's use of arguments from the Witherspoon Institute, the conservative organization that funded the Regnerus study "so that defenders of traditional marriage would have a published article in a 'respectable' social science journal to cite."[70] Given the strong scientific consensus about same-sex parenting reflected in the Prop. 8 trial testimony, conservative opponents have a strong incentive to work aggressively to challenge the professional consensus if they are to have any hope of defending governments' protection of opposite-sex-only marriage under the rational basis test.

Lambda Legal has higher hopes for a federal challenge to Nevada's ban on same-sex marriage. Lambda's complaint, filed in April of 2012, reflects the rapidly evolving federal equal protection jurisprudence, driven by courts and the executive branch, in its full-throated defense of a legal liberal interpretation of the Equal Protection Clause as applied to relationship equality, both in terms of sexual orientation and sex. Interestingly, gone were arguments about fundamental rights and due process, perhaps a signal that litigators have seen the "lack of history and tradition" writing on the wall, as even the most liberal judges have difficulty justifying this interpretation. According to Lambda, the state's constitutional ban on same-sex marriage and the domestic partnership law places same-sex couples in a "second class status and inflicts serious and irreparable harm upon Plaintiffs and other same-sex couples and children" and "denies same-sex couples equal dignity and respect," the complaint reads. While the utility of fundamental rights arguments may be waning, a sex-based discrimination argument was included in the complaint. As the complaint states, "Plaintiffs have failed to conform to the prevailing and State-enforced stereotype that men should marry women and that women should marry men."[71] Of course, Lambda is requesting the opposite of Kay's approach in Hawaii. They are asking judges to be more aggressive than the Ninth Circuit in *Perry* and to dismiss the attempts by Democrats to make the best of a bad situation for relationship equality in Nevada. In other words, for Lambda, gradualism is no longer enough.

PREDICTION FOR THE SUPREME COURT

A wave of same-sex marriage cases is headed to the Supreme Court after years of activist avoidance of the high court. As of this writing, the Supreme Court has started review of the Ninth Circuit's *Perry* decision. Interestingly, Olson and Boies asked the court not to take the case, allowing the Ninth Circuit decision to stand, thus legalizing same-sex marriage in California only. This is a shift from their initial "all the way to the Supreme Court" approach. Of course, a reversal would be a devastating loss for same-sex-marriage advocates. In addition, the court granted *certiorari* in the *Windsor* case, after the Second Circuit Court of Appeals upheld Judge Jones's opinion in that case.

As was stated at the start of this chapter, it is difficult to envision that the Supreme Court would rule expansively on a right to same-sex marriage under either fundamental rights or equal protection analysis, given the current ideological makeup of the court and the implications of challenging state constitutional bans on same-sex relationships more broadly. Some conservatives, like Scalia, are quite hostile to the idea of marriage equality, or at least a judicial role in its creation and enforcement. We can very likely also place Clarence Thomas and Samuel Alito in this camp. The stance of the chief justice, a conservative, is more complicated to predict, given that he is also concerned with the court's image. As public opinion trends in the direction of support for marriage equality, he may not want to create a precedent that places the court clearly on the wrong side of history. This does not mean that he will vote to create a broad right to same-sex marriage, simply that he may not support a sweeping denial of any legitimate constitutional protection for same-sex couples.

Indeed, the most interesting vote on the case may not be a vote on the merits, but the vote to grant *certiorari*, which is granted when four justices agree to hear and decide a case. Fearing what the more conservative members may do with a potential majority opinion, the court's liberals (Ruth Bader Ginsburg, Stephen Breyer, Sonia Sotomayor, and Elena Kagan) may have voted against granting *certiorari*. Alternately, they may agree with the Obama administration's position that sexual orientation discrimination should be reviewed under heightened scrutiny and desire to push the court in the same direction, but this may be done more safely in the DOMA challenges. For both ideological wings of the court, however, the vote of Anthony Kennedy, both on *certiorari* and the merits, is crucial, as was discussed in the analysis of the Ninth Circuit's opinion. It is quite likely that the court will invalidate DOMA, however. Much more legal momentum exists for this outcome, as illustrated by the cases discussed above. It is more difficult to imagine an expansive ruling in *Perry*.

NOTES

1. See Thomas M. Keck, *The Most Activist Court in History: The Road to Modern Judicial Activism* (Chicago: University of Chicago Press, 2004).

2. See Michael J. Klarman, *From Jim Crow to Civil Rights: The Supreme Court and the Struggle for Racial Equality* (New York: Oxford University Press, 2004).

3. *National Federation of Independent Business v. Sibelius*, 567 U.S. __ (2012).

4. Jeffrey A. Segal and Harold J. Spaeth, *The Supreme Court and the Attitudinal Model Revisited* (New York: Cambridge University Press, 2002).

5. Alexander Hamilton, et al., *The Federalist* (New York: Modern Library), 504.

6. Lee Epstein, et al., "Constitutional Interpretation from a Strategic Perspective," in *Making Policy, Making Law: An Interbranch Perspective*, Mark C. Miller and Jeb Barnes, eds. (Washington, DC: Georgetown University Press, 2004), 170–88.

7. Barry Friedman, "The Politics of Judicial Review," *Texas Law Review* 84 (2005), 257–337.

8. For more on new institutionalist approaches, see Howard Gillman and Cornell Clayton, eds., *The Supreme Court in American Politics: New Institutionalist Interpretations* (Lawrence: University Press of Kansas, 1999); and Michael McCann, *Rights at Work: Pay Equity Reform and the Politics of Legal Mobilization* (Chicago: University of Chicago Press, 1994).

9. 434 U.S. 374 (1978), 384.

10. 517 U.S. 620 (1996), 633.

11. *Romer v. Evans*, 635.

12. *Romer*, 652–53.

13. 539 U.S. 558 (2003), 567, 574.

14. *Lawrence v. Texas*, 578.

15. *Lawrence*, 601.

16. Kevin O'Hanlon, "Judge Strikes Down Nebraska's Same-Sex Marriage Ban," *Associated Press*, May 12, 2005. The quote is from David Buckel, senior staff attorney at Lambda Legal.

17. *Citizens for Equal Protection v. Bruning*, 368 F. Supp. 2d (D. Neb., 2005), 987.

18. *Citizens for Equal Protection v. Bruning*, 455 F.3d 859 (8th Cir. Neb., 2006).

19. Andrew DeMillo, "Gay Marriage Supporters Discouraged by Federal Court Ruling," *Associated Press*, July 14, 2006.

20. *Wilson v. Ake*, 354 F.Supp.2d 1298 (M.D. Fla. 2005).

21. *Smelt v. County of Orange*, 447 F.3d 673 (9th Cir. 2006).

22. Bob Egelko, "Judge Calls Defense of Marriage Act Legally Sound," *San Francisco Chronicle*, June 17, 2005, A4.

23. The case is *Bishop v. United States*, United States District Court, Northern District of Oklahoma, Case No. 04-CV-848-TCK-TLW.

24. Margaret Talbot, "Gay Marriage, *Perry v. Schwarzenegger*, and the Supreme Court," *New Yorker*, January 27, 2010; Ned Martel, "New Head of Human Rights Campaign Aims to Stop Losing Streak for Gay Marriage," *Washington Post*, July 25, 2012, http://www.washingtonpost.com/politics/new-head-of-human-rights-campaign-aims-to-stop-losing-streak-for-gay-marriage/2012/07/25/gJQARmNt9W_print.html.

25. Talbot.

26. Jesse McKinley, "Two Ideological Foes Unite to Overturn Proposition 8," *New York Times*, January 11, 2010, A9.

27. Trial transcript, *Perry v. Schwarzenegger*, United States Northern District of California, No.C 09-2292-VRW, January 11, 2010, vol. 1, 109.

28. Trial transcript, January 11, 2010, vol. 1, 116.

29. Trial transcript, *Perry v. Schwarzenegger*, United States Northern District of California, No.C 09-2292-VRW, January 12, 2010, vol. 2, 247.

30. Trial transcript, *Perry v. Schwarzenegger*, United States Northern District of California, No.C 09-2292-VRW, January 13, 2010, vol. 3.

31. Trial transcript, *Perry v. Schwarzenegger*, United States Northern District of California, No.C 09-2292-VRW, January 15, 2010, vol. 5, 1025.

32. See trial transcript, *Perry v. Schwarzenegger*, United States Northern District of California, No. C 09-2292-VRW, January 21, 2010, vol. 8. The text of Tam's letter can be found at http://www.afer.org/press-releases/statement-on-supreme-court-decision-on-prop-8-cameras/.

33. See trial transcript, *Perry v. Schwarzenegger*, United States Northern District of California, No. C 09-2292-VRW, January 25, 2010, vol. 10; January 26, vol. 11.

34. See trial transcript, *Perry v. Schwarzenegger*, United States Northern District of California, No. C 09-2292-VRW, January 26, 2010, vol. 12. Blankenhorn's testimony begins in vol. 11.

35. David Blankenhorn, "How My Views on Gay Marriage Changed," *New York Times*, June 23, 2012.

36. *Perry* v. *Schwarzenegger*, 704 F. Supp. 2d 921 (N.D. Cal., Aug. 4, 2010), 993.

37. *Perry* v. *Schwarzenegger*, 1002–3.

38. Kevin Fayle, "Gay Judge's Prop 8 Decision Survives Bias Claim," Findlaw.com, June 14, 2011, http://blogs.findlaw.com/courtside/2011/06/gay-judges-prop-8-decision-survives-bias-claim.html.

39. *Arizonans for Official English v. Arizona*, 520 U.S. 43 (1997).

40. *Perry* v. *Brown*, 671 F.3d 1052 (9th Cir., Feb. 7, 2012), 1072.

41. *Perry* v. *Brown*, 1085.

42. *Perry* v. *Brown*, 1092.

43. *Perry* v. *Brown*, 1113.

44. Letter from U.S. Attorney General Eric Holder to Speaker of the House of Representatives John Boehner, February 23, 2011.

45. Felicia Sonmez and Ben Pershing, "House Republicans Take Action to Defend the Defense of Marriage Act," washingtonpost.com, March 4, 2011, http://voices.washingtonpost.com/2chambers/2011/03/house_republicans_take_action.html.

46. Brief for the Bipartisan Legal Advisory Group of the United States House of Representatives, *Gill v. Office of Personnel Management*, First Circuit Court of Appeal, Case No. 10-2204, September 22, 2011, 7.

47. Intervenor-Defendant's Sur-Reply in Opposition to Plaintiff's Motion to Summary Judgment, *Pedersen v. Office of Personnel Management*, Civil Action No. 3:10-cv-1750 (VLB), U.S. District Court, District of Connecticut, October 5, 2011, 9.

48. *Gill v. Office of Personnel Management*, 699 F. Supp. 2d 374 (D. Mass. 2010), 396–97.

49. *Massachusetts v. Department of Health and Human Services*, 698 F. Supp. 2d 234 (D. Mass. 2010), 249.

50. The author of the opinion, Michael Boudin, was appointed by George Bush; Sandra Lea Lynch was appointed by Bill Clinton; and Juan Torruella was appointed by Ronald Reagan.

51. *Massachusetts v. Department of Health and Human Services*, 682 F.3d 1 (1st Cir. 2012), 12.

52. Adam Liptak, "In the Next Term, a Possible Rematch on a Different Law," *New York Times*, July 10, 2012, A14.

53. *Massachusetts v. Department of Health and Human Services* (1st Cir. 2012), 15.

54. *Pedersen v. Office of Personnel Management*, slip opinion, Civil Action No. 3:10-cv-1750 (VLB), U.S. District Court, District of Connecticut, July 31, 2012, 98–99.

55. *Golinski v. Office of Personnel Management*, 824 F. Supp. 2d 968 (N.D. Cal. 2012), 974–76.

56. *Golinski*, 992.

57. *Windsor v. U.S.*, slip opinion, United States District Court, Southern District of New York, Case No. 1:10-cv-08435-BSJ-JCF, June 6, 2012, 3–5.

58. Basil Katz, "Defense of Marriage Act Unconstitutional: Judge," Reuters, June 6, 2012.

59. *Windsor*, 10.

60. *Windsor*, 24.

61. *Dragovich v. United States Department of Treasury*, slip opinion, United States District Court, Northern District of California, Case No. 4:10-cv-01564-CW, May, 24, 2012, 18.

62. Julia Preston, "Confusion Over Policy on Married Gay Immigrants," *New York Times*, March 30, 2011, A14.

63. The group sponsoring the suit, Immigration Equality, asserts: "The lawsuit will help defeat   DOMA."   http://www.immigrationequality.org/issues/couples-and-families/doma-lawsuit-faqs/.

64. *Lui v. Holder*, slip opinion, Case No. 2:11-CV-02167-SVW (C.D. Cal. Sept. 28, 2011).

65. *Jackson v. Abercrombie*, slip opinion, Case No. 11-00734-ACK-KSC, (D. Haw. August 8, 2012), 101.

66. *Jackson v. Abercrombie*, 6.

67. *Jackson v. Abercrombie*, 6.

68. Mark Regnerus, "How Different Are the Adult Children of Parents Who Have Same-Sex Relationships? Findings from the New Family Structures Study," *Social Science Research* 41:4 (July 2012), 752–70. Tom Bartlett, "Controversial Gay Parenting Study is Severely Flawed, Journal Audit Finds," *Chronicle of Higher Education*, Percolator Blog, July 26, 2012, http://chronicle.com/blogs/percolator/controversial-gay-parenting-study-is-severely-flawed-journals-audit-finds/30255. Robert George is a senior fellow at the Witherspoon Institute.

69. *Jackson v. Abercrombie*, 115.

70. Arthur S. Leonard, "Federal Court Rejects Hawaii Marriage Challenge," Leonard Link blog, http://newyorklawschool.typepad.com/leonardlink/2012/08/federal-court-rejects-hawaii-marriage-challenge.html.

71. Complaint, *Sevick v. Sandoval*, United States District Court, District of Nevada, Case No. 2:12-cv-00578, April 10, 2012, 3, 26, 28.

Chapter Nine

Conclusion

Regardless of the outcome on the Supreme Court, the political and legal movement for marriage equality has been enormously consequential. While significant barriers remain, public opinion has shifted in favor of same-sex marriage, as several national polls indicated by 2011 and 2012. Given the fact that younger people are more supportive, this trend will likely continue. The question remains whether policy and law will catch up, and how quickly. Certainly, support from the Supreme Court could accelerate this process, but avoidance of the issue could confirm the status quo of a patchwork of state legal protections and prohibitions. A strong opinion from the court (one striking down all state amendments) could trigger a short-term backlash, as opponents of marriage equality defend state autonomy and the traditional values of many states, but this would likely wane, given the overall trend in public opinion in the direction of support for marriage equality.

Indeed, events in 2012 reflected both significant change and continued resistance. After Vice President Joe Biden indicated his support for marriage equality on *Meet the Press*, increased pressure was placed on Barack Obama to declare his support, a change from his "civil unions but not marriage" position. Shortly thereafter, Obama declared his support for marriage equality, leading to speculation that the change in position would hurt him with socially conservative Democrats, especially socially conservative African Americans. His decision appears to have created the opposite effect, however. Polls captured significant increases in support for same-sex marriage among African Americans after the president sided strongly with marriage equality, especially in Maryland, where this block of voters significantly affected the outcome on the referendum on the same-sex marriage law in November of 2012. In the wake of Obama's announcement, both the NAACP and the National Council of La Raza announced support for marriage equality. Thus, the legal liberal civil rights paradigm appears to be trumping that of religious traditionalism on sexuality and gender. More broadly, Obama's shift in position appeared to have little effect on his reelection and his overall standing with voters.

Next, the Democratic Party endorsed marriage equality, for the first time, in its 2012 national platform. The platform reads:

> We support the right of all families to have equal respect, responsibilities, and protections under the law. We support marriage equality and support the movement to secure equal treatment under law for same-sex couples. We also support the freedom of churches and religious entities to decide how to administer marriage as a religious sacrament without government interference. We oppose discriminatory federal and state constitutional amendments and other attempts to deny equal protection of the laws to committed same-sex couples who seek the same respect and responsibilities as other married couples. We support the full repeal of the so-called Defense of Marriage Act and the passage of the Respect for Marriage Act [a proposed law that would repeal DOMA].

The framing of the issue as one of religious freedom is particularly interesting, beyond the clear endorsement of legal liberal principles.

This, of course, contrasts with the Republican Party national platform. The platform, however, muted the explicitly anti-gay and theological justifications for marriage-equality opposition, instead relying mostly on neoconservative arguments, with a notable, though arguably hollow, nod to legal liberalism:

> The institution of marriage is the foundation of civil society. Its success as an institution will determine our success as a nation. It has been proven by both experience and endless social science studies that traditional marriage is best for children. . . . Furthermore, the future of marriage affects freedom. The lack of family formation not only leads to more government costs, but also to more government control over the lives of its citizens in all aspects. We recognize and honor the courageous efforts of those who bear the many burdens of parenting alone, even as we believe that marriage, the union of one man and one woman must be upheld as the national standard, a goal to stand for, encourage, and promote through laws governing marriage. We embrace the principle that all Americans should be treated with respect and dignity.[1]

The argument about the threat of same-sex marriage, though not from (presumably heterosexual) single parents, to children is combined with the threat that marriage equality poses to freedom itself. While many within the party are openly challenging this approach, the party is still overwhelmingly opposed to relationship equality. Given the connection between the party and the Religious Right, this will not soon change. As we have seen, a handful of Republican state legislators were instrumental in enacting equality policies in the Northeast, but they were lone voices in their party. Thus, the future of marriage equality in the United States may depend significantly on the fortunes of the Democratic Party in Washington, D.C., and in the states.

RELIGION AND POLITICAL CULTURE: THE CHICK-FIL-A CONTROVERSY

The cultural battle over a fast-food chicken restaurant in the summer of 2012 illustrates the short-term barriers to the nationalization of marriage equality policy in the United States and highlights the strong connection between religion and political opposition to same sex–relationship recognition. In addition, opponents of marriage equality were emboldened by supporters' invocation of negative freedom arguments to defend that opposition. Indeed, what began as a strong critique of those opposed to equality for same-sex couples ended as a victory for the opposition, as their rights of expression were seen by the media and the public as trumping equality concerns.

The controversy began when the president of Chick-fil-A, Dan Cathy, made statements through Christian media outlets reflecting his belief in the "biblical definition of the family unit." As he stated in a radio interview, "As it relates to society in general, I think we are inviting God's judgment on our nation when we shake our fist at him and say, 'We know better than you as to what constitutes a marriage.'"[2] Cathy is a Southern Baptist, and his company is privately held and run according to his religious principles. Indeed, *Forbes* described the company as a cult in a 2007 profile.[3] Restaurants are closed on Sundays and prospective franchisees are asked about their religion and marital status. The company is headquartered in the South, which is also the location of most of their restaurants, a region where relationship equality policies are virtually nonexistent.

In response to these statements, pro–marriage equality activists and politicians condemned what they considered to be his discriminatory statements, including the mayor of Boston, Thomas Menino, who wrote the company indicating that the city would oppose the company's efforts to open a franchise in the city. A city council member and the mayor of Chicago, Rahm Emanuel, took similar positions. However, this resulted in a backlash, including from many in the lesbian and gay rights movement, that this was a violation of First Amendment rights. On a separate front, activists called for a "kiss-in" of same-sex couples at Chick-fil-A restaurants. In response, former presidential candidate and social conservative Mike Huckabee called for a Chick-fil-A appreciation day. As he posted on his Facebook page, "The goal is simple: Let's affirm a business that operates on Christian principles and whose executives are willing to take a stand for the Godly values we espouse by simply showing up and eating at Chick-fil-A on Wednesday,

August 1. Too often, those on the left make corporate statements to show support for same sex marriage, abortion, or profanity, but if Christians affirm traditional values, we're considered homophobic, fundamentalists, hate-mongers, and intolerant." The day was very well attended with customers explicitly stating solidarity with Cathy and Huckabee or their right to express their opinion. The kiss-in was less successful, and many in the lesbian and gay rights movement viewed the episode as a loss. Thus, Cathy was supported by religious moralism and libertarianism, the potent forces in American politics that act as a significant constraint on sexuality-based equality movements. Indeed, the turnout on August 1, and many of the statements of attendees containing overt hostility for sexual minorities, evoked Jonathan Goldberg-Hiller's description of the movement for the Hawaii amendment in 1998 discussed in chapter 1—an attempted purging of sexual minorities from the culture, law, and politics of the polity.

Babst's argument about bans on same-sex marriage amounting to a religious establishment is confirmed by this book's examination of the close ties between organized religion and the movement to prevent marriage equality. This is further confirmed through an examination of worldwide developments. More secular politics provides the setting for the expansion of relationship recognition politics, while political religion is a barrier, especially when parties reflecting traditional religious views hold power, as the discussion in chapter 3 demonstrates.

FEDERALISM

Federalism has given unique power to religious conservatism in the United States, as a result of the state definition of marriage and the existence of state-based citizen initiatives and referenda, a potent mix of institutions not seen in most other liberal democracies confronting the question of marriage equality. At the same time, federalism allowed for legal and political innovation in the movement for same-sex marriage. In the end, this is the defining aspect of the movement for marriage equality in the United States and its backlash and is the primary reason for the lack of a definitive national approach. It is also why the Supreme Court will likely be reluctant to be the institution that fully nationalizes policy on its own through aggressive adjudication against state bans on same-sex relationship recognition.

For marriage equality advocates to overcome the limits of federalism for their cause, the Supreme Court will need to invalidate state amendments, or voters will need to repeal them. The backlash has locked policy into place in many states, and repeal of these policies could take several decades without leadership from the Supreme Court. Thus, the only path possible for marriage equality advocates to achieve any change, through the states, also created a strong barrier to the realization of their goals. While, in retrospect, some might argue that the movement for marriage equality was premature, it was the natural outgrowth of changes in law and politics, especially on gender and the family, and by legal consciousness–driven rights claiming by same-sex couples in response to these changes, as was explored in chapter 2.

COURTS AND SOCIAL CHANGE

Given this state of affairs, it is tempting to assert that, in Rosenbergian terms, litigation for marriage equality has not achieved its desired results, instead only triggering a backlash that will make achieving marriage equality more difficult. However, scholars have increasingly argued that this litigation has achieved significant social and political change.[4] This book has documented the new relationship equality–protective policies that have been created directly, or indirectly, in response to litigation. In all regions of the country, except the South, same-sex marriages, civil unions, or domestic partnerships are recognized. In addition, a significant shift in the framing of the issue has occurred. When the second phase of the movement started in the 1990s, same-sex marriage was considered a radical idea outside of activist circles. In 2012, marriage equality is the policy preference of the sitting president and the Democratic Party.

This reflects a notable shift in public opinion. In 1996, Gallup began asking the question, "Do you think marriages between same-sex couples should or should not be recognized by the law as valid, with the same rights as traditional marriages?" In that year, 27 percent of respondents said yes and 68 percent said no. By 2011, the percentage responding yes increased to 53 percent to 45 percent no.[5] Other polls began to register majority support by 2011 and 2012. A *Washington Post* poll found 53 percent support for same-sex marriage, up from 37 percent in 2003.[6] Many commentators have noted that such rapid change has occurred with few social issues. Much of the increase in support for marriage equality comes from younger citizens who have come of age in a period where the movement for marriage equality was highly visible in the courts and in the public arena. Of course, Rosenberg argues that this change resulted from cultural factors (such as the more open portrayal of homosexuality in the media) and grassroots politics, rather than litigation. However, the previous pages discuss in great deal the connection between litigation and policy change in the direction of marriage equality. Certainly, litigation alone did not achieve these results, but it was a decisive factor.

Understanding the true role played by litigation in achieving social change requires a revisiting of the methods of court decision making discussed in the last chapter. In particular, we must expand our understanding of

judicial decisions beyond the strategic model. Rosenberg's perspective embraces this approach. Recall that under this model, the power of judges is
sharply limited by other political actors and public opinion. Judges may
desire to take the law in a new direction, but potential backlash from elected
officials and the public constrain what is actually possible. This certainly
describes some judicial decision making on the question of same-sex marriage, especially the reluctance of more liberal state and federal judges to
push legal interpretation toward more protection for same-sex couples. For
instance, recall judge George Bundy Smith from the New York Court of
Appeals. Though a liberal, he was hoping for reappointment by Republican
George Pataki and ruled with the more conservative judges in that case.

However, this approach fails to explain the judicial assertiveness explored
in this book, most notably in Iowa in 2009. Looking through the prism of
new institutionalism, we see that a judge's conception of the requirements of
the law can matter—it can drive outcomes regardless of the political consequences. This, too, is not a uniform rule, but it was seen repeatedly in the
previous pages. More broadly, litigation alters politics by placing issues and
claims for rights, blocked from genuine consideration in the majoritarian
political arena, on the public agenda. It legitimizes those issues and claims
when judges rule them to be legitimate. In this sense, then, litigation is
constitutive, in that it can alter the political status quo rather than only being
defined by the status quo. This may be true even when litigation is unsuccessful. Douglas NeJaime calls this "winning through losing." As he states,
"When a court validates a claim, the group's claim enjoys the legitimacy that
comes with the state's approval. When a court rejects the group's claim,
however, the demand that the legal claim embodies might be made more
pressing and the deprivation more acute. That is, the denial of the claim
might serve to highlight more intensively the injustice suffered by the
group."[7] Thus, losses can increase political and legal mobilization by the
losers. We saw this in states like Oregon, Washington, New York, and Maryland, where activists pursued aggressive legislative strategies after high court
losses in those states.

In the end, the position that courts cannot achieve social change is driven
by a normative stance that courts *should not* achieve social change, given
their lack of democratic accountability.[8] But, this leads to empirical blind
spots. According to Jane Schacter, "Any romanticized picture of judges as
countermajoritarian revolutionaries, single-handedly making policy more
progressive, is empirically unsustainable. But we should not replace one
piece of mythology with another. The notion that the institutional properties
of courts disable them from ever driving social change in a significant way
has its own caricature qualities."[9] She argues for an embrace of the "variabil-
ity, contingency, and complexity," that typifies litigation-based mobilization,

and this book has utilized precisely that approach in noting both the power of the backlash, with its distinct institutional and cultural foundations, and the real progress that has resulted from marriage equality litigation.

NOTES

1. "We Believe in America," 2012 Republican Platform, http://www.gop.com/wp-content/uploads/2012/08/2012GOPPlatform.pdf, 31.

2. Kim Severson, "Chick-fil-A Thrust Back into Spotlight on Gay Rights," *New York Times*, July 26, 2012, A13.

3. Emily Schmall, "The Cult of Chick-fil-A," Forbes.com, July 23, 2007, http://www.forbes.com/forbes/2007/0723/080.html.

4. See, for instance, Thomas Keck, "Beyond the Backlash: Assessing the Impact of Judicial Decisions on LGBT Rights," *Law & Society Review* 43:1 (2009), 151–85; Susan Gluck Mezey, *Queers in Court: Gay Rights Law and Public Policy* (Lanham, MD: Rowman & Littlefield, 2007); Jason Pierceson, *Courts, Liberalism, and Rights: Gay Law and Politics in the United States and Canada* (Philadelphia: Temple University Press, 2005).

5. Frank Newport, "Half of Americans Support Legal Gay Marriage," *Gallup.com*, May 8, 2012, http://www.gallup.com/poll/154529/Half-Americans-Support-Legal-Gay-Marriage.aspx.

6. "Same-Sex Marriage, Gay Rights," PollingReport.com, http://pollingreport.com/civil.htm.

7. Douglas NeJaime, "Winning through Losing," *Iowa Law Review* 96:941 (2011), 985.

8. See Jason Pierceson, "Deconstructing the Backlash: Same-Sex Marriage Litigation and Social Change in the United States and Canada," in Jason Pierceson, Shawn Schulenberg, and Adriana Piatti-Crocker, eds. *Same-Sex Marriage in the Americas: Policy Innovation for Same-Sex Relationships* (Lanham, MD: Lexington Books, 2010), 161–80.

9. Jane Schacter, "Sexual Orientation, Social Change, and the Courts," *Drake Law Review* 54:861 (2006), 863.

Index

Abercrombie, Neil, 100, 229
abortion rights, 17, 55
ACLU. *See* American Civil Liberties Union
ACLU v. Alaska, 103
Action Wisconsin, 121, 126
activism, 40, 64, 160; of African Americans, 170; grassroots, 78, 104–106, 107, 128; in Hawaii, 95, 99; legislation and, 31; litigation and, 6; in 1970s, 31–35; public, 27; social, 134; in West, 199
Adams, Richard, 35
Adams v. Howerton, 35, 228, 229
ADF. *See* Alliance Defense Fund
adoption rights, 123; in Ecuador, 76; in France, 58; in Illinois, 135; in Indiana, 141; in Portugal, 59; registered partnership and, 58, 59, 62; in Scandinavia, 55; South Africa support of, 68; in Uruguay, 75; in Wisconsin, 124
advocacy, 41–46, 62, 168–169
Affordable Care Act, 206, 225
African American activism, 170
African National Congress Party (ANC), South Africa, 69
African traditionalism in South Africa, 69
AIDS crisis, 45, 56, 64
Alaska, 19, 100–103

Alaska Civil Liberties Union Ex Rel. Carter v. Alaska, 102
Alliance Defense Fund (ADF), 125, 171, 195
American Civil Liberties Union (ACLU), 37; Action Wisconsin and, 121, 126; on domestic partnerships, 93; on Hawaii's civil unions, 100; in Illinois by, 137; Lesbian and Gay Rights Project of, 89; Maryland lawsuit by, 168; in Montana, 199; in Washington, 182; Wisconsin litigation by, 120–123, 126
American Family Association, 132, 192
amicus briefs, 127–128, 142, 162
ANC. *See* African National Congress Party
antidiscrimination law, 36, 57, 92, 119, 134, 195
anti-gay politics, religious and moral roots of, 13–17
Argentina, 73, 75, 79–80
Aristotle, 7
Arizona, 34, 179, 193–194
Asia, 81
attitudinal model, 207
Australia, 70–73
Australian Christian Lobby, 71

Baehr, Nina, 93
Baehr v. Lewin, 93, 96, 97, 99, 106, 111, 229
Baker, Jack, 28, 33

Baker v. Nelson, 28, 33, 138, 139–140, 224
Baker v. State of Vermont, 106, 107, 111, 168, 230
bankruptcy, 229
Basic Rights Oregon (BRO), 180
Becket Fund for Religious Liberty, 162
Belgium, 57, 59
benefits: death, 138; domestic partnership in Alaska, 100, 101, 102; domestic partnership in Wisconsin, 120, 123; federal, 98; military, 229; parental relationship, 44; same-sex couple, 43–46, 54, 57, 64, 76, 108, 137, 155, 228; social policy, 12, 31, 54; social welfare, 54, 64
Bickel, Alexander, 4
Biden, Joe, 235
Bill of Rights, negative rights of, 18
Bipartisan Legal Advisory Group (BLAG), House, 223–224, 227
Blankenhorn, David, 219
Boies, David, 97, 214, 215, 218
Bonauto, Mary, 105, 108, 110, 158
Bowers, Shellie, 91
Bowers v. Hardwick, 70, 88, 89, 90, 91, 206, 210, 211
Boy Scouts, 154
Brady, Bill, 135
Branstad, Terry, 2, 132
Braschi v. Stahl Associates, 45, 164
Brause, Jay, 101
Brazil, 73, 77–78
Britt, Harry, 43
BRO. *See* Basic Rights Oregon
Broad Front, 75
Brown, Jerry, 42, 192, 193
Brown v. Board of Education, 205, 218
Burke, Thomas, 6
Burns, Michael Floyd, 32
Burns, Walter, 95
Bush, George W., 15, 66, 214
Bush v. Gore, 214

Cady, Mark, 131, 132
California, 1, 42, 43–44, 160, 179, 186–193, 187–190. *See also* Proposition 8 in California; Proposition 22 in California
Cameron, David, 60

Cameron, Edwin, 68, 70
Canada, 62, 64–67. *See also* Supreme Court of Canada
Catholic Charities, 135–136
Catholic Church: in Colombia, 76, 77; conservative activists in, 160; religious opposition from, 74, 155; in Spain, 59; in Wisconsin, 120, 122
Chang, Kevin, trial of, 97, 215, 220
Charter of Rights and Freedoms, Canada, 52, 64, 67
Chick-fil-A controversy, 237–238
child: best interest of the, 54; custody cases, 37; development, 96, 97, 128, 217; of same-sex couples, 205; welfare of, 131, 165, 217
Christian Coalition, Hawaii, 100
Christian Democrats, Germany, 60
Christie, Chris, 155–156
Citizens Constitution, Brazil, 77
Citizens for the Protection of Marriage (CPM), 143
Civil Liberties Union, Alaska, 102, 103
civil partnerships: in Ireland, 61; Labour Party in United Kingdom on, 60; in South Africa, 69
civil rights, 2, 27, 130; argument, 219; New Zealand law for, 72; relationship equality as, 160
Civil Rights Act (1964), 206
civil unions: in Australia, 70; in Ecuador, 75; Hawaii on, 99–100; in Illinois, 119; in Iowa, 127; law, 155; in Mexico, 78; in New Hampshire, 161; New Zealand law for, 72; religion and, 137; Rhode Island bill on, 162; in Uruguay, 75; in Vermont, 106–108, 127; Wisconsin amendment on, 122, 123
cohabitation, 42, 64; in Brazil, 78; Colombia on, 76; frameworks, 19; in Illinois, 134; law, in Sweden, 57; social welfare benefits in Europe, 54
Colombia, 73, 76–77
Colorado, 34, 36, 179, 196–197
Commission on Sexual Orientation, Hawaii, 96
Common Benefits Clause, Vermont, 105, 106
common law marriage, 65, 68

companionate marriage, 40, 41
Connecticut, 1, 157–159
conservatism, 160; neo, 14; religious, 16, 19, 62, 67, 132, 139; of Tea Party movement, 16
Conservative People's Party, Denmark, 56
constitution: Iowa amendment to, 132, 133; of North Carolina, 171. *See also* liberal constitutionalism
Constitution, U.S., 6; equality and individual rights principles, 9; Fourteenth Amendment, 10, 10, 11, 218; Supreme Court interventions for, 4; Tenth Amendment, 225
Constitutional Council of France, 52
Constitutional Court: Colombia, 76; South Africa, 68–69, 70
controversial politics, 4
Convention on the Rights of the Child, 70
Cory, Donald Webster, 25–27, 41
court-facilitated change: in Argentina, 79–80; in Brazil, 77–78; in Colombia, 76–77; in Mexico, 78–79
court made me do it argument, 3
Court of Appeal, New Zealand, 72
Court of Cassation, France, 58
courts, 1; democracy role of, 4; federal, 1, 20, 205, 214–222; on heterosexual marriage right, 10; Illinois wariness of, 134; Latin America role of, 74, 80; social change and, 4–5, 239–240; Uruguay and Ecuador change without, 75. *See also* Supreme Court
CPM. *See* Citizens for the Protection of Marriage
Culver, Chet, 2, 132; court made me do it argument by, 3; on Iowa Supreme Court decision, 3
Cuomo, Andrew, 163, 166, 166–167, 170
Customary Marriages Act, South Africa, 69

Daughters of Bilitis (1953), 25, 27
Dean, Craig, 40, 89–90, 91
decentralization: Burke on, 6; of political systems, 5
decision making models, 207–209; attitudinal model, 207; legal model, 208; new institutionalism, 208; strategic

model, 207
Defense of Marriage Act (1996), 1, 87, 89, 205, 206, 222; on federal benefits, 98; Social Security and, 12; Wyden negative freedom focus on, 18. *See also* DOMA
Defense of Marriage Act (1998), of Iowa, 129
deferential rational basis test, 11
deinstitutionalism of marriage, 219
Delaware, 171
democracy: courts and judges role in, 4; in Latin America, 74; liberal, in South Africa, 70
Democratic Party, 33; in Illinois, 133; in Iowa, 132; marriage equality 2012 endorsement, 236; same-sex marriage endorsement, 32–33; in Washington, 184; in Wisconsin, 120
Denmark, 55–57
Designated Beneficiaries Act, Colorado, 196
discrimination: employment, 17, 33; Fourteenth Amendment on, 10; gender, 29, 37, 39, 89, 90, 94, 95, 101; racial, 29, 39; against sexual minority, 131, 217, 224. *See also* antidiscrimination law
divorce, 40–41, 162; lesbian case of, 198; no-fault, 36, 37, 41, 42; women's rights movement on, 41
Dixon, Arrington, 35, 37
Dixon bill in Washington, D.C., 35–41; GAA and, 36, 37; Kameny on, 36; NOW support of, 40; religious opposition to, 37
Doe v. Reed, 185
DOMA, 223; federal challenges for, 227–229; in Florida, 213; litigation, 222; Massachusetts challenge of, 224; sexual orientation and, 226; Supreme Court and, 222, 232; Tauro and, 225; unconstitutionality of, 223, 226, 228; in Washington, 184. *See also* super-DOMA amendments
domestic partnership: ACLU on, 93; Australia registries, 71; benefits in Alaska, 100, 101, 102; benefits in Wisconsin, 120, 123; in California, 186;

Michigan Supreme Court on, 143;
    municipal laws for, 31; in 1977, 41–46;
    in Oregon, 181; Spain registries, 59; in
    Washington, D.C., 89, 92
domestic partnership law, 43–44, 155; in
    California, 43; in Hawaii, 95, 98; in
    Nevada, 179; in New Mexico, 195; in
    Washington, D.C., 89, 92; in
    Wisconsin, 124
Domestic Relations Act (1909), 164
"Don't Ask, Don't Tell" repeal, 16
Doyle, James, 120, 123
Dragovich v. Department of Treasury,
    227–228
Dugan, Gene, 101
Dworkin, Ronald, 4

East (U.S.): Connecticut, 1, 28, 157–159,
    209, 210; Delaware, 171; Maine, 160;
    Maryland, 36, 168–171; New
    Hampshire, 160–162; New Jersey,
    154–157; New York, 1, 29, 44,
    163–168; Rhode Island, 162
Ecuador, 73, 75
Egan v. Canada, 65
Eighth Circuit Court, 213
elimination of sodomy laws, 18, 56, 88,
    172
employment discrimination, 17, 33
Employment Non-Discrimination Act
    (ENDA), 15
Equal Employment Opportunity
    Commission, 29
equal protection argument, 10, 154, 190; in
    Hawaii, 94; by Lambda Legal, 157; for
    sexual orientation, 40, 122; by Supreme
    Court, 209–212
Equal Protection Clause, 11, 89, 91, 94,
    231
Equal Rights Amendment (ERA), 30;
    gender discrimination and, 37, 39;
    same-sex marriage as argument against,
    40; in Washington, 29
equality: constitutional principle of, 9;
    popular vote on, 2
Equality Maryland, 168, 170
Equality Project, South Africa, 68
ERA. *See* Equal Rights Amendment
Eskridge, William, 26, 56, 89

EU. *See* European Union
Europe, 61; cohabitation rights in, 42; legal
    protections for same-sex couples in, 54;
    LGBT advocacy network in, 62;
    nonjudicial politics in, 54; relationship
    equality trend in, 57–63; resistance to
    same-sex marriage policies, 60–63;
    same-sex marriage developments in, 19
European Convention on Human Rights,
    63
European Court of Human Rights, 52, 62
European Parliament, 62
European Union (EU), 62, 63

Fair Courts for Us, 132
Fair Wisconsin, 146n28
family: of affinity, 46; best interest of the
    child standard, 54; member, same-sex
    partner as, 45; social welfare policy
    and, 12, 54
Family Forum, Hawaii, 230
Family Research Council, 14, 132, 162
federal challenges for Supreme Court,
    227–229
federal courts: on Proposition 8, 1, 205,
    214–222; in same-sex marriage debates,
    20
federal policy, 115n35
federal protection from employment
    discrimination, 17
federalism, 1, 19, 206, 238; Burke on
    decentralization of, 6; role of, 5–6; U.S.
    marriage equality movement role in, 20
Finland, 55, 57
Florida, 42, 213
Focus on the Family, 192
Foley, Dan, 93, 95
foreign policy, 51
forum shopping, 88, 106
Fourteenth Amendment, 10, 10, 11, 218
France, 58, 63
Freedom to Marry Taskforce, Vermont,
    104, 107
Friedlander, Ezra, 142
Full Faith and Credit Clause, U.S.
    Constitution, 99, 127
fundamental right: Lambda Legal on, 154,
    164; to life partner, 101; marriage as,
    10, 28, 40, 188; same-sex marriage as,

94, 154, 183, 220

GAA. *See* Gay Activists Alliance
Gallagher, Maggie, 142, 191
Gay Activists Alliance (GAA), 29, 36, 37
Gay and Lesbian Advocates and Defenders
  (GLAD), 105, 158, 224–227; litigation
  strategy, 110; Massachusetts litigation
  sponsored by, 108; Rhode Island and,
  162
gay liberation movement, 32, 38
gender: -neutral marriage, 101, 220;
  politics of, 37; roles, 23
gender discrimination, 89, 90; ERA and,
  37, 39; Hawaii prohibition of, 94, 95;
  marriage license denial as, 101; racial
  discrimination and, 39; in Washington,
  29
gender law revolution, 39–40
George, Robert, 8, 191
Georgia, 88
Germany, 60
Gill, Patrick, 89–90, 91, 92
GLAD. *See* Gay and Lesbian Advocates
  and Defenders
Goldberg-Hiller, Jonathan, 13, 173, 238
Golinski, Karen, 227
Golinski v. OPM, 227–228
Goodridge v. Department of Public Health,
  109–111, 162, 180, 212
government: on sex perverts and sexual
  deviants, 24; sexual minority hostility
  by, 23
grassroots activism, 78, 104–106, 107, 128
Greaney, John, 111, 112
Griswold v. Connecticut, 28, 209, 210

hate crime, 198
Hawaii, 1, 19, 93–100, 230; Nevada and,
  229–230
Hernandez v. Robles, 165, 166, 230
heteronormative marriage, 25–26, 35
heterosexism, 9, 42, 151
heterosexual marriage: accidental
  procreation by, 141; courts on right to,
  10; neoconservatism support of, 14
*High Tech Gays v. Defense Industrial
  Security Clearance Office*, 227, 228,
  230

Hill, Irving, 35
Hinkle, Phillip, 140
Hochberg, James, 96
Holder, Eric, 223–224
The Hollow Hope (Rosenberg), 5
homophile movement, 27, 38
homophobia, 33, 69, 74, 151
The Homosexual in America (Cory), 25–27
homosexuality: as illness, 31; as immoral
  sexual practices, 15; perversion of, 14;
  as sin, 13; sodomy and, 24
Howell, Kenneth, 8–9
Human Rights Act: New Zealand, 72;
  Washington, D.C., 90
Human Rights and Equal Opportunity
  Commission, 70
Human Rights Campaign, 44, 214
Human Rights Committee International
  Covenant of Civil and Political Rights,
  United Nations, 72
Hungary, 62
Hunter, Nan, 89, 215

Iceland, 55, 57
ICLU. *See* Indiana Civil Liberties Union
Illinois, 119, 133–137
Illinois Religious Freedom Protection and
  Civil Union Act, 135
illness, homosexuality as, 31
immigration, 229; same-sex marriage for
  purposes of, 34, 35
Immigration and Naturalization Service,
  35
Indiana, 140–142
Indiana Civil Liberties Union (ICLU), 141,
  142
individual rights, 4; Canada legislative
  branch on, 64; constitutional principle
  of, 9; liberal constitutionalism for, 7
Industrial Revolutionary Party, Mexico, 79
inequality: of French PACS, 63; political
  and social, 8
institutionalism, 240; new, 208
International Covenant on Civil and
  Political Rights, 70
interracial marriage, 28, 112, 164, 216
Iowa, 1, 129–130; citizens lack of support
  in, 2; Lambda Legal in, 126–127, 128;
  litigation strategy in, 119, 126–128,

133; political reaction in, 131–133;
religious conservatism in, 132
Iowa Family Policy Center, 127
Iowa Supreme Court, 2, 19, 108, 119; on
constitution requirement of same-sex
marriage, 130; Culver on decision of, 3;
election of 2010, 2, 3, 132; opinion of,
130–131
Ireland, 61

Johnson, David K., 25
Jones v. Hallahan, 29
judges: democracy role of, 4; trial court,
94, 95, 146n56
judicial activism, 2, 95
judicial minimalism, 105
judicial review: Bickel on, 4; Dworkin on,
4
judicialization: in Canada, 65, 66; of
politics, 52; in South Africa, 68
"just world syndrome" in South Africa, 70

Kameny, Franklin, 27, 31–32, 36, 40
Kennedy, Anthony, 9, 206, 210–211,
221–222
Kinsey, Alfred, 24
Kramer, Richard, 187–188

Labour Party, United Kingdom, 60
Lambda Legal Defense and Education
Fund, 44, 88, 90, 108, 215; on AIDS,
45; on Alaska litigation, 101; in
Arizona, 194; equal protection
argument by, 157; on fundamental
rights, 154, 164; grassroots activism
and, 128; on Hawaii civil unions, 100;
in Illinois by, 137; in Iowa, 126–127,
128; on legalization of same-sex
marriage, 156; in Nevada, 230; in
Washington, 182
Latin America, 73–80; courts role in, 74,
80; public opinion in, 74; sex role in,
73; sexuality history in, 73; sodomy
decriminalization in, 73
Lavender Scare (1930s), 24, 25, 26
law: antidiscrimination, 36, 57, 92, 119,
134, 195; civil unions, 155;
cohabitation, 57; divorce, 41; family,
44–45; gender, 39–40; gender-neutral

marriage, 101; marriage equality, 92;
New Zealand, 72; politics and, 1;
reciprocal beneficiaries, 98; resistance
to, 38. *See also* domestic partnership
law; sodomy laws
Lawrence v. Texas, 9, 110, 172, 182, 188,
190, 194, 206, 210, 211, 212–213
Law v. Canada, 65
legal consciousness, 38–39, 46, 239
legal model, 208
legalization of same-sex marriages: in
Argentina, 79; in Brazil, 78; in Canada,
63, 64, 67; in Iowa, 133; Lambda Legal
on, 156; majority rule for, 3; in
Massachusetts, 151; in New York, 1; in
Portugal, 59; in Scotland, 60; in South
Africa, 51, 63; in Spain, 59, 80; in
Washington, D.C., 27, 31–32, 33,
35–37, 93, 168
legislation, activism and, 31
lesbian and gay rights, 17, 32; public
activism for, 27; relationship equality
and, 19; Republican Party opposition
to, 17; U.S. movement for, 19
lesbian and gay rights, 1950–1990, 23–46;
Cory on, 25–27; Dixon bill in
Washington, D.C., 35–37, 40; domestic
partnerships, 1977, 41–46; early
movement in U.S., 23–25; same-sex
couples marriage licenses, 34–35;
same-sex marriage activism (1970s),
31–35; same-sex marriage cases, early,
27–30; same-sex marriage in 1970s,
37–41
Lesbian and Gay Rights Project, of ACLU,
89
Lewis v. Harris, 154, 156
LGBT rights, 189; Alaska political
environment and, 101; in Canada, 64;
Doyle support of, 120; ERA and, 39;
Illinois support of, 133; majoritarianism
and, 130; movement in world, 51; as
religious freedom violation, 15; in
Uruguay, 75
liberal constitutionalism, 7, 9–11, 181
liberal democracy in South Africa, 70
Liberal Party, Canada, 66
libertarian jurisprudence, 101
libertarian political agenda, 25, 26

Life Partnership Act, Germany, 60
Ling-Cohan, Doris, 164–165
Lingle, Linda, 99, 100
litigation, 52, 65, 119–125; activism and, 6; in Alaska, 19, 101, 102; in California, 187–190; DOMA, 222; federal after *Lawrence*, 212–213; in Hawaii, 19, 92, 93–95; in Massachusetts, 19, 108–109; national groups for, 88; New York failure in, 164–166; religious and moral roots of, 13–17; same-sex marriage opposition from, 5, 17; in Vermont, 19, 104–106; in Washington, D.C., 19; Wisconsin ACLU, 120–123, 126
litigation avoidance strategy, 137; in Illinois, 119, 133–137; in Minnesota, 138
litigation strategy, 88; of GLAD, 110; in Iowa, 119, 126–128, 133
Love Makes a Family for adoption rights, 123
Loving v. Virginia, 28, 29, 94, 110, 169, 182, 188, 209

M. v. H., 65
Madigan, Lisa, 135, 137
Madigan, Michael, 134–135
Maine, 160
majoritarian morality, 17
majoritarian political process, 52
majoritarianism, 130
majority rule: for legalization of same-sex marriages, 3; limits on, 3; minority rights and, 4
The Manhattan Declaration: A Call of Christian Conscience (2009), 8, 15–16, 21n26, 133
Marbury v. Madison, 226
marriage: amendment in Wisconsin, 122, 123; common law, 65, 68; companionate, 40, 41; Cory's heteronormative bias for, 25–26; definition between one man and one woman, 96, 173; deinstitutionalism of, 219; as fundamental right, 10, 28, 40, 188; gender-neutral marriage, 101, 220; heterosexual, 10, 14, 141; as institution, 111; interracial, 28, 112, 164, 216; law

and social policy benefits of, 12, 31, 54; legal and economic protection of, 12; mental and physical health in, 217; Mexico state definition of, 79; as oppressive, 7, 11; plural, 3, 16, 69; for procreation, 7, 8, 29, 91, 94, 95, 105
Marriage Act: Australia, 70; South Africa, 69
marriage equality: Biden support of, 235; Democratic Party 2012 endorsement of, 236; enactment in South Africa, 68; Kameny on, 27, 31–32; law, in Washington, D.C., 92; Obama on, 170, 173, 235; as religious freedom violation, 15; in Scandinavia, 55; Supreme Court on, 29; traditional gender roles reinforcement by, 23; Washington bill on, 185
marriage license application, 31, 33–35, 101; in Alaska, 101; in Arizona, 34; in California, 42; in Colorado, 34, 36; in Hawaii, 93; in Indiana, 141; in Maryland, 36, 168; in New Mexico, 195; in New York, 163; in New Zealand, 72; in Oregon, 179
Marry Me Minnesota, 139
Marshall, Margaret, 110–111
Maryland, 36, 168–170
Massachusetts, 1, 19, 108–113, 154, 179; *See also Goodridge v. Department of Public Health*
Mattachine Society (1950), 25, 31
Maynard v. Hill, 209
medical profession, sexual minority hostility by, 23
Metropolitan Community Church, 32
Mexico, 73, 78–79
Meyer v. Nebraska, 209
Michigan, 142–143
Midwest, 119–144; Illinois, 119, 133–137; Indiana, 140–142; Iowa, 1, 2, 3, 19, 119, 126–133; Michigan, 142–143; Minnesota, 28, 29, 137–140; Ohio, 143; relationship equality in, 19; Wisconsin, 119–125, 146n28
Milford v. Worcester, 111
military: benefits, 229; gays and lesbians ban in, 75

Minnesota, 28, 29, 137–140; *See also Baker v. Nelson*
minority rights, 4
Montana, 199
moral arguments: liberal constitutionalism and, 10; against same-sex relations, 42
morality-policy politics, 130
Mormon Church, 101, 191, 191–192
municipal employees, domestic partnership law for, 43–44
Murray, Susan, 104, 106

National Assembly, France, 58
National Center for Lesbian Rights, 187
National Coalition for Gay and Lesbian Equality, South Africa, 68
National Federation of Independent Business v. Sibelius, 225
national groups for litigation, 88
National Organization for Marriage, 132, 139, 142, 160, 191, 218
National Organization for Women (NOW), 37, 39, 40
natural law, 7–11; Howell on, 8–9; politics of disgust and, 9
Neary, Jeffrey, 127
Nebraska, 212
negative rights, U.S. focus on, 18
neoconservatism, 14
Netherlands, 57, 59
Nevada, 179, 194, 229–230
New Hampshire, 160–162
new institutionalism, 208
New Jersey, 1, 154–157
New Mexico, 179, 195
New York, 1, 29, 44, 163–168
New York Court of Appeals, 44
New Zealand, 70–73
Newsom, Gavin, 38, 39, 179, 187, 195
NGOs. *See* nongovernmental organizations
Ninth Circuit Court of Appeals, 185, 215, 221–222, 227, 229
no-fault divorce, 36, 37, 41, 42
nongovernmental organizations (NGOs), 62
nonjudicial politics in Europe, 54
North Carolina, 171–173, 171, 173
Norway, 55, 56, 57

NOW. *See* National Organization for Women

Obama, Barack, 138, 140, 170, 173, 193, 223–224, 235
observational approach to political theory, 7
Office of Personnel Management (OPM), 227–228
Ohio, 143
Olson, Ted, 97, 215
one man and one woman marriage definition, 96, 173
OPM. *See* Office of Personnel Management
Oregon, 179, 179–183
OutFront Minnesota, 139

PACS in France, 57–58; inequality of, 63; legal protection for same-sex couples by, 58
parental relationship, benefits secured through, 44
parenting rights: in Denmark, 56; New Zealand on, 72; in Scandinavia, 55; in U.S., 54
parliamentary supremacy: in Canada, 52; in New Zealand, 72
parliamentary systems in Europe, 54
Pataki, George, 166, 239
Perez v. Sharp, 110, 188, 190
perversion of homosexuality, 14
philosophical conflict, 7–11; liberal constitutionalism, 9–11; natural law, 7–9
Pizer, Jennifer, 108, 215
Planned Parenthood, 16
plural marriage, 3, 16, 69
policy diffusion, 56
policy stagnation in U.S., 6
Polikoff, Nancy, 12, 20n18, 88, 216
political and legal culture, 18–19, 237–238
political environment, 101
political inequality, 8
political reaction: in Hawaii, 95–96; in Iowa, 131–133; in Massachusetts, 111–113
political systems: in Brazil, 77; decentralization of, 5; individual rights

protection by, 4
political theory, 7
politics: anti-gay, 13–17; controversial, 4; of disgust, 9; gender, 37; judicialization of, 52; law and, 1; morality-policy, 130; nonjudicial in Europe, 54; revolution in, 39–40; sexual orientation, 37
Portugal, 57, 59
privacy jurisprudence, 28, 30, 93, 101
procreation, 230; accidental in heterosexual marriage, 141; justification, 154; marriage for, 7, 8, 29, 91, 94, 95, 105; of same-sex couples, 131; sex for, 8
Proposition 8 in California, 20, 42, 97, 131, 186, 206; federal courts on, 1, 205, 214–222; Mormon Church support of, 191, 191–192; Ninth Circuit Court of Appeals, 221–222; religion role in, 98; trial and Walker opinion on, 215–221; Walker overturn of, 179
Proposition 22 in California, 186, 187, 188
public activism for lesbian and gay rights, 27
public opinion: in Latin America, 74; in Minnesota, 137

quasi-marriage, 35
queer theory, 7, 12
Quinn, Pat, 135, 137

racial discrimination, 29, 39
reciprocal beneficiaries law in Hawaii, 98
registered partnership: adoption rights, 58, 59, 62; in Denmark, 55; in Netherlands, 59; in Switzerland, 61
Registered Partnership Act, Denmark (1989), 55
relationship equality, 19, 46, 81; Alaska litigation for, 102; Brady support of, 135; in Brazil, 77; death benefits bill for, 138; Europe trend for, 57–63; EU support of, 63; France's civil PACS on, 58; in Germany, 60; global resistance to, 81–82; Latin America courts and, 80; in Midwest, 19; policy in Belgium, 59; religious opposition to, 135; by Socialist People's Party in Denmark, 55; in Southern and Eastern Europe, 61;

state policies of, 152; in Western and Central Europe, 61; Wisconsin litigation for, 119–125
relationship recognition, 108; Canada on, 64–65; Washington, D.C. on, 92
religion: civil unions and, 137; homosexuality as sin, 13; membership, on Commission on Sexual Orientation, 96; political culture and, 237–238; Proposition 8 role of, 98; sexual minority hostility by, 23; shadow establishment of, 17; U.S. marriage equality movement role of, 20
religious activism, 8
religious and moral roots of anti-gay politics and litigation, 13–17
religious conservatism, 19, 62; in Canada, 67; in Iowa, 132; in Minnesota, 139; in Republican Party, 16
religious freedom, 18, 236; Catholic Charities on, 135–136; Illinois on, 135–136; LGBT rights as violation of, 15; marriage equality as violation of, 15
religious marriage: of Brause and Dugan, 101; of Spainhour and Burns, M.R., 32
religious opposition, 3; from Catholic Church, 74; to civil unions in Hawaii, 99; to Dixon bill in Washington, D.C., 37; to relationship equality, 135; in United Kingdom, 60
Religious Right, 31, 154; gay rights ordinance repeal by, 42; Republican Party and, 236; in South, 172, 173
Republican Party, 16; in Alaska, 100; lesbian and gay rights opposition by, 17; on Planned Parenthood, 16; religious conservatism of, 16; Religious Right and, 236; Tea Party movement and, 16; 2012 national platform, 236; in Wisconsin, 120
revolution, 39–40
Rhode Island, 162
Robinson, Beth, 104, 106
Roe v. Wade, 209
Romer v. Evans, 206, 210, 212–213, 221, 222
Romney, Mitt, 111–112
Rorex, Clela, 34, 38, 39
Rosenberg, Gerald, 5, 239

same-sex communities, 24
same-sex couples, 70; benefits for, 43–46, 54, 57, 64, 76, 108, 137, 155, 228; cohabitation rights for, 42; common law marriage and, 68; Europe legal protections for, 54; family law and policy changes for, 44–45; marriage license application by, 33–35; procreation of, 131
same-sex marriage, 1, 57, 59, 60, 66, 75; activism in 1970s, 31–35; advocacy in 1977, 41–46; Branstad arguments for, 2; child development and, 96, 97, 128, 217; Democratic Party endorsement of, 32–33; as fundamental right, 94, 154, 183, 220; in Midwest, 119–144; New Zealand lawsuit, 72; in 1970s, 37–41; opposition from litigation, 5, 17; progress 2004-2012, 151–173; prohibition in 1977, 42; radical critiques of, 11–12; religion opposition to, 3; state ban of, 153; Supreme Court and, 205–232; trial, 97
same-sex relations, 24; Denmark recognition of, 51; as family of affinity, 46; moral argument against, 42; partner adoption, 44; in world, 53
Scalia, Antonin, 211, 231
Scandinavia, 55
Schwarzenegger, Arnold, 187
scientific method of political theory, 7
Scotland, 60
separate but equal argument, 107–108, 158
sex: Latin America role of, 73; perverts, 24; for procreation, 8
Sexual Behavior in the Human Male (Kinsey), 24
sexuality, 9, 73
sexual minority, 14; Canada on, 65; Denmark commission on, 55; discrimination against, 131, 217, 224; ENDA and, 15; France bias against, 57; legal and political movement to regulate, 24; religion, medical profession and government hostility toward, 23; social mobilization of, 24; Texas hostility toward, 172; Uganda hostility toward, 81

sexual orientation, 94; deferential rational basis test and, 11; DOMA and, 226; equal protection argument for, 40, 122; politics, 37; protection, in South Africa, 67; Vermont antidiscrimination laws on, 104
sexual practices, immoral, 15
shadow establishment of religion, 17
Sharp, David, 160
Singer, John, 29
Singer v. Hara, 39, 182
Smith, George Bundy, 166, 239
Snyder-Hall, Claire, 10
social activism, 134
social change, courts and, 4–5, 239–240
Social Democrats, Germany, 60
social inequality, 8
social mobilization of sexual minority, 24
social welfare: benefits, 54, 64; policy, 12, 54
Socialist Party, 58, 59
Socialist People's Party, Denmark, 55
sodomy: homosexuality and, 24; Latin America decriminalization of, 73; Vermont on, 107
sodomy laws: Canada repeal of, 64; elimination of, 18, 56, 88, 172; in Georgia, 88; South Africa repeal of, 68; unconstitutionality of, 44
South, 171–173
South Africa, 51, 63, 67–70, 111
South America, 19
Southern Poverty Law Center, 192
Spain, 57, 59, 80
Spainhour, Jack Allen, 32
Spedale, Darren, 26, 56
spouse definition, 64, 121, 156
stare decisis doctrine, 52, 74
State v. Lopez, 162
Stonewall Riots (1969), 13, 27, 32, 121
strategic model, 207
Sunstein, Cass, 91, 105
super-DOMA amendments, 108, 197; in Arizona, 193; in Indiana, 140; in Michigan, 142; in Nebraska, 212; in Ohio, 143; in Wisconsin, 119, 138
Supreme Court, 4; BLAG and, 223–224, 227; controversial politics and, 4; DOMA and, 222, 232; on equal

protection and right to marry, 209–212; federal challenges, 227–229; foreign policy and, 51; GLAD cases, 224–227; individual rights protection by, 4; on majoritarian morality, 17; on marriage equality, 29; on marriage as fundamental right, 28; models of decision making, 207–209; Nevada, Hawaii and, 229–230; as policy maker, 205–206; prediction for, 231–232; Proposition 8 and, 214–222; after *Romer* and *Lawrence*, 212–213; same-sex marriage and, 205–232. *See also* Iowa Supreme Court

Supreme Court of Canada, 52; *Egan v. Canada*, 65; *Law v. Canada*, 65; *M. v. H.*, 65; on same-sex marriage constitutionality, 66

suspect classification, 11

Sweden, 55, 57

Switzerland, 61

Take Back Vermont, 107

Tanner v. OHSU, 180–181, 183

Tauro, Joseph L., 225, 226

Taylor, Camilla, 126, 128

Tea Party movement: conservatism of, 16; Republican Party and, 16

Tenth Amendment, 225

Texas, 172

Traditional Family Coalition, 218

traditional marriage, 36, 198

trial court judges, 94, 95, 146n56

Tribe, Lawrence, 88, 91, 113n3

Turner v. Safley, 182, 210

Uganda, 81

unconstitutionality, 44, 129; of DOMA, 223, 226, 228; of Full Faith and Credit Clause, 99, 127; of sodomy laws, 44

United Kingdom, 60

United States (U.S.): Canada versus, in legalization of same-sex marriages, 64; early lesbian and gay rights movement in, 23–25; lesbian and gay rights movement in, 19; negative rights focus of, 18; parenting rights in, 54; policy stagnation in, 6; state constitutional ban

of same-sex marriage, 6; state recognition of same-sex marriage, 6

universal health-care system, 12

unmarried cohabitation, 42

Uruguay, 73, 75

U.S. *See* United States

Vermont, 1, 19, 103–108, 127, 154

Walker, Vaughn, 97, 179, 215–221, 229

Washington, 29, 39, 179, 182, 183–185

Washington, D.C., 19, 89–92, 170–171; legalization of same-sex marriage in, 27, 31–32, 33, 35–37, 93, 168. *See also* Dixon bill in Washington, D.C.

welfare: child, 131, 165, 217; Norway state of, 57

West (U.S.), 179–200; activism in, 199; Arizona, 34, 179, 193–194; California, 1, 42, 43–44, 160, 179, 186–193; Colorado, 34, 36, 196–197; Montana, 199; Nevada, 179, 194, 229–230; New Mexico, 179, 195; Oregon, 179, 179–183; super-DOMA amendments in, 197; Washington, 183–185; Wyoming, 198

West, Jason, 38, 39

Windsor, Edith, 228

Windsor v. U.S., 227–228

Wisconsin, 119, 119–125, 126, 138, 146n28

Wisconsin Family Action Christian advocacy group, 124

Women's Law Center of Maryland, 168

women's rights movement, 39, 131; on divorce laws, 41; on gender discrimination, 39

world, 51–82; Australia and New Zealand, 70–73; Canada, 63–67; Europe, 19, 42, 54–63; global resistance in, 81–82; Latin America, 73–80; same-sex relationship recognition in, 53; South Africa, 67–70

Wyden, Ron, 18

Wyoming, 198

Zablocki v. Redhail, 209

About the Author

Jason Pierceson is associate professor of political science at the University of Illinois, Springfield. His research interests include public law, political theory, and the politics of sexuality. He is the author or coauthor of several books on same-sex marriage, including *Same-Sex Marriage in the Americas: Policy Innovation for Same-Sex Relationships* and *Courts, Liberalism and Rights: Gay Law and Politics in the United States and Canada.*